H INGE POINTS

HINGE POINTS

An Inside Look at North Korea's Nuclear Program

Siegfried S. Hecker

with Elliot A. Serbin

Stanford University Press
Stanford, California

Stanford University Press
Stanford, California

Printed in the United States of America on acid-free, archival-quality paper

Library of Congress Cataloging-in-Publication Data

Names: Hecker, Siegfried S., author.
Title: Hinge points : an inside look at North Korea's nuclear program /
  Siegfried S. Hecker ; with Elliot A. Serbin.
Description: Stanford, California : Stanford University Press, [2023] |
  Includes bibliographical references and index.
Identifiers: LCCN 2022015242 (print) | LCCN 2022015243 (ebook) | ISBN
  9781503634459 (cloth) | ISBN 9781503634473 (ebook)
Subjects: LCSH: Nuclear weapons—Korea (North) | Nuclear arms
  control—Korea (North) | Korea (North)—Foreign relations—United
  States. | United States—Foreign relations—Korea (North)
Classification: LCC UA853.K7 H43 2023 (print) | LCC UA853.K7 (ebook) |
  DDC 355/.03355193—dc23/eng/20220819
LC record available at https://lccn.loc.gov/2022015242
LC ebook record available at https://lccn.loc.gov/2022015243

Cover design: David Drummond
Cover photograph provided by the author

*In memory of Professor John Wilson Lewis, whose boundless energy
and dedication to a peaceful and prosperous Korean Peninsula
inspired my North Korea work and this book*

Contents

figures follow page 208

Preface

"Would you like to see our product?" asked Dr. Ri Hong Sop, director of North Korea's Yongbyon Nuclear Scientific Research Center. He peered at me expectantly from across a table in a small, nondescript conference room. We were inside North Korea's Radiochemical Laboratory, a massive complex where the North had allegedly extracted the bomb fuel for its nascent nuclear weapons program. "You mean the plutonium?" I replied cautiously, somewhat taken aback by the question. Well, yes, Ri replied and motioned to a colleague in a white lab coat who promptly left the room to retrieve the material. Within minutes, I was holding a nearly half-pound piece of funnel-shaped plutonium in my hands in a sealed glass jar.

This event was the crowning moment of my first and most improbable visit to North Korea in January 2004. It was nearly forty years after I had first held plutonium in my gloved hands as a summer student at the Los Alamos laboratory in New Mexico, the birthplace of the nuclear bomb. It was not so much the presence of plutonium that surprised me—although bringing it into a conference room was unusual—but rather that the North Koreans would show their plutonium to me, the former director of the Los Alamos lab. Perhaps even more surprising, why would their nuclear specialists give me such a revealing tour of their facilities? As I discovered, they were eager to show the outside world that their nuclear facilities were operating and what they had accomplished. Although I was visiting with

Stanford University Professor John W. Lewis in a nongovernmental, unofficial (typically called Track 2) capacity, North Korean officials viewed my association with Los Alamos as a valuable conduit to the U.S. government.

I knew my way around nuclear facilities and nuclear weapons, having worked at Los Alamos for several decades, including serving for nearly twelve years as the laboratory's fifth director. I had visited the nuclear weapons facilities of Russia, China, the United Kingdom, and France. Although my expertise was primarily in the technical domain, I was no stranger to political and diplomatic issues, having worked closely with UK and French colleagues to develop cooperative programs to keep the Soviets at bay during the Cold War. As the Soviet Union disintegrated, I worked with Russia and several other former Soviet states to help them mitigate the nuclear security and safety challenges resulting from the Soviet collapse. I had also worked with China's nuclear complex to assist its nuclear specialists in protecting and safeguarding their nuclear materials, and later in joining forces to help prevent nuclear terrorism. I had also just begun to take a closer look at the India–Pakistan conflict, an antagonistic relationship for over fifty years that had risen to alarming levels when both countries declared themselves nuclear powers after conducting nuclear tests in 1998. North Korea was not on my horizon. I was not keen to visit.

What I saw and experienced during that first visit shattered my preconceived notions about the Democratic Peoples' Republic of Korea (DPRK). How could a country that ranks in the bottom 10 percent of the world's economies—in which hundreds of thousands of its citizens starved to death in the 1990s—possibly muster the means to build the bomb? And now, why did this country, generally viewed as the equivalent of an astrophysical black hole from which nothing can escape, open its main nuclear complex to me and allow its nuclear professionals to brief me on the status and plans for that complex?

Most importantly, the visit alarmed me. I thought about how the George W. Bush administration had failed to anticipate the technical consequences and ensuing nuclear security risks of its political decision to walk away from a diplomatic agreement that had halted activities at the nuclear complex for eight years. I reported my findings at a congressional hearing for what marked the beginning of a nearly two-decade endeavor to better assess North Korea's nuclear program and mitigate the risk it posed to our

Northeast Asian allies, South Korea and Japan, and U.S. assets in the region and at home. This journey took me back to North Korea each of the next six years. Each trip brought more information about the nature of the nuclear program, the personalities of my North Korean interlocutors, and the inner workings of their bureaucracy. The surprises never stopped coming.

Since my last visit in November 2010, North Korea's nuclear facilities have been off limits to all outsiders. I watched from afar as the North showed off one nuclear advance after another. I continued to update my technical analysis, followed political developments closely, and provided advice to our government and to allies. I was frustrated by how successive U.S. administrations were not able to prevent a country with such a weak hand from becoming one of fewer than ten countries in the world to possess a nuclear arsenal, and one of only three that might target the United States. My analysis of how this happened, what could have been done differently, and the lessons learned for future administrations are the subject of *Hinge Points*.

HINGE POINTS

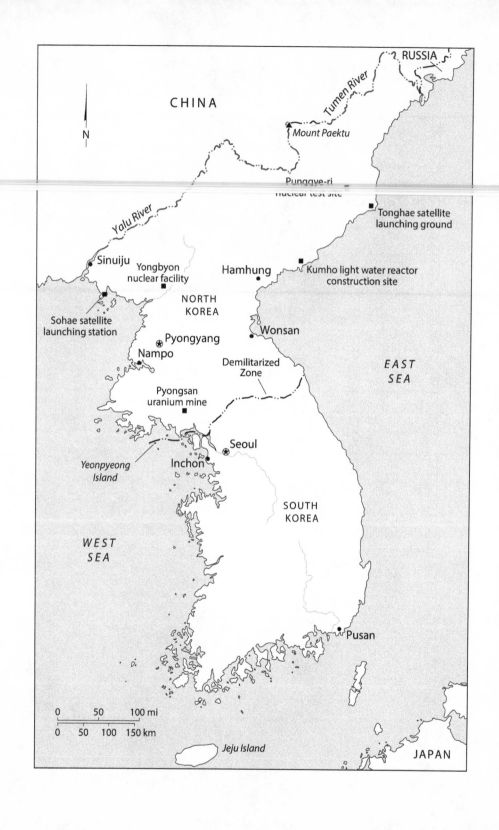

CHINA

Tumen River

N

Mount Paektu

RUSSIA

Punggye-ri
nuclear test site

Yalu River

Tonghae satellite
launching ground

Sinuiju

Yongbyon
nuclear facility

Hamhung

Kumho light water reactor
construction site

NORTH
KOREA

Sohae satellite
launching station

Pyongyang

Wonsan

Nampo

*EAST
SEA*

Demilitarized
Zone

Pyongsan
uranium mine

Seoul

*Yeonpyeong
Island*

Inchon

SOUTH
KOREA

*WEST
SEA*

Pusan

| 0 | 50 | 100 mi |
| 0 | 50 | 100 | 150 km |

Jeju Island

JAPAN

1   Introduction

Mount Mantap was never the tallest peak in North Korea's rugged Hamgyong range. As day broke on September 3, 2017, it was about to become even shorter. Throughout the morning, North Korean scientists and technicians busied themselves at the base of one of Mantap's slopes preparing for what they hoped would be a watershed moment in the development of their country's nuclear program. During the last weeks of August, they had readied diagnostic instrumentation, fortified construction efforts, and assembled and emplaced a nuclear device within the tunnels that burrowed deep into the mountain, which had already been shaken by five previous nuclear tests.[1] Now, they reviewed instruments and equipment housed in sheds outside the north portal, and trudged through a muddy courtyard to the command center, where they waited anxiously for the results of their years of effort. At 12:36 PM, the mountain shook. Within a fraction of a second, a powerful nuclear reaction took place, blossoming violently with devastating heat and pressure. It annihilated the test device, blasting a large spherical cavity within

---

1. Frank Pabian, Joseph S. Bermudez Jr., and Jack Liu, "North Korea's Punggye-ri Nuclear Test Site: New Media Reports of an Imminent Sixth Test Again Cannot Be Corroborated," *38 North* (August 30, 2017), https://www.38north.org/2017/08/punggye083017/

the mountain, and—unexpectedly—dropping Mantap's 2,205-meter peak by half a meter and bulging it out sideways about 3.5 meters.

The ensuing 6.3 magnitude earthquake set off by the explosion reverberated throughout North Korea, into neighboring China and South Korea, and around the world. It triggered the sensors of the U.S. Geological Survey and the Comprehensive Nuclear Test Ban Treaty Organization, which monitor the globe for seismic activity.[2] Just hours before the blast, the Central News Agency (KCNA) had released photos showing North Korea's leader, Kim Jong Un, inspecting a nuclear device. In one remarkable photo, Kim appears not giving orders but almost as the student, attentively following the instructive gesture of Dr. Ri Hong Sop, identified as director of the Nuclear Weapons Institute. Following the test, the Nuclear Weapons Institute called the test device a two-stage thermonuclear bomb—that is, a hydrogen bomb—small enough to fit inside the nose cone of the North's long-range missiles, photos of which had been conspicuously displayed on the wall behind Kim.[3]

It remains impossible to determine whether the North had tested the device shown in the photos, but the explosion yield estimated from seismic data was 200 to 250 kilotons,[4] about fifteen times the size of the August 1945 Hiroshima explosion and consistent with a yield from a hydrogen bomb. The last time a device of such power was detonated anywhere in the world was in a May 1992 nuclear test in China. The United States and the Soviet Union had not exceeded a blast of 150 kilotons since they signed the Threshold Test Ban Treaty in 1974. Regardless of the exact design of the North's

2. Earthquake Hazards Program, "M 6.3 Nuclear Explosion—21 km ENE of Sengjibae-gam, North Korea," *USGS* (September 3, 2017), https://earthquake.usgs.gov/earthquakes/eventpage/us2000aert/executive#executive; CTBTO estimate was magnitude of 6.1. See Technical Findings, "3 September 2017: North Korea Announced Nuclear Test," *CTBTO* (September 7, 2017, updated April 12, 2018), https://www.ctbto.org/the-treaty/developments-after-1996/2017-sept-dprk/technical-findings/

3. David Sanger and Choe Sang-Hun, "North Korean Nuclear Test Draws U.S. Warning of 'Massive Military Response,'" *New York Times* (September 2, 2017), https://www.nytimes.com/2017/09/03/world/asia/north-korea-tremor-possible-6th-nuclear-test.html

4. Dimitri P. Voytan, Thorne Lay, Esteban J. Chaves, and John T. Ohman, "Yield Estimates for the Six North Korean Nuclear Tests from Teleseismic *P* Wave Modeling and Intercorrelation of *P* and *Pn* Recordings," *JGR: Solid Earth* 124, no. 5 (May 2019): 4916–4939, https://doi.org/10.1029/2019JB017418

test device, there was no doubt that North Korea had demonstrated a new capability to inflict damage on a massive scale.

Following the nuclear test, on November 28, North Korea launched an unarmed ballistic missile almost 4,500 kilometers into space before its pieces fell back to Earth in the Sea of Japan. The U.S. government and independent analysts quickly assessed that the missile, dubbed Hwasong-15 by the North, had intercontinental range, meaning that it could put the entire United States within reach.[5] North Korean state media released photos of Kim, illuminated against a towering, camouflaged transporter-erector-launcher (TEL), inspecting the missile before launch as well as Kim watching images of the missile's flight path from an observation station. The Hwasong-15 test was the latest in a robust development schedule that the North had followed throughout 2017, during which it tested several ballistic missiles with newfound intermediate and intercontinental range.

All told, these two major events—the North's test of a likely hydrogen bomb in September and a new intercontinental ballistic missile (ICBM) in November—underscored what had been a dangerous and unsettling year on the Korean Peninsula. The significant advancement of North Korea's nuclear arsenal exacerbated the existing military threat that the North's conventional, chemical, and nuclear forces posed to the United States and its allies in Northeast Asia. While North Korea would need more testing to improve the safety, reliability, and performance of its nuclear-tipped ICBMs, events in 2017 served notice that it was well on its way. The North had already demonstrated that it almost surely could reach South Korea or Japan with nuclear-tipped missiles, and now there was, for the first time, a possibility that it could reach the U.S. mainland as well. In less than six years after assuming the reins of the Kim dynasty in North Korea, the young Mr. Kim had fulfilled the dreams of his father Kim Jong Il, and grandfather Kim Il Sung, to possess a sufficiently menacing nuclear arsenal to deter the United States.

What made 2017 especially dangerous was that these rapid-fire technical developments took place as the political relationship between Washington and Pyongyang had become increasingly tense. The provocative rhetoric and

5. David Wright, "North Korea's Longest Missile Test Yet," *All Things Nuclear* (November 28, 2017), https://allthingsnuclear.org/dwright/nk-longest-missile-test-yet

threats of military force by both Kim Jong Un and U.S. President Donald Trump—backed by their respective nuclear arsenals—posed a great risk to international security. As Trump's advisors debated whether the United States should initiate a "bloody nose" strike—a limited, preventive U.S. attack on North Korea's nuclear assets and/or its short- and long-range delivery systems—Trump threatened that North Korea's continued missile and nuclear development would be "met with fire and fury like the world has never seen." And he stood before the UN General Assembly in September 2017 to warn "Rocket Man" that, if forced to defend the U.S. or its allies, he would "have no choice but to totally destroy North Korea." Kim Jong Un responded in a statement with a ferocity that stunned even North Korean diplomats and caused many Americans to scramble for their dictionaries: "I will surely and definitely tame the mentally deranged U.S. dotard with fire."

The fear of nuclear war in 2017 was heightened because so little was known at the time about the two leaders with their fingers on the nuclear button. Kim Jong Un, who had assumed power in North Korea in late 2011, was young and viewed in the United States as inexperienced and unpredictable. The U.S. news media often portrayed him as crazy or homicidal. Even less was known about the military leadership that commanded his strategic rocket forces. President Trump was equally inexperienced and, arguably, even more unpredictable. Compounding the problem was the lack of a regular, direct line of communication between Washington and Pyongyang.

North Korea was able to build its present-day nuclear arsenal against all odds and often in plain sight despite being in the crosshairs of every U.S. administration for the past thirty years. Every American president has vowed either to not let North Korea obtain the bomb or, once that ship sailed, to achieve its full disarmament. The North's nuclear program was restrained but not eliminated during the Clinton administration; challenged, demonstrated, and then unleashed during the George W. Bush administration; greatly expanded during the Obama years; and became a menacing threat during Trump's first year when Washington and Pyongyang nearly stumbled into a nuclear confrontation in 2017. A year of rapprochement in 2018 was followed by Kim Jong Un pulling back from diplomacy. The North has continued to cement its status more convincingly than ever as a state with a nuclear arsenal. This is the stark reality that leaders of the past three administrations must live with and that the current administration faces. It cannot be explained away or left on the foreign policy back burner indefinitely.

A DIFFERENT VIEW

As I got more deeply involved in the Korean nuclear issue, it became increasingly clear to me that there was a dismayingly misleading narrative in the United States about how North Korea progressed from zero nuclear weapons in 2001 to an arsenal of close to fifty weapons some twenty years later. The conventional wisdom I encountered again and again was that good faith American efforts to halt the North's nuclear program were circumvented by the North's repeated violations of diplomatic agreements. Over the years, I found this perspective to be neither true nor helpful. It lets Washington off the hook too easily for its own failures and does not tell us why we are in the current predicament. Rather than cling to an unflinching belief in North Korea's perfidy and to a narrative that the Kims trapped Washington in manipulative cycles of "provocation, extortion, and reward," this book takes a fresh look at North Korea's technical and political developments and how they are intricately intertwined.

Technical advances or setbacks in the North's nuclear program opened or closed diplomatic options, just as diplomatic advances sometimes were a brake on technical progress. Failures in the laboratories or on the testing grounds may have required turning to diplomacy to buy time to correct problems. At other junctures, diplomatic progress gave Pyongyang new reasons to consider throttling back technical advances. At the same time, active diplomacy and agreements sometimes constrained technical options by limiting specific steps (such as tests) or allowing on-site presence of inspectors. In the subsequent chapters, I detail how these technical and diplomatic developments proceeded over two decades.

Moreover, the close and parallel examination of technical and political developments is crucial because *perceptions* of technical capabilities can be as important as reality. In other words, one must differentiate what Pyongyang wants Washington to believe from the reality on the ground. Over the years, Pyongyang has publicly hyped its nuclear and missile advances more often than it has tried to hide them. Separating perceptions from reality requires a certain level of in-country presence. U.S. intelligence agencies had little, if any, assets in North Korea, which combined with the closed nature of the regime, made it a difficult intelligence collection target. The intelligence community was dramatically wrong in several of its key North Korea estimates, and even when correct, the information was often not packaged in a manner useful to negotiators and, just as often, was not used effectively or manipulated by the policymakers who worked with negotiators.

As the North Korean nuclear drama unfolded, I had the benefit of a front-row seat, beginning with my first visit in 2004. My assessment of the North's nuclear journey was informed by the extraordinary access Pyongyang gave me to its nuclear facilities and its nuclear staff for seven consecutive years. I was there by invitation, not as an inspector. Rather than hiding its nuclear progress, Pyongyang sought a certain level of transparency, primarily to try to convince Washington that it had a credible nuclear deterrent. My access to its nuclear facilities and the level of discussion with the North's technical experts went far beyond what they typically shared with inspectors or what they professed through government propaganda. There was little posturing because they understood that I knew my way around nuclear facilities and nuclear weapons.

I began my involvement with North Korea with pretty much a blank slate. Although while at Los Alamos I had traveled to most countries with nuclear programs, I had not visited the Korean Peninsula and had little understanding of Korean history and culture. As it turned out, I was fortunate. My early visits provided a crucial education on the political front, thanks to Stanford University Professor John W. Lewis, who assembled his Track 2 delegations with individuals who had intimate and longstanding experience on North Korea. Lewis was a respected Asia specialist who had been engaged in Track 2 dialogue with China in the 1970s and with North Korea beginning with his first trip in 1989. He recruited Charles L. (Jack) Pritchard, an experienced diplomat and Northeast Asia expert who had just left government service, to join us for the first three visits. Pritchard had firsthand experience negotiating with North Korea from serving on the National Security Council and then as the State Department's chief North Korean negotiator. Robert L. (Bob) Carlin was another key member of Lewis's team. He first tackled the North Korea conundrum in 1974 as a CIA analyst. Later, he was chief of the Northeast Asia Division in the State Department's Bureau of Intelligence and Research (INR), where he took part in all phases of U.S.–North Korea negotiations from 1992 to 2000. Carlin served in the Korea Energy Development Organization (KEDO) created to supply North Korea with electricity-producing nuclear reactors as part of the Clinton administration's 1994 Agreed Framework nuclear deal. Beginning in 2006, Carlin joined us for visits to North Korea. I found Lewis and his colleagues to be indispensable tutors on politics and diplomacy.[6]

I learned quickly that Lewis and his team were highly respected in Pyongyang and had access to key government officials. This work was Track 2 at its most effective: people on each side with intimate familiarity with the politics and diplomatic record but who were not bound by the strictures of formal government negotiations. They were able to probe diplomatic openings, uncover potential red lines, and transmit warning signals. On the American side, the Track 2 engagements also provided a measure of continuity, which was typically lost within the government during presidential transitions. This was important because the North Korean side maintained continuity. For example, some of the key North Korean officials present during negotiations for the Clinton era nuclear deal are still there for President Biden's term some twenty-five years later.

For seven consecutive years, from 2004 to 2010, Pyongyang gave us access to high-level diplomats, nuclear experts, and nuclear facilities. We used those visits to gain critical insights into the North's nuclear developments and surmise how Pyongyang tied these to its political strategy. Pyongyang used our visits to signal its capabilities and its political interests to Washington. It ended with a 2010 visit in which North Korea surprised us and the rest of the world by revealing a modern centrifuge facility, demonstrating that in addition to their plutonium path to the bomb, they also had a plan with uranium.

After 2010, our Stanford University team continued to follow the North's nuclear developments, but now from afar. We were greatly aided by the emergence of readily available commercial satellite imagery. Our team of experienced analysts benefited from what we had learned during our visits to

6. Pritchard published a memoir of his government service work in North Korea. Charles L. Pritchard, *Failed Diplomacy* (Washington, DC: Brookings Institution Press, 2007). Carlin co-authored the third edition of the classic *The Two Koreas: A Contemporary History* with Don Oberdorfer (New York: Basic Books, 2014). Lewis published several influential books on China. For instance, see John Wilson Lewis and Xue Litai, *China Builds the Bomb* (Stanford: Stanford University Press, 1988).

the nuclear complex.[7] Pyongyang also chose to selectively reveal its nuclear and missile advances. When the North stepped up its missile launches, it would augment the findings of foreign governments with its own propaganda. It routinely publicized photos of missiles, launch videos, technical details, and flight trajectories—often shown as being viewed by Kim Jong Un. New military systems, such as missiles and TELs, were displayed at huge military parades. Kim Jong Il and Kim Jong Un were shown visiting key defense facilities, inspecting critical equipment required to support the nuclear program.

Nuclear tests created their own observables by making the ground shake and triggering seismic signals that were registered by instruments around the world. The magnitude of the seismic rumbles allowed us to estimate the power of the explosions, which, in turn, provided clues as to how rapidly North Korea was enhancing its nuclear firepower. To augment what could be assessed from such measurements, and to make sure outsiders would not underestimate its capabilities, Pyongyang took the extraordinary step of publicizing photos of Kim inspecting two of its modern bomb designs. To ensure they lost nothing in translation, state media displayed nuclear missiles and drawings in the background of the bomb mock-ups to send the message that the nuclear devices would fit onto its missiles.

Pyongyang had moved on from our visits to using other means to lift the curtain to its nuclear progress, including missile launches, seismic signals, photographs, and videos. Our team also used these indicators to continue to assess the North's nuclear trajectory, side by side with tracking the political developments. I continued to have regular contact with the American negotiation teams in all U.S. administrations and compared notes with Chinese, Russian, and South Korean government officials, scholars, and practitioners. Consultations with the Chinese, in particular, underscored the folly of U.S. administrations looking to China to solve the North Korea problem.

Bob Carlin was able to continue to track the political state of play with visits to North Korea in an unofficial capacity through 2017. Fortunately, Carlin was a seasoned veteran of official negotiations with North Korea

---

7. Over the years the Stanford University team consisted of affiliates Chaim Braun, Nick Hansen, Frank Pabian, and Allison Puccioni, and former students Niko Milonopoulos, Sulgiye Park, and Elliot Serbin.

and an astute observer of how Pyongyang functions and how it manages the news. He had experience on the ground through his more than thirty visits to North Korea over the years. Carlin was also adept at deciphering North Korean announcements and statements. To know what's important in Pyongyang's pronouncements, one must understand who said what and whether it is just propaganda or smokescreen. In fact, a few years ago, a contact at the North Korean Mission at the UN confided, "Mr. Carlin is able not only to read between the lines of Pyongyang statements, but he also reads between the words."

NORTH KOREA'S DUAL-TRACK STRATEGY

By tracking the nuclear and political developments side by side, how they intersected or diverged, it became clear that Pyongyang has followed a dual-track strategy of diplomacy *and* nuclear development. I was able to identify a number of key events—"hinge points" I call them—in which Washington failed to weigh the risks and rewards presented by a particular combination of diplomatic and technical factors. Contrary to the prevailing view in Washington that North Korea only used diplomacy to buy time for its nuclear program, it was Kim Il Sung, the country's founder, who, in the early 1990s, seriously explored a long-term strategic relationship with the United States through diplomacy. Whereas accommodation with Washington was in his view the best path to survival given the dramatic geopolitical upheavals at the end of the Cold War, a time when North Korea felt abandoned and even threatened by both Russia and China, Kim Il Sung insisted such accommodation be based on the projection of strength, not weakness.[8]

By this time, North Korea's economy and conventional military were increasingly falling behind South Korea's and, of course, the North was heavily outmatched by the United States. The only projection of strength would have to come from the North's nuclear program, making it a top priority for the regime. By choosing to pursue diplomacy *plus* nuclearization, not one or the other, North Korea has been able to hedge against failure in one track

---

8. Mike Chinoy, *Meltdown: The Inside Story of the North Korean Nuclear Crisis* (New York: St. Martin's Griffin, 2009), 3. (Chinoy's assessment of what Kim Il Sung said at a Pyongyang meeting he attended with evangelist Billy Graham).

or the other and mitigate the risks inherent in the vicissitudes of the post–Cold War international system and its own authoritarian domestic politics.

North Korea's determination to build a nuclear weapon option to deter a United States that remained the North's central adversary was resolute, if not always predominant. Pyongyang has alternated prioritizing one track or another over the last thirty years but has not made the strategic decision to irrevocably commit to a single track. While the North has slowed its nuclear progress at times, it has never fully abandoned the nuclear track. But the realization and permanent pursuit of a credible nuclear deterrent were not necessarily preordained, despite the attention and resources that North Korea has devoted to its nuclear development. By leaving open the possibility of success in either track and taking advantage of the flexibility this afforded them in their dealings with the United States, the Kims have sought a measured degree of insurance for the long-term survival of the country and the regime. In other words, each of the Kims at times seriously pursued diplomacy to reach strategic accommodation with Washington, which in turn opened the way for agreements that would retard further development of the nuclear weapons program.

Washington, however, had a singular focus on denuclearization. It ruled out a political middle ground by forcing Pyongyang early on to choose between diplomacy *or* the nuclear program. It failed to deal with Pyongyang's dual-track strategy, missing key opportunities for diplomacy and misinterpreting some of the North's actions, which led to bad decisions—the hinge points I mentioned above. The resulting bad decisions by Washington had bad consequences, leading to a state of nearly continuous crisis for twenty years and one of the greatest security risks the United States faces today.

Washington consistently failed to recognize and/or cope effectively with North Korea's dual-track strategy. The North was often moving on two parallel fronts—the technical/military front to build a nuclear arsenal or earn foreign currency through nuclear or missile exports and the engagement/diplomacy front to explore strategic accommodation with the United States. Even when Washington suspected that the North was moving on parallel tracks, it did not deal effectively with Pyongyang. Washington's North Korea policies seldom incorporated sound technical analysis, either because such analysis was not sought out by the policymakers or because it was contrary to Washington's policy assumptions and political priorities.

The logic guiding the North's dual-track strategy is pragmatic and has steadied the hand of Pyongyang as the mantle of leadership passed down from founder Kim Il Sung upon his death in 1994 to his son Kim Jong Il, and to his grandson Kim Jong Un, in 2011. All three Kims have, to different degrees, found it useful to implement elements of the dual-track strategy. On the one hand, diplomatic engagement could normalize relations with North Korea's chief antagonist, the United States, neutralizing an outsized military threat, counterbalancing against regional competitors, and potentially freeing up resources to concentrate on the economy. On the other hand, the acquisition of a nuclear arsenal could also neutralize the threat of the United States and its regional allies via different means: deterring and protecting the regime from aggressive neighbors and an implacably hostile United States. Equally or perhaps more importantly, the strength of a nuclear arsenal could force Washington to take Pyongyang seriously, to deal with it on the diplomatic track.

Pyongyang realized long ago that to develop the technical foundations for nuclear and missile programs requires time and significant resources. To succeed, the North pursued these programs with great tenacity, although at times the pace and extent were contingent on what was achievable on the diplomatic front. I believe that each of the Kim regimes had a genuine interest in diplomacy, beginning with Kim Il Sung's strategic vision of normal relations with the United States. Over the years, his son and grandson also explored such strategic accommodation at times. All three, however, believed that while exploring diplomacy, nuclear weapons could not be relinquished until accommodation had been achieved to their satisfaction.

At some key decision points, Pyongyang accelerated the nuclear hedge too soon instead of giving diplomacy more time to bear fruit. Whereas technical development is subject to the laws of physics, diplomacy can change reality as it progresses. What is impossible today often becomes conceivable tomorrow. Even if the Kims believed they wouldn't abandon their weapons at any given moment, it is possible to imagine and work toward circumstances in which they may view it in their best interest to do so. Unfortunately, decisions at each hinge point facilitated the North's almost unfettered expansion of its nuclear and missile programs, making a path to the elimination of such weapons increasingly difficult. Nevertheless, declaring that Kim Jung Un will never give up his weapons is counterproductive. We simply don't know—and likely, neither does he.

PLAN OF THE BOOK

In *Hinge Points*, I take the reader on a journey that tracks the nuclear and political developments side by side, how they intersected or diverged over the past twenty years. The journey is complex but ultimately necessary to see what I saw, hear what I heard, and understand what, in my view, best explains one of Washington's greatest foreign policy failures. The reader doesn't have to be a nuclear scientist or an expert in nuclear weapons to grasp the interplay between diplomatic and technical developments. In the early chapters I provide an inside view of the North's nuclear complex and its technical staff based on my seven visits. Meetings with North Korean diplomats convinced me that they were able to integrate technical and diplomatic developments, in stark contrast to what happened in Washington from the George W. Bush administration through the Trump years. The chapters describing the seven visits are separated by chapters that analyze the political climate, particularly as it played out in Washington and Pyongyang, to highlight the importance of following both technical and diplomatic developments. The political analysis is not meant to constitute a diplomatic history or a detailed description of the negotiations process during the past twenty years.[9]

After describing my last visit to North Korea in 2010, I continue to integrate the technical analysis with the political and diplomatic developments chronologically through the Obama and Trump administrations. I describe the hinge points that took us further and further down the road to a North Korea with a growing, and more sophisticated, nuclear arsenal. Both Washington and Pyongyang squandered opportunities. In many of these cases, had Washington properly incorporated a sensible risk analysis of the technical factors into policy decision-making, it may have been able

---

9. The reader is referred to detailed histories such as Joel S. Wit, Daniel B. Poneman, and Robert L. Gallucci, *Going Critical: The First North Korean Nuclear Crisis* (Washington, DC: Brookings Institution Press, 2004), addressing the early years of the crisis; Mike Chinoy's *Meltdown* for the Clinton years; and Oberdorfer and Carlin's *Two Koreas* for a comprehensive history through 2012.

to implement a reliable long-term process to freeze, roll back, and eventually eliminate the North's nuclear program, rather than see it advance.

The tragedy, in my view, is that Washington, no matter who was in the White House, failed to conduct a technically informed risk/benefit analysis. Instead, American political leaders and policymakers made decisions that let political or ideological prejudices win out over decisive analysis. Over and over, these political decisions that failed to incorporate a clear-eyed evaluation of their technical consequences opened the door for North Korea to expand its nuclear program. Political leaders in Washington relied on their own (often misguided) assumptions about North Korea's motivations for developing its nuclear program and engaging in diplomacy. Many American policymakers have resisted engagement with the Kim regimes on what they cite as moral grounds: These reigns were considered reprehensible with horrendous human rights violations, and they were likely to cheat on every agreement reached. Washington's policies were also hampered by the corrosive effects of differing and dueling ideologies, poisonous disagreements and infighting within administrations, and a lack of continuity within and across U.S. administrations. Similar mistakes were made over and over. While North Korea's leadership remained focused as it transitioned from one Kim to another, Washington vacillated.

I acknowledge that over the years many issues have plagued U.S. decision-making about the North Korea nuclear question. These issues have been debated by politicians, documented by scholars, and examined in the news media and scores of books. I benefited from reviewing memoirs, commentaries, and scholarly works. This book focuses on two primary failings that have received little attention: first, the absence of full recognition of North Korea's dual-track strategy to pursue diplomacy *and* nuclear development; second, Washington's seeming inability to incorporate technically informed risk/benefit analysis in its decision-making.

The nuclear issue is, of course, not the only one that impedes peace and security on the Korean Peninsula, but it continues to cast a larger and darker shadow over everything else as the North's arsenal grows more and more dangerous. Thus, I focus on the nuclear issue because its resolution is necessary, although I realize not sufficient, to resolve decades of enmity.

2   Nuclear Background

Nuclear energy can electrify the world, or it can destroy it. This was recognized immediately after the discovery of fission—the splitting of the atomic nucleus—in Germany in 1938. The energy released in splitting the atomic nucleus is one hundred million times the energy generated from the electrons that orbit the tiny nucleus—through chemical reactions such as burning fossil fuels or through electronic processes. Controlled fission of the elements uranium and plutonium in nuclear reactors produces heat that can be converted to electricity.[1] In very different configurations, uranium or plutonium can be fissioned in an uncontrolled, chain reaction to produce bombs of enormous destructive power. One of the limitations to the greater use of nuclear reactors to produce clean electricity has been

---

1. Uranium (element 92) and plutonium (element 94) are part of the row of heavy, radioactive elements called actinides in the periodic table. Their nuclei are unstable resulting in their disintegration and transmutation into daughter elements through radioactive decay. Uranium and plutonium are designated by the *atomic numbers* of 92 and 94: that is, the number of protons (positive charges) in their nucleus. The nucleus captures the same number of electrons to make the atom neutral. The chemical properties are determined by the electrons. The nuclear properties are determined by the number of protons and neutrons (neutral or uncharged particles) in the nucleus. Different *isotopes* of an element, such as U-235 and U-238, have the same chemical properties but different numbers of neutrons. U-235, for example, has 143 neutrons, and U-238 has 146 neutrons, giving them different nuclear properties.

that the technologies for both peaceful and military applications of nuclear energy are largely interchangeable and interdependent—the dual-use dilemma.[2]

In the United States, nuclear fission was pursued first for military purposes with the Manhattan Project. The U.S. government believed itself to be in a race to beat the Germans to the bomb during World War II—although the bombs were ultimately used to end the war with Japan. The awesome power of the first fission bombs was unleashed in the bombing of Hiroshima on August 6, 1945, and of Nagasaki three days later, with the destructive power of 15 kilotons (15,000 tons) and 21 kilotons of TNT equivalent, respectively. Fortunately, these remain the only times that nuclear weapons have been used in warfare.

Over the next couple of decades, the United States and the Soviet Union increased the destructive power to megatons (millions of tons) of TNT equivalent with the development of fusion, or so-called hydrogen bombs, in which enormous energy is released by fusing heavy forms of hydrogen under intense pressures and temperatures. Such bombs have been exploded only in test devices, many of them to frightening effects in the atmosphere. Although the nuclear taboo, or what might be called the no-nuclear-use norm, has held for more than seventy-five years, it is alarming that the American public no longer fears nuclear explosions as much as they once did—knowing that they would be unmitigated catastrophes to be avoided at any cost. Recent research suggests that public opinion is unlikely to be a serious constraint on any president contemplating the use of nuclear weapons in the crucible of war.[3]

How do we warn the public more than seventy-five years after Hiroshima and Nagasaki (and nearly fifty years after the end of atmospheric nuclear testing) of the awesome destructive power of nuclear explosions—as we think about these weapons in the hands of North Korea's leaders? I have found the words of Tatsuichiro Akizuki, a Nagasaki doctor and eyewitness

2. D. E. Lilienthal, C. I. Barnard, C. A. Thomas, J. R. Oppenheimer, and H. A. Winne, *Acheson-Lilienthal Report: Report on the International Control of Atomic Energy* (Washington, DC: U.S. Government Printing Office, 1946).

3. Scott D. Sagan and Benjamin A. Valentino, "Revisiting Hiroshima in Iran: What Americans Really Think About Using Nuclear Weapons and Killing Noncombatants," *International Security* 42, no. 1 (Summer 2017): 41–79.

to the city's destruction, to be the most sobering account of the horrific scene of an atomic bombing and why these weapons must never be used again:

> Trees on the near-by hills were smoking, as were the leaves of sweet potatoes in the fields. To say that everything burned is not enough. It seemed as if the earth itself emitted fire and smoke, flames that writhed up and erupted from underground. The sky was dark the ground was scarlet, and in between hung clouds of yellowish smoke. Three kinds of color—black, yellow and scarlet— loomed ominously over the people, who ran about like so many ants seeking to escape. . . . But that ocean of fire, that sky of smoke! It seemed like the end of the world.[4]

By August 1945, tens of millions of people had been killed in the war with conventional weapons. Cities like Dresden and Tokyo had been almost totally destroyed by Allied firebombing. What was different about Hiroshima and Nagasaki was that their destruction did not require 300 planes to drop thousands of bombs—it was one plane, one bomb, one city destroyed, and approximately one hundred thousand people killed. In the case of Nagasaki, it was around 6 kilograms of plutonium, the size of a grapefruit, that provided the nuclear bomb fuel. For Hiroshima, it was some tens of kilograms of uranium. If the situation on the Korean Peninsula ever degenerates to the point of a nuclear confrontation, it could result in hundreds of thousands, if not millions, of military and civilian casualties in the region, including many of the 200,000 Americans living in South Korea. Even a single nuclear weapon detonated above Seoul or Tokyo would kill at a massive scale; a 10-kiloton warhead could result in over 77,000 dead, while a 250-kiloton warhead, an explosive yield similar to the device North Korea tested in September 2017, could kill over 600,000.[5]

Today, there are fewer than ten countries that are known to possess nuclear weapons. The five permanent members of the UN Security

4. Tatsuichiro Akizuki, *Nagasaki 1945: The First Full-Length Eyewitness Account of the Atomic Bomb Attack on Nagasaki* (London: Quartet Books, 1981), 4.

5. Nukemap 2.7, *Nuclearsecrecy.com*. Data for a yield of 10 kilotons, https://nuclearse-crecy.com/nukemap/?&kt=10&lat=37.566536&lng=126.977969&hob_psi=5&hob_ft=2207&-casualties=1&fallout=1&psi=20,5,1&zm=13 Nukemap 2.7, *Nuclearsecrecy.com*. Data for a yield of 250 kilotons, https://nuclearsecrecy.com/nukemap/?&psi=20,5,1&casual-ties=1&fallout=1&linked=1&kt=250&lat=37.566536&lng=126.977969&hob_psi=5&hob_ft=6454&zm=11

Council—the United States, Russia, China, the United Kingdom, and France—are specifically acknowledged as nuclear weapon states in the Nuclear Nonproliferation Treaty (NPT). India and Pakistan, non-signatories to the NPT, declared themselves to be nuclear weapons states with nuclear tests in 1998 after decades of covert nuclear weapon development. Israel is also not a signatory of the NPT. Its nuclear status is unclear as the Israeli government neither admits nor denies the possession of nuclear weapons, and the U.S. government's position is that it does not know. South Africa is the only country that built nuclear weapons and relinquished them voluntarily. Ukraine, Kazakhstan, and Belarus inherited some of the Soviet Union's nuclear weapons without operational controls for those weapons upon its dissolution but were then persuaded to return them to Russia.

North Korea signed the NPT in 1985 but withdrew in 2003. Pyongyang declared itself to be a nuclear power with a nuclear test in 2006 and continued to develop a threatening nuclear arsenal and the means to deliver it during the next fifteen years. I briefly explain the technical fundamentals of the nuclear technologies required for a nuclear arsenal to help the reader navigate the North's nuclear developments and how these affected Pyongyang's diplomacy with Washington.

TECHNICAL REQUISITES FOR A NUCLEAR ARSENAL

To field nuclear weapons requires bomb fuel, weaponization, and means of delivery. Although several of the heavy elements could possibly fuel fission bombs, only uranium and plutonium have been used because of their suitable physics and engineering properties.[6] Specifically, the isotopes uranium-235 and plutonium-239, are the fissile forms of these elements that have fueled bombs, as well as nuclear reactors. Hydrogen bombs require the heavy isotopes of hydrogen—namely deuterium and tritium—to create nuclear energy by fusion. Weaponization involves the design, building,

---

6. Plutonium and some uranium isotopes are *fissile*—that is, they can sustain a chain reaction required for reactors or bombs triggered by neutrons of any energy and release more neutrons when they fission. Their *critical mass*—the smallest amount of fissile material needed for a sustained nuclear chain reaction—is sufficiently small for practical nuclear weapon devices. Although these elements are unstable, their *half-lives*—the time for one-half of the element to decay—is sufficiently long for practical use. For a helpful nuclear primer, see Richard L. Garwin and Georges Charpak, *Megawatts and Megatons: The Future of Nuclear Power and Nuclear Weapons* (Chicago: University of Chicago Press, 2002).

and testing of nuclear weapons. The nuclear devices then require integration into the means of delivery. The three components require very different technical capabilities and industrial bases. North Korea was able to develop all three of the essential components over several decades.

1. Bomb Fuel

Natural uranium consists of 99.3 percent uranium-238 and 0.7 percent uranium-235. The difference results from the two having decayed over geologic time scales because of their greatly different half-lives.[7] To make uranium suitable for bombs, it must be almost pure uranium-235, that is, it must be concentrated (enriched) in the isotope U-235 to a level of roughly 90 percent. This isotope is fissile and in the fission process releases energetic neutrons that can cause other nuclei to fission—that is, support a chain reaction.[8] U-235 and U-238 are virtually identical chemically, but differ in their physical properties, notably their mass. The slight difference in mass allows the isotopes to be separated and makes it possible to increase the percentage of U-235. Almost all present and historic enrichment processes, directly or indirectly, make use of this small mass difference.

Nuclear reactors can operate with much lower enrichment levels of uranium fuel. Some reactor designs can use natural uranium as fuel combined with moderators that slow neutrons sufficiently to sustain a chain reaction. Over the years, "heavy" water (in which the heavier isotope deuterium replaces ordinary hydrogen) or graphite have been used as moderators in reactors dedicated to plutonium production for weapons. For electricity production, it is much more effective to enrich natural uranium to 3 to 5 percent U-235 combined with "light" (regular) water as a moderator and typically also as the coolant. Centrifuges have become the technology of choice to enrich uranium from its 0.7 percent U-235 content in natural uranium, to 3 to 5 percent for reactors, or 90 percent for weapon-grade uranium, by taking advantage of the slight mass differences in the isotopes. A cascade

7. U-238 is much more stable with a half-life of 4.5 billion years compared to 700 million years for U-235.

8. A nuclear chain reaction is a self-sustaining sequence of fission reactions in which neutrons emitted during fission produce an additional fission in at least one further nucleus. This nucleus in turn produces neutrons, and the process repeats. The process may be controlled in nuclear reactors or uncontrolled in nuclear explosions.

of centrifuges rapidly spin (at almost 100,000 rpm) uranium hexafluoride (UF_6) gas to separate the heavy from the light isotope. Centrifuge technologies are sophisticated and demanding. Only a small number of countries in the world have developed such capabilities.

Enriching uranium suffers from the dual-use dilemma because at low levels of enrichment, the uranium is used to fuel power reactors to make electricity but at high levels it can be used as bomb fuel. The International Atomic Energy Agency (IAEA) classifies any enrichment level of 20 percent U-235 and above as highly enriched uranium (HEU) and potentially weapon usable.[9] The centrifuge technologies required for producing low-enriched uranium (LEU) (below 20 percent) are the same as those required for producing HEU; only the details of the centrifuge cascades differ. Moreover, enriching natural uranium to LEU levels for reactors requires more than half of the work to achieve the 90 percent levels for weapon grade. In other words, producing LEU gets you halfway to HEU.

Because of the short half-lives (in geologic time) of its isotopes, plutonium is virtually nonexistent in nature.[10] It is produced in nuclear reactors when U-238 reactor fuel absorbs neutrons and transmutes to the element plutonium. The isotopic mix of plutonium created in reactors depends on reactor design, reactor fuel, and operational conditions. Unlike uranium, virtually all plutonium isotopes are fissile, but weapon-grade plutonium typically contains greater than 93 percent isotope Pu-239. Heavy water and graphite-moderated reactors using natural uranium fuel, typically in metallic form, are the favored pathways for weapon-grade plutonium production. Light water reactors using low-enriched uranium fuel, typically in oxide form, are operated in an electricity-producing mode and yield plutonium with much higher concentrations of Pu-240 and Pu-241, making that plutonium less desirable for weapon applications. Nevertheless, any uranium-fueled reactor will produce neutrons, and those neutrons will produce plutonium.[11] Interestingly, near the end of the operational cycle,

9. Although at 20 percent enrichment the critical mass is about 800 kg, far too heavy to be a practical weapon.

10. The half-life of Pu-239, the predominant isotope in weapon-grade plutonium, is 24,100 years.

11. A more detailed treatment of proliferation concerns is presented in Siegfried S. Hecker, Matthias Englert, and Michael C. Miller, "Nuclear Non-proliferation," in *Funda-*

about half the energy in uranium-fueled reactors is generated by fission of the plutonium that has been bred into the reactor fuel.

Plutonium produced in all reactors is created in combination with numerous fission products. Together they are present in the used (spent) uranium fuel. To be used for nuclear weapons, the plutonium must be separated chemically from that mix—what is called "reprocessing" of spent fuel. The chemistry and chemical engineering of reprocessing developed during the Manhattan Project is still the prevalent one in use today. This PUREX process (plutonium uranium reduction extraction) also has dual-use applications. It is used to produce bomb-grade plutonium metal but is also used by several countries to extract plutonium to feed back into the reactor fuel stream for generating electricity.

The production of plutonium bomb fuel requires a large infrastructure—together called "fuel-cycle facilities." These including mining of uranium (or purchase of uranium ore), chemical processing to prepare uranium (or uranium oxide) reactor fuel, nuclear reactors to produce plutonium from the uranium, and chemical facilities to reprocess (chemically extract) plutonium from the spent reactor fuel. Fuel-cycle facilities require significant financial investments and technical workforce. Some of the facilities, such as reactors, have reasonably large footprints that can be detected by the national technical means (NTM) of verification employed by intelligence agencies or by commercial satellite imagery. Others, such as centrifuge facilities, have very small footprints and are easily hidden.

In addition to the fissile materials, plutonium and uranium, hydrogen bombs require deuterium and tritium for fusion bomb fuel. Fusion bombs are typically called hydrogen bombs or thermonuclear weapons. Deuterium and tritium[12] can also be used to enhance the yield of a fission bomb by a process called "boosting"—that is, having fission produce some fusion, which in turn helps to boost further fission reactions. Deuterium and tritium will also be the essential fuel for future civilian nuclear fusion reactors.

---

mentals of Materials for Energy and Environmental Sustainability, edited by David S. Ginley and David Cahen (pp. 162–177) (New York: Cambridge University Press, 2011).

12. Deuterium is a stable isotope of hydrogen with a nucleus comprised of a proton plus a neutron. Tritium consists of a proton and two neutrons. It is unstable and radioactively decays (to helium-3) with a half-life of 12.32 years.

2. Weaponization

The weaponization stage consists of designing, building, and testing of nuclear weapons. This stage requires an understanding of physics, not only nuclear physics, but also hydrodynamics, condensed matter physics, and many other aspects of physics under extreme conditions. Likewise, it needs chemistry, engineering, and materials expertise, especially for nuclear materials and high explosives. It also involves manufacturing know-how and equipment, such as machining and welding. Most of these processes and operations are conducted in buildings and spaces that are undetectable by overhead satellite imagery. Explosive compression of spherical objects in "cold tests" with surrogate materials are telltale signs of weapons development. These would be conducted covertly but are more difficult to hide. Nuclear testing is the most distinct indicator of a nuclear weapons program. Underground nuclear tests, such as those conducted by India, Pakistan, and North Korea during the past twenty-five years, send distinct seismic signals that are easily picked up around the world in seismic monitoring stations.

Unlike the fuel-cycle activities, which have legitimate civilian use, some of the weaponization activities do not. The requisite knowledge base for weaponization includes nuclear physics, computers, and high explosives. All of those have dual-use applications, enough so that interest in any of them, by a non-nuclear weapon nation, is not in itself a tipoff that the nation is working toward nuclear weapons. However, interest in neutron initiators[13] and/or high-explosive lenses would be such a warning, so research in either of these would be carried out covertly. Some such activities are easier to conceal than others. The biggest weapons-specific activity is a nuclear test, which as history has demonstrated is difficult to hide.

Fission bomb designs remain similar to the two families developed during the Manhattan Project (Figure 1). The bomb detonated over Hiroshima was an HEU-fueled gun-type device. This design is technologically straightforward—two subcritical masses of HEU are joined at high speed by a propellant in a gun barrel. The gun-assembly technology only works with HEU because it is not sufficiently rapid to work for plutonium. The second

---

13. Neutron initiators provide a burst of neutrons used to kickstart the chain reaction at the optimal moment as the bomb materials are explosively compressed in a nuclear device.

design, the implosion device shown in Figure 1, uses powerful chemical explosives to rapidly compress a subcritical mass of either plutonium or HEU. This design fueled with plutonium was detonated over Nagasaki.

In the early 1950s, both U.S. and Soviet scientists developed and tested hydrogen bombs based on the principle of compressing and fusing deuterium and tritium. Los Alamos scientists Edward Teller and Stanislav Ulam developed the breakthrough "radiation implosion" for a usable hydrogen bomb. The concept was a two-stage thermonuclear bomb. It channels the radiation from a fission bomb, the primary, to compress the secondary that contains deuterium/tritium fusion fuel. Hydrogen bombs can be developed with virtually unlimited destructive power. The most powerful hydrogen bomb ever tested by the United States was the Castle Bravo test at 15 megatons in March 1954 at Bikini Atoll, Marshall Islands, in the Central Pacific. The Soviets detonated a 100 megaton–class device at an intentionally reduced half yield of 50-plus megatons above the island of Novaya Zemlya in October 1961.

Deuterium accounts for approximately 0.02 percent of all naturally occurring hydrogen atoms in ocean waters. It is readily separated from ordinary hydrogen in water by distillation. Tritium can be produced in nuclear reactors by neutron bombardment of lithium-6, which is one of the two stable isotopes of lithium, the lightest of all metals. It co-exists in nature at 12.5 percent with the predominant isotope lithium-7 and is easily separated. Early in the development of the hydrogen bomb, it was discovered that tritium can be generated *in situ*, that is, during the nuclear detonation, by bombarding lithium-6 deuteride in the fusion secondary with neutrons from the imploding primary.

3. Delivery Systems

Nuclear bombs and warheads must also be integrated into delivery vehicles. The Hiroshima and Nagasaki fission bombs were delivered by B-29 bombers, appropriately modified to carry the first atomic bombs. Air delivery remains an important part of the "U.S. triad"—air, land, and sea delivery. In addition to gravity bombs, the United States employs air-launched cruise missiles with nuclear warheads. However, the most common delivery systems today are ballistic missiles, either land based or sea based on submarines. North Korea has several aircraft (the Russian Ilyushin-28, its Chinese version, the H-5, and the Russian MiG-23) that could be configured to carry nuclear weapons, but all indications are that Pyongyang decided early on to concentrate on missiles as the mode of delivery.

Delivery systems can be used to launch conventional or nuclear bombs. Short-range rockets are produced in many countries to deliver chemical explosives. In fact, there is a huge international market for these—both overt and covert. For example, during the 2021 Israel–Palestine crisis, over 4,000 rockets loaded with conventional explosives were fired from the Gaza Strip toward Israel. Israel responded with nearly 1,000 targeted air attacks. The crises resulted in nearly 300 people killed and thousands injured on the two sides. If one rocket were tipped with a nuclear bomb, even of modest yield, it could have killed hundreds of thousands and would have changed the face of the Middle East forever.

The proliferation of missiles with delivery capabilities for weapons of mass destruction is regulated by the Missile Technology Control Regime (MTCR),[14] an informal political understanding among thirty-five-member states that seek to limit the proliferation of missiles and missile technologies. Nevertheless, countries such as North Korea, Iran, Pakistan, and India have acquired missile technologies capable of carrying nuclear warheads.

Longer range rockets can be used for intercontinental ballistic missiles (ICBMs) or for space launch vehicles. They differ in detail and operations, but the technologies are also largely interchangeable and interdependent. Rockets for space launches are typically fueled with liquid propellant just prior to takeoff and are launched from fixed sites. Solid-fuel rocket motors are preferred for nuclear-tipped missiles because they can travel safely while fueled and therefore can be prepared for launch more rapidly and are more readily obscured. In addition, solid-fuel missiles can be launched from road-mobile transporter erector launchers (TELs) or from submarines. Intermediate and long-range nuclear-tipped missiles require greatly miniaturized nuclear warheads

14. "Missile Technology Control Regime (MTCR)," *Nuclear Threat Initiative*, https://www.nti.org/learn/treaties-and-regimes/missile-technology-control-regime-mtcr/ The MTCR complements the Nuclear Nonproliferation Treaty to deal with missile proliferation concerns.

that are sufficiently robust to survive the entire flight trajectory: launch, space flight, and atmospheric reentry. The final integration for nuclear warheads is accomplished through the command-and-control structure that links the military to the country's leadership.

NORTH KOREA'S EARLY NUCLEAR DEVELOPMENT

A brief review of how North Korea joined the elite club of nations with nuclear weapons will be helpful for understanding more recent developments. Contrary to what is generally believed in the West, the North's nuclear weapons quest was not supported by the governments of the Soviet Union/Russia or China. It was a determined effort to develop indigenous capabilities while taking advantage of every hole in a leaky international export control system to acquire nuclear and missile technologies.

Following Japan's surrender in August 1945, with little forethought, the United States and the Soviet Union divided the Korean Peninsula into two zones of control along the 38th parallel. The Red Army occupied the North, the U.S. Army the South. The Soviets installed the young Kim Il Sung to lead in its zone; the United States selected the Western-educated Syngman Rhee. Neither accepted the idea of a perpetually divided country. Kim's attempt at forceful reunification led to a brutal three-year civil war (1950 to 1953) that quickly escalated to an international conflict. The United States entered within days of the outbreak to aid the South. Months later, the newly established People's Republic of China (PRC) sent "volunteers" to aid the North. The war devastated the entire peninsula. It left roughly one-tenth of the total population killed, wounded, or missing. An estimated 180,000 Chinese soldiers died supporting the North, and 36,000 American soldiers died supporting the South.[15]

Technically, the Korean War has not ended; it was suspended in July 1953 by an armistice that remains (more or less) in effect—awaiting formal, final agreement over terms of peace. The two Koreas are still

---

15. Many American estimates were that closer to 1 million Chinese died, but Chinese military officials claimed 180,000 at the sixtieth anniversary of the war. *China Daily* (June 29, 2010), http://www.china.org.cn/china/2010-06/28/content_20365659.htm

separated by one of the most heavily fortified zones in the world, the 2-mile-wide demilitarized zone (DMZ). During the first several decades after the war, the North and the South "grappled unceasingly for advantage and supremacy over each other—and with the great powers outside."[16] In the late 1980s, the Republic of Korea (ROK), or South Korea, made a transition from a military dictatorship to a democracy, harnessing its resources and talents to build one of the most advanced and prosperous economies in the world. A strong military alliance with the United States allowed it to focus on manufacturing and exporting consumer goods, such as Hyundai autos and Samsung electronics, rather than building the bomb.

North Korea, or the Democratic Peoples' Republic of Korea (DPRK) remained under the dictatorial rule of the Kim family. The leadership mantle was handed down from its founder Kim Il Sung, to son Kim Jong Il in 1994, to grandson Kim Jong Un in 2011. Through close association with the communist regimes, though never formally joining the Soviet bloc, Kim Il Sung was able to rebuild the North after nearly total obliteration during the war. Its state-controlled economy was more successful than the South's, and the North was visibly better off economically than the South through the 1960s and into the 1970s. However, by the early 1980s, the advantage shifted as the North ran into the same fundamental limitation of communist economies that led to the decline and demise of the Soviet Union in the 1980s.

Despite having signed mutual defense treaties with the Soviet Union and China in 1961, and literally weeks after a U.S.–ROK treaty, North Korea refused to entrust its security to either of its big neighbors. It built one of the world's largest armies and began to explore building the bomb. The origin of Kim's interest in bombs remains unknown, though some observers posit that it began after the United States considered using nuclear weapons to bring the Korean War to an early end. Pyongyang signed cooperative agreements with Moscow as early as 1952 to train technicians and scientists in general areas of science. The agreements provided opportunities for students and graduates from North

---

16. Don Oberdorfer and Robert Carlin, *The Two Koreas: A Contemporary History,* 3rd ed. (New York: Basic Books, 2014), 6.

Korea to complete their education at Soviet universities and institutes. In December 1952, even as the Korean War was still underway, Kim Il Sung established a research institute of atomic energy under the DPRK Academy of Sciences. DPRK–Soviet cooperation was greatly expanded later under the Soviet "Atoms for Peace" umbrella. Kim sent hundreds of students and researchers to Soviet universities and nuclear research centers, such as the Joint Institute for Nuclear Research in Dubna. Several newly established North Korean scientific centers—the Institute of Nuclear Physics, the Institute of Atomic Energy, and the Kim Chaek University of Technology—participated in joint projects at Dubna on fundamental research and civilian nuclear applications.

The Soviet–North Korean nuclear cooperative treaty in 1959 led to the construction in the 1960s of the IRT-2000 Soviet research reactor and other key nuclear facilities in the newly created nuclear research complex, 8 kilometers from the provincial city of Yongbyon and 90 kilometers north of Pyongyang. These were some of the basic steps— educating scientists and technicians and acquiring a small reactor that would provide a platform for learning and hands-on experience—that would prove crucial to the North's subsequent efforts to build the bomb.

The Soviets were mindful of the dangers and pressured Kim to remain on the civilian path as a condition for their continued assistance. In the meantime, North Korea expanded its domestic institutions to educate nuclear specialists and used Soviet-supplied research facilities to train them. The specialists honed their skills by upgrading the Soviet research reactor to achieve higher performance. North Korea joined the IAEA in 1974, giving it access to the vast IAEA literature and experience base, all of which helped Pyongyang gather scientific and technical materials for the creation of its nuclear energy complex. Even as it took advantage of this trove of information, the North only allowed IAEA access to their Soviet-supplied facilities until the early 1990s.

When the North went in search of light water reactors for its civilian energy program, Moscow refused until the North agreed to join the NPT in 1985. By then, Pyongyang had spent two decades building indigenous nuclear capabilities. It was also well on its way toward constructing its own graphite-moderated (also called gas-graphite) reactor. Such reactors do not need enrichment of the uranium fuel but require the spent fuel to be reprocessed for safety reasons because it is chemically unstable. Reprocessing allows the extraction of plutonium for bombs. The graphite-moderated reactors designed and built at Yongbyon resemble the British reactor at Calder Hall, which was the first commercially successful nuclear power station reactor in the world but had also been used to produce plutonium for Britain's nuclear weapons program. The Calder Hall reactor blueprints and details were declassified in the 1950s. The reprocessing facility built a few years later at Yongbyon, the crucial second part of plutonium production for bomb fuel, resembles the civilian Eurochemic facility in Mol, Belgium. The blueprints for this plant were published in Belgium, and the diagrams of the production processes were in IAEA publications in the 1970s. The ambitious construction activities at Yongbyon became visible to U.S. reconnaissance satellites in the early 1980s, but these did not make international headlines until 1989 when some of the satellite images reached the public.

The Yongbyon 5 MWe reactor became operational in 1986, producing small amounts of electricity for the site and the nearby city, as well as accumulating plutonium in the spent reactor fuel. There was no one on the ground to watch or inspect the activities (although Pyongyang had signed the NPT in 1985) because the North did not permit IAEA inspectors at the reactor site or associated facilities until 1992. By that time, Pyongyang had all the pieces in place for the plutonium fuel cycle. It was capable of producing approximately 6 kilograms (roughly one bomb's worth) of weapon-grade plutonium per year once it overcame startup problems. The fuel fabrication and reprocessing facilities were operational. Two bigger gas-graphite reactors, designed for 50 and 200 megawatt-electric power, were under construction.

NORTH KOREA'S EARLY MISSILE PROGRAM

North Korea's missile program dates to the 1960s, about the same time it built its first nuclear facilities.[17] It first acquired coastal defense missiles, short-range surface-to-surface missiles, and multiple rocket launchers (MRLs) with conventional munitions from the Soviet Union

---

17. Joseph S. Bermudez Jr., "A History of Ballistic Missile Development in the DPRK," Occasional Paper No. 2, Center for Nonproliferation Studies (November 1999).

in the early 1960s. By 1965, Kim Il Sung decided to seek indigenous ballistic missile capability though he continued to rely on Soviet assistance. In 1971, he also turned to China, which itself had relied heavily on Soviet assistance in prior years. The Hamhung military academy was created to train North Korean specialists in missile development. Over the next five decades, North Korea expanded its missile capabilities both to ensure its security and to export for foreign currency.

North Korea took a big step in missile development when it reputedly purchased its first Soviet Scud-B liquid-propellant missiles from Egypt in the late 1970s or early 80s and signed a technology acquisition and cooperation agreement with Egypt. It began a Scud-B missile reverse-engineering program for what it called the Hwasong-5 missile. Between 1986 and 87, the North entered serial production for these missiles and exported them to Iran, which was mired in war following the attack by Iraq. North Korea followed with the development of the Hwasong-6 (Scud-C) with a longer range of 500 kilometers and an improved guidance system. By 1999, North Korea was estimated to have produced 600 to 1,000 Hwasong-6 missiles, of which some 300 to 500 were believed to have been exported to Iran, Syria, and Libya for hundreds of millions of dollars.

The Hwasong-6 was superseded by the substantially more capable Nodong-1. It is a medium-range missile with a range of 1,200 to 1,500 kilometers, which gave North Korea the ability to strike Japan for the first time. North Korea used its extensive illicit procurement network to buy components for the missiles and its TELs, which enabled mobile missile launching platforms. Iran funded much of North Korea's development and acquired the right to produce its own version called the Shahab-3. The Nodong has also been exported to Egypt and Libya. Pyongyang had burgeoning missile cooperation with Pakistan as well. All Scud variants and the Nodong missiles are capable of delivering nuclear warheads. For example, by 1958, the Soviet nuclear arsenal included the Scud-A with a 50-kiloton nuclear warhead. The Soviets also developed several different warheads for the Scud-B missiles that were deployed with nuclear yields between 5 and 70 kilotons.

The North's rapid sequence of missile development is believed to have been possible only with a high level of foreign technical assistance, primarily from the Soviet government. However, with the collapse of the Soviet Union, hundreds of missile scientists and engineers from former Soviet states began to sell their services abroad. In contrast, the scientists and engineers at the Russian nuclear weapons institutes, with few exceptions, were patriots who did not want to sell their skills and expertise overseas.[18] Russian missile exporters found eager buyers in Pyongyang. In the mid-1990s, North Korea unsurprisingly also began to develop long-range rockets, both for potential space flight and for long-range missiles.

THE START OF NUCLEAR DIPLOMACY

Just as the Yongbyon nuclear reactor complex was coming online in the late 1980s, North Korea had to deal with monumental geopolitical upheaval wrought by the dissolution of its benefactor, the Soviet Union, and the consequent loss of economic support from the Soviet-bloc countries. The North was suddenly cast adrift. Almost overnight it lost a large percentage of its petroleum imports, sources of raw materials, and markets. By 1992, the Soviet Union's security assistance and financial support that had undergirded the North Korean state collapsed. The North's future relationship with Russia was cast into doubt. A new Russian state under the leadership of Boris Yeltsin ended military aid to Kim Il Sung's regime in Pyongyang. Yeltsin had a personal antipathy toward the North and, against the strenuous objection of many of his foreign policy advisors, moved the weight of Russian involvement on the peninsula from Pyongyang to Seoul. The conventional military parity that the Korean People's Army had maintained against U.S. and South Korean forces across the DMZ was lost.

At the same time, China, North Korea's other key benefactor during the Cold War, was taking steps to forge a new political and economic relationship with South Korea. In 1992, while Pyongyang was engaged in an extensive dialogue with Seoul, Beijing established diplomatic relations with South Korea, a step that shocked and angered Pyongyang.

18. The patriotic response of the scientists and engineers of the Russian nuclear weapons institutes after the dissolution of the Soviet Union is chronicled by both Russians and Americans in *Doomed to Cooperate*, edited by Siegfried S. Hecker (Los Alamos: Bathtub Row Press, 2016).

More than that, Pyongyang redoubled its resolve never to trust anyone else for its security.

Kim Il Sung, in his typical pragmatic and calculating manner, decided that developments called for a major reorientation of DPRK policy. He made, but did not announce, a strategic decision to seek improved relations with the United States as a buffer against a hostile Russia and an unreliable China. As the Soviet Union collapsed, President George H. W. Bush took unilateral actions to reduce nuclear deployments that were part of Washington's deterrent against the Soviet Union. The goal was to ease the pressure on Soviet President Mikhail Gorbachev, who was struggling to keep his failing state from splintering and his nuclear weapons safe and secure. Bush announced the unilateral withdrawal of all land- and sea-based tactical nuclear weapons worldwide. Though the U.S. policy to "neither confirm nor deny" made it impossible for Washington to specifically state nuclear weapons had been withdrawn from South Korea, the South's president, Roh Tae Wu, was able to announce, "As I speak, there do not exist any nuclear weapons whatsoever anywhere in the Republic of Korea," a statement crafted to meet the DPRK position that inter-Korean nuclear talks could not move ahead as long as U.S. nuclear weapons were on the peninsula.[19]

Soon after, in early 1992, the North and South signed a joint declaration that committed both countries to "not test, manufacture, produce, receive, possess, store, deploy or use nuclear weapons" and "not possess nuclear reprocessing and uranium enrichment facilities."[20] The George H. W. Bush administration signaled willingness to open a diplomatic track between the United States and North Korea if Pyongyang accepted IAEA safeguards on its nuclear program, a move that North Korea had been resisting for years.

19. Robin Bulman, "No A-Arms in S. Korea, Roh Says," *Washington Post* (December 19, 1991), https://www.washingtonpost.com/archive/politics/1991/12/19/no-a-arms-in-s-korea-roh-says/b62e8f9e-fd08–498e-abd7–0d81184f1073/

20. "Joint Declaration on the Denuclearization of the Korean Peninsula," *Ministry of Foreign Affairs: Republic of Korea*, https://www.mofa.go.kr/eng/brd/m_5476/view.do?seq=305870&srchFr=&srchTo=&srchWord=&srchTp=&multi_itm_seq=0&itm_seq_1=0&itm_seq_2=0&company_cd=&company_nm=&page=6&titleNm=

By 1992, North Korea had taken a big step toward the nuclear weapons option. It had successfully demonstrated that the ostensibly civilian Yongbyon nuclear complex could produce weapon-grade plutonium by extracting small amounts of plutonium from the 5 MWe reactor's spent fuel in its newly operational Radiochemical Laboratory. As Washington became increasingly concerned about the North's nuclear weapons ambitions, Kim Il Sung and his son Kim Jong Il realized the DPRK could leverage its nascent program into improving relations with the United States. That set the stage for U.S.–DPRK talks in June 1993, resulting in the first nuclear deal, the Agreed Framework, signed in October 1994.

THE AGREED FRAMEWORK: A DEEP PARTISAN DIVIDE

The 1994 Agreed Framework was a diplomatic deal to constrain, roll back, and eventually eliminate the North's nuclear weapons program in exchange for energy assistance, the provision of a civilian nuclear energy program in the North, and normalization of U.S.–North Korea relations. To the Americans, the Agreed Framework was primarily a nonproliferation document designed to keep North Korea from a nuclear arsenal. To Pyongyang, it was to be a step toward the strategic alignment with Washington envisioned by Kim Il Sung at the end of the Cold War. In effect, the Agreed Framework was a set of guidelines that, if implemented carefully, could provide the time and space necessary to avoid future crises, such as those in the spring of 1993 and May 1994.

In September 1992, after years of trying, the IAEA was granted access to inspect key nuclear facilities in Yongbyon. The inspectors discovered discrepancies in North Korea's plutonium declaration and demanded special inspections of two sites. On March 12, 1993, Pyongyang announced its intention to withdraw from the NPT in three months, citing Article X (1), which provides for withdrawal in the event that supreme national security interests have been jeopardized. In June, the two sides opened talks, producing a joint statement in which Pyongyang announced it would suspend withdrawing from the treaty "as long as it considers necessary." That stopped the process a day before the withdrawal would have become legally effective and averted a serious confrontation.

Since the North was technically still in the NPT, and because part of the U.S.-DPRK discussions in June and then in July had included Washington's insistence that IAEA inspectors stay and IAEA monitoring of the facilities at Yongbyon continue, the nuclear facilities remained under IAEA inspections. In March 1994, however, IAEA inspectors were denied access to the Radiochemical Laboratory. The IAEA Board of Governors approved a resolution calling on North Korea to fully comply with its inspection request. In May, North Korea began unloading the spent fuel elements from the 5 MWe reactor without the cooperation and supervision of IAEA inspectors. Defense Secretary William Perry considered the fuel unloading to be a red line requiring U.S. action, including preparation for bombing key facilities in the Yongbyon nuclear complex to prevent the North from gaining access to the plutonium in the fuel elements.

Robert Gallucci, the very able and experienced diplomat heading the U.S. negotiations team, realized that the deal as consummated did not rule out all potential routes to bombs and missiles, but he believed it covered the greatest risks at the time—namely, the plutonium pathway to the bomb. North Korea had agreed to freeze plutonium operations at Yongbyon, including its 5 MWe reactor and plutonium reprocessing facility, along with halting construction of two much larger reactors that would have been able to produce close to 300 kilograms of plutonium annually by the early 2000s. Tighter restrictions that would explicitly cover missiles and uranium enrichment, the second path to the bomb, were believed to be beyond reach and/or not verifiable. The potential proliferation risk of providing two light water reactors to North Korea was viewed as manageable, and the costs were to be shouldered primarily by South Korea and Japan.

The provision of heavy fuel oil by the United States was also seen as reasonable considering the freeze of operations at Yongbyon. It was especially important to North Korea as it was experiencing a disastrous economic and food crisis in the 1990s. Gallucci and colleagues also structured the deal as a political framework, not a treaty, so as to avoid requiring congressional approval. There was little love lost for North Korea in U.S. policy circles or, for that matter, among the U.S. public.

The Agreed Framework had a rocky journey from the beginning. In Washington, there was no stomach for helping out a disdained regime that looked to be sinking into a swamp of its own making. In Seoul, ROK President Kim Young Sam bitterly opposed the deal primarily because he felt Seoul was kept out of the negotiations process. Though he had been prepared for a summit meeting with Kim Il Sung in early July 1994, he viewed Kim's death later that month as the beginning of the end of the regime, and he did not want to do anything that would make things easier for Kim's son.

A still greater challenge was the fact that a couple of weeks after the agreement was signed, U.S. elections resulted in a complete flip from Democratic majorities in the House and the Senate to Republican majorities. North Korea policies proved to be a perfect partisan divide in Congress. Virtually all of Clinton's actions to meet American obligations were intensely opposed by the Republican-controlled Congress. As Victor Cha and David Kang point out in their 2004 debate on North Korea policy, the Agreed Framework had become such a partisan issue that one could not tell whether detractors objected to the merits of the policy or the policy's association with the Clinton administration.[1]

Washington was continually challenged to uphold its end of the deal, especially for actions that required financial outlays needing congressional approval, such as the provision of heavy fuel oil. The provision of the light water reactors was, if anything, an even bigger challenge. The reactors were to be financed and constructed by the Korean Energy Development Organization (KEDO), an international consortium made up of the United States, South Korea, and Japan, later to be joined by the European Union. Though the provision of the LWR's was part of the agreement, Congress refused to join in funding the $2 billion project—that was left to the South Koreans and the Japanese.

In August 1998, North Korea launched what was initially thought to be a two-stage ballistic missile over Japan. Although it turned out to be a failed launch of a three-stage rocket, it contributed to the Agreed Framework edging toward collapse. The rocket launch and the intelligence leak of a new site that the Defense Intelligence Agency considered an underground

---

1. Victor D. Cha and David C. Kang, "The Debate over North Korea," *Political Science Quarterly* 119, no. 2 (Summer 2004): 229–254.

nuclear reactor ignited a political firestorm in Washington. President Clinton appointed Perry, former secretary of defense, as special envoy to review U.S. policy with North Korea to avoid another crisis. Perry consulted with the governments of South Korea and Japan, and then visited Pyongyang in what became known as the Perry Process. Several rounds of discussions culminated in 1999 with a report recommending the United States pursue a verifiable suspension and eventual dismantlement of the North's nuclear and long-range missile activities. In turn, the report recommended that the United States take steps to address the North's security concerns and establish normal relations. In addition, Washington would begin to ease its economic sanctions against North Korea. In an unusual step, Perry took the results of the review to Pyongyang to meet with a range of DPRK officials. North Korea responded positively, and in line with one of Perry's recommendations, agreed in September 1999 to freeze its missile testing for the duration of the talks. But, other than the missile launch moratorium, Pyongyang was slow to respond to the diplomatic opening created by the Perry Process. It wasn't until September 2000 that North Korea tried to put the relationship on firmer footing before the end of President Clinton's term, perhaps by making major progress on nuclear and missile issues.

During the last few months of 2000, several key steps were taken to fundamentally change the relationship between Pyongyang and Washington. Finally reciprocating Perry's May 1999 visit to Pyongyang, in October 2000, Kim Jong Il sent his most senior military official, Vice Marshal Jo Myong Rok, to Washington with a letter for the president. On October 10, Clinton met Jo at the White House. Jo told Clinton that if he came to Pyongyang, "Kim will guarantee all your security concerns."[2] The State Department's Wendy Sherman, who had been to Pyongyang with Perry, later said that when Jo and Clinton shook hands at the farewell, "We all knew there was something real here. Kim Jong Il was ready to deal."[3]

At the conclusion of Jo's visit to Washington, the two sides issued the Joint Communiqué, capping what was clearly the high-water mark of

2. Mike Chinoy, *Meltdown: The Inside Story of the North Korean Nuclear Crisis* (New York: St. Martin's Griffin, 2009), 25.

3. Ibid.

U.S.–North Korea relations.[4] In the document, the two sides agreed that they would fundamentally improve their bilateral relations, that neither government would have hostile intent towards the other, and that they would "make every effort in the future to build a new relationship free from past enmity."

Ten short days after Jo's visit, Secretary of State Madeleine Albright was welcomed to Pyongyang. The discussion between Albright and Kim Jong Il seemed to promise a new and different future. Albright stressed that the missile issue was of central importance, not only for the North's own development, but also for their export to countries of concern. In a remarkably candid comment, Kim Jong Il said that the DPRK was selling missiles to Iran and Syria to earn badly needed foreign currency. He added that if Washington guaranteed compensation, they were prepared to suspend the exports.[5]

The Agreed Framework was heavily criticized for not eliminating North Korea's nuclear program, but as Gallucci pointed out in an interview a few years later, it never claimed to do so. He regarded it "as a good deal, in our interest, because over time, we'd be better off with the deal than without it. It wasn't perfect."[6] It is probably for this reason that Clinton listed North Korea at the bottom of the list of future security problems for the United States when he gave the customary briefing to President-elect Bush during the transition period.

MELTDOWN

As the Bush administration entered the White House in January 2001, the signals from the North were still largely positive. Pyongyang expressed public support for a continuation of Clinton policies as captured in the 2000 Joint Communiqué. However, there was unease in Pyongyang. Some North Korean officials expressed concern to their American counterparts

4. "U.S.-D.P.R.K. Joint Communique," *U.S. Department of State* (October 12, 2000), https://1997-2001.state.gov/regions/eap/001012_usdprk_jointcom.html (accessed April 13, 2022).

5. Madeleine Albright, *Madam Secretary: A Memoir* (New York: Miramax Books, 2003), 463.

6. "Interview with Robert Gallucci," *PBS Frontline* (March 5, 2003), https://www.pbs.org/wgbh/pages/frontline/shows/kim/interviews/gallucci.html

about possible changes in U.S. policy being pushed by what they called conservative hard-liners. The North Koreans had good reason to be concerned because their relations with Washington would soon sink into a deep ideological abyss.[7]

The Bush administration brought in hard-line conservatives that had been biding their time (and sharpening their knives) during the Clinton terms. Vice President Dick Cheney and Secretary of Defense Donald Rumsfeld brought teams of neoconservative advisors and assistants. Two of the most outspoken, John Bolton and Robert Joseph, moved into influential positions in the State Department and National Security Council, respectively. The hard-liners had railed against the Clinton administration's nuclear accord with North Korea. They viewed North Korea's approach as a cycle of provocation, crisis, and temporary resolution to buy time for its nuclear program.

Although different camps in the administration continued to spar about how to proceed with North Korea, the hard-line advisors had pretty much set the tone into the spring and summer. There was general agreement that greater pressure was required to compel North Korea to finally make a strategic choice between its nuclear weapons program or regime collapse. The terrorist attacks by Al-Qaeda on the World Trade Center and the Pentagon on September 11, 2001, transformed the Bush administration's calculations about the nature and magnitude of global threats as it cast the world more starkly in terms of "good and evil." This dramatic worldview trickled down to North Korea policy, resulting in a focus on North Korea as a sponsor of international terrorism and as a potential proliferator of weapons of mass destruction.

The Bush administration's rhetoric in late 2001 and through the winter and spring of 2002 ratcheted up tensions to all but completely close the door to a diplomatic solution to the nuclear issue. In his January 2002 State of the Union speech, President Bush singled out North Korea as part of a new focus for America's war on terror, throwing it into an "axis of evil" along

---

7. See two insiders' intricate accounts of events in Chinoy's *Meltdown* and Don Oberdorfer and Robert Carlin, *The Two Koreas: A Contemporary History*, 3rd ed. (New York: Basic Books, 2014).

with Iraq and Iran. Pyongyang soon worried that U.S. regime-change efforts would first concentrate on Iraq, then move on to North Korea or Iran.

In March 2002, leaked public reports of the Bush administration's Nuclear Posture Review indicated that North Korea was among six countries that the administration did not rule out as possible targets of U.S. nuclear weapons. Pyongyang argued that this position was contrary to commitments that the United States had made under the Agreed Framework and the 2000 Joint Communiqué. The "axis of evil" comment and the Nuclear Posture Review would often be cited in the coming years by Pyongyang as evidence of Washington's hostile policy.

In the summer of 2002, the intelligence community provided an updated assessment of the North's covert uranium enrichment program. The new intelligence report included evidence of Pyongyang's massive procurement efforts for materials and components for a centrifuge program. These efforts dated back to the late 1990s and reached into Europe and Asia, with distinct tracks leading to A. Q. Khan's laboratory in Pakistan. Clinton's Assistant Secretary of State Robert Einhorn said in subsequent interviews that the Clinton administration knew Pyongyang had an enrichment effort in the late 1990s. However, they were not able to determine how large it was and, for several reasons, decided to tackle the issue later.[8] In September, John McLaughlin, the deputy CIA director, briefed the White House that it had high confidence that the North was acquiring materials consistent with a centrifuge program, but they did not know where such a program was based or how far along it was.[9]

The briefing and the accompanying intelligence report were sufficient to deal the deathblow to the Agreed Framework, which had already been on life support. According to John Bolton, the report was "the hammer [he] had been looking for to shatter the Agreed Framework."[10] Hard-line Bush administration officials like Bolton characterized the intelligence as evidence of "cheating" and as a "moral affront" that necessitated punishment.[11]

8. Patrick McEachern, *Inside the Red Box: North Korea's Post-Totalitarian Politics* (New York: Columbia University Press, 2010), 82.

9. Ibid., 102.

10. John Bolton, *Surrender Is Not an Option: Defending America at the United Nations and Abroad* (New York: Threshold Editions, 2008), 106.

11. Oberdorfer and Carlin, *The Two Koreas*, 364.

Even less hawkish elements of the Bush administration could not dispute the veracity of the intelligence.

But through much of 2002, North Korea still appeared to favor dialogue. Kim Jong Il had introduced major economic reforms in July for which the North needed a less threatening external security environment. That required building bilateral relations with its neighbors—notably Japan— and further buttressing relations with European countries and the United States. Much to Washington's surprise—and to the surprise of virtually everyone in Japan, including senior Japanese officials—Japanese Prime Minister Junichiro Koizumi flew to Pyongyang in September for a summit with Kim Jong Il, with the two sides agreeing to move toward Japan–North Korea normalization.[12]

Notwithstanding Kim's plans, a diplomatic confrontation in October 2002 precipitated, in rapid fashion, the end of the Clinton-era Agreed Framework and the resurrection of North Korea's fissile materials production. During a meeting in Pyongyang, James Kelly, assistant secretary of state for East Asian and Pacific Affairs, accused the North of pursuing the uranium enrichment path to the bomb, charging that Pyongyang had breached its obligations under the Agreed Framework. The American delegation interpreted the response of the North Korean diplomats to be tantamount to an admission. Although American and North Korean accounts of what transpired at the meeting differ, the meeting marked a major turning point in North Korea's nuclear program.[13] The U.S. delegation used the secure communications channel in the British embassy in Pyongyang to send an urgent message back to Washington. It was titled "North Koreans Defiantly Admit HEU Program." These six words proved to be the final nail in the coffin of the Agreed Framework.[14] Almost every senior official that read those words came to the same conclusion, even though a closer reading of the summary and reconstructed transcript belied the accuracy of that

12. The meeting was the result of years of secret contacts between Tokyo and Pyongyang.

13. The meeting is described in considerable detail in Chinoy, *Meltdown*; Oberdorfer and Carlin, *The Two Koreas*; and Charles L. Pritchard, *Failed Diplomacy* (Washington, DC: Brookings Institution Press, 2007).

14. Oberdorfer and Carlin, *The Two Koreas*, 364.

headline. Although key officials in the administration were divided on next steps, there was no doubt that the Agreed Framework was beyond saving.

In a clear sign that the Agreed Framework had collapsed, Washington cut off the KEDO heavy fuel oil shipments to North Korea. On December 12, two days after the last drop of November's heavy oil shipment was un-loaded in Nampo and further shipments were suspended, the DPRK Foreign Ministry announced the North would "immediately resume operation and construction of facilities [in Yongbyon] to generate electricity."[15] The Foreign Ministry pointed to a passage in the Agreed Framework that linked KEDO's supply of heavy fuel oil to the North's obligation to freeze its reactor and related facilities. The bottom line was "no heavy fuel oil, no freeze."

North Korea proceeded methodically to bring the Yongbyon nuclear complex back to life. The IAEA was told to remove its seals and monitoring cameras from the North's nuclear facilities, and when it failed to act, North Korean technicians removed the seals themselves. They began to move fresh fuel elements into the reactor for its eventual restart. By the end of the year, the IAEA inspection team was sent back to Vienna because, as North Korean authorities pointed out sarcastically, there was nothing left for them to do. By January 2003, the 5 MWe reactor was put back in operation to produce more plutonium. The Radiochemical Laboratory was reactivated to harvest the plutonium that had been stored in the spent fuel pool for eight years. Pyongyang, with no small measure of chutzpah, took the position that it was simply resurrecting the clock from its prior warning in 1993, so that only one day was required to leave the NPT. It served notice that it was no longer committed to its status as a non-nuclear weapons state.

AS NORTH KOREA BUILDS THE BOMB, WASHINGTON SITS IDLY BY

In light of these developments, Washington's strategy quickly coalesced into an approach that eschewed diplomacy in favor of containment through escalating pressure—namely, by trying to curb Pyongyang's trade with its neighbors and intercept imports and exports related to its weapons programs. The effect of this policy response was that Pyongyang was able to take full advantage of Washington's long leash and patience

15. Ibid., 379.

and proceed full speed ahead with its nuclear program with few tangible consequences. Without a plan of action to counter the reprocessing of plutonium, the Bush administration turned instead to prevent North Korea from exporting nuclear materials and technologies.[16]

By accusing Pyongyang of a covert uranium enrichment program and killing the Agreed Framework, the administration had allowed the North to take decisive and threatening steps toward the bomb by reactivating its plutonium complex. Though highly enriched uranium could be used as bomb fuel, it is not as potent as the plutonium that the North would surely recover within six months. Despite the intelligence community's claims that the North already had enough plutonium for a bomb or two, as subsequent chapters will make clear, it is unlikely that North Korea had more than a kilogram or two—that is, not enough for any nuclear bombs before 2003.

However, even if North Korea had enough plutonium for one or two bombs, to downplay, as the Bush administration did, the importance of extracting another 25 to 30 kilograms, sufficient for four to six nuclear devices, is simply inexcusable. In addition to increasing the export threat, this amount gave the North enough material to refine their fabrication techniques, conduct additional experimental tests, and, when necessary, conduct a nuclear test. It opened the floodgates for North Korea, unencumbered, to rapidly build nuclear weapons. The voices of Bolton, Cheney, Rumsfeld, and their allies drowned out the more sensible but less influential voices of Colin Powell and Condoleezza Rice. Moreover, there was no nuclear expert at the decision-making table to warn of the dire technical consequences of walking away from the Agreed Framework and letting the North restart the Yongbyon nuclear complex.

The lack of a cohesive, robust response can also be attributed in part to the fact that North Korea was simply not a high priority for the administration or the American public in 2003. U.S.–North Korean relations played out in the shadow of the Bush administration's invasion of Iraq and the demise of Saddam Hussein. It was a swift victory followed soon by an endless quagmire. The contrast between the administration's Iraq

16. David E. Sanger, "Bush Shifts Focus to Nuclear Sales by North Korea," *New York Times* (May 5, 2003), https://www.nytimes.com/2003/05/05/world/aftereffects-the-asian-arena-bush-shifts-focus-to-nuclear-sales-by-north-korea.html

and North Korea policies was striking. It reveals how poorly the Bush administration framed and managed the North Korean nuclear issue—or, rather, one might argue, the more consequential invasion of Iraq. Simply put, the United States invaded Iraq, in part, because some in the administration believed Saddam Hussein had nuclear weapons, which he did not. They concurrently killed the Agreed Framework because of concerns that North Korea was covertly seeking nuclear weapons and then stood idly by as North Korea built the bomb in relatively plain view. But a simple appeal to the distractions of the Iraq War does not fully explain the slow, almost apathetic, response by the Bush administration to North Korea's renewed nuclear development in 2003. Every administration must balance competing foreign policy priorities.

In the view of one close observer, the Bush administration was not only unfocused but also plagued by incompetence. The officials influencing North Korea policy held myriad misconceptions, misperceptions, and frankly dodgy assumptions about North Korea that crowded out reality. Because they viewed it as impossible to negotiate directly with Pyongyang—believing such talks to be a trap designed to catch U.S. diplomats, as they believed happened to the Clinton administration—the Bush administration adopted a multilateral negotiating format. China was seen as an intermediary and influential patron of the North. The Bush administration chose not only to involve China but also to cede the leading role to Beijing.[17] China arranged some desultory three-party discussions (North Korea, China, and the United States), followed by Pyongyang grudgingly agreeing to participate in what became known as the Six-Party Talks (which also included South Korea, Japan, and Russia).

The administration adopted a two-pronged approach in which it would pursue diplomacy through the six-party process while also pushing for tougher measures from the international community to punish Pyongyang for further transgressions. It launched the global Proliferation Security Initiative (PSI) in late May 2003. Designed to prevent the trafficking of weapons of mass destruction, their delivery systems, and related materials to and from states and non-state actors, the initiative naturally focused on North Korea as a major target. Although this initiative had a rocky start, it

17. Pritchard, *Failed Diplomacy*, 63.

has over the years been supported by several U.S. administrations and has been generally viewed as a positive contribution to nonproliferation and counterterrorism efforts. But its effect on North Korea has been offset by the North's uncanny ability to work around these obstacles, much as it has been able to work around UN sanctions over the years.

North Korea followed its own dual-track strategy. The nuclear track was focused on building the bomb and putting the pieces in place to test a nuclear device. The Yongbyon complex was back in full swing, and uranium enrichment efforts were surely accelerated. Concurrently, Pyongyang pursued the diplomacy track. Although it agreed to participate in the Six-Party Talks, it wanted to deal exclusively with Washington to resolve the nuclear issue, which had always been its preferred diplomatic track. That was the message conveyed to John Lewis during his August 2003 visit. Ambassador Ri Gun, Lewis's host and deputy director of American Affairs at the North's Foreign Ministry, denied that North Korea had a uranium enrichment program but told Lewis they would again entertain a plutonium freeze and would not transfer weapons or nuclear materials.

The first round of the Six-Party Talks held in Beijing in late August achieved no breakthrough. Both sides stuck to their scripts. The North called for the United States to meet its obligations under the Agreed Framework. The Americans demanded that North Korea unconditionally agree to "complete, verifiable, and irreversible dismantlement" (CVID) of its nuclear program before the United States would take any action to provide security guarantees.[18] Pyongyang announced that it saw no need for further talks and put the formal negotiations on hold.[19] Vice President Cheney who had insisted on the CVID language stayed true to his hard-line ideology, reportedly telling the U.S. team, "I have been charged by the president with making sure that none of the tyrannies in the world are negotiated with. We don't negotiate with evil;

18. John Pomfret, "U.S., North Korea Don't Bend on Arms," *Washington Post* (August 28, 2003), https://www.washingtonpost.com/archive/politics/2003/08/28/us-north-korea-dont-bend-on-arms/8eaf608e-a9ba-4af0-b2ba-cb8ec35af95c/

19. Joseph Kahn, "Korea Arms Talks Close with Plans for a New Round," *New York Times* (August 30, 2003), https://www.nytimes.com/2003/08/30/world/korea-arms-talks-close-with-plans-for-a-new-round.html.

we defeat it."[20] Accordingly, the plans for a December resumption of Six-Party Talks were scrapped.

At that point, Pyongyang decided to take a different tack and invited John Lewis back to North Korea. It was this invitation that brought me to North Korea in January 2004 for the improbable trip to its Yongbyon nuclear complex.

20. Pritchard, *Failed Diplomacy*, 103.

4 "Would You Like to See Our Product?"

"But John, I don't want to go to North Korea," I told Professor Lewis in October 2003 when he asked me to accompany him on the trip. At the time, I was a senior fellow at the Los Alamos National Laboratory. I had returned to the research world a few years earlier after serving nearly a dozen years as director of the lab. I was deeply ensconced trying to unravel the scientific mysteries of plutonium and working collaboratively with Russian nuclear weapons experts to help them mitigate the nuclear dangers that arose after the dissolution of the Soviet Union. I was also looking for ways to strengthen the relationship with the Chinese nuclear complex because I thought China might face similar nuclear security challenges to those Russia was experiencing. Going to North Korea was the last thing on my mind. Little did I realize that all the years at the lab working on plutonium and other nuclear materials had prepared me well for this trip to North Korea, a place that offered a daunting set of new, complex issues to unknot and understand.

John Lewis had returned from his eighth visit to North Korea in fourteen years in August 2003. His North Korean interlocutors told him that they had thought restarting the Yongbyon nuclear complex would bring Washington back to the diplomatic table, but that hadn't happened. For Lewis, it was time to act.

I told Lewis that I had little to contribute to his visit, and (here I played my hole card) since I was still employed by the Los Alamos National Laboratory with plenty of security restrictions, it would be nearly impossible to get Washington's approval for the trip. But John was known for his persistence. He said the North Koreans told him they might take him to the Yongbyon nuclear complex, from which international inspectors and U.S. technical personnel had been expelled with the demise of the Agreed Framework. As a political scientist, he said, he didn't know the difference between a reactor and a centrifuge (which, of course, was not true), so it was important I come along. I gave in, taking comfort in believing that the prospects were slim to none of getting approval from Washington. Besides, getting the North Koreans to allow a former director of the Los Alamos National Laboratory to tour their nuclear center seemed just as unlikely.

I was nearly correct about the U.S. government. Officials in the Bush administration, particularly those in the White House, did not want me to go. There was an enormous mistrust of North Korea and concern that Pyongyang would use my visit purely as a propaganda coup, which turned out not to be so. As a Los Alamos lab employee, I needed travel approval from the lab's governmental sponsor, the Department of Energy's National Nuclear Security Administration (NNSA). Travel to North Korea also required what is called "country clearance" approval from the State Department.

To my surprise, the trip was approved. Ambassador Linton Brooks from the NNSA—a wise and experienced diplomat—thought the trip was a good idea since the government had no other eyes on North Korea at the time. Lewis managed to get the same response from Dr. Thomas Fingar, head of the Bureau of Intelligence and Research (INR) in the State Department, to obtain the country clearance.

Even so, the opposition made itself felt. To express their displeasure with my visit, National Security Council officials advised the CIA not to give me background briefings on the North's nuclear program. Fortunately, several Los Alamos colleagues, who had been involved in inspections and verification activities in North Korea during the Agreed Framework, shared some of the necessary technical background. Some of them also had experience as technical advisors to previous U.S.–DPRK negotiations. They provided an overview of the diplomatic backdrop and gave me a glimpse of the rigid formalities in the six-party negotiations.

Lewis asked Jack Pritchard, who was then at the Brookings Institution following his U.S. government service, to join our delegation. We were also to be accompanied by two U.S. Senate Foreign Relations Committee staffers, both Northeast Asia specialists, who were on their own fact-finding visit: W. Keith Luse worked closely with Senator Richard Lugar who chaired the committee, and Frank Jannuzi who supported Senator Joseph Biden, ranking member on the Democratic side.

I traveled to Washington, DC, twice in December to meet with key government officials. Although the Bush administration did not allow me to meet with CIA analysts, I was able to learn much from colleagues in the Department of Energy's NNSA and in the National Academies of Sciences and Engineering. On the technical side, there was much uncertainty about what North Korea had accomplished at the Yongbyon nuclear complex since all inspectors were ejected a year earlier. On the diplomatic front, there were deep divisions of opinion within the government. The administration seemed focused on the aftermath of the invasion of Iraq. North Korea was not top priority.

Throughout the winter holidays, I remained convinced that the trip would not occur, but all governmental approvals arrived, and Lewis got final confirmation from the North that we were expected in Pyongyang on January 4, 2004. At 7 AM on Friday morning, January 2, I was at home in Los Alamos, bags packed, brushing my teeth, when my wife called out, "ABC News is on the phone." This was definitely not what I wanted to hear. The reporter wanted to know about what she called my "imminent" travel to North Korea. How the hell did that happen, I asked myself. The whole idea had been to keep this trip out of the public eye. I mumbled that I was just about to depart for China but didn't know about North Korea.

Technically that was prevaricating, but it was close enough to being true since I still did not believe I would get the required visa in Beijing to visit the North. I immediately called NNSA head Linton Brooks to tell him that the cat was out of the bag. Brooks was unflappable, "Yes, I know, it was on the front page of USA Today, and I already had a call from the White House wanting to know what the hell Hecker was doing going to North Korea."[1]

1. Barbara Slavin, "N. Korea OKs U.S. Visit to Complex," USA Today (January 2, 2004), https://usatoday30.usatoday.com/news/world/2004-01-02-korea-usat_x.htm

Brooks said he told them that he approved the trip because we might learn something. I discovered later that when President Bush saw the paper, he went ballistic. "I didn't authorize this," he fumed to Condoleezza Rice, "Shut it down."[2] Rice called Secretary Powell, who in turn called Senator Biden because his staffer, Frank Jannuzi, was scheduled to go on the trip. Powell told Biden that the White House objected, but when Biden asked, "Are you, sir, saying it would be unhelpful for them to go?" Powell replied "No, I can't say that. I am just telling you what I'm told to communicate." Biden responded, "Fine, they'll go."

THE IMPROBABLE VISIT TO NORTH KOREA

With the okay from Linton Brooks, I flew to Los Angeles and then to Beijing, where I met up with John Lewis and the others. The next morning, we were off to the North Korean consulate. Much to my surprise, the visa process took less than thirty minutes and 830 renminbi ($84 at the time). Visas in hand, the next stop was the Beijing office of Air Koryo, the state-owned national airline of North Korea, to buy our $310 ticket to Pyongyang.

Tuesday morning, several foreign reporters showed up at our hotel and began quizzing Lewis about the trip. That was just a taste of what we would face at the airport. The scene there was chaotic. Some fifty news media representatives were waiting. They followed us through the airport—pushing, shoving, and yelling questions. Fortunately, at 6 foot 2 inches, Lewis had a huge stride and that made it difficult for them to keep up. I was at some disadvantage at 5 foot 10, but I had always been active athletically so I managed.

Since the Bush administration opted not to give me detailed intelligence briefings on the Yongbyon facilities, I relied on briefings from my Los Alamos colleagues and on a book by David Albright and Kevin O'Neill of the Institute for Science and International Security (ISIS),[3] carefully examining what was known about North Korea's nuclear program up to 2000.[4] The

2. Mike Chinoy, *Meltdown: The Inside Story of the North Korean Nuclear Crisis* (New York: St. Martin's Griffin, 2009), 198.

3. ISIS was a perfectly good acronym until the Middle East terror group became known by it. We can now refer to Albright's organization as the "good" ISIS.

4. David Albright and Kevin O'Neill, eds., *Solving the North Korean Nuclear Puzzle* (Washington, DC: Institute of Science and International Security, 2000).

book proved enormously helpful to me in understanding North Korea's decades-long quest for nuclear technologies and was my trusted companion on the flights all the way to Pyongyang and during down time in the hotel.

The trip from Beijing to Pyongyang was short. The Air Koryo plane was familiar—a Soviet-era Ilyushin 62, the Soviet's first narrow-body, long-range jetliner that began service in the Soviet Union in the 1960s. I'd been on similar planes during my many trips to Russia in the 1990s and early 2000s and had no worries about their ability to stay in the air. There was a long taxiway to the passenger terminal after landing in Pyongyang. When I saw the huge portrait of Kim Il Sung overlooking the parking tarmac, it suddenly hit me: This was going to be the adventure of a lifetime.

Ambassador Ri Gun met us in the cold, spartan arrival hall. He would be our host, or what American visitors typically called their North Korean "minders," for the next four days. But Ri was much more than a minder; he was knowledgeable and efficient, obviously operating under explicit instructions to make our trip successful and to smooth over any problems. Both John Lewis and Jack Pritchard had known Ri for many years, either from his former position at the DPRK UN mission in New York or his participation in the numerous rounds of U.S.–DPRK negotiations that took place from 1993 to 2002. Ambassador Ri is sometimes described as tough, even irascible. But I found him friendly and sociable. He spoke excellent American English and was very much at ease, with a quick, often mischievous smile exposing several gold-rimmed teeth. Even from his post in Pyongyang, he followed the American scene closely. He seemed to be amused by all the U.S. media coverage that the trip had already received and particularly that the only name mentioned by the Western press was mine.

Ambassador Ri had hired two drivers in Toyota Land Cruisers, to be paid for by us,[5] to take us to our hotel on the banks of the Potonggang, a small, well-behaved river that winds its way through part of Pyongyang before emptying into the larger Taedong River that bisects the capital. The drive into the city was mostly along deserted streets; the air was layered with smog, not from cars but rather from the aged, coal-fired power plant on the edge of the city. The lobby of the hotel was quiet and, somewhat incongruously I thought, adorned with Christmas decorations. We were

5. Professor Lewis had grants from private U.S. foundations to pay our travel expenses.

assigned spacious suites on the eighth floor of the nine-story hotel. The suites were Soviet style with wide sofas, oriental rugs, small bathrooms, and soft mattresses. And much like the Soviet hotels I had stayed in, they were surely wired for sound and possibly cameras, although I didn't see any. Since the hotel sits in a park-like setting, the view from our windows, though it was the middle of the winter, was serene.

For the trip, I carried few personal effects. We had no doubt that everything about our presence would be subject to monitoring and surveillance by DPRK security. I brought neither a cell phone nor a computer because I was forewarned by John Lewis that I would not be able to use them. A few years later, foreigners could use cell phones while in-country, but we weren't yet at that happy point. I did bring a camera but was advised to ask permission before taking photos.

Ambassador Ri met us in the hotel lobby that afternoon to explain the agenda prepared for our visit. On Wednesday, we would meet with officials from the Committee for the Promotion of International Trade (CPIT) and the DPRK Academy of Sciences (KAS) in the morning, and then with Vice Minister of Foreign Affairs Kim Gye Gwan at the ministry in the afternoon. On Thursday, they would take us to the Yongbyon nuclear center for the day. Friday would include meetings with Colonel General Ri Chan Bok of the Korean People's Army and a trip to one of the markets. Saturday morning, we would board the flight back to Beijing. I found out later, the trip to Yongbyon was what interested Ambassador Ri the most since he had never been allowed to visit the nuclear facility. The Yongbyon visit was, of course, also my highest priority. I believed that a current technical assessment would help to better understand the military threat and the diplomatic landscape.

The most important issue to resolve was whether the spent fuel rods that were stored in a cooling pool during the Agreed Framework had been reprocessed to extract weapon-grade plutonium. It was also important to find out if the Yongbyon reactor was operating at full power. The U.S. intelligence community was uncertain. Although the community has many smart analysts, without inside information they were mostly in the dark about what had transpired at Yongbyon since the international inspectors were expelled. It was important to get these answers to be able inform the political assessment of how much more dangerous North Korea's nuclear program had become since the demise of the Agreed Framework and to get an indication of where the program was heading. If the North Koreans took us to Yongbyon and if I could successfully engage the nuclear specialists, I might be able to answer some of these questions.

After the meeting with Ambassador Ri, we asked if we could take a walk along the river. I had learned during the many dozens of international trips I had taken that getting out into the sunlight and open air after arrival was one of the best ways to beat jet lag. I didn't know what to expect here in North Korea and was surprised by the bemused looks we got from the young children we met along the way. Since no one knew ahead of time we'd be out for a walk in that place at that time, I thought it unlikely these were little actors sent to impress us. As I accumulated more experience interacting with North Koreans, it became clear to me that, at least at the human level, the cold, frightening image of the country I had envisioned was quite mistaken. What I should have realized was that here, as elsewhere, I would encounter what I'd experienced on all my travels—a warm humanity that, given the opportunity, could peek through what otherwise appeared to be forbidding and impenetrable political barriers.

INITIAL DISCUSSIONS AT THE
MINISTRY OF FOREIGN AFFAIRS

For me, the Wednesday meeting with Vice Minister Kim Gye Gwan was an important and eye-opening lesson in diplomacy. Kim had had extensive contact with Americans, having led the North Korean delegations during official consultations and negotiations with the United States during the Agreed Framework years. Given his own extensive experience, much of it dealing with Kim, Jack Pritchard led the discussion from our side. Throughout the meeting, I was impressed by how effectively Kim expressed the North Korean position (although he knew English, he spoke Korean interpreted by Ms. Choe Son Hui, who later rose to high-level positions in the ministry), and how detailed an understanding he had of American politics. Looking back, I find it remarkable that so many of the issues we discussed then remain the same after all these years, with the notable difference being that the North had just begun to build a bomb then but has a menacing nuclear arsenal now.

Vice Minister Kim welcomed us by acknowledging that our visit could have "great symbolic significance." Pritchard told him that even though we were a private group, we were there to talk about the main issues—that is, their nuclear program—and he emphasized the importance of our upcoming trip to Yongbyon. Kim brightened at the mention of the Yongbyon visit. "We view the delegation's visit to Yongbyon as a way to help contribute to breaking the stalemate and opening up a bright future," he said. Kim continued:

> "We will not play games with you. Our primary reason for inviting you is to ensure transparency and thereby reduce all the assumptions and errors. We want you to take an objective look, and we will leave the conclusions to your side. This is why the inclusion of Dr. Sig Hecker is so significant. His presence will allow us to tell you everything. This is an extraordinary approval by us."

Of course, they didn't tell us "everything," but as it turned out, the visit gave us invaluable insights into their technical developments and their political thinking.

Pritchard affirmed our group's interest in transparency and emphasized that we were not approaching the visit with the mindset of inspectors. Pyongyang, as I learned, has a pained reaction to the word "inspection" and the implied infringement on its sovereignty, particularly in the context of what had happened in the nuclear inspections in Iraq and how that led to the subsequent U.S. invasion. Kim wholeheartedly agreed with how Pritchard had framed our visit and promised to provide us enough access to come away with a good understanding. He told us that we would not be allowed to take photos at the nuclear center, adding with a chuckle, "I hope you don't memorize too well."

Kim and Pritchard agreed that prior cooperation on Yongbyon, such as the re-canning of the spent fuel rods during the Agreed Framework period, was a success story. But Kim lamented that those times were long gone—that "all those efforts have gone to zero." He pressed the need for Washington to reverse its "hostile policy" and emphasized that the DPRK would "maintain our principles even if we are killed doing so." His statement was not delivered in a bellicose manner, more as a simple statement of fact. He maintained that a peaceful resolution through dialogue was still possible, but that Washington would need to show initiative in response to what he called the flexibility and concessions offered by the North. Pritchard conceded that the North had been flexible in its engagement in the early rounds of the Six-Party Talks but noted that it would be difficult to proceed diplomatically if the process did not move past North Korea's intransigence and opacity regarding the uranium enrichment issue. At that point, there might well have been a drum roll and trumpets since the issue of the North's uranium enrichment program had become central to the dispute between Washington and Pyongyang. It was why the Agreed Framework had abruptly ended in 2002, and although it wasn't why I had come along to visit Yongbyon, it would be a dark cloud hanging over the entire trip.

Pritchard then recounted the notorious October 3, 2002, meeting in Pyongyang, which he had attended, when Assistant Secretary James Kelly told the North Koreans that the United States had "clear and compelling" intelligence that the North had a covert uranium enrichment program. Pritchard told Kim that he himself was "satisfied" with that intelligence. Kim was immediately dismissive: "It was fabricated, just like the August 1998 Kumchang-ri accusation about a clandestine underground nuclear reactor." Pritchard pressed the point, advising Kim that regardless of his position—or what anyone else in the room believed to be true about the enrichment issue—what truly mattered was that the United States now "believes that the DPRK has an HEU program based on the intelligence" and thus the "complete, verifiable, irreversible resolution of this HEU issue is mandatory." Kim began warming to the exchange, for he knew his brief on the subject well:

> "In October 2002, we were looking forward to something new. We thought it was a time to rejoice that the U.S. delegation was coming to Pyongyang. When Kelly walked in, he presented fabricated information and put pressure on North Korea. He behaved rudely, not like a guest should behave in our culture. Vice Minister Kang [Sok Ju] thought that the U.S. had come to our country in a high-handed manner. This is why I so strongly denied his [Kelly's] allegation that first day, and I maintain that we have nothing to do with an HEU program."

At this point, John Lewis tried to give Kim a face-saving way out by suggesting that perhaps the North had gas centrifuge equipment not for an HEU program but for other scientific uses. Kim did not fall for that, responding categorically, "With respect to any so-called HEU program, we do not have any facilities or scientists dedicated to such a program." It was clear by that point that we would get no further on uranium enrichment in this conversation.

Kim turned the focus to the stalled Six-Party Talks and proposals for how to resolve the impasse. He offered as a first step to freeze the North's nuclear program—including no manufacturing, no testing, and no transferring of nuclear weapons. In return, the North would need to receive something, as a freeze could not be "cost free." Kim proposed that the United States take certain actions that were anathema to Washington at the time but would later become central to the 2007 and 2008 disablement process: the removal of North Korea from the list of state sponsors of terrorism; the lifting of sanctions; and the provision of energy, including heavy fuel oil, by the North's neighboring states. He stressed that such moves would be seen as part of a process in which the United States demonstrated respect for North Korea's sovereign rights.

We continued the discussions about the North's proposal for a freeze in a somewhat more congenial atmosphere that night at dinner. This was the first time I had been privy to diplomatic discussions about North Korea with such depth and candor. Kim laid out what he called the fundamental policy choice facing Washington. He said, "You have three options: to live with a nuclear nation, to settle the nuclear issue peacefully with us, or to go to war. We are prepared for war, but once you have the will to settle this issue, it will be easy to solve." In early October, Pyongyang had announced that the Yongbyon nuclear center "made a switchover" in the purpose of reprocessing its spent fuel from civilian needs to its weapons program with the goal of "increasing its nuclear deterrent force."[6] Now, a few months later, Kim's comment about living with a "nuclear nation" clearly fell in line with Pyongyang's carefully orchestrated public strategy throughout 2003, giving notice that it had built the bomb and would reap the benefits for its national defense.

I intervened to shift the conversation to the technical issues. I told Kim that I saw our delegation's role as trying to add clarity and understanding to the nuclear problem. Scientists and engineers had an obligation to work together to implement and subsequently verify the political decisions on

6. DPRK Foreign Ministry Spokesman, "DPRK to Continue Increasing Its Nuclear Deterrent Force," *KCNA* (October 2, 2003).

the nuclear issue. Borrowing language from my experience working with Russian nuclear experts, I ventured that our visit to Yongbyon the next day would begin to foster an atmosphere of mutual respect and trust that would eventually help us achieve successful implementation and verification. I emphasized that we must work together and that there should be no surprises. I explained that I would share my assessment of what I saw at Yongbyon first with them before reporting back to the U.S. government.

Kim was amenable to this plan: "It sounds quite good. Our scientists will welcome you, and we agree that this is a visit, not an inspection." Kim appeared enthusiastic about our visit to Yongbyon, but he also expressed concerns about their efforts to be transparent. He said, "The U.S. might claim that this visit proves that the DPRK has crossed a red line when it restarted the [5 MWe] reactor. Can we be sure that the U.S. will refrain from action if it declares that we have gone beyond its red line? Bush will not be happy." As such, he mused, Washington might arrive at a new pretext for initiating an attack against the North. He returned to the upcoming Yongbyon trip and emphasized that despite the risks, "We want you to make a fair assessment. It's a difficult mission, but I believe you will conclude that the DPRK can do what you Americans have done," which I took as a not-so-veiled way of saying that, like us, they could make nuclear weapons.

Kim's remarks were more than standard talking points. Throughout 2003, the Bush administration seemed to downplay that North Korea expelled all inspectors and restarted its plutonium production complex. Apparently, the U.S. posture was more than just irritating to Pyongyang. The North Koreans were convinced that the benefits of getting Washington to acknowledge that they were on their way to building bombs outweighed the risk that the United States would react negatively and aggressively to the information that emerged from our visit.

VISIT TO THE YONGBYON NUCLEAR COMPLEX

On Thursday morning, the North Koreans waited in front of the hotel to take all five members of our delegation to Yongbyon. We were accompanied by Kim Chol Nam (deputy director of the General Bureau of Atomic Energy), a young official from the General Bureau, and Ambassador Ri Gun. A black sedan led our two Land Cruisers all the way to Yongbyon, guiding us through busy Pyongyang intersections and then along a well-built but deserted four-lane highway to the north. As we left the capital, we were greeted with a thick layer of snow on the ground and a brilliant blue sky.

After a little more than one hour, we turned off onto a dirt road toward the city of Yongbyon. The route ran along the Nine Dragon (Kuryong) River, whose distinctive curve around the nuclear facility was very familiar to anyone who views satellite photographs of Yongbyon. As we drove along the river on the way to the Yongbyon nuclear facility, we saw people on foot, some pulling handcarts or guiding oxcarts, while some were on bicycles. We saw dozens of people leveling the dirt road with shovels and brooms. It showed me just what an aberration the nuclear program was in this poor country.

The nuclear center is in its own "closed" city behind a security gate, reminiscent of Russia's closed nuclear cities with gray Soviet-style administrative buildings and apartment complexes. The monuments here, of course, commemorated Kim Il Sung and Kim Jong Il rather than Lenin. After a second security gate and passport checks, we entered the nuclear complex. We were greeted at the guesthouse and given an initial orientation by Dr. Ri Hong Sop, director of the nuclear center. He introduced us to several senior managers. I would eventually get to know Li Yong Ho, the head of the safeguards section, quite well because he would accompany me during all my visits to Yongbyon.

Director Ri carried most of the conversation—through an interpreter—in a professional and confident manner. He explained that their superiors instructed him to show us certain facilities within the complex. Ri also praised the cooperation with American technical experts during the Agreed Framework. I thought this was a good start. On our side, Lewis turned to me to lead the discussion after a few introductory remarks. I emphasized that we were not there as inspectors (teeing off from the conversation with Vice Minister Kim the night before) but rather as professional colleagues looking to clarify the status of Yongbyon.

Director Ri kicked off the substantive exchange by describing in detail the technical specifications and construction history of the 25 megawatt-thermal (MWth) (5 megawatt-electric, MWe) small experimental power reactor, proudly asserting that no aid or help was given to the North. He explained that the North also had plans for a 50 MWe plant and a 200

MWe plant. While the initial goal had been to get the 200 MWe power plant online by 2002—a target set by the Supreme People's Assembly—the 1994 Agreed Framework had not only frozen the 5 MWe plant but also stopped construction on the two larger reactors. Ri explained that the 5 MWe plant had now been restarted. None of this was new, and I began to worry whether we would get to what was of real interest. I needn't have been concerned because in the next breath, Ri promised that we would see and confirm that the reactor was operating now and that all 8,000 spent fuel rods in the spent fuel rod storage pool had been removed and sent to the Radiochemical Laboratory.[7]

Director Ri told us he was not sanguine about resuming progress on the stalled larger reactors. He said restarting construction of the 50 MWe eight years after stopping it would be very difficult. Later, when we drove by that reactor, Ri told Lewis, "Every time I drive by the reactor, I feel very sad. It has been reduced to rubbish." This certainly seemed true. The concrete was cracked, the steel girding of the building adjacent to the reactor building was badly rusted, and there was junk everywhere. Though no one knew the fate of this reactor at the time, I strongly suspected it was not salvageable. We learned during future visits that the North continued to have hope for the 50 MWe reactor, but ultimately neither it nor the 200 MWe reactor would ever be completed—an unsung benefit of the Agreed Framework.

Ri explained that after a visit to the 5 MWe reactor, we would break for lunch and then see the Radiochemical Laboratory, where North Korea reprocessed the plutonium from the spent fuel. Ri then put some meat on the bones. He told us that by June 2003 the entire load of 8,000 fuel rods had been brought to the laboratory and reprocessed using the PUREX method—referring to the standard chemical processing method for plutonium extraction. He said that the reprocessing took six months to complete, but it had gone smoothly. Although the facility generally had a very high level of radiation, portions of the building now had a low radiation hazard because the reprocessing campaign had finished. This would allow us to examine the facility to see specific signs that they had finished reprocessing.

When I asked Director Ri about the product of the reprocessing, he said simply, "You will see the actual product." I didn't realize at the time what

7. The Radiochemical Laboratory is the North's plutonium reprocessing facility.

he meant by this, but it piqued my interest. Perhaps the visit really would encompass more than just a verbal overview and whirlwind tour. Ri told us we were forbidden to take pictures, which was not surprising but turned out to be annoying when North Korean photographers who had accompanied us took hundreds of photos and several videos. At least we were able to obtain some of these for our use after the trip. With that last instruction, we were back in the cars and proceeded through a third security gate to the complex. Ambassador Ri Gun ended up not accompanying us to the nuclear facilities. Director Ri had John Lewis join him in his official car, while the rest of us followed in the two Toyotas.

THE 5 MWe REACTOR

At the 5 MWe reactor complex, we were met by the elderly chief engineer, Li Song Hwan, and several of his staff. As we entered the building, we saw numerous workers mostly dressed in the proper protective attire: yellow protection suits, yellow hats, white gloves, but wearing black tennis shoes. It was bitterly cold in this building, so note-taking was a challenge. We made our way into the main reactor control room, which looked like a throwback to 1950s operations at Los Alamos, except for a few early-generation Philips computer monitors and a Sony TV display monitor. Chief Engineer Li pointed out that the monitor indicated the reactor was running at 100 percent of thermal power, and the generators were producing 2.18 megawatts electricity. After restarting the reactor in February, he said, it now operated at its rated power. Now that the supply of heavy fuel oil from the Americans had been cut off, Li said they used the heat from the reactor to operate a boiler that supplied heat to the entire complex. Judging from the temperature inside the reactor building, they must have decided not to waste too much of the heat in their lab buildings.

This was my chance to dive into less sensitive technical areas and see if Chief Engineer Li—who told us he'd been there for many years—was prepared to give us a complete picture of reactor operations. I first asked several specific questions based on problems such as fuel rod cladding failures that the reactor was believed to have experienced early in its operations before the IAEA visit in 1992. I hoped the answers could help illuminate how reliable the reactor would be now that it had been restarted. Li said they had experienced only one rupture of the fuel cladding during current operations. Director Ri, up to then content to let Li do the talking, added that they were quite satisfied with the reactor's performance after having been frozen for eight years, and they expected it to be operational for a long time, meaning several decades. Ri said they had enough fuel for one more 5 MWe reactor charge. Since they were not in a hurry to make more new fuel, part of the Fuel Fabrication Facility was operational while part of it was under maintenance, according to Ri.

We walked upstairs to the reactor hall viewing room. Through the glass, we could see the top of the core of the reactor and the huge refueling machine behind it. I noticed only one refueling machine though the North had used two in 1994 when it decided to unload the reactor in a hurry before the Agreed Framework. There were three technicians on the floor vacuuming around the perimeter of the reactor core. Everything was spotless. Li provided us with specific design details that were well known to the IAEA and U.S. technical teams who had access to the reactor during the Agreed Framework. My overall impression of the reactor was that the facility was very clean, but the control and electronics, while functional, were outdated.

After about an hour at the reactor, we proceeded to the spent fuel storage pool next door. What had transpired at the pool since North Korea restarted operations at Yongbyon in January 2003 was one of the big mysteries we hoped to solve with our visit. The pool was just that: a pool of water nearly 25 feet deep, designed to store the spent fuel rods after they were unloaded from the reactor after about two or three years of operation. Having so much uranium undergo controlled fission produces a lot of heat and radioactive fission products whose radioactivity must be dissipated once removed from the reactor. The spent fuel rods would typically sit in the pool for about three months before they could be safely transported to the reprocessing facility at a different location in the center. The heat produced during reactor operation is used to produce steam, which drives turbines and generates electricity. Reactor operations also produce plutonium, which can be extracted to make bomb fuel in the reprocessing facility.

During the Agreed Framework, the spent fuel from the reactor's last cycle had been under the watchful eye of IAEA inspectors as it sat in the cooling pool. The problem went beyond mere surveillance, however. The fuel rods were clad in a magnesium alloy, which requires that technicians closely control the chemistry of the pool water to avoid cladding corrosion

and failure. The North Koreans failed to do that, and therefore they justi-
fied the need to reprocess the spent fuel after short storage times for safety
reasons. This is exactly what the United States had tried to avoid because

part of the Agreed Framework, the U.S. government agreed to re-can the
spent fuel rods in the pool. That required draining the canisters of water
and backfilling them with an inert gas, allowing for longer-term storage
until the rods could be shipped out of the country, theoretically putting the
plutonium beyond the North's reach. The re-canning effort turned out to
be an enormous job and was only completed a few years before our visit.
Although by the time we arrived in January 2004, the North Koreans had
publicly claimed that the fuel rods had been taken out of the pool and reprocessed in the Radiochemical Laboratory, U.S. intelligence agencies had
been unable to confirm their removal.

The North Koreans were determined to convince us that the fuel rods
had been taken out of the pool. Although this would seem to be a simple
task, it was anything but that. Director Ri and his team took us into the
spent fuel building where we were asked to put on some primitive protective
gear (smocks, cloth skull caps, and booties) and proceed to the observation
platform overlooking the pool.

The pool appeared to be early Soviet-style with 1950s vintage safety
precautions. Technicians walked along the narrow top ledge of the pool
with no guardrail and no handheld radiation measuring equipment. I also
didn't see any radiation alarms. Since we carried no radiation monitors, I
followed the example set by the Yongbyon director. I assumed he would not
jeopardize his own health if radiation levels were dangerously high. The pool
itself was divided into two halves with a crane separating the two sides. We
could only see the front side. As I looked into that front half of the pool, I
saw that about one-third of the canisters were missing, one-third were in
place without lids, and the other third still had lids secured with bolts.[8] I
wanted to ask Director Ri if they carried out only a partial unloading of the
spent fuel, but he suggested we continue our conversation in the conference

8. I learned later that the United States had supplied 400 canisters to accommodate
the 8,000 fuel rods at 20 per canister. From what I could see, there were 15 canisters in a row
across the width of the pool and about 20 to 30 rows deep. In other words, there were about
400 canisters total in the pool.

room outside where there was no radiation hazard. The spent fuel building was the most problematic in terms of radiation exposure because spent fuel rods contain fission products that emit highly penetrating gamma radiation. Though the North insisted the rods had already been removed, I wasn't so sure. If the rods were still there, we had to rely on the water in the pool to shield us from residual radiation.

In the conference room, Director Ri explained the technical and logistical steps that the North went through to remove the fuel rods from the U.S.-supplied canisters and deliver them to the reprocessing plant. Ri maintained, unconvincingly I thought, that the initial reason for reprocessing the spent fuel in early 2003 was "safety," but then the purpose changed to respond to what he vaguely termed "the international situation," mirroring the position of the Foreign Ministry in its October 2003 announcement on the reprocessing. I assumed that was his way of saying that they had decided to extract plutonium for nuclear weapons. Carefully, so as not to seem too contradictory, I expressed doubt that all the fuel rods were gone on the grounds that as far as I could see, some canisters still had the lids on. Chief Engineer Li was ready with a proposal. We could go back in, and I could select a canister at random that would be opened to see if it was empty or not.

I returned to the pool without my American colleagues because I thought there was no reason to potentially expose my colleagues to additional radiation. As suggested by Chief Engineer Li, I picked a closed canister at random—the one seven rows back and four canisters in from the right. There was nothing distinctive about it. It was as random as I could get. The crane was moved over the selected cannister, and two workers leaned over dangerously, using a long tool to remove the bolts. When they removed the lid, I couldn't quite see in, so I asked to have them bring the underwater light they had close by in the pool and move it above the canister. That allowed me to confirm that my randomly selected canister was empty. Li asked if I wanted to pick another canister for them to open, but I told him that one was good enough for me.

Back in the conference room, we had a long, candid conversation with Director Ri. We asked about the Agreed Framework freeze at Yongbyon and its effect on his facility. He said the freeze was a great burden for them. He noted that the people at Yongbyon—about 100 working on the reactor and 1,000 in total at the center—were not involved with the KEDO light water construction project on the east coast and were not affected by its termination. Ri said what worried him was that if Yongbyon were closed, his workers would all lose their jobs. The concern for his staff was what

heard the same sentiment expressed by those in charge of similar Russian facilities in the 1990s.

We also talked about safeguards, meaning how they protected and controlled their nuclear materials and facilities. Ri told us that Yongbyon had two levels of security guards: protective services from their own facility wearing blue uniforms and a second level comprised of soldiers from the Korean People's Army. The army, he explained (though none of us asked), was there "because you [the United States] are threatening to attack." We returned to the main guesthouse to break for lunch. The American canning teams had used the dining room over the many years of their operations, and the waitress seemed pleased to see Americans again. After a nice Korean lunch with beef and kimchi, we folded ourselves back into the cars and drove through the second checkpoint, which was manned by very stern-looking military guards—no smiles, no nodding of heads. They checked our credentials. Director Ri had told us that we were going to a more secure area than the one in which the reactor was located.

In transit, Lewis asked Director Ri if Kim Jong Il had ever visited the Yongbyon nuclear center. Ri said, "No, we wouldn't allow him to come because of concern for his safety," which I interpreted as concern about radiation exposure. Perhaps that is why Ambassador Ri also chose to sit out the lab tour.

THE RADIOCHEMICAL LABORATORY

Chief Engineer Li greeted us at the laboratory. He detailed the history of the facility, explaining how it was designed by their scientists and technicians and constructed by their own efforts from 1986 to 1990. Li said that they conducted a trial with real materials in March 1990 to test the equipment and confirm the ability to reprocess spent fuel, ultimately processing 80 fuel elements and extracting 60 grams of plutonium. The North's claim of having extracted only 60 grams of plutonium was heavily disputed. IAEA Director General Hans Blix later claimed it was hundreds of grams, but some American intelligence estimates believed it to be many kilograms. Li repeated that the facility had been reactivated when the Agreed Framework fell apart. All 8,000 spent fuel rods were reprocessed between mid-January and the end of June 2003.

Li walked us slowly through the six stages of reprocessing at the laboratory and patiently answered my barrage of questions. John Lewis and I were taking detailed notes since we may well have been the first Americans through that facility. Li and his colleagues were very knowledgeable about all aspects of the PUREX process used to extract plutonium from the spent fuel. The facilities, though dated, were functional and adequate for the job. But ultimately, I was not able to confirm they had reprocessed all 8,000 fuel rods six months ago as they claimed. The rods might no longer be in the cannisters in the spent fuel pool as they demonstrated, but that didn't necessarily mean they would all be reprocessed in a single six-month campaign. It was important to confirm that they had completed the reprocessing because it would determine the size of the weapon-grade plutonium inventory, which would bound the estimates of how many weapons the North could produce.

We eventually proceeded downstairs to a small conference room for additional discussion. What transpired there turned out to be the highlight of the entire visit. Director Ri turned to me for comments and questions. I repeated that the big question for us was the reprocessing product. Without hesitation, Ri asked if I wanted to see their product. This threw me. Did it mean what I thought it meant? "You mean the plutonium?" I asked. Ri replied as if I had asked exactly what he wanted me to ask. "Yes," he said, "if you wish." If I wished! The good director knew exactly what I wanted.

As Ri motioned for one of his people to go out into the hallway, I realized they had carefully planned all of this. They wanted me to see the product. Moments later, technicians brought a maroon-colored metal box, about the size of a big shoe box, into the room. Clearly, they had not just been walking around in the hallway with a box of plutonium. That stuff is much more valuable than gold—once out of the gloveboxes (stainless steel enclosures with rubber gloves used to handle plutonium safely), it is kept locked up in a vault. Without a word from Director Ri, they opened the metal box and took out a somewhat smaller white wooden box with a slide-off top. Removing the top revealed two glass jars—my immediate impression was recycled marmalade jars—set in Styrofoam. The jars were closed with screw-on lids and sealed with transparent tape. So far so good,

I thought, since for safety reasons it was important the plutonium be in a fully sealed container.

Director Ri pointed to the jars. "This one," he indicated which one he

one has 150 grams of plutonium oxalate." I was somewhat surprised to see plutonium oxalate, which in the United States we typically don't store for extended periods since plutonium is much more stable if stored in the oxide rather than the more reactive oxalate form. How, I asked innocently, did they get from the oxalate to the metal? Ri undoubtedly knew I was trying to understand as much as possible about how much they knew about plutonium and how they get it from the reprocessed plutonium to plutonium metal in bomb-usable form. "We use the tetrafluoride/calcium reduction process," he said without hesitation. I took the next step, asking if they also used iodine. In the coy manner he would adopt many times with me over the years, he didn't answer the question directly but would point me in the right direction. Ri said, "I am not authorized to explain the whole system of making plutonium, but you know how it works." With that, we both knew we had set the rules of engagement. Ri would be open to my asking more and more detailed questions about their program, scientist to scientist. He would answer some things, parry others, and for the rest, he would just say he was not authorized to tell me.

The metal piece in the first jar was the shape of a thin-walled funnel that I estimated to be 1/8- to 3/16-inch thick, about 3 inches at the base, 1 inch on top, and about 1½ inches tall, like a truncated ice cream cone. The surface was rough, certainly not machined, but rather more like an as-cast piece. When I showed puzzlement at the shape, Director Ri told me—knowing full well what he was revealing—that it was "scrap" (that is, the end piece) from their recent casting.

I figured I just hit pay dirt. All the time spent working on plutonium at Los Alamos came in handy. That cast shape was confirmation that the North Koreans not only knew how to make plutonium metal, but they also knew quite a bit about plutonium casting and alloying. During the Manhattan Project, my predecessors at Los Alamos had discovered that to make something such as a bomb core, they had to add a bit of another element to pure plutonium—that is, to alloy it. It turns out that pure plutonium has one of the highest densities of any element, close to 20 grams per cubic centimeter (nearly twice that of lead). Alloying pure plutonium makes it easier to manufacture and results in more desirable engineering properties, but it lowers the density to less than 16 grams per cubic centimeter. In fact, if they told me the exact density, I could quite accurately determine the amount of the alloying element. The specifics are quite important in weapon design, but the generalities have been declassified for over fifty years.

I was quite sure that I would not get a direct answer to my next question, about the exact nature of the plutonium, so I thought I would be clever and ask indirectly by inquiring about the density. Director Ri didn't hesitate for even a heartbeat. "It's between 15 and 16." When I raised my eyebrows, he added quickly, "It's alloyed." When I asked what they use to alloy plutonium, he fell back to what I knew he would say—that he wasn't authorized to tell me. But then he added, "Besides, you already know."

Ri knew that if he had given me a specific number for the density, say 15.8, it would tell me how much of the alloying element they use, which in turn would give me more information about their bomb design than I am sure was allowed. His answer of "15 to 16" told me they use the form of plutonium with good engineering properties, just as we do in the United States, without giving away too much. It isn't classified that the alloying element of choice is gallium. I have written many unclassified research articles on Pu-Ga alloys, but the tacit knowledge to make plutonium, purify it, alloy it, cast it, and machine it needs to be learned in a laboratory. It was clear from what I saw and heard that the North Koreans knew how to do so, and they didn't learn that overnight.

I decided it was worth the risk to press on with my questions about the plutonium. I asked how much of the plutonium from the 8,000 spent fuel rods they had processed into metal. Ri said they make the metal as they need it, but unsurprisingly he wasn't going to tell me what the North's plutonium metal bomb fuel inventory was. He confirmed that they had gloveboxes for handling the plutonium in the building. He said they first practiced with the gloveboxes during the 1990 hot test, removed them before the IAEA inspections in 1992, and returned them back to the facility immediately after January 10, 2003. I expressed surprise that they could move gloveboxes in so quickly, but Ri referenced the speed of the Manhattan Project to convince me that it was quite possible that North Koreans could also operate on an expedited timetable. The subtext of his remarks may well have been that he thought I was belittling their capabilities, and he wanted to make clear they were every bit as capable as anyone else, including the United States. My being surprised by how quickly they restored the plutonium labs was

a year in today's regulatory environment.

At this point, I thought about how I was going to explain in Washington what we had just witnessed. I could say that the North was very knowledgeable about plutonium and their "product" looked like plutonium, but I had no way to positively confirm it. It turned out they had no radiation monitoring equipment in the room, nor had we seen any during the rest of the visit. When I departed Los Alamos on this trip, I did not take such equipment with me because I was concerned that if I showed up with radiation monitors, they would think I was trying to get sensitive information and, therefore, would not take us to the nuclear facility. On balance, I thought it was worth the risk to go without them.

After the workers left with the metal box, I asked Director Ri if they could bring it back, explaining to my American colleagues that the glass, or even plastic, easily shields plutonium's alpha radiation, so there shouldn't be any danger. In fact, the alpha radiation is even stopped by human skin. However, one needs to avoid inhaling or ingesting plutonium as it could cause cancer if it enters the body. This was only moderately reassuring, I realized, but my colleagues decided to remain in the room.

I realized it would be good to explain myself to Director Ri. Though not as sensitive as radiation monitors, I decided that my hands could function well enough under the circumstances as a substitute. I asked Ri if I could hold the glass jar with the metal to see if I could get a sense of the temperature and the density of the product. He had no objection. In fact, he might have been amused, though nothing showed on his face. The workers brought back the box, gave me a pair of orange plastic gloves perfectly adequate for the job, and allowed me to take out the jar with the plutonium metal.

I tried to assess if the jar was heavy enough to hold nearly a half-pound, or 200 grams, of plutonium. It felt about right. The second clue was to see if the jar was warm. It wasn't particularly warm. When I told Ri, he replied that was because the concentration of Pu-240 was low. He knew what he was telling me with that remark. The fact is, the lower the Pu-240 content, the less heat is generated and the better weapon-grade plutonium it would be. I couldn't be sure of the Pu-240 content, but the jar was slightly warm in a place where everything else was very cold—it ranged from cold to frigid inside the buildings—confirming that it had a radioactive product inside. The reason for its being slightly warm, of course, was that although plutonium's alpha radiation cannot penetrate the glass jar, it does generate heat.

I did want to check the gloves I was wearing for potential external plutonium contamination from handling the jar. There was some possibility that the outside of the jar had become contaminated when they inserted the plutonium sample. That likelihood was much greater for the jar with the plutonium oxalate powder, which is one reason I never asked to handle it. Checking for potential plutonium contamination is done with an alpha radiation probe that one slowly waves like a wand over the gloves. So, I asked Director Ri if I could get my gloves monitored before I removed them. His colleague waved out into the hallway, and almost immediately a technician entered with what looked like a Geiger counter strapped to his waist. Again, I don't believe someone just happened to be walking the halls with a monitor. I thought it was unusual that he appeared with a Geiger counter because that is not the proper way to check for plutonium's alpha contamination. As the technician approached the box, the counter went off, giving my colleagues pause. Judging from the tone of his voice, I think Director Ri told the technician to get the metal box with the plutonium the hell out of the room. At that point, the counter quieted down, and the technician scanned my gloved hands.

The irony of it all was that the Geiger counter was able to pick up the weak gamma radiation from the plutonium inside the jar, therefore confirming for me that the piece inside the jar was radioactive—without much question now that it was plutonium. As for the gloves, the Geiger counter did not go off because it was unlikely to pick up minute amounts of residual plutonium left on them. So, I knew that I had to follow standard Los Alamos protocol on how to slip off the gloves, carefully grabbing an end and turning them inside out.

The Radiochemical Laboratory was the last stop on our facilities tour, but our conversation continued as we drove around the Yongbyon complex back to the guesthouse for closeout discussions. John Lewis received some important information about uranium enrichment from the North Korean officials in the institute's car. Lewis was told that North Korea developed a small pilot uranium enrichment program in the 1980s with centrifuges they managed to buy (most likely through third parties) from the Urenco conglomerate in the Netherlands. That program was kept in place, Lewis

in the Radiochemical Laboratory. At that point, believed to be in the early 1990s, Pyongyang decided to shut down the enrichment effort in favor of the plutonium route. All scientists who had been devoted to the enrichment effort were transferred to other jobs, and no further action was taken with respect to enrichment, Lewis was told. These comments were subsequently denied when Lewis brought up this conversation during our visit the following year. In retrospect, it's not clear whether this was a completely fabricated account fed to Lewis, or if it was only partially fabricated, meaning that they did stop the enrichment program in 1992, but restarted it again in around 1998 when they got a small number of centrifuges from A. Q. Khan.

Back at the guesthouse, Director Ri seemed very relaxed and prepared to hear what he called my "objective" comments. I said I was convinced that there were no fuel rods in the pool as they took the extraordinary step to open a randomly selected storage canister for me to inspect. As for the question of fuel reprocessing, I said that I received a lot of indirect evidence, but I couldn't say definitively that the Radiochemical Laboratory operated for six months in the first half of 2003 or that they reprocessed all the fuel. I noted that he had showed me what he called the product, plutonium, that resulted from the reprocessing, but I couldn't tell if it came from the most recent reprocessing campaign or an earlier one.

Ri listened attentively, nodding occasionally—whether in agreement or simply acknowledging that he understood my point. When I had finished, he replied evenhandedly, without obvious irritation or disappointment:

"Today, we were authorized to show you the status of our working facilities. My job was just that. It was not to show you proof that everything had been reprocessed. To prove that the plutonium metal we showed you was from the last campaign would require that we measure the ratio of americium to plutonium-241."

He left unstated that they had no intention of telling me that. Then he continued as if to underline the points he had hoped we would come away with. "Yes, the reprocessing is all done. Yes, the products were plutonium oxide, and we have finished processing the plutonium oxide into metal. Our next step will be to reprocess what's in the 5 MWe reactor now. We don't know when that will be." He left that hanging in the air, a not very subtle threat—albeit said in an even tone—that there was more plutonium for their bomb program in the reactor, and they would take it out when their superiors in Pyongyang wanted more plutonium.

Just as the day's light was fading, we went outside for pictures. We asked Director Ri to send us copies of the photos that had been taken during our visit and perhaps later also send us copies of some of the video footage. As we were getting ready to depart, Ambassador Ri Gun, who had waited the entire time at the guesthouse, came up to toast me—with a glass of water. "I want to thank you," he said, smiling. "If it wasn't for your visit, I would have never been able to come here." He did not seem to have minded not having to trudge along into the nuclear facilities.

As we were heading up one of the hills in the countryside on the drive back to Pyongyang, we followed a couple on a bicycle. A woman was sitting sideways on the luggage carrier behind a man who was peddling. When he heard the cars approaching, the man turned around and lost control, sending both tumbling to the ground with what seemed embarrassed laughter. I'll never forget the smile on the face of the young lady as we passed by. As we drove closer to Pyongyang, we were greeted by a full orange moon rising, a moment of unexpected beauty in the so-called hermit kingdom.

BACK TO DIPLOMACY

Our group had dinner alone at the hotel that night to recap the extraordinary access we had been given. After dinner, I began to write up my observations and what I would tell Vice Minister Kim Gye Gwan at dinner the next night. On Friday, our schedule called for a meeting with Korean People's Army General Ri Chan Bok—pretty much a de rigueur session with a KPA general for delegations such as ours. General Ri was the chief delegate of the talks at Panmunjom on issues about the demilitarized zone. He was a familiar face to Western visitors. A short, almost grandfatherly looking man at this point in his life, the general knew the party line to a T. He could alternate with lightning speed between being jocular and acid depending on the subject under discussion. Essentially, the meeting told us nothing, but it was a chance to hear the standard line well delivered:

"We think that we can develop our economy and improve the people's live-lihood only when we can protect our country from outside threats of force against us. Our only option for now is to have these [nuclear] weapons so

do not want to have nuclear weapons in our country or any other place in the world. But your president says he will attack us with nuclear weapons, so we must have nuclear weapons to protect ourselves."

Having just been to Yongbyon, which Ri surely knew, we didn't tell him that based on what we had seen, we didn't think they had much, if any, of a nuclear arsenal yet.

Back at the hotel, we prepared for dinner with Vice Minister Kim Gye Gwan. John Lewis, Jack Pritchard, and I met with Ambassador Ri Gun to present a summary of our Yongbyon visit, which in his words was designed so we could see the North's "deterrent." I told him that while the nuclear specialists at Yongbyon showed us much and told us a great deal about the process of producing plutonium metal from spent fuel, there are additional steps required to move from plutonium metal to a nuclear device. I told him it takes three requisites for the technical part of a deterrent—the bomb fuel, weaponization, and the integration into a delivery system. I asked Ri if we could talk to anyone involved in these other steps.

I also told Ri that I found their technical specialists competent and their facilities to be dated but clean and functional. Ri was perplexed, asking why I could not reach stronger conclusions about their nuclear program given the high level of capabilities that I had witnessed. I said that while I found the Yongbyon workforce to be knowledgeable about reactor physics, chemical engineering involved in reprocessing, and plutonium metallurgy, creating a nuclear device from plutonium metal requires a very different skill set and different facilities. For plutonium metallurgy you also need to be able to cast plutonium, heat treat, and machine the parts. For weapon design you need physics, computing, and expertise in explosives, non-nuclear tests, and a lot of other materials. Ri countered with, "Why didn't you ask about these yesterday?" John Lewis told Ri that when we asked Director Ri Hong Sop to see things beyond the plutonium metal, he said he showed us all that he was authorized to discuss.

I added that the experts at Yongbyon were likely not the right people to ask about the other activities because I suspected those functions didn't take place there. Ri Gun said that he would inquire about what could be done for us to see other parts of the nuclear program. He apparently did that. On Saturday, as we were departing for the plane back to Beijing, he said it was not possible to arrange other visits so quickly but encouraged me to make the request during my next visit. I was curious to find out how much they might be willing to reveal to convince me they had a credible deterrent. At the time, I believed they had passed a critical milestone—producing weapon-grade plutonium—but were still a long way from a deterrent.

Our five-member delegation had dinner with Vice Minister Kim, Ambassador Ri, Ms. Choe Son Hui (who handled the interpretation), and three members of their staff at the Mokran Restaurant in the hotel. Lewis began by exploring what we should say about the visit after we returned to the United States. Both sides stressed that the purpose was to add clarity and understanding of the critical issues and that we had exchanged a wide range of opinions on ways to get to those issues. Kim, who understood the sensitive nature of U.S. delegations possibly being used for propaganda purposes, said he didn't think they would have much to say publicly about our visit. "We'll say you were shown all the sites you requested, and the visit adds clarity and understanding to the current situation." As it turned out, that was almost exactly the line the North took in its public report on our trip.

Vice Minister Kim ordered scotch, with water and ice. He asked me if U.S. nuclear scientists drink a lot of alcohol. I said, "Not particularly." Kim, who has a good sense of humor, said he was told that nuclear scientists drink a lot of alcohol because of the radiation, so they can flush their system. The Russian scientists like to drink vodka, I added, to which Kim proclaimed, "All Russians like to drink."

The conversation turned to my assessment of what we had seen at Yongbyon. I kept in mind the concern of my visit being used by the North for propaganda, particularly considering the Bush administration's concerns. Moreover, this being my maiden voyage to North Korea, a country with which I had no experience, I knew little of its politics, history, and culture. Hence, I was determined to stick to my knitting—that is, technical assessments.

I told Vice Minister Kim that I wanted to share my impressions with the group in the spirit of preventing any surprises. At this point, Kim opened a writing pad and began to take notes himself while Ms. Choe interpreted.

Although Kim obviously understood English well, he still chose to use interpretation in both directions. He clearly wanted us to know that he took my findings seriously and likely also used the notes to help prepare his own ~~report to the leadership.~~

I told Kim we had a useful day at Yongbyon because the cooperation from their nuclear scientists was outstanding. I was impressed by their professional competence, and the facilities themselves were adequate for their intended job, though I was disappointed that we did not see some facilities I had hoped we could visit, such as the Fuel Fabrication Facility or anything required to go from plutonium metal to a nuclear device. We told him that these were not on our original wish list, and Director Ri Hong Sop told us it was too late to get approval to see anything beyond the original request.

I went through what we saw at Yongbyon step by step, much as I did for Ri Gun. I explained that what they called their "product" had the right appearance to be plutonium, and while I did not monitor it with any instruments, I believed they demonstrated the capability to extract plutonium from the spent fuel. I further detailed what I did *not* see—the full set of capabilities required for a nuclear deterrent. That is, I was not shown enough to convince me that they could make a device or deliver it. I concluded:

> "Let me repeat that you have given us great clarity about your ability to make metal. This is important for two reasons. First, it can positively impact the current dialogue related to the freeze and to dismantlement, and second, it can help scientists get prepared to implement a freeze. Our visit to Yongbyon yesterday was a first step toward a peaceful resolution of the nuclear issue."

Kim listened to this summary with clear interest and then replied, "Our scientists at Yongbyon understood the points that you have just made." He must have gotten a readout from Director Ri since Ambassador Ri Gun did not tour the nuclear facilities himself. He continued:

> "They did not want to convince you beyond that. We do understand there is still some ambiguity. Once said, your statement, of course, will arouse ambiguities around the world. So, if the world will have less ambiguity, that's good, otherwise too bad."

Vice Minister Kim said he hoped that I would draw more definitive conclusions, but he recognized that it was difficult to do so from a scientific perspective. He said: "I understand you are a scientist, and you must tell it the way it is. I would like you to make this report to your government. Don't add anything and don't subtract anything."

But when I told Kim that I forgot to mention one more ambiguity, he cut in even before I could mention it with, "I should quote a line from one of your famous movies, *Gone With the Wind,* 'Frankly, my dear, I don't give a damn.'" I had been told that the North Korean leadership likes American movies, but the exquisite timing of his comment still amazed me. He did quickly come back and say, "Nevertheless, we believe that this visit will contribute toward the peaceful resolution of the crisis. We wanted to add clarity so that the policies people draft have some relation to reality. It is a first step, and there will be more," implying they were planning on future visits.

Kim then shifted the discussion to ask me how much plutonium is needed to make a bomb. I countered by asking, "How much is in your bombs?" Kim—who likely had no idea but was being a good diplomat—came back right away with a shrewd reply, "Same as yours." When I asked, "Like the Nagasaki bomb or modern ones?" Kim again parried, probably just to make things interesting, "The modern ones." Kim likely was not privy to a lot of technical detail about nuclear weapons from his own government. It is interesting to note, however, that he was much better informed the next time we met. At the conclusion of the dinner, Kim said he hoped that my observations would help break the impasse between our two countries.

BEYOND NUCLEAR

John Lewis was convinced that resolution of the nuclear crisis required an understanding far beyond the nuclear issue. I also believed that it was important to understand a country for its people, customs, history, and institutions. I benefited greatly because on each trip to North Korea, Lewis made sure we visited many other places and organizations. In that spirit, Lewis had arranged a tour around Pyongyang and a visit to one of the large markets, as well as the DPRK Academy of Sciences and the Committee for the Promotion of International Trade (CPIT); these visits were laid out according to the schedule we'd received upon our arrival. Keith Luse and Frank Jannuzi, who had accompanied us to Yongbyon, were also keenly interested in the tour stops that had broader economic and cultural content.

Lewis was able to continue his ongoing discussions on the North's economic reforms with the regional director of CPIT. I was impressed with the director's willingness and candor in discussing North Korea's economy. the past ten years but had rebounded in the past year. Their industry and agriculture sectors were recovering, and exports were as well, citing the benefits of Kim Jong Il's economic reforms of July 2002. However, the lack of electricity remained the biggest challenge across all sectors of their economy. Our discussions with an official of the Korea Academy of Sciences did little to enlighten me about the state of science in the North. Meeting with us was clearly not his choice.

After lunch on Friday, we visited the Tong-il Street Market, a huge building packed with what seemed to be thousands of people. It was a madhouse. All vendors wore red uniforms, and most returned my smiles with friendly smiles of their own. I felt no sense of animosity. There were lots of Chinese goods in the market, from batteries to bed headboards. There was also an abundance of fruits, vegetables, and meats—which I found surprising even if the shoppers were likely only Pyongyang's elite. In fact, when I showed my wife the photos of the red tomatoes and other vegetables, she said, "I wish we could get that at our Smith's grocery store here in Los Alamos in January." I bought five small wall paintings. After all, how often do you get to buy something made in North Korea?

Back at the hotel, I asked Ambassador Ri Gun if he could get us copies of some of the photos they took at Yongbyon. He said he would have them before we left, but on Saturday morning as we were ready to depart, he said he was unable to get them. He promised to send them to us through the UN mission in New York.

BACK TO BEIJING

Returning to Beijing on Saturday morning, we hoped there would be less pandemonium at the airport with the press. A reporter from Agence France-Presse (AFP) had contacted John Lewis by phone at the Potong-gang Hotel, offering to organize a single press session for the news media at the airport upon our return, in stark contrast to the chaotic scene at the airport on our way to Pyongyang.

Upon arrival, the AFP reporter spotted John Lewis and took us to where he had miraculously arranged a hundred or so reporters gathered to ask questions about our visit. It was still chaotic, but much less so than racing through the airport with a pack of reporters at our heels. John addressed the throng briefly, but they clearly wanted more information about the nuclear issues, so he turned it over to me. I spent the next few minutes trying to tell them as little as possible. I said we visited the Yongbyon nuclear complex and were treated very professionally by very competent nuclear specialists. I certainly had no intention of briefing the international news media before reporting the findings back home to my government. Luse and Jannuzi had already arranged to have me testify at a hearing of the Senate Foreign Relations Committee in Washington, DC, on January 20.

Once out of the airport, the few days in China were productive. The laws of physics and chemistry are in force equally around the world, but the practical application differs from country to country. The U.S. experience in developing its nuclear weapons program plays a large part in American views of how other countries developed their own programs, and to some extent this is misleading. Over time and many conversations, we learned how the Chinese perspective and experience informed their analysis of the North Korean program. For a start, we had incredible access to Chinese authorities that John Lewis, along with Stanford University colleague Xue Litai, forged while writing *China Builds the Bomb*, the seminal book on China's nuclear program, published in 1988.[9] From that experience, Lewis had established contacts sustained over the years with key Chinese nuclear experts. I had been to China twice in 1994, including a visit to the Mianyang nuclear weapons institute (a Chinese counterpart to Los Alamos) in Sichuan Province, to explore cooperative efforts with the Chinese nuclear weapons complex on nuclear materials security and safeguards. On Monday, we participated in an international topical seminar on Northeast Asia security and stability, organized by the scientists I had met in 1994 and those with whom Lewis had stayed in touch for many years. Since our trip to North

9. John Wilson Lewis and Xue Litai, *China Builds the Bomb* (Stanford: Stanford University Press, 1988).

Korea was current news, I had to mention the visit to Yongbyon but did not provide any details.

The seminar and the visits in Beijing painted a picture quite different

ington solve the North Korean nuclear problem. Former Chinese diplomats and retired military officers maintained that China was opposed to North Korea building the bomb, but it was not willing to bring the Kim regime to its knees to stop them. They put much of the blame for Pyongyang's pursuit of the bomb in Washington's lap. They said that Beijing stepped in during the current crisis primarily as an honest broker and to avoid a North Korea–U.S. military confrontation, not to assist Washington. Beijing's priorities were to preserve peace and stability in Northeast Asia, rather than join Washington's single-minded drive for denuclearization. After listening to the Chinese perspective, I found it puzzling that the Bush administration, and later the Obama administration, looked to China to rein in North Korea's nuclear program.

At the seminar, a Chinese nuclear scientist presented a remarkably insightful technical assessment of North Korea's nuclear project. His principal conclusion was that North Korea had already spent several decades developing its nuclear weapons program. He stated that North Korea was not just interested in building a nuclear device but rather a nuclear weapon that could be mounted on a missile to defend itself from a threat by the United States. He concluded that North Korea had the ability to produce a crude atomic bomb, but he was not sure whether it was able to produce a nuclear warhead to put atop a missile.

I have continued to compare assessments on the North's nuclear progress with Chinese nuclear experts ever since. Based on their own experience in the 1960s, the Chinese experts have good insight into how a fledgling nuclear weapons program can be developed with crude technical capabilities during difficult economic times. It was a mistake, they warned, for us to see the development of the North's preparations through the prism of the U.S. experience. In turn, the Chinese experts valued our opinions because we'd been able to visit North Korea's nuclear facilities, which none of them were allowed to do until September 2007, when two of them were on a China–U.S.–Russia team to verify North Korean disablement. No Chinese nuclear experts have been to North Korea since then, as far as we know.

REPORTING ON THE TRIP BACK HOME

Once back in the United States, the most daunting task was to deal with the dozens of news media inquiries. With help from the public affairs offices at Los Alamos and Stanford, we developed a communications strategy that we hoped could accurately (always the goal but not always reached when dealing with the press) convey the visit to the public. I had learned from the many years as director at Los Alamos that it was crucial to have the story in writing. I decided to incorporate the major findings into a written statement for the Senate hearing scheduled for January 20.

By this time, I had also learned how politically charged and partisan the North Korean situation was. Officials from the previous Clinton administration were openly critical of the Bush administration for having abandoned what they considered a deal that almost resolved the decades-old Korean Peninsula crisis. On the other side were the Bush administration's hard-liners, who in John Lewis's view, had managed to kill the agreement and were determined to bring the Kim regime to its knees. I did not belong in either camp. My job was to provide the best possible technical assessment of what we found in North Korea. However, as I got more deeply involved in the North Korea quandary in subsequent years, I was able to witness firsthand the disastrous results of the hard-liners' ideology turned into action.

The written statement for the hearing record gave me the opportunity to provide details that I thought were important for both policymakers and the public. It was distributed to committee members and staff as well as to relevant U.S. government agencies and, the morning before the open hearing, to the press. The night before the hearing, I also sent a copy of the statement to the DPRK mission at the UN to transmit it back to Pyongyang. I wanted Pyongyang to get the story directly from me, not just from news reports.

I was especially careful in the written statement to tell it the way I saw it and not to speculate or get into political judgments. I presented my views carefully and conservatively. My approach was to describe each of the facilities we visited by stating what the North Koreans told us, followed by what I saw, and then what I believed it meant.

As we approached the end of the week before the hearing, I got a call from Senator Lugar's office telling me that the White House objected to the hearing being held on the same day that President Bush was scheduled to present his State of the Union address. White House officials were concerned that the hearing would dominate the news headlines. We quickly developed an excellent alternative—that is, the hearing on January 20 would be held in closed session to allow for classified discussion and avoid news media

I had hoped to have the photos that I requested of our visit to the Yongbyon nuclear complex when I left Pyongyang. John Lewis had checked with the DPRK mission at the UN in New York and was told the photos were on the way to Los Alamos via DHL, the international express shipping company, and got a tracking number. On Monday January 19, as I was about to depart Los Alamos for Washington with no shipment in sight, I called DHL. They tracked down the order and put me in touch with the driver on the phone. He was looking for my address in Los Alamos, but the problem was that he was in the small town of Los Alamos, California, not New Mexico. I asked him to have the package delivered to the L'Enfant Plaza Hotel in Washington, DC, where I would be staying the next few days. Amazingly, the photos arrived there in time for me to take them to the Senate hearing the next day.

The closed hearing of the Senate Committee on Foreign Relations was unlike anything I had ever experienced. Senator Lugar, committee chair, and Senator Biden, ranking minority member, told me that they knew I had a lot to report from the trip to North Korea, so I should take as much time as I needed. And that's what I did. If they were willing to listen, I was willing to talk, and I explained in much more detail than a normal hearing would allow. And despite the detail, as the hearing progressed, I had the feeling that the eight senators were paying attention to every word I said. I was able not only to report on my findings from the Yongbyon visit, but also explain what these meant. It was like giving a Nuclear Weapons 101 lecture at the university. In fact, one of the most preeminent of the senators with nuclear knowledge asked at one point when I was explaining the spent fuel pool and the absence of the spent fuel rods, "Dr. Hecker, could you explain what's a fuel rod?" Since the hearing was closed (meaning classified, no press), there was no posturing and little politicking. I had been called to some thirty hearings at Senate and House committees over the years, especially during my Los Alamos directorship. This was by far the most satisfying.

After three hours, the hearing adjourned, but Senator Biden was interested in more details, so we convened in a small, classified meeting room for another hour. During the private session, I found Biden refreshingly engaged, incredibly interested in the details, and very knowledgeable.

The next morning, the open hearing began at 9 AM in a hearing room in the Hart Senate Office Building that was packed with senators, staffers, and news media. Senator Lugar opened the session by thanking me for an informative session the day before. This hearing followed a more normal path. Both Senators Lugar and Biden made opening statements. Lugar focused on the importance of the Six-Party Talks, the role of China, the human rights problems in North Korea, and the Bush administration's objective of a peaceful and diplomatic settlement. Biden praised our closed session the previous day, calling it "one of the most informative meetings that this committee has held, ever" because, in his words, I had "the rare and unique capacity . . . to be able to translate that [plutonium and nuclear issues] to a group of educated women and men . . . and for us to understand what's at stake here." Biden also emphasized that it was important that policymakers understand and inform themselves on technical matters. That was music to my ears because I had been carrying that message to Washington for over a decade. For nearly the next two hours, I presented my findings much as I did at the final dinner with Vice Minister Kim Gye Gwan in Pyongyang, in what I'd consider to be a cross between a public seminar and a class lecture.

Naturally, the news media were hot on my trail for interviews. Even though I said virtually the same thing to all of them, the stories and commentary came out differently. The *Wall Street Journal* ran a scathing editorial titled "North Korean Reruns," slamming what it called our "Potemkin tour of North Korea" and praising the Bush administration for its resolve not to fall for the same "plutonium stunt" that the North had used to "hoodwink" the Clinton administration into the Agreed Framework. Obviously, not everyone was prepared to listen to what was a straightforward account. As I knew then and the rest of the U.S. government has found out since, there was nothing Potemkin, or make-believe, about what we had seen at Yongbyon. Whereas the Washington hard-liners could have used my report to demonstrate North Korea was intent on building the bomb, they preferred to denigrate the report of someone who had been allowed to visit the North's nuclear facilities. As I witnessed after all my visits, they were not interested in factual reports. They already had made up their minds about North Korea.

I had gone to North Korea to help provide insight to an important national security concern. What I had not expected, in retrospect somewhat naively even after all my years of dealing with the U.S. government, was that

ideologies. It rapidly became clear to me that the hard-liners in the Bush administration had no desire to resolve the nuclear crisis short of regime change, along the lines of what they had just unleashed on Iraq. I had witnessed members of the Bush administration twisting intelligence reports to incorrectly conclude Iraq had nuclear weapons to fit their political agendas. I became more determined than ever to provide sound scientific analysis and advice on international nuclear matters, both to our government and to the public.

While in Washington, I watched closely for news out of North Korea on the trip. After the North Korean official news agency released a Foreign Ministry statement giving a brief report right after our trip, Pyongyang was silent on the subject. The single release was very much in the spirit of what Vice Minister Kim had told us—that they would not use the visit as a propaganda stunt and would not have much to say about it publicly. The North's report followed the lines of our discussions at the dinner, saying the visit had been intended "to ensure transparency and clear up ambiguities," concluding that if some modicum of clarity was achieved, "it would serve as a substantial foundation for a peaceful settlement of the nuclear issue." One could interpret that language however one wanted, but I thought the key was that it left the door open to dialing down tensions and having additional talks. The statement was noticeably free of bellicose language—no threats about the North's nuclear program and none of the bald choices that General Ri had laid before us.

Back in Los Alamos, I worked with our medical staff to try to measure the amount of radiation that I may have been exposed to in Yongbyon. A variety of tests confirmed that I had no excess internal gamma radiation from possible residual fission products at the spent fuel pool and no pickup of measurable plutonium from my handling of the "product." As primitive as radiation protection looked over there, the water in the spent fuel pond and the plastic orange gloves had done their job.

I also worked with my colleagues at Los Alamos to gain greater confidence in my findings from the trip. The simulations we carried out at the lab confirmed with greater certainty that the glass jar I held in Yongbyon did indeed contain plutonium. I was convinced that the Yongbyon scientists and engineers could make weapon-grade plutonium and that North Korea's claim to have reprocessed all 8,000 spent fuel rods was believable. It was also clear that during the Agreed Framework, North Korea had likely kept a hedge by continuing its weapon design and weapon R&D activities outside of Yongbyon. In that case, even though there was no direct evidence, I was willing to bet that North Korea had now produced a rudimentary nuclear device or two of the Nagasaki type from the most recently reprocessed plutonium. That meant the stakes were very high.

5   Disastrous Consequences of Bolton's Hammer

I was alarmed by the political implications of what we had seen in North Korea. If, as I thought, North Korea had built the bomb, how could the Bush administration have walked away from the Agreed Framework on the grounds that the North was pursuing another path? The uranium path that they suspected would take years to develop, yet by abandoning the freeze on Yongbyon's plutonium facilities, Washington opened the door to the North building plutonium bombs.

Even though I knew that the Bush administration was preoccupied with events in Iraq, I was surprised that the administration downplayed our report of the nuclear advances North Korea had made. Before I describe the political developments ahead of my next visit to North Korea in August 2005, in this chapter I take a closer look at what was at stake when the administration abrogated the Agreed Framework and the dire consequences of Bolton's "hammer." It killed the Agreed Framework to the delight of the hard-liners, but it allowed the North to proceed with the plutonium path to the bomb. Not even the most rudimentary risk/benefit analysis would have led Washington to this decision. Whereas it may have been an ideological victory for the hard-liners, it was disastrous for U.S security.

NUCLEAR PROGRAM AT FULL SPEED AHEAD

As bad a decision as killing the Agreed Framework was, not being prepared for the consequences was even more dangerous. Freezing the Yongbyon plutonium complex was the central element of the Agreed Framework. Although it was fully recognized that this was only one step toward
the elimination of the North's nuclear weapon program, it was the most
urgent: Shutting down plutonium production and extraction meant no
bomb fuel. Indeed, from 1994 to 2002, no plutonium was produced. Had
there been no such deal (Agreed Framework), the North could have operated its 5 MWe reactor and at the same time completed the two larger reactors that were under construction in 1994. That would have given it the
capacity to produce nearly 300 kilograms of plutonium annually. Washington still reaps the benefits of the 5 MWe reactor not operating for eight
years and of construction of the two larger reactors being abandoned, because now, more than twenty years later, I estimate North Korea's total
plutonium inventory to be less than 50 kilograms.

Although plutonium production was frozen, even during the Agreed
Framework's last years there were concerns about the clandestine pursuit
of uranium enrichment. North Korea also undoubtedly kept weapon design
and missile development programs active during that time. Such efforts were
essentially impossible to track and were not verifiable. Signing the Agreed
Framework in 1994 was a sensible risk-based decision by Washington. It
stopped the most dangerous and imminent part of North Korea's nuclear
weapon program because no plutonium, no bombs. It was understood that
the freeze of Yongbyon facilities would allow North Korea to rapidly reconstitute the plutonium operations, but that was an inevitable result of the
give-and-take of negotiations. North Korea was not a conquered country,
as their diplomats kept reminding the Americans. In the "Confidential
Minute" adopted at the end of the negotiations, Pyongyang agreed dismantlement of the reactors and related facilities would begin when the
first LWR unit was completed and would be finished at completion of the
second unit.[1] The transfer out of North Korea of the spent fuel stored in

1. "1994 U.S.-DPRK Agreed Framework Confidential Minute" (October 21, 1994).
https://www.documentcloud.org/documents/2829751–1994-U-S-DPRK-Agreed-Framework-
Confidential-Minute.html

the pool would also begin after the completion of the first LWR unit. In
the meantime, IAEA inspectors and U.S. technical teams had access to the
Yongbyon plutonium facilities.

sortium resulted in Americans getting access to the northeast part of the
country at the Kumho site and put them in close contact with North Korean
officials and technical specialists. The very idea of Washington orchestrating
the construction of the LWRs was vehemently opposed by the hard-liners.
They considered LWRs an unacceptable proliferation risk. Moreover, providing them with the reactors was seen as rewarding bad behavior. This
was another example of allowing ideology to blind good decision-making.
Although neutrons, which are produced in all reactors, can be used to produce plutonium, the likelihood of North Korea repurposing the civilian
electricity-producing reactors to make plutonium was small. There were
also strong safeguards in place: The reactors were to be built with foreign
technologies, operated with foreign assistance, and reliant on supply of
foreign fuel, which could be cut off at the first sign of a violation. Besides,
once the LWRs had been completed and were providing electricity for this
energy-starved country, the Kim regime would have had to think twice
before it allowed the country to go dark again.

The LWR opponents never allowed for the prospect that the KEDO
projects could have benefits—such as potentially transforming the confrontational relations between the United States and North Korea as part of the
broader goal of normalization by having North Koreans and Americans
work side by side for a decade or so on such a high-visibility energy project.
Objections were also voiced that the United States was providing financial
assistance for the LWR, although finances were borne by South Korea and
Japan. KEDO also had the benefit of possibly convincing South Korea and
Japan that Washington was interested in a long-term transformation of its
relations with Pyongyang.

The Clinton administration stuck to the Agreed Framework even when
Pyongyang strained relations, as it did openly with the Taepodong-1 launch
in August 1998 and when evidence emerged that it was covertly pursuing a
uranium centrifuge acquisitions program in the late 1990s. Remaining in
the Agreed Framework was a good risk/benefit tradeoff because the Clinton administration knew that Pyongyang could quickly reconstitute the

Yongbyon complex should it terminate the agreement. However, the Bush administration walked away from the deal and gave North Korea access to 25 to 30 kilograms of plutonium in the spent fuel—the final missing piece Pyongyang needed to build the bomb—which it did within the next year. The United States needed to deal with the uranium enrichment issue, but it made more sense, and was less of a risk, to do that within the framework of the diplomacy already underway rather than blowing that up and starting from zero, or in this case, from a much worse situation.

All indications are that in the 1990s, Pyongyang gave priority to diplomacy in its dual-track approach. It came close to reaching strategic accommodation with Washington by the end of 2000. But it also kept the nuclear weapon option open in case diplomacy failed. The Yongbyon facilities were frozen, not eliminated, while Pyongyang gauged whether and how fast Washington would move to normalize relations. Technologies and materials for uranium enrichment were procured to explore the second path to the bomb, if needed. Little was known about Pyongyang's weaponization activities. However, based on my visit, I concluded that the North had continued its nuclear weapon design and engineering; plutonium metallurgy and fabrication; and research on high explosives, detonators, and neutron source—all away from the Yongbyon complex. North Korea also likely continued to prepare for eventual underground nuclear testing and persisted in its work on short- and medium-range missile delivery capabilities.

North Korea was also keeping some of its nuclear facilities operational to earn foreign currency. As discovered in 2004, Pyongyang was involved in the sale of uranium hexafluoride (the key precursor for uranium enrichment) to Libya's nascent centrifuge program a few years earlier.[2] And in an incredibly audacious move, not discovered until 2007, North Korea embarked on building a plutonium production reactor for Syria, a decision likely made in the late 1990s. Upon subsequent examination of satellite imagery, it was confirmed Syria had broken ground at Al Kibar, on the banks of the Euphrates River, by 2001 for what later was determined to be such a

2. David E. Sanger and William J. Broad, "Evidence Is Cited Linking Koreans to Libya Uranium," New York Times (May 23, 2004), https://www.nytimes.com/2004/05/23/world/evidence-is-cited-linking-koreans-to-libya-uranium.html

reactor.[3] These nuclear exports not only raised much needed foreign currency for the regime, but also helped to keep its nuclear workers occupied and exercised. The nuclear exports constituted a much more serious risk

these exports had the potential of supporting nuclear weapons programs in an already unstable part of the world.

The prevalent view in the United States was that Pyongyang was never serious about diplomacy and about giving up its nuclear weapon quest. In his book, Thae Yong-ho, a North Korean defector, claimed that diplomacy in the 1990s was pursued only to buy time for the regime to develop a nuclear arsenal.[4] On the other hand, William Perry, Madeleine Albright, Wendy Sherman, and others who dealt with the North Korean regime in 2000 are all of the mind that the North's diplomacy during this time was genuine. Perry, who in 1994 as secretary of defense had prepared plans to bomb the Yongbyon nuclear facilities, has stated that he believed Washington and Pyongyang were only months away from resolving the nuclear issue at the end of 2000.[5]

It is certainly possible that the Kims believed diplomacy would serve them well even if it did not result in a nuclear deal because it might get Washington to dial-back pressure at a time when the North was facing grim economic times. Pyongyang also benefited from KEDO providing heavy fuel oil during the country's dire energy shortages, though the fuel oil had only limited utility and was delivered intermittently, a schedule that some in the North thought was a deliberate effort on Washington's part to further undermine the DPRK economy. Diplomacy yielded benefits, but the primary reason, I believe, is that Pyongyang had hoped it would lead to an end of enmity. I disagree with the notion that the Kims were engaging in diplomacy simply to buy time to build up the nuclear program. Halting

3. Director General, IAEA Board of Governors, "Implementation of the NPT Safeguards Agreement in the Syrian Arab Republic" (May 24, 2011), https://www.iaea.org/sites/default/files/gov2011-30.pdf

4. Thae Yong-ho, personal discussions with author, Seoul (September 14, 2017). The book was published in the Korean language and has not been translated to English. Its title is translated as *Cryptography from the Third-Floor Secretariat* (Korean: 3 서기실의 암호; Hanja: 3層 書記室의 暗號).

5. William J. Perry, *My Journey at the Nuclear Brink* (Stanford: Stanford University Press, 2015), 167.

Yongbyon operations and stopping the construction of the two bigger re-actors set back Pyongyang's ability to produce plutonium and tritium, a serious disadvantage that cannot be overcome by uranium enrichment, no matter how much enriched uranium North Korea would eventually pro-duce. Whereas the Agreed Framework may have relieved pressure on the regime during the economically disastrous 1990s, it crippled its plutonium production capability, from which it still has not recovered as of this writing.

In 2003, with the Agreed Framework dead, Pyongyang switched prior-ities in its dual-track strategy. Building the bomb now became the primary objective. This was made easier because the North had expelled Americans and IAEA inspectors. Even so, Pyongyang also continued to keep the diplo-matic channels alive well into 2004 and 2005, both as a hedge in case weap-ons development ran into difficulty and to allow the North to diplomatically probe where the American red lines were for potential military action.

All facets of the bomb program likely progressed rapidly during this time. The Yongbyon complex, back in full swing, was producing more plu-tonium. During this time, although Washington did not know it then, the reactor engineers and construction specialists were assisting Syria in build-ing a slightly larger version of the 5 MWe reactor. The nuclear test site at Punggye-ri was being readied for a nuclear test, which required both careful preparation of tunnels that would have to be sealed to safely contain the blast and sophisticated instrumentation to measure the device's performance.

North Korea's uranium enrichment program was also picking up speed. If, as we learned during our 2004 visit, the North had previously explored centrifuge technologies in the 1980s but set them aside in the early 1990s, the program started up again, apparently in the late 1990s, with the procure-ment of a small number of centrifuges from A. Q. Khan.[6] At some point, the program was put into higher gear, which the intelligence community began tracking through the North's procurement of centrifuge technology and materials. However, there was no evidence that North Korea possessed in 2004 or before a production-level facility capable of making sufficient

---

6. A. Q. Khan was a Pakistani nuclear scientist generally credited with having been the father of Pakistan's nuclear weapon program, but he was also a notorious nuclear prolifera-tor.

uranium to create a weapon. They were probably at least a few years away from that capability.

More evidence of Khan's dealings with North Korea began to emerge

try's nuclear weapon aspirations and relinquished its uranium centrifuge purchases. Gaddafi subsequently provided a treasure trove of intelligence information about Libya's primary supplier, namely Khan. Khan's network included North Korea, which in collaboration with him sold a critical part of an enrichment program—uranium hexafluoride (UF_6)—to the Libyans.[7] At the time, the Yongbyon complex was able to produce uranium tetrafluoride (UF_4), which is the precursor for producing uranium metal required to manufacture fuel rods for the 5 MWe reactor. But it did not have the facilities for the subsequent fluorination step from UF_4 to UF_6. Those facilities must have been outside of Yongbyon, and likely had been there for several years before the Libya sale. That capability was likely also used to produce UF_6 for North Korea's clandestine enrichment efforts at the time.

The Libya saga also provided deeper insights into A. Q. Khan's flagrant international proliferation business and his dealings with Pyongyang. Upon his arrest by the Pakistani government in early 2004, Kahn confessed to some of his nuclear business activities with North Korea.[8] The CIA concluded in March 2004 that this assistance included a comprehensive package of uranium hexafluoride, centrifuges, and "one or more warhead designs."[9] Pakistan's president Pervez Musharraf corroborated that assessment by stating in his memoir that Khan delivered a couple of dozen centrifuges, mostly of the primitive type, to North Korea.[10] In addition, Pakistan's Khan Research Laboratory in Kahuta trained North Korean engineers and technicians in centrifuge operations. In his confession, Khan claimed that on one of his visits to North Korea in the late 1990s, he was shown three nuclear devices in a secret tunnel. Khan may have made this claim to absolve himself of responsibility for the North's success in building bombs, but it

7. Sanger and Broad, "Evidence Is Cited Linking Koreans to Libya Uranium."

8. Pervez Musharraf, *In the Line of Fire: A Memoir* (New York: Free Press, 2006).

9. David E. Sanger, "U.S. Widens View of Pakistan's Link to Korean Arms," *New York Times* (March 14, 2004), https://www.nytimes.com/2004/03/14/world/us-widens-view-of-pakistan-link-to-korean-arms.html

10. Musharraf, *In the Line of Fire.*

is not credible. In fact, when during a subsequent visit, I asked Ambassador Ri Gun about Khan's claim to have visited North Korea some thirteen times and having been shown North Korea's weapons, he categorically said Khan lied. He only visited twice, Ri said, and was never shown nuclear weapons.

North Korea likely assembled its first bomb in late 2003 or early 2004 according to designs it had been developing since the 1990s. These designs benefited from the series of cold tests using surrogates for the plutonium core begun in the late 1980s and apparently picked up again as soon as the Agreed Framework ended. These tests were crucial in helping North Korean specialists construct a complex implosion system with high-explosive lenses and detonators. The tests and R&D on materials for the implosion design surely continued throughout the 1990s, even during the period of the Agreed Framework. And these efforts were almost certainly aided by nuclear device design information supplied by Khan. North Korean nuclear experts also must have been working closely with their missile experts and the military to begin to integrate their warhead designs into the North's missile force.

The Khan revelations also provided information about the North's missile export business. The exchange of some of Pakistan's centrifuge technology information with North Korea in return for Pyongyang's missile know-how date back to the visit of Benazir Bhutto, Pakistan's prime minister, in 1993. By the early 2000s, North Korea was exporting missiles and missile technologies to numerous countries in the Middle East. Its cooperation with Pakistan and Iran likely proved valuable to North Korea's own missile program. This was important because North Korea had agreed to a missile test ban in the final years of the Clinton administration and continued that into the early Bush years. But even with the missile test ban, North Korea must have continued to improve its longer-range missile capabilities late in the Clinton years and early in the Bush years. In summary, when the Americans walked away from the Agreed Framework, they opened the door for North Korea to put the Yongbyon nuclear complex back in full swing and to accelerate the efforts it had been pursuing covertly.

KEEPING THE DIPLOMACY DOOR OPEN

Washington continued to flirt with the appearance of serious diplomacy in 2004, but its policies only resulted in lost time. The Bush administration had decided that it must deal with Pyongyang multilaterally, particularly getting help from China. It tied itself to the ineffective six-party process and remained hampered by divisions within its policymaking apparatus. Pyongyang, for its part, kept the diplomacy door ajar while it was moving

The second round of talks was held in late February 2004. The American negotiator, James Kelly, was instructed to stick to the CVID (complete, verifiable, irreversible dismantlement) formula and to push for a complete disclosure at the start, including uranium enrichment. The Bush hard-liners were looking to duplicate their success in Libya, with the goal of swift dismantlement up-front, rather than a "pay-as-you-go installment plan."[11] The North was looking for a "freeze for compensation" deal. It continued to deny a uranium enrichment program. Unsurprisingly, the talks ended without progress.

Over the next few months, Washington continued to press China to get North Korea to make progress on U.S. terms. Vice President Cheney presented evidence about the North's uranium enrichment program to President Hu Jintao and other Chinese leaders in Beijing. He warned them that "time is not necessarily on our side."[12] Indeed, by the end of April, a new consensus U.S. intelligence assessment determined that North Korea already possessed two to eight weapons.[13] The high end exceeded my estimate. However, China was not swayed to do Washington's bidding with the North, and Pyongyang simply continued to enhance its nuclear program. At another round of the Six-Party Talks in June, Washington and Pyongyang claimed to have softened their demands, but they continued to talk past each other. No meaningful progress was made.

During the rest of the year, Pyongyang appeared to be playing a clever six-party card by insisting on preconditions to get them to return to the talks. In late September before the UN General Assembly, Vice Foreign Minister Choe Su Hon laid out the new conditions that needed to be overcome

11. Glenn Kessler, "U.S. Will Stand Firm on N. Korea; Arms Talks to Set Stage for Demands," *Washington Post* (February 16, 2004): A17.

12. Joseph Kahn, "Cheney Urges China to Press North Korea on A-Bombs," *New York Times* (April 15, 2004), https://www.nytimes.com/2004/04/15/world/cheney-urges-china-to-press-north-korea-on-a-bombs.html

13. Glenn Kessler, "N. Korea Nuclear Estimate to Rise; U.S. Report to Say Country Has at Least 8 Bombs," *Washington Post* (April 28, 2004): A1.

to resume the Six-Party Talks, including that in exchange for movement toward disarmament, the United States must move to normalize relations and provide economic compensation.[14] The other parties, especially the United States, were so anxious to get Pyongyang back to the negotiating table that they appeared to measure diplomatic progress simply by that fact alone, rather than real headway.

Choe further stated that the DPRK had "made clear that we have already reprocessed 8,000 fuel rods and transformed them into arms." There could only be one type of "arms" this could be—nuclear—but Choe's statement pulled up just short of making that explicit. That was left for a high-level Foreign Ministry statement five months later, in February 2005—only weeks after the start of the second Bush term. The statement announced that the North had "manufactured nukes for self-defense"—in effect, the formal announcement that the DPRK had crossed the threshold to become a nuclear power. Amazingly, this did not create a greater sense of urgency in Washington, which saw it as a ploy by Pyongyang to gain leverage.

The reelection of George W. Bush to a second term marked a gradual shift in Washington's approach to North Korea, buttressed by key personnel changes. Condoleezza Rice's appointment as secretary of state moved the United States toward reviving the Six-Party Talks. Rice recommended Christopher Hill for the next assistant secretary of state for East Asian and Pacific Affairs, replacing James Kelly at the helm of the U.S. negotiating team. Hill, an experienced and well-traveled diplomat, wanted a longer leash than his predecessor. Other notable personnel changes impacted the direction of the interagency fight on policy. These included John Bolton's move, at the urging of Rice, from undersecretary of state for arms control to ambassador to the United Nations, which removed him from a day-to-day role in policymaking on North Korea. He was replaced by the equally hawkish Robert Joseph, a skilled bureaucrat, who moved over from his nonproliferation portfolio at the NSC.

Pyongyang watched closely for signs that the second Bush administration would take a different approach. That didn't go so well when, at her confirmation hearing, Condoleezza Rice, almost as a throwaway comment,

14. Colum Lynch, "North Korea Resists Talks on Nuclear Arms: Meeting by U.S. Election Is Unlikely," *Washington Post* (September 28, 2004): A21.

referred to North Korea as one of the "outposts of tyranny" in the world.[15] Then in his State of the Union speech, Bush called on North Korea to abandon its nuclear ambition, asserting, "America will stand with the allies of

Pyongyang's perspective, these comments confirmed the hostile intent of the second Bush administration.[17]

Throughout the spring, Pyongyang continued to enhance its nuclear program and publicly define its nuclear status. On May 11, North Korea claimed that it removed another batch of 8,000 spent fuel rods from its 5 MWe reactor,[18] which likely provided additional plutonium for another two bombs. The Bush administration stood by, frustrated and hamstrung, with one senior administration official stating, "There is a lot of symbolism and taunting here."[19] What Washington feared was much more than symbolism, namely a nuclear test, but Pyongyang held back for the time being.

The administration's priority on North Korea was to make another attempt to compel China to wield its influence. Rice, Cheney, and others hoped that China would increasingly desire to be seen as a responsible "stakeholder" in the international system, one that would be willing to take decisive actions on North Korea.[20] They, like other U.S. officials before and after them, misjudged China's interest. Whereas Beijing opposed North Korea's acquisition of nuclear weapons, maintaining regional stability was a higher priority. Yet, Beijing was displeased with the North's overt nuclear development announced earlier in the year because of its destabilizing effect on the region. There is little doubt that China's behind-the-scenes political

15. "The Nomination of Dr. Condoleezza Rice to Be Secretary of State," Hearing Before the Committee on Foreign Relations, United States Senate (January 18 and 19, 2005), https://www.govinfo.gov/content/pkg/CHRG-109shrg22847/pdf/CHRG-109shrg22847.pdf

16. George W. Bush, "State of the Union Address," *The White House* (February 2, 2005), https://georgewbush-whitehouse.archives.gov/news/releases/2005/02/20050202-11.html

17. Victor Cha, *The Impossible State: North Korea, Past and Future* (New York: Harper-Collins, 2012), 427.

18. DPRK Foreign Ministry Spokesman, "Spent Fuel Rods Unloaded from Pilot Nuclear Plant," *KCNA* (May 11, 2005).

19. James Brooke, "North Koreans Claim to Extract Fuel for Nuclear Weapons," *New York Times* (May 12, 2005), https://www.nytimes.com/2005/05/12/world/asia/north-koreans-claim-to-extract-fuel-for-nuclear-weapons.html

20. Associated Press, "Cheney Says China Must Press N. Korea on Weapons," *Washington Post* (May 30, 2005): A18.

pressure played a role in bringing the North back to the table, although Beijing's overall effort fell far short of what Washington wanted.

The diplomatic currents turned favorable as Ambassador Hill spent the spring of 2005 searching for a new way to resume diplomacy, developing an overriding vision to guide U.S. policy and a set of principles to discuss in the negotiations.[21] This vision was based on the realization that the framework for negotiations was conceptually flawed. The United States had to offer Pyongyang a much richer agenda for diplomatic action than had been presented in the past. In fact, the new approach to policy proceeded essentially in the same manner as that of the Clinton administration, which was to reach an "agreement in principle" and then follow it with practical steps. These efforts finally resulted in Hill and Kim Gye Gwan having a bilateral meeting, although it required help from the Chinese. Chinese diplomats had arranged a trilateral dinner meeting in Beijing, then conveniently did not show up, leaving Hill and Kim to talk.[22] Kim told Hill that the North would attend the next round of Six-Party Talks in Beijing at the end of July.

What accounted for this change in Pyongyang's position? In announcing the North's return to the negotiating table, the Foreign Ministry cited the fact that the United States took steps to roll back its hostile policy and moved to hold bilateral talks within the framework of the Six-Party Talks.[23] Although that may have helped bring Pyongyang back to the talks, what wasn't acknowledged was that the entire negotiating ground had shifted. The original purpose of the Six-Party Talks was to prevent the North from going nuclear. Now that the North had formally declared itself to be a nuclear weapons state, the Six-Party Talks would have to completely refocus or, as ultimately happened, fail.

Washington and Pyongyang relayed muted or modest goals for the upcoming negotiations. Although Hill was empowered, to some degree, to use

21. Mike Chinoy, *Meltdown: The Inside Story of the North Korean Nuclear Crisis* (New York: St. Martin's Griffin, 2009), 236.

22. Charles L. Pritchard, *Failed Diplomacy* (Washington, DC: Brookings Institution Press, 2007), 110–111.

23. Glenn Kessler, "N. Korea Agrees to Rejoin Talks; Nuclear Arsenal on Table After Year-Long Boycott," *Washington Post* (July 10, 2005), https://www.washingtonpost.com/archive/politics/2005/07/10/n-korea-agrees-to-rejoin-talks/7f10e9bb-ff9e-44fd-830a-3f971c-1c716c/

his own judgment and to have some bilateral contact with the North, he would still have to work against skeptical hard-liners in Washington who did not want him to make inappropriate concessions.[24] The Chinese side

ing the language of a joint statement patterned on the 1992 North–South declaration. Nevertheless, the parties could not reach agreement on a joint statement, so China announced a three-week recess for the talks with the goal of reconvening at the end of August.

Progress had stalled primarily over the issue of North Korea retaining a civilian nuclear power program. American negotiators resisted the concession on light water reactors because they did not trust North Korea with any nuclear capability, which would by definition be dual use.[25] After the talks ended, Ambassador Hill asserted publicly that there was "a bit of a problem" with regard to the peaceful nuclear program, since Pyongyang "proudly proclaimed it was making bombs from this research reactor" in the past, blatantly taking advantage of the dual-use nature of the technology.[26] Furthermore, from the perspective of hard-liners in the Bush administration, the prospect of providing the North with light water reactors raised the specter of Clinton's hated Agreed Framework; "people just went ballistic" over the proposition and proffered up significant resistance to Rice and others at the State Department who were considering a change in policy on the issue.[27] The issue of whether the North had a right to peaceful nuclear energy and, specifically, whether a joint statement would promise new light water reactors, loomed over the parties. With the United States seemingly hardened in opposition, John Lewis and I again boarded a flight to Pyongyang.

24. Chinoy, *Meltdown*, 241–242.

25. Cha, *Impossible State*, 261.

26. Joel Brinkley, "North Korea Says U.S. Alone Is Holding Up 6-Nation Nuclear Talks," *New York Times* (August 10, 2005), https://www.nytimes.com/2005/08/10/world/asia/north-korea-says-us-alone-is-holding-up-6nation-nuclear-talks.html

27. Chinoy, *Meltdown*, 244.

6   Back to North Korea: "No LWR Till Pigs Fly"

On a hot and humid day in August 2005, the plane touched down at Pyongyang's Sunan Airport. As we rolled toward the terminal building, I had no reservations this time about what I'd gotten myself into. Unlike my first visit, I looked forward to this one without the irrational worry in the back of my mind that I'd somehow end up being detained in the North. Based on my first visit, I concluded that the North Koreans wanted me to report back to Washington what they had shown and told me about their nuclear program.

It had been almost eighteen months since my last visit. I estimated that the North had 25 to 30 kilograms of bomb-grade plutonium, enough for four to six bombs. Based on what I knew about the nuclear weapons programs of other countries, I had concluded the North may have produced several simple nuclear devices. However, since the North had not conducted a nuclear test, no one could be sure whether their scientists, engineers, and technicians had mastered the art of building a plutonium bomb. I hoped that this visit would shed more light on how far they had come. Based on my experience during the first visit, I expected them to raise the curtain enough to see some hard evidence.

As the plane pulled up the terminal, we were told to stay in our seats as the airport crew rolled out a red carpet. A red carpet, I thought to myself!

This surely was a sign that the North had been pleased with the first visit. At a New York nonproliferation conference in August 2004, at which Ambassador Ri Gun participated, Ri told John Lewis that Pyongyang was satisfied

> "When Hecker was at Yongbyon he said that he would only report on what he actually saw and could scientifically confirm. We watched what happened when your group returned to the U.S. and received so much publicity, and Hecker did exactly what he said he would do. We greatly respected that."

It turned out, of course, the red carpet was not for our delegation. It was for the vice president of Zambia and his entourage who were on the same flight. We hadn't seen them on board because they were in the first-class cabin. Once the VIPs were off the plane, we followed. Our delegation—John Lewis, Jack Pritchard, and me—was met by Foreign Ministry officials, who took us to the Potonggang Hotel, the same place we stayed previously. On reviewing the week's schedule arranged for us, I discovered to my dismay that Yongbyon was not on the list.

I was anxious to go back because little was known about what had transpired at Yongbyon since our visit. No outsiders had access. I had a long list of questions for the Yongbyon nuclear specialists, and I had hoped to visit the nuclear facility again to judge for myself. It was important to find out how well the 5 MWe reactor was operating and what the status and reconstruction plans were for the two larger reactors. I was also curious to find out if their technical specialists would say anything about the uranium enrichment program.

Although a visit to Yongbyon was not on the agenda, they had arranged for a productive visit. However, it took a while before I understood why they invited me back. Our previous trip confirmed beyond any reasonable doubt, even to the nonbelievers in the administration who had characterized my first visit as one to a Potemkin village, that North Korea had put the Yongbyon complex back into the plutonium production business and that it had proceeded to build nuclear weapons. The question of uranium enrichment remained unresolved. The North adamantly denied having admitted to a centrifuge program at the infamous October 2002 Pyongyang showdown with Assistant Secretary James Kelly, but there was continuing evidence that they did have at least a fledgling enrichment program, one they surely intended to expand.

We met Ambassador Ri Gun for lunch before a meeting at the Ministry of Foreign Affairs with Vice Minister Kim Gye Gwan. I asked Ri about a high-level Foreign Ministry statement from February 10 that the North had manufactured nuclear weapons, the first such official pronouncement. Ri Gun had hinted that much during our 2004 visit when he mentioned the North's "nuclear deterrent." I reminded Ri that when we departed in 2004, he told me I should ask to see the next stage of their nuclear program. At that, Ri broke into a mischievous grin. "You should see our nuclear weapons—why not? You should go there." He was most likely just displaying his puckish sense of humor. When I later saw Ri's boss, Vice Minister Kim Gye Gwan, he put that idea to rest quickly. "You have to be kidding. You can't see our nuclear weapons. They are secret."

DISCUSSIONS WITH DIRECTOR RI HONG SOP

Dr. Ri Hong Sop, director of the Yongbyon nuclear center, met with us in a Potonggang Hotel conference room. He was accompanied by several officials from the General Department of Atomic Energy, Kim Myong Gil from the Ministry of Foreign Affairs, along with a notetaker and an interpreter. Dr. Ri was courteous and professional, but not nearly as relaxed and open as he had been throughout our visit to his Yongbyon complex in 2004. He said he had been asked to come and answer my questions to help resolve the nuclear issue. Ri closed off any efforts on my part to wrangle a visit to the site by saying, "You cannot visit Yongbyon this time because we are currently reprocessing spent fuel. This, as you know, creates high radioactive background from the release of isotopes iodine-131 and krypton-85." That seemed like a logical precaution to me. We would have to wait for another time to get back to Yongbyon.

Nevertheless, having the Foreign Ministry, most likely with approval from Kim Jong Il, bring Dr. Ri from Yongbyon to talk to us was reassuring. It would have been easy just to tell me he sends his regards but that he is too busy in Yongbyon. Instead, I realized that keeping me informed was part of Pyongyang's playbook. But I still hadn't figured out why. They weren't looking to make propaganda hay out of my visits, and—given what they had let me see on my first visit—they weren't trying to dupe me.

Although I was quite disappointed not to return to Yongbyon for another look, the discussions with Director Ri provided answers to my most important technical questions, reinforcing the impression that the North was serious about giving the outside world a look at their developing nuclear weapons program in a way no other country had done. Some of the details

note-taking skills) because they are crucial to an assessment of how much plutonium North Korea had produced and what the additional production prospects were at the time. The details would be important for verification purposes if the two countries were able to strike another deal. Director Ri Hong Sop answered my questions honestly and candidly. When I got into a particularly sensitive area, he let me know he was not allowed to comment on that. I will summarize the essence of our dialogue organized by facility, only occasionally providing a direct account. The reader will find some highly technical questions and answers, which I have included both for the historical record and to show how free of cant Director Ri's answers were. In other words, contrary to conventional American wisdom, it is possible to get straight answers from North Koreans.

The 5 MWe Reactor

Ri told us that the 5 MWe experimental reactor had operated continuously from January 2003 until mid-March 2005. It was shut down to discharge the spent fuel in April. It took one month to remove all 8,000 fuel rods. The reactor was serviced in late April and May, recharged with fresh fuel, and restarted in mid-June. The reactor was operating at 25 MWth (mega-watt-thermal)—its original design output.

Western nuclear experts believed that in the 1990s the reactor never achieved its design power, but rather ran at 20 MWth. The power level is important to estimate the amount of plutonium produced. Ri told us that during the early startup period following the 1986 commissioning of the reactor, they kept the reactor output very low. They ran a lot of tests. They had to learn how to replace damaged fuel rods while the reactor was operating. It took a long time to find the damaged fuel rods in the core. Ri said they kept the output of the reactor low from 1986 to 1994. They solved these problems when the reactor was restarted in January 2003. He said, "We have been running at full power of 25 MWth since." He added that they had inserted some dummy (inert) steel rods into the core in place of fuel rods to help them maintain a flat neutron flux, crucial for efficient operations.

I was curious why they decided to shut the reactor down and remove the spent fuel rods after only two years, when he told us in 2004 that they could run the reactor virtually indefinitely. Ri explained there were two reasons. First, they needed to examine the integrity of the fuel rods that were loaded in January 2003 because these were fabricated before the Agreed Framework. Hence, they were ten years old when they were loaded into the reactor. Second, they wanted to extract the plutonium. Ri told us that the fuel rods and the magnesium alloy cladding were in good shape when they examined them after the recent reactor run. Ri added, "We could have run the reactor much longer."

I asked how long they kept the rods in the pool before reprocessing. Ri said they had intended not to store the spent fuel for long in the pool. As of the time of our visit (August 25, 2005), the radioactivity of the rods was low enough for safe removal, he said. Hence, almost all spent fuel rods were out of the pool. Ri said they had already reloaded fresh fuel into the reactor from another batch manufactured before the Agreed Framework. The reactor could now be run as long as desired.

The Radiochemical Laboratory

Ri explained that the process had shifted to the Radiochemical Laboratory—the reprocessing center. After the period of cooling was over in late June, they immediately started reprocessing. He told me that as he had explained in 2004, the original throughput capacity of the facility was 375 kilograms of uranium per day. But, within the last year they modified the facility to increase the throughput by 1.3 times (to roughly 487 kilograms of uranium per day). He said, "We changed the box-type mixer/settlers to vertical pulsed columns. With the increase in capacity, the processing of the 8,000 rods is in a late stage now."

In the early 1990s, when IAEA inspectors got access to the Radiochemical Laboratory, they concluded it had two reprocessing lines, but whether there was one or two processing lines had never been resolved. When I asked Ri, he clarified that they used only one line for reprocessing; the second was a spare used for waste management. Thus, they defined the reprocessing capacity of the plant as 375 kilograms of uranium per day. During the 2004 visit, when Ri showed me the plutonium metal, he called it their "product." I asked him if they also took the current reprocessing campaign all the way to a plutonium metal product. I added that I was somewhat surprised in that it would be much easier to store the product in plutonium oxide form—it keeps better. Ri said they still take the process all the way to plutonium

used to build nuclear devices, which require metal, not oxide.

I was curious what they did to trap the fission gases that are generated during reprocessing. As well as being a potential health risk, they are also indicators of reprocessing activities if they escape into the atmosphere. I asked if they use filters to trap the dangerous fission gases. Ri told me that they trap iodine-131 gases, but there are no filters for krypton-85 (which is true because it is a noble gas that does not react chemically). Ri said, "We would need to condense the gas at very low temperatures. We need to make greater efforts to trap the krypton gas." He added correctly that trapping the noble gases is still under investigation worldwide. I asked if they were concerned about worker safety from the radioactive gases inside the building. Ri replied that he was not concerned about the gases inside the building because they have a powerful ventilation system, but that there are concerns about radiation outside the building. I thought to myself that was one reason for why they needed medical isotopes—it's to treat people for radiation exposures, as explained below.

The 50 MWe and 200 MWe Reactors

I asked Ri about the construction status of the 50 MWe and 200 MWe reactors. He said they had completed the design for restarting the 50 MWe reactor and were preparing the construction worker teams for this reactor. On the 200 MWe reactor, they were still studying what to do. The investment for rebuilding would likely be greater than the investment for a new one, but he indicated they may have a methodology for recovering its construction. Ri said, "On the 50 MWe reactor, some parts can be recovered and some of the old, fabricated parts can be installed. We will build—or rebuild—this reactor on the current site." I was curious if there was anything inside the 50 MWe reactor building at the time it was halted. Ri told us it had the containment vessel in place, but no core. The core was fabricated elsewhere. Some of the parts had been finished by 1994, but not installed. Ri added that they were planning to use the current containment structure.

I was curious about how long it would take to complete the construction of the 50 MWe reactor. Ri said he was confident construction would start soon, but he couldn't give the details. He added with a smile, "We have been very busy." And so, they had. I asked if fuel fabrication would present a problem for the reactor. Ri didn't think so because the fuel was the same and the cladding (the metallic casing in which the fuel is contained) almost the same for the 50 MWe as for the 5 MWe reactor. The cladding for the 200 MWe reactor, he told us, was more complicated. The reason I asked these questions is that completing these reactors would dramatically increase the North's plutonium production capacity. Ri put things in perspective, telling us that these issues were all manageable; the real problem with these reactors was the "outmoded design of the graphite-moderated natural uranium reactor." In other words, they had recognized that these reactors were a dead end for electricity production. Countries such as the UK and France had replaced them with light water reactors for electricity generation. His comment also indicated that North Korea was seriously interested in nuclear electricity—not just producing plutonium for bombs—for which these reactors were well suited.

Not surprisingly, the outside world had concerns about the safety of North Korea's nuclear reactors. I asked Ri what kind of regulatory system and inspection processes they had in place for reactor construction and operations. Ri replied that the State Nuclear Regulatory Commission had jurisdiction. The commission was a separate governmental department, not part of the General Department of Atomic Energy. The nuclear center had to apply to the commission for a license for the startup of the reactor. Upon further questioning, Ri told us that once the license was issued, the commission had no more role in reactor operations. The Yongbyon facility had its own inspectors who reported to Director Ri, but he said that only occurs when there was a problem. The inspectors, he said, have the authority to shut the reactor down if they found a serious problem. Whereas it was comforting that they had some inspection processes in place, what Ri described fell far short of having an independent regulatory authority to ensure safe reactor construction and operation.

Director Ri was remarkably candid responding to the litany of questions I posed about what may seem like technical minutiae. He didn't have to provide such precise, detailed answers, but he must have decided it was better to level with another technical person than to reply "no comment" or make things up. As it turns out, during subsequent visits to Yongbyon in 2007 and 2008, I was able to corroborate the veracity of his replies. I

were essential to estimating North Korea's plutonium inventory, which, in turn, governs the size of their arsenal. The status of the construction of the bigger reactors was important because it would give them more than a tenfold increase in plutonium production capability. I was surprised that Director Ri still had hopes of completing the 50 MWe reactor considering how badly it had deteriorated during the Agreed Framework; Ri had told John Lewis during the drive-by in 2004 that he was saddened that they had been so close to finishing the reactor and now "it had turned to rubbish."

The Fuel Fabrication Facility

Director Ri explained they had produced metal fuel rods, but not the magnesium alloy (Magnox) cladding, for the 50 MWe reactor before the Agreed Framework. The dimensions of these rods differed slightly from the 5 MWe reactor rods. They had not produced any new fuel rods since 1994. Ri said that during the Agreed Framework, some of the Fuel Fabrication Facility corroded to the point of collapse. I was curious if they had produced any fresh uranium tetrafluoride (UF_4), which can be used to make metal fuel rods or to make uranium hexafluoride (UF_6), which is a required precursor for uranium enrichment. Ri said they had not made any since the Agreed Framework. This was important because they could have made the tetrafluoride at Yongbyon and shipped it to a covert facility to turn into the hexafluoride for centrifuge operations. Director Ri told me that they were refurbishing one fabrication line to be able start making fuel for the 5 MWe reactor the following year. They had no plans to make fuel for the 50 MWe or 200 MWe reactors, which suggested they were not as close to completing the 50 MWe reactor as he had implied in the earlier response.

The IRT-2000 Reactor

I asked Director Ri about medical isotope production at Yongbyon. He said they made their own isotopes in the IRT reactor, the small research reactor built by the Soviets in the 1960s. There was a large demand for isotopes from hospitals. He explained that they used a research building behind the IRT reactor. Over the years, they have used the reactor to produce iodine-131, which is used for thyroid cancer treatment. He told us that once I-131 is produced in the reactor, it is transferred via a connected airpipe to an adjacent hot cell facility where it is extracted.[1] Ri lamented that they had only been able to operate the IRT reactor intermittently because the enriched uranium fuel elements were supplied by the Soviets. After the Soviet Union collapsed in 1992, Russia no longer supplied fuel for the reactor.

Director Ri explained that when it began operation, the IRT power was 2 MWth (megawatt-thermal). They increased it to 8 MWth by themselves by purchasing fuel enriched to 80 percent from the Soviets. Ri said the fuel elements were changed from "rod-type fuel to multiple-tube rods." They had also purchased fuel enriched to 36 percent because that was the enrichment level the Soviets preferred. Ri told us they would like to purchase more fuel and continue to produce isotopes. Right now, "if we were able to get fuel, we would prefer it to have 80 percent enrichment."

Ri told me that they stored the spent fuel elements of the IRT-2000 in a pool located in the reactor building. The facilities were all under IAEA inspection since the early 1970s. The IRT-2000 complex was not included in the Agreed Framework. Ri said the IAEA came to the facility only once. They had little interest because the reactor was not viewed as being significant from a proliferation perspective. I was interested in the reactor's history and status because it could have been used to produce plutonium and some tritium despite its small size. Director Ri told me that they used to do interesting research with the IRT reactor but had to give that up when they could no longer get fresh fuel elements. Ri said that whereas getting new fuel was the most pressing issue, they also had concerns about the longevity of the reactor. They would have to replace the reactor lining, he said. If that was done, it would last another twenty to thirty years. I had not realized that the IAEA had taken little interest in the status of that complex during its Agreed Framework inspections of plutonium production facilities.

1. A hot cell facility is a heavily shielded laboratory with remote handling for highly radioactive materials.

I asked if North Korea had other isotope production facilities. Director Ri told me there was only one other, a small cyclotron in Pyongyang that made short-lived isotopes. Ri lamented the fact that they had so little capac-

business for them. He added, "It's the kind of business we are looking for."

Nuclear Weapons Production

I tried to engage Director Ri on the larger questions, such as Yongbyon's role in the North's nuclear weapons. I mentioned that earlier in 2005 the government announced that North Korea had manufactured nuclear weapons. I asked him what role Yongbyon played beyond plutonium production. Ri replied that plutonium production was its only role. Once produced, the plutonium went somewhere else. In an uncharacteristically evasive manner, he said, "I don't know what happens beyond that."

This was clearly a topic that Ri had been told not to discuss by his superiors. Although I believed that Yongbyon was the only facility in which they produced plutonium (in the reactor), extracted plutonium (in the Radiochemical Laboratory), produced and purified the metal (a set of laboratories that I was not able to visit until 2007), and that this product was then taken to another location (as Ri said), it was inconceivable that Ri and his plutonium specialists had no connection to that facility.

CIVILIAN NUCLEAR ENERGY AND PROLIFERATION RISKS

I was interested in getting Director Ri's views on the potential nuclear weapons threat from LWRs. Ri explained that if the fuel was burned out to its rated power in an LWR, there was only a theoretical potential to use it to manufacture nuclear weapons. Some countries may be concerned about the risk, but he thought it was practically impossible. The concern about nuclear weapons should not be used as a reason to stop building LWRs, he added.

What about graphite-moderated reactors, I asked. Ri said in that case it depends more on the operating conditions. If the total burn-up of the fuel is 3,000 MWth-days/ton of uranium, then there is no chance of using it to make a nuclear weapon. But he added—correctly, in my opinion—it also depends on the weapon manufacturing capability of the country. In other words, it depends on the sophistication of their design and manufacturing proficiency. He was telling us that they did not possess the capabilities to use fully burned-up fuel.

I asked Director Ri how they would address the proliferation concerns associated with LWR fuel cycles. On the front end, he said they would not do their own enrichment but rather buy the fuel from the outside. On the back end, disposition of the spent fuel would depend on the kind of arrangement they had with the fuel supplying country. He told me that if they would have to handle their own spent fuel, they could modify the Radiochemical Laboratory to accept the LWR oxide fuel, but it would be best to just send the fuel back to the country of origin.

We talked about the early years of their nuclear reactor programs. I was curious about how they decided which reactors and fuel cycles to pursue. Ri said that in the 1970s, before they had any reactors beside the IRT-2000 research reactor, they investigated all possible technologies. They concluded that the only ones they could pursue by themselves were the graphite-moderated reactors because the fuel did not require enrichment, which they were not able to do. As for now, they can solve any technical problems related to graphite-moderated reactors, but if the country adopted the LWR route, they would need help with fuels and some of the technologies. Ri asked me "Would your people be willing to be involved with us on LWRs?"

Though I believed it would be sensible for the United States to be involved with the North's LWRs, I passed on answering since that was the U.S. government's call. Director Ri's views on the risks of the two types of reactors to be used for weapon-grade plutonium production were technically accurate. In other words, whereas it is theoretically possible to make plutonium for weapons in an LWR, why would they want to do so? They already had an effective plutonium production reactor and designs for much larger ones. Besides, they were willing to take necessary safeguards to assure the Americans that they were not diverting an LWR to military use.

These discussions demonstrated how well-versed Director Ri was on proliferation issues associated with various reactors and their fuel cycles. The approaches he advocated for North Korea were sensible and the safeguards provisions solid.

Director Ri was not inclined to answer questions outside the technical sphere. When John Lewis asked him if he and his people would be involved in technical working groups if such were established as part of the six-party process, Ri said that was up to the Foreign Ministry. When Jack Pritchard asked where the personnel for the KEDO project came from and who they report to, Ri simply said he didn't know, which is difficult to believe. He

not from his center but rather from universities. Ri also told us that the specialists in the Yongbyon complex had little connection with the DPRK Academy of Sciences.

The only time Director Ri became visibly agitated was when Lewis recalled that during the January 2004 visit, he was told that Yongbyon had purchased a small number of gas centrifuges from Urenco to pursue uranium enrichment in the 1980s, like other countries had done. And then in late 1992, they discontinued the enrichment work when they were convinced that the Radiochemical Laboratory could reprocess plutonium. Director Ri denied having made such statements. He told Lewis his understanding was "incorrect." They had investigated the different ways to achieve nuclear power and settled on the graphite-moderated reactors. They never had spare resources to pursue two paths. He said, "We never purchased gas centrifuges."

It was not surprising that Ri was disconcerted since he was asked that question in the presence of officials from the General Department of Atomic Energy and the Ministry of Foreign Affairs. In the intervening eighteen months between our visits, the North Korean government had gone on record vehemently denying any centrifuge activities. Vice Minister Kim later told us the same in no uncertain terms. On this point, Director Ri knew he had to stick to the government line, even though he also knew it wasn't true.

When I asked Ri at the end of the meeting if he had any questions for me, he said, "What will you do with this knowledge?" John Lewis replied first, saying that this visit was low profile compared to the very high-profile visit in 2004. I told Ri that we would return to our country and relay what we saw here. After the January 2004 visit, I was asked to give a report to the U.S. Congress. I had sent a copy of this report to the DPRK Ministry of Foreign Affairs. I presented Ri with a copy of the report. I also gave him a copy of an article I had written for a U.S. National Academy of Engineering publication about the January 2004 trip.[2]

2. Siegfried S. Hecker, "The Nuclear Crisis in North Korea," *The Bridge* 34, no. 2 (June 1, 2004), https://www.nae.edu/7452/TheNuclearCrisisinNorthKorea

DISCUSSIONS WITH VICE MINISTER KIM GYE GWAN

We had three sessions with Vice Minister Kim Gye Gwan—one in the Ministry of Foreign Affairs and two dinners. He had just returned from Beijing during the recess in the fourth round of the Six-Party Talks. Kim was not at the first session of the talks in August 2003. It wasn't until the second round in February 2004 that Pyongyang had upped the representation to his level. He led the North's delegation for all subsequent rounds. Kim pointed out what he saw as obstacles to fruitful conversations with the Americans at these talks. For example, there were six parties representing their states around a huge table, all conversations interpreted into five languages with no official record of the proceedings. Subtleties were lost, he said, in the process of translation, which moved very fast. During the last session, there was a written statement of principles, which was prepared by the Chinese side, but it was only in English (we found out later that one of our Chinese interlocutors, Yang Xiyu of the Chinese Foreign Ministry, drafted the statement).

Kim told us that he viewed unofficial discussions, such as those with us, as especially important because of the weaknesses of the six-party format. These discussions might have been "unofficial" to Kim, but in the formal atmosphere of the Foreign Ministry's large conference room with its polished mahogany tables and red velvet upholstered chairs, Kim's presentation was delivered more like established North Korean talking points than casual discussion. Kim laid out North Korea's position on denuclearization, the sequencing of denuclearization with normalization of relations, and the North's right to peaceful use of nuclear energy. Kim told us more than once that they had reached a strategic decision to give up all nuclear weapons and all elements of their nuclear weapons program. He complained that the United States saw denuclearization only as something for the North to do, whereas Pyongyang insisted that the entire Korean Peninsula be denuclearized. To Jack Pritchard, who had dealt with the North Koreans when he was in the U.S. government, Kim's presentation sounded like a broken record. Kim's pitch also begged the question that if they were so committed to a denuclearized Korean Peninsula, why were they moving on all cylinders to make nuclear weapons? It was clear that given the setting, Kim would stick to the North's official positions, so we saved the big questions for the less formal atmosphere at the two dinners.

As we had hoped, in contrast to the stiffness in the Foreign Ministry, the two dinners felt quite different—informal with a mix of humor though still with an occasional defiant tone. Vice Minister Kim asked us to tell the

He said they understood the benefits of an LWR over graphite-moderated reactors for electricity production. They had tried to get the Soviet Union to supply LWRs, but they said no.[3] They tried France and Canada, and they said no. Russia, under Boris Yeltsin, who has little sympathy for the DPRK, stopped the project cold. Kim said they wound up building the graphite-moderated reactors because they could do so by themselves, albeit at great sacrifice by the people in Yongbyon.

I gave Kim a detailed accounting of what I learned from my discussions with Director Ri Hong Sop. The bottom line was that they were proceeding full steam ahead at Yongbyon with the plutonium program. I said we also discussed concerns over the proliferation potential of LWRs and asked Kim to address what safeguards the North would be willing to implement to prevent the pursuit of civilian nuclear energy being diverted to nuclear weapons. Kim said they were willing to put the LWR under complete IAEA safeguards. If that didn't allay U.S. concerns, they were prepared to let the United States operate the reactor until the North rejoined the NPT and allowed IAEA inspections. At that point, the LWR could be turned over to the DPRK. The DPRK, he said, was ready to return to the NPT and abide by IAEA inspections as soon as relations with the United States were normalized. To address U.S. concerns about enrichment, Kim said the North could go one of two ways: build an inspected enrichment facility or buy enriched fuel from the outside until U.S. concerns were removed. If the North ended up keeping a graphite-moderated reactor, they were prepared to stop reprocessing was well as to agree not to reprocess LWR spent fuel.

Kim had clearly done his homework. These would be remarkable concessions from the North Korean side, albeit at this point they were only promises. His grasp of nuclear fuel cycles and nonproliferation safeguards had improved immensely from our discussions in 2004. He said the right

3. That's not quite the way it was. The Soviets did promise to build four light water reactors but insisted that the North sign the Nuclear Nonproliferation Treaty first. The North did, but the Soviet Union got no farther than preliminary siting exploration before it started to come apart.

things, as far as he went. What he left out was that Yongbyon was proceeding full tilt with their plutonium program. They were also helping the Syrians build a graphite-moderated plutonium production reactor (which the United States did not know at the time, and it is likely that Kim Gye Gwan did not either). And somewhere in North Korea, they were ramping up their uranium centrifuge effort. The North was prioritizing the nuclear track but was exploring keeping diplomacy alive.

Kim had still more to say about LWRs. He said that the provision of such a high-tech facility as an LWR would mean that they could trust the Americans. It would prove Washington's words that it considers the DPRK to be a sovereign nation. "This is the key to everything! Whatever difficulties exist can be unlocked by this key," Kim said. He was not being sarcastic as best as I could tell. His was precisely the reasoning that some of the more astute proponents of the Agreed Framework and the KEDO project believed to be the North's view of the Agreed Framework. But the LWRs were an anathema to the hard-liners.

At one point the conversation got around to the upcoming, annual U.S.–ROK joint military exercises. Kim got testy and then defiant when Jack Pritchard told him not to focus so much on the exercises. Kim said, "We [the DPRK] should have nuclear weapons. Is it God who decides that we can't have nuclear weapons? All of us are equal. We are born equal! Koreans and Americans are equal." Kim went on to accuse the United States of trying to dominate the whole world with its nuclear weapons. He said the DPRK believes that the Americans attacked Iraq because it didn't have nuclear weapons. He said that at the NPT Review Conference (in May 2005), the United States refused to pledge not to use its nuclear weapons against non-nuclear weapon states and did not rule out making new special nuclear weapons. This somewhat surprising tirade on the part of the otherwise very professional, composed Kim soured the atmosphere for a few minutes.

I tried to get Kim back to telling us why they invited me if they knew I could not get back to Yongbyon. Kim's answer was serpentine but ended up again with LWRs: "To tell the American people the reality of our position. We understand the tradeoffs between graphite-moderated reactors and the LWR. That's why we want an LWR." In effect, he was again acknowledging what the North had admitted when they first raised the idea of trading their graphite-moderated reactors for LWRs in June 1993—LWRs were good for electricity and poor for bombs, whereas graphite-moderated reactors were good for bombs, but poor for making electricity. Later he added, somewhat ambiguously, "You will be our guarantee that technical measures can be

LWR agreement." Then, in typical fashion, he backed up and added the additional qualifier: "We are very clear—as relations are normalized and there is no U.S. threat along with greater trust, we will abandon all our nuclear weapons."

So, which was it? Were LWRs the key or was it "no U.S. threat"? Kim said that under the right circumstances they would abandon "all" their nuclear weapons, but since they hadn't tested anything, were they playing with chips they didn't really have, not yet anyway? Quite frankly, I was surprised how far Kim said they would be willing to go to assure the United States and the international community that they would not divert LWR civilian reactors to weapons use. These were precisely the conditions the United States imposed on South Korea before helping it to build LWRs—that is, no enrichment and no reprocessing. By contrast, the Japanese managed to keep and exercise both options when they struck a deal with the United States long before the South Koreans did. The only way to understand the U.S. rejection of such an offer was to believe that North Korea would never abide by the safeguard conditions it had promised. But that is exactly what the hard-liners in the Bush administration believed, as I found out when I briefed administration officials back in Washington upon my return.

Lewis and Pritchard had several exchanges with Kim about normalization and denuclearization and how the North viewed the necessary sequencing of steps. Kim said Pyongyang did not insist that normalization must come first. He told us that we each can do something at the beginning. The DPRK could, for example, make a commitment to return to the NPT and abide by the IAEA. As for the United States, it could say that it would not threaten North Korea or use nuclear weapons and would commit to normalization. Each should jot down the steps it expects it would take and then work out a sequence of actions. Kim said, "We have already agreed to have words for words and actions for actions." He added, "Right now, we are still at the stage of words for words."

Before the visit, I had taken a close look at North Korea's overall energy situation to see if LWRs really made sense for them at this time. I familiarized myself with the extensive work that Peter Hayes of the Nautilus Institute had done in North Korea. I went prepared with very specific recommendations based on Hayes's work. These included upgrading all phases of the energy sector—production, transmission/distribution, and use. The entire industrial infrastructure required upgrades and replacements. I found out later that the KEDO organization had also examined using gas-fired plants in place of the LWRs, but that idea didn't take off.

I told Vice Minister Kim that if I were his science advisor, I would recommend requesting U.S. assistance with conventional energy. Kim listened patiently. Perhaps my lengthy explanation allowed him a chance to rest and to eat his dessert in peace. I stressed that this approach would bring badly needed electricity to their country in about a year, rather than the decade required for nuclear electricity. Besides, without a massive upgrade of the electricity grid, it would not be safe to hook an LWR into their current electrical grid. And even with an upgraded grid, an LWR could be shut off with the click of a switch by the outside powers even once it was operating because North Korea is not able to provide its own fuel.

Kim was not swayed by my arguments. He said that the matter of conventional power stations was covered in depth with experts at the last session of the Six-Party Talks. "We said thanks, but we need LWRs." I refused to give up. I told Kim that I recognized the symbolic and political nature of the nuclear energy option, but I wanted to stress that from a practical standpoint, a massive upgrading of their conventional energy infrastructure and an immediate supply of conventional energy was a much better choice. If energy is needed now, I said, then nuclear is not the preferred option.

At that, Kim got testy. I guess I had managed to get under his skin because he replied defiantly, "You are the only foreign scientist who has talked to the Yongbyon scientists" (here, Kim excluded the American scientists and IAEA inspectors who were given access to Yongbyon during the Agreed Framework):

> "This is a privilege and reflects our trust in you. The DPRK and the U.S. are in a state of cease fire. We are in a state of war. We cannot give you access to our nuclear weapons. We cannot show you everything. We are doing everything that you [the U.S.] can do. We can make a nuclear weapon out of 5 kg of plutonium, just as you can. If you can put the weapon on a missile, so can

we. If you can put it in a backpack, we can, too. We can do what other nations can do. We are not bluffing. My nation has experienced a war with the United States. You should not doubt what we have. If you can give us the LWR, then

This was pure North Korean pride bubbling up, along with exasperation that I wasn't getting his point. I could have poked him that the nuke in a backpack was a bit over the top, but I could tell he was just blowing off steam.

Kim continued, returning to the question of the LWRs:

"I told Chris Hill that the LWR is the key to the agreement. I told him why. That is, I told him enough so he would know that without it there is no way out, and there would be no point in wasting any more time with each other. There would be no point to continue."

Kim concluded with, "No LWR, no deal." That was the bottom line he wanted us to convey to Washington.

We saw less of Ambassador Ri Gun than we had on our previous trip, but we had an interesting discussion at a lunch at which he asked what the United States would be prepared to do to help the Yongbyon staff transition from nuclear weapons work to civilian activities. Ri was quite familiar with how Washington had helped the Russian nuclear workers as part of the Cooperative Threat Reduction programs implemented when the Soviet Union dissolved. These programs were designed to help create new jobs for critical personnel and to retrain them to acquire relevant new skills for the civilian economy. Ri told us that he was not so concerned about the technically skilled people at Yongbyon, of which he said there were only a few thousand, but rather with retraining the nontechnical and support personnel. He said that the nearby city of Yongbyon was and still is a major silk-producing area. Perhaps one could develop silk factories in the area to provide employment for such workers? Could a program be arranged that would supply a silk factory to employ some of the nuclear center support personnel? I mentioned that very similar measures were taken to work with the Russian nuclear cities.[4]

4. Siegfried S. Hecker, ed. *Doomed to Cooperate* (Los Alamos: Bathtub Row Press, 2016).

In a lighter moment at lunch, I said jokingly, "Ri Gun, I understand that Kim Jong Il has a large collection of American movies." (He was reputed to have a library of some 10,000 of them.) Ri nodded, "That's right." I continued, "I have been told you also like American movies. Is that so?" Ri smiled, "That's right." "So," I ventured, "what's your favorite American movie?" Ri's smile broadened, "*Rambo.*" I smiled back and thought, why am I not surprised?

As during our 2004 visit, the delegation had several additional meetings. Once again, we met with General Ri Chan Bok. Again, we didn't cover much new ground, but we did get the sense that North Korea had not formulated a nuclear posture or a concept of deterrence, despite using deterrence to justify its nuclear program. We also visited again with representatives of the Korean Academy of Sciences and the Committee on the Promotion of International Trade. John Lewis also arranged a visit to the headquarters of the Academy of Agricultural Sciences and an agricultural cooperative farm in the outskirts of Pyongyang. Although not my main focus, all of these meetings were useful in helping me fill in the huge blank spots I had about the North. I appreciated the deeply held view Lewis had that a better understanding of the North's people and institutions was going to be crucial if we were ever going to develop the comprehensive approach required to solve the nuclear problem.

John was also able to arrange visits to the Mangyongdae Students' and Children's Palace to see impressive musical and dance performances by talented children. The sight of first- or second-grade girls in traditional Korean dress playing on a kayagŭm, a twelve-stringed zither considered the Korean national instrument, is vividly etched in my memory. I have often used the photos I took in my public talks on North Korea to stress that whereas Americans tend to demonize the North Korean regime, we should not demonize its people. We also attended the Arirang Festival at the massive 114,000-seat Rungrado 1st of May Stadium. The festival is an impressive mass gymnastics and artistic performance that involves some 100,000 performers.

These were mostly obligatory cultural visits that our North Korean hosts wanted us to see. In addition, we returned to the Tong-il Street Market we had visited in 2004. It had some 500 private vendors selling fabric, fruits, nuts, electronics, and shoes. As before, it was jammed with people. I asked for permission to take some photos. Ambassador Ri who accompanied us got approval from the market manager. So, as we entered, I started snapping away until Ri said, "Not so many." I did catch him checking out the

market contained—most of which seemed to be made in China—and how many people were buying things. We were told the number was in the tens of thousands on the weekends. These visits showed me things I hadn't expected and made me realize how wrong a lot of the conventional wisdom was about North Korea.

As we departed on Saturday morning, I was quite satisfied with the visit despite not being able to visit Yongbyon. The session with Director Ri Hong Sop had been very useful in providing an update of the nuclear activities, and the frank discussions with Vice Minister Kim were important to convey to Washington. In Beijing, John Lewis had arranged more meetings with influential Foreign Ministry officials and scholars from several institutes. They conveyed the sense that Beijing did not want Pyongyang to continue to pursue nuclear weapons, but it was not willing to implement sufficiently dire sanctions to topple the regime. Peace and stability came first, nuclear developments second, in China's priorities. To the Chinese, it was chaos and indecision in Washington that caused, or at least contributed to, the crisis on the peninsula.

BACK IN THE UNITED STATES

On the way back to Los Alamos, I stopped at Stanford University to begin my first full week in my new place of work. In early 2005, the Department of Energy decided it would open the bidding on the contract to operate the Los Alamos National Laboratory. The laboratory had been operated by the University of California as a public service since the Manhattan Project. But in 2005, the government decided it had to find better ways to incentivize contractors like the University of California. Competing the contract to include for-profit organizations was its preferred path. I thought that was a monumental mistake. The nuclear weapons business is an inherently governmental job, not one that should be driven by financial incentives and profits. Part of the attraction of joining the laboratory some forty years earlier had been the academic influence of the University of California. I decided to retire from the laboratory at the end of the contract year,

June 30, and at the urging of the always persuasive Professor Lewis, agreed to come to Stanford as a visiting scientist for a year.

While still at Los Alamos in 2003 and 2004, I had also witnessed how members of the Bush administration twisted intelligence reports to fit their political agendas in Iraq and North Korea. By this time, it had become clear just how disastrous that was for Iraq and how badly things had gone in North Korea. Joining Stanford's Center for International Security and Cooperation (CISAC) appeared an ideal way for me to provide sound scientific analysis and advice on international nuclear matters to our government and to the public. The move to Stanford University, where I have now been for more than sixteen years and remain as an emeritus research professor and emeritus senior fellow, allowed me to better fulfill the role of an honest technical broker.

Thanks to John Lewis's professional friendship with Secretary Condoleezza Rice, who had been a postdoctoral fellow at CISAC, we were in her office at the State Department on September 8, soon after the return from our second visit. Secretary Rice had asked Ambassador Chris Hill and Philip Zelikow, her special advisor, to join us. I summarized my findings and recommendations on five briefing charts. I told Secretary Rice that on the technical front, we found that the 5 MWe reactor had operated for roughly twenty-six months at full power, and Director Ri was confident it could run for decades more. Since our last visit, the North Koreans had improved their reprocessing efficiency and speed. They were just completing their second full reprocessing campaign and most likely had extracted 10 to 12 kilograms of plutonium, sufficient for two additional bombs. Director Ri was still making plans to resume construction of the 50 MWe reactor that had sat idle during the previous ten years. What we saw during our 2004 visit seemed to indicate that the reactor was not salvageable, but Director Ri was still exploring how to complete it. The 200 MWe reactor, he said, would require starting over, so it was most likely lost.

Our best estimate was that North Korea may have produced as much as 45 kilograms of weapon-grade plutonium, and, if it completed the 50 MWe reactor (or began new construction), its annual capacity would increase to approximately 60 kilograms a year—a very big deal because that would mean a lot more bombs. Based on our discussions with the North Korean technical experts, we had to assume that North Korea has produced a few simple, primitive nuclear devices similar to the Nagasaki bomb. We were not able to assess if the devices were missile capable. The bottom line, I concluded, was that North Korea was moving full speed ahead with its

I explained that, whereas in 2004 John Lewis was told that North Korea performed some uranium centrifuge experiments, during this visit, Director Ri denied that they had any uranium enrichment activities despite what we considered to be strong evidence to the contrary. Whatever the real situation was, plutonium itself represented the major threat. And how much plutonium they had was important: It not only determined the number of weapons, but also their ability to test weapons and the potential of export.

We explained Vice Minister Kim's determined pitch for a light water reactor. I described my efforts to convince Kim that it would be much more effective to provide much needed electricity with a massive upgrade to their conventional energy capabilities. His response was dismissive, explaining that he understood his country better than we did. He concluded that conversation with—and here I used his exact words—"No LWR, no deal."

We mentioned the safeguards that Kim clearly stated the North was willing to implement to give Washington assurances of no diversion to weapons use. I showed Secretary Rice the chart in which Director Ri and I summarized the potential weapons risks of LWRs versus graphite-moderated reactors of the type that North Korea was currently using to produce plutonium. Director Ri and I agreed that both fuel cycles can lead to nuclear weapons, although the graphite-moderated reactors were much more suitable. In both cases, there were technical measures that could be taken to reduce the risk of diversion. In the end, I told Secretary Rice, the level of risk that is deemed acceptable was a political decision.

I told her that if North Korea was prepared to give up its nuclear weapons and its program, then proceed down a path that included an LWR sometime in the future, that was a good deal—it was worth the risk, particularly considering the alternative of no agreement and continued plutonium production. Agreeing to an LWR could be done without allowing uranium enrichment or reprocessing in North Korea. In fact, Vice Minister Kim had indicated they would not insist on such. John Lewis and I suggested that the administration keep the KEDO organization intact for now to allow for a future LWR. Secretary Rice did not argue that point, although

Hill announced eleven days later at the next session of Six-Party Talks that KEDO would be terminated at the end of the year. She was quite engaged throughout the presentation, thanked us for the update, and asked me to talk to Bob Joseph since a previous commitment prevented his attendance at this session.

I met with Bob Joseph in his State Department office the next day. In June 2005, he had succeeded John Bolton as undersecretary of state for arms control and international security, having moved over from heading counterproliferation activities at the National Security Council. Joseph was known to be as much of a defense hawk as John Bolton, but with much deeper scholarly credentials and greater experience in nuclear matters. He had served in several policy roles in the Reagan and George H. W. Bush administrations along with academic positions at the National Defense University and the Naval War College. He was the U.S. chief negotiator with Libya in 2003 to convince Gaddafi to give up his WMD programs. Joseph was instrumental in creating the Proliferation Security Initiative, a coalition of countries willing to cooperate to stop illicit transfers of WMD materials and technologies. He was also the architect of the George W. Bush administration's Global Initiative to Combat Nuclear Terrorism.

Joseph's credentials clearly demonstrated that he was an experienced policy professional, not a nuclear neophyte. I expected him to be able to weigh the risks of an LWR in North Korea versus the risks of the path North Korea was on—producing plutonium and building bombs. I gave Joseph the same briefing and conclusions I had given earlier to Secretary Rice. My technical arguments about the potential risks of diversion of LWRs and the current grim situation of the North producing more plutonium in the graphite-moderated reactor got nowhere. My explanation of the safeguards the North was willing to implement to assure no diversion from an LWR to weapons fell on deaf ears and a closed mind. Joseph said that having the North retain any nuclear capabilities, and particularly to provide such capabilities to them, even an LWR, was unacceptable. He said that they have cheated on every agreement they have ever signed, and they will continue to do so. I shouldn't have been surprised because it was Joseph and his staff who tried to stop me from going to North Korea in 2004 when they served in the White House.

During his years in government and academe, Joseph promoted a muscular U.S. foreign policy. He viewed arms control agreements as limiting U.S. freedom of action. He believed negotiations with regimes like North

As Mike Chinoy points out in *Meltdown,* Joseph viewed the Agreed Framework as nothing but appeasement, the worst diplomatic trash in U.S. history.[5]

I wasn't exactly an academic pussycat, having spent most of the past four decades at Los Alamos helping to deter the Soviet Union. However, I viewed the North Korean situation very differently than Bob Joseph did. To me it was a matter of making a technically informed risk assessment. I believed that we had more to gain by agreeing to the North's right to nuclear energy than to denying it and having them continue on the dangerous path they were on. For Joseph, it never got to that sort of tradeoff. I had the sense it was a matter of ideological opposition. Risk analysis be damned.

I also met with Ambassador Christopher Hill to follow up on the session with Secretary Rice. Hill was wired very differently from Bob Joseph. He didn't display ideological blinders, but rather took the pragmatic approach to look for what it would take to make a deal. He had to work in the caustic DC environment that often made it more difficult to negotiate a way forward inside the U.S. government than with North Korea. It was difficult, he said, to work in a setting in which people worry about the most remote possibilities to block a path forward. He was not adamantly opposed to providing an LWR if that was going to help get to a deal, although it would be best if one could consider it later. Hill emphasized that the mood in Washington was any agreement would have to go beyond the Agreed Framework. This time the North would have to give up the plutonium and eliminate the facilities. Hill said he was ready to go to Pyongyang the next day to start some interactions, get things in motion, and solve the rest along the way. He fully understood my emphasis on doing whatever we could to limit more plutonium production. He told me some years later that what he remembered from this meeting was my bottom line: "It's the plutonium, stupid."

5. Mike Chinoy, *Meltdown: The Inside Story of the North Korean Nuclear Crisis* (New York: St. Martin's Griffin, 2009), 44.

I met with several other groups in the State Department, including the affable Joe DeTrani, Hill's deputy, who had the patience to listen to my technical assessment of the visit along with parts of my Nuclear Weapons 101 and 102 lectures. I visited the Department of Energy and various intelligence organizations. In all visits, I stressed the importance of understanding the North's nuclear progress and the nuclear trajectory they were on.

THE MAKING OF ANOTHER HINGE POINT

The following week, Chris Hill, Joe DeTrani, and several other officials I had briefed were back in Beijing for the second session of the fourth round of Six-Party Talks. As it turned out, the Bush administration managed to turn this event into another hinge point where bad decisions would wind up having bad consequences.

When the talks resumed the week of September 13, the Chinese produced draft after draft trying to satisfy the three main parties—North Korea, Hill, and his opposition hard-liners back in Washington. One draft contained only a general reference to peaceful nuclear use but had the words, "the United States stated that it recognizes and respects the sovereignty of the DPRK, and that it undertakes to take steps to normalize its relations with the DPRK, subject to bilateral policies and dialogue." The hard-liners in Washington removed the "bilateral dialogue" since that was still an anathema to them. The North Koreans returned the favor and now insisted on specific reference to an LWR. The talks were deadlocked again.[6]

Hill realized that he had to find a way to address the North's demand for LWRs. He echoed the discussion I had in his office—that is, if North Korea got out of the nuclear weapon business, rejoined the NPT, and allowed IAEA inspections, there would be no harm to agreeing to discuss the LWR issue.[7] Hill called Secretary Rice to convince her to accept the latest round of Chinese drafts, which cleverly read, "The DPRK stated that it has the right to peaceful uses of nuclear energy. The other parties expressed their respect and agreed to discuss, at an appropriate time, the subject of provision of a light-water reactor to the DPRK."

6. Ibid., 246.
7. Ibid., 247.

Hill convinced Rice to go with this draft for the joint declaration. However, she insisted that at the final plenary session, Hill would present a unilateral American statement providing the U.S. interpretation of the joint

agenda anytime soon. Years later when I asked Professor Rice, who was back at Stanford by that time, whether our trip in 2005, and our report to her the week before the talks reconvened in Beijing, had any impact. She told me that our findings and advice helped her to counter the hard-liners who objected to any mention of LWRs. However, when she approved the American unilateral statement as shown below, she must have realized that the North Koreans would walk away.

Hill thought he had the battle won. He had kept his team pretty much in the dark because according to Hill, "Even on the negotiating team, there was considerable mistrust at every stage." When the hard-liners on Hill's team in Beijing found out, they were furious. When Victor Cha, who was serving in the NSC at the time, saw the draft, he objected to a different issue—namely, the use of "peaceful coexistence." Cha, a Korean American scholar, had a deep understanding of the Korean Peninsula. He felt that the term had too much of a Cold War flavor that didn't belong in the declaration. He called his boss at the NSC, Steve Hadley, who proceeded to talk to Rice. She in turn called Hill in the morning Beijing time, just as he was about the head in for the final formal session of the announcement. Much to Hill's dismay, Rice told him to take it out. It took an enormous diplomatic effort involving Hill and his Chinese counterpart, Wu Dawei, along with Secretary Rice and her counterpart, Foreign Minister Li Zhaoxing, to come to a compromise that Hill proposed. When he phoned Rice to ask if instead of the phrase "peaceful coexistence" they could use "existing peacefully together," Rice said sure.[8] The Chinese were in utter disbelief but decided to go with it as a translation correction.

The joint declaration was designed to be a statement of principles, with implementation to be worked out by the parties subsequently. The following summarizes the key provisions:[9]

8. Christopher Hill, *Outpost: Life on the Frontlines of American Diplomacy: A Memoir* (New York: Simon & Schuster, 2014), 239.

9. "Joint Statement of the Fourth Round of the Six-Party Talks," *U. S. Department of*

1. The goal is verifiable denuclearization of the Korean Peninsula in a peaceful manner. The DPRK committed to abandoning all nuclear weapons and existing nuclear programs. It will return at an early date to the NPT and IAEA safeguards. The 1992 Joint Declaration of the Denuclearization of the Korean Peninsula should be observed and implemented by all. The DPRK stated that it has the right to peaceful uses of nuclear energy. The other parties expressed their respect and agreed to discuss, at an appropriate time, the subject of the provision of light water reactor to the DPRK.

2. To respect each other's sovereignty, exist peacefully together, and take steps to normalize their relations.

3. The Six Parties undertook to promote economic cooperation in the fields of energy, trade, and investment, bilaterally and/or multilaterally.

4. Joint efforts by the six parties for lasting peace and stability in Northeast Asia.

5. To proceed in a phased manner in line with the principle of "commitment for commitment, action for action."

6. To hold the fifth round of the Six-Party Talks in early November 2005.

With Hill working the "peaceful coexistence" issue down to the wire, little time was left to look at the unilateral American statement that Rice had insisted be read once the joint declaration was signed. Crafting this statement was left to the Deputies Committee back in Washington. This turned out to be the revenge of the hard-liners—a poison pill addition to the joint statement. The statement was drafted by Bob Joseph, Deputy National Security Advisor J. D. Crouch, and NSC nonproliferation head, John Rood.[10] Hill recounts that his first time reading the closing statement that had been prepared for him in Washington was in the large conference room at the final session of the Six-Party Talks.[11] Chinoy quotes Hill's reaction when he saw it as, "Oh shit. I can't believe this."

State Archive (September 19, 2005), https://2001-2009.state.gov/r/pa/prs/ps/2005/53490.htm

10. Chinoy, *Meltdown*, 250.

11. "North Korea–U.S. Statement," *U.S. Department of State Archive* (September 19, 2005), https://2001-2009.state.gov/r/pa/prs/ps/2005/53499.htm

Chinoy states that Hill felt it was "bloodcurdling, impolite, and rude, deliberately designed to goad the North Koreans into being angry." Hill did the best he could, hoping that it would wind up being only a minor irritant because it

proceeded to read it, albeit reluctantly, but as Chinoy noted, Hill later realized he had made a big mistake, as did the other parties in the room.

Strangely, Hill's own account in *Outpost,* published nine years after the events of September 2005, downplays the caustic nature of the statement. Hill writes, "The substance of the statement was fine, although the tone didn't quite achieve the near-euphoric atmosphere in the room."[12] The line that concerned him was, "the United States will take concrete actions necessary to protect ourselves and our allies against any illicit and proliferation activities . . . " He thought the appropriate time to consider an LWR was sufficiently well defined as requiring the elimination of all nuclear weapons and all nuclear programs. And this would be verified to the satisfaction of all parties by credible international means, including the IAEA. What troubled Hill more was that the U.S. Treasury Department had just announced designating the Macao-based bank, Banco Delta Asia, as a primary money-laundering concern, and threatening concrete U.S. actions could derail the joint statement.

Don Oberdorfer and Robert Carlin in *The Two Koreas* and Mike Chinoy in *Meltdown* point out that the unilateral statement defining the U.S. position not only made an "appropriate time" as virtually never, but it also used language that appeared to deliberately provoke a North Korean rejection. It didn't just settle for verifiable denuclearization, but it specifically called for "All elements of the DPRK's past and present nuclear programs—plutonium and uranium—and all nuclear weapons will be comprehensively declared and completely, verifiably, and irreversibly eliminated"—the CVID language that North Korea had rejected in the past. The statement also said that the North's "right" for peaceful uses of nuclear energy should be premised upon the completion of verification of the DPRK's elimination of all nuclear weapons and programs and be in full compliance with the NPT and IAEA safeguards. In other words, as Pyongyang would hear it, the North's "right" was contingent on it bowing to U.S. demands for the prior elimination of

12. Hill, *Outpost,* 240.

its nuclear weapons program. In effect, this undid the careful phrasing that allowed the joint statement to be completed.

As if that wasn't enough, Hill went on to read, "I would like to note also that the United States supports a decision to terminate KEDO by the end of the year"—leaving no hope of resurrecting the multinational LWR construction. But the hard-liners were not yet done. They defined outstanding issues that needed to be discussed: "human rights abuses, biological and chemical weapons programs, ballistic missile programs and proliferation, terrorism, and illicit activities."

Victor Cha, who was sitting across from Kim Gye Gwan at the session, reports that Kim set aside his prepared remarks and said, "I see that we have climbed one mountain—only to find a taller one ahead," a polite way of saying the Americans moved the goalposts and North Korea got screwed.[13] The next day Pyongyang made it clear how Hill's statement changed the game. In a very quick and obviously angry Foreign Ministry statement, the North declared that the United States should not even dream of the issue of the DPRK's dismantlement of its nuclear deterrent before providing LWRs, a physical guarantee for confidence building. Some Americans suggested that this proved their point that the North would never stick to what it had agreed. Hill and others knew Pyongyang was responding to what had been a deliberately provocative move by the hard-liners in Washington.

So, in what Hill had termed the six-party gathering's euphoric atmosphere, the hard-liners had just destroyed whatever progress had been made. Instead of sending the delegations off to plan implementation of a sensible, hard-won joint statement, they were heading, in the words of Oberdorfer and Carlin, "toward a train wreck."[14] In about a year's time, we found out it was worse than that: It opened the door to North Korea's first nuclear test, which changed everything.

This episode illustrates another case of how Washington's hard-liners were able to take advantage of the divisions, mistrust, and confusion to push their ideology at the expense of sensible risk management. The disastrous direction came not from an overt decision from President Bush

13. Chinoy, *Meltdown*, 251.

14. Don Oberdorfer and Robert Carlin, *The Two Koreas: A Contemporary History*, 3rd ed. (New York: Basic Books, 2014), 409.

or Secretary Rice, but instead it was cleverly inserted into the process to undermine a deal. While Hill's effort to come to closure was focused on the six-party joint statement, Bob Joseph and company managed to hijack

in the American unilateral statement that Chris Hill read to the dismay of all the other parties, with the likely exception of the Japanese.

What I found particularly discouraging was that a week before the Six-Party Talks reconvened, I had given Secretary Rice my assessment of the status and direction of the North's nuclear program based on our August visit. I made it clear that the North was proceeding full steam ahead on all fronts of its nuclear program—building bombs, making plutonium, preparing for a nuclear test, and likely making missile advances. I advised that our focus should be on stopping these advances. Moving out quickly on the agreed joint statement would have slowed all of these and brought international inspectors back into the Yongbyon nuclear complex. I had also argued that agreeing that Pyongyang had the right to civilian nuclear energy and providing an LWR sometime down the road were a price worth paying.

I thought Secretary Rice and Ambassador Hill resonated with most of my recommendations, but clearly Bob Joseph did not. Most likely my report gave him additional reasons, in case any were needed, to thwart Hill's progress in Beijing and help to derail the talks. The combination of insisting on complete, verifiable, irreversible disarmament; the announcement of the end of KEDO; and defining the "appropriate time" as a distant date proved to be the hard-liner's triumph, like what John Bolton and his hammer accomplished when they smashed the Agreed Framework three years earlier. Apparently, Secretary Rice didn't appreciate the impact Joseph's poison pill unilateral statement, which she approved, would have, or, like Ambassador Hill, had hoped it could be finessed. Joseph, on the other hand, had no intention to finesse. When, less than a year later, Joseph was asked to define what the "appropriate time" for an LWR meant, he told the next South Korean six-party envoy, Ambassador Chun Yung-woo, "No LWR till pigs fly."[15]

15. "Chief Negotiators' Advice: Next Steps on North Korea," *International Crisis Group*, webinar with comments by Ambassador Chun Yung-woo (June 15, 2020), https://www.crisisgroup.org/how-we-work/events/chief-negotiators-advice-next-steps-north-korea

We will likely never know if Pyongyang considered the joint statement to be a serious step toward resolution of the nuclear crisis. The U.S. hard-liners, of course, believed the answer was no. The unilateral American statement they crafted undermined the joint statement and made sure it would not be tested. In *Failed Diplomacy*, Jack Pritchard reminds us that hard-liners firmly believed North Korea could not be trusted with any kind of peaceful nuclear program.[16] He points out that they hijacked the official process, in this case the six-party negotiations, to make policy through talking points, rather than official government agreements.

Why did Vice Minister Kim Gye Gwan go to such lengths to line up support for an LWR in the runup to the joint statement? He made his pitch with the individual delegates of the parties, with visiting U.S. congressional representatives, with CNN's Mike Chinoy, and with our Stanford delegation. As pointed out in Chapter 3, when the Bush administration killed the Agreed Framework in 2002, Pyongyang appeared to switch the priorities in its dual-track strategy. Nuclear pursuit supplanted diplomacy as the primary track. With Washington, somewhat surprisingly, keeping a diplomatic path open thereafter, did the North use that diplomacy track strictly to buy time for its nuclear development, or did diplomacy have a chance? Vice Minister Kim certainly gave us the impression that he believed diplomacy had a chance, but it required that he be able to get an agreement for an LWR. Yet, he also must have realized that the best chance for an LWR, namely the KEDO multinational consortium, was on life support following the death of the Agreed Framework.

Although we have no way of knowing what Kim Jong Il was thinking, it is quite logical to assume that he may have given Vice Minister Kim the green light to try one more time after the demise of the Agreed Framework to see if he could strike a denuclearization for normalization deal that included LWRs, because as he explained to our Stanford delegation, the LWRs had symbolic significance far beyond their energy benefits. Besides, at this point, North Korea had at best a few primitive bombs and had not tested them. Moreover, it did not have a proven missile system that could deliver

16. Charles L. Pritchard, *Failed Diplomacy* (Washington, DC: Brookings Institution Press, 2007).

such a bomb reliably. Diplomacy was also critical for Kim Jong Il, who had instituted major economic reforms in 2002. For those to succeed, he needed a benign external security environment—not exactly what he faced with

try, though they had no intention of stopping their nuclear quest during such an exploration.

It appears that Kim Gye Gwan got very close to a deal. He was willing to accept the "appropriate time" language for an LWR but was devastated by the unilateral American statement that not only spelled out how distant that time was, but also piled on the other provisions that provoked Kim to reply we now have a "taller mountain to climb." When Hill announced that the KEDO project would be officially terminated by the end of the year, Kim must have seen he was at the end of his rope. In Pyongyang, it would be back to prioritizing the nuclear track over diplomacy. That's exactly what happened.

7   Kim Jong Il: Buying Time

By the time Kim Gye Gwan returned home from the Six-Party Talks in Beijing, the die was cast. Whatever chance he may have had to resurrect diplomacy and forge a deal had vanished. Based on the North's actions over the next year, I posit that Kim Jong Il decided to again prioritize the nuclear track over diplomacy. The most important next steps were a nuclear test and a long-range missile test. Both had been in the works for some time, but they still required a final push to pull off within the next year. The role of diplomacy post-September 2005, Kim Gye Gwan must have been told, was now to buy the time and space for these nuclear and missile advances, rather than to get to a nuclear deal. The North likely knew this would be a risky dance because such tests, or even their preparation, could trigger an American military response. What happened, in fact, was that Kim Gye Gwan choreographed a delicate process that allowed Pyongyang to conduct its first nuclear test a year later while the Bush administration foundered in indecision and infighting.

The North Koreans decided not to disavow the joint statement, but to use it. For their own reasons, China and South Korea also did what they could to keep it alive. The American side, however, continued to plough along the hard-line route in succeeding statements and meetings, underscoring that the Bush administration was never serious in negotiating the joint statement in the first place. The administration had lost support at home for the Iraq

War, negotiations with Iran were going nowhere, and the president had low approval ratings after the government's poor response to Hurricane Katrina, so signing the joint statement, it was hoped, would give the administration

In the days following the joint statement, administration officials continued to toe the hard line. Secretary Rice insisted that disarmament by the North must come first, before the United States would be willing to even "discuss" an LWR.[2] President Bush said that although verification provisions were not in the joint statement, they would be necessary. Some administration officials suggested that the verification of any agreement would have to be conducted by Americans given unhindered access throughout the country. Clearly, all of these were non-starters for the North, yet the Foreign Ministry gave the impression it still "committed itself to dismantling the existing nuclear weapons program, returning to the NPT, and allowing inspections by the IAEA."[3] These comments, however, were more consistent with the North buying time for its nuclear advances by staying engaged in diplomacy.

In early October, Ambassador Hill said the United States was preparing to press the North Koreans on tangible, specific steps that would "translate the pact's ambiguous language into a more concrete set of obligations." He added, "The first step is to declare what they have. And we hope the declaration is complete. It's very important that it's complete, because we do have to overcome a lot of mistrust."[4] This statement was a clear reference to the uranium enrichment program, which had not been admitted to or disclosed during the talks. That would eventually have to be followed by a

1. Glenn Kessler and Edward Cody, "N. Korea, U.S. Gave Ground to Make Deal; Long Process Looms on Nuclear Accord," *Washington Post* (September 20, 2005): A1.

2. David E. Sanger, "Yes, Parallel Tracks to North, But Parallel Tracks Don't Meet," *New York Times* (September 20, 2005), https://www.nytimes.com/2005/09/20/politics/yes-parallel-tracks-to-north-but-parallel-tracks-dont-meet.html

3. Colum Lynch, "N. Korea Urges U.S. to Give Reactor for Nuclear Program," *Washington Post* (September 23, 2005), https://www.washingtonpost.com/archive/politics/2005/09/23/n-korea-urges-us-to-give-reactor-for-nuclear-program/735196fe-9482-4393-b977-965ace36f81d/

4. Peter Baker and Glenn Kessler, "U.S. to Push Koreans on Nuclear Program," *Washington Post* (October 5, 2005), https://www.washingtonpost.com/archive/politics/2005/10/05/us-to-push-koreans-on-nuclear-program/e8c3cb7f-4260-4e30-8245-920f266cde1c/

full declaration of the weapons program. Hill must have realized by that point that the provisions in the American unilateral statement and these demands didn't have a snowball's chance in hell with the North.

On October 14, a DPRK delegate to the UN General Assembly reiterated the North's position on the LWR. But by October 18, a DPRK Foreign Ministry spokesman appeared to be changing the tune to focus instead on its unhappiness about the Banco Delta Asia (BDA) sanctions, mocking Washington about making much ado about the DPRK's presumed "illegal deals such as drug deals and counterfeit notes."[5] The U.S. Treasury Department had begun to tighten the screws on the DPRK a month earlier. It turned out the BDA sanctions had not only made $25 million of North Korea's assets in the bank inaccessible but were beginning to make it difficult for Pyongyang to deal in the international market for legitimate as well as illegitimate business. How much of the intense focus the Kim Jong Il regime placed on the BDA issue over the next year resulted from the actual pain incurred in the North, perhaps including the financial dealings of the Kim family, versus the North using the sanctions as a convenient stalking horse to return to serious diplomacy or just to otherwise occupy the Americans is still not clear today. In most likelihood, it was some of both.

BDA SANCTIONS DOMINATE DIPLOMACY
IN THE SHORT TERM

Kim Gye Gwan led the North's delegation to the next round of the Six-Party Talks in Beijing in early November. The Chinese side said it hoped to finally make substantive progress to begin putting into practice the broad principles outlined in the September agreement. Both the American and North Korean sides, on the other hand, appeared resigned, as Chris Hill stated, to talking about how to go forward. Hill later complained that the North continued to want a "slow, more deliberate process."[6] Meanwhile, Kim Gye Gwan, as reported by Chinese state media, called the current round of talks a "beacon guiding the six parties toward progress . . . but

5. DPRK Foreign Ministry Spokesman, "U.S. Anti-DPRK Diatribe Assailed," *KCNA* (October 18, 2005).

6. Jim Yardley, "Six-Nation Talks on North Korea Resume in China," *New York Times* (November 10, 2005), https://www.nytimes.com/2005/11/10/world/sixnation-talks-on-north-korea-resume-in-china.html

that beacon, at present, is far away, and moreover, the mist on the ocean is thick and sometimes it blurs the beacon."[7] He was buying time.

On November 12, the talks ended with an inconclusive and irresolute

dropped the LWR issue for the time being. No agreements were forged, and no schedule was set for another meeting. At the end of November, a DPRK Foreign Ministry spokesman addressed the upcoming termination of KEDO. The statement mentioned that the United States had already stopped construction for two years, so the end was just a matter of time. It used this example of U.S. noncompliance with its commitments to justify why any agreement with the Americans must abide by the principle of simultaneous actions. "Now that the construction of the LWRs came to a final stop, the DPRK is compelled to blame the U.S. for having overturned the Agreed Framework and demand it compensate for the political and economic losses it has caused to the former."[8]

There was no way this was going to happen, and Pyongyang certainly knew it. When on a freezing morning in early January 2006 the last ship carrying the remaining KEDO workers left port, they watched nearly a decade of effort, and more than a billion dollars (mostly provided by South Korea and Japan) disappear from view.[9] What a sorry end to what could have permanently changed U.S.–North Korea relations for the better. Completing the construction of the two LWRs by KEDO could have transformed the relationship between the United States and its allies and North Korea. It would, indeed, have signaled the end of what Pyongyang called Washington's "hostile intent." To Seoul and Tokyo, it would have demonstrated that Washington was serious about a long-term diplomatic relationship with the North. Moreover, even at the time of its termination, the KEDO organization had become an important window into North Korea. As Don Oberdorfer and Robert Carlin point out, "In some respects, KEDO was more effective than the six-party talks in dealing with the North on a multilateral

7. Ibid.

8. DPRK Foreign Ministry Spokesman, "DPRK FM Spokesman Demands U.S. Compensate for Political and Economic Losses," *KCNA* (November 28, 2005).

9. Don Oberdorfer and Robert Carlin, *The Two Koreas: A Contemporary History*, 3rd ed. (New York: Basic Books, 2014), 413.

basis."[10] The American KEDO workers and officials had feet on the ground in North Korea, and they were in constant contact with their North Korean counterparts. With the death of KEDO, yet another point of contact inside North Korea was lost.

During the early months in 2006, most communications and discussions were focused on the BDA issue. Hill offered to have Treasury experts brief the North on what he called a law enforcement issue. The North rode this point for all it was worth to justify not getting back to the talks. Then, on March 8, North Korea tested two short-range missiles, its first in six years. The next day, U.S. and North Korean officials utilized the New York channel to meet at the UN. The North again warned the United States to ease up on the BDA sanctions; otherwise, it would continue to abstain from the Six-Party Talks.

But by this time the Bush administration believed that its efforts against Banco Delta Asia had been successful, considering the tactic far more effective than anyone had dreamed because foreign banks had taken notice and were curbing their relationships with North Korea. Even better, Pyongyang was very vocal about its displeasure—according to one satisfied U.S. official, the sanctions really struck a nerve. The sanctions were pushed by U.S. hard-liners and empowered them in the aftermath, showing the apparent effectiveness of an approach that favored pressure and eschewed the Six-Party Talks, concluding that the negotiations were unlikely to succeed unless they were accompanied by these direct, punitive actions. The strategy was "squeeze them, but keep the negotiations going," hoping for the talks to "serve as little more than a vehicle for accepting North Korea's capitulation."[11] The North responded by moving toward more confrontational measures by late summer.

Little did the Bush administration seem to realize it was playing right into Pyongyang's hands—buying time to prepare for major steps forward in its missile and nuclear programs. While the BDA pressure may have hurt, it was not going to break the regime, although Pyongyang was surely

10. Ibid.

11. Joel Brinkley, "U.S. Squeezes North Korea's Money Flow," New York Times (March 10, 2006), https://www.nytimes.com/2006/03/10/politics/us-squeezes-north-koreas-money-flow.html.

concerned that the U.S. Treasury would use the sanctions as a tool to completely cut North Korea off from the international financial system. The sanctions also served a useful purpose, providing convenient cover for the

after the obvious failure of the diplomatic track in September 2005.

THE NORTH BREAKS ITS MISSILE TEST MORATORIUM

The first of these steps was reported by the U.S. intelligence community on June 17, when it spotted signs that the North was preparing to test a long-range missile. Pyongyang had already announced in March 2005 that it no longer felt its 1999 self-imposed missile-test moratorium was still in effect. That announcement had come only a month after the North declared that it had become a nuclear weapon state, a one-two punch that Washington seemed to shrug off at the time. The Bush administration and South Korea viewed the current launch preparations as designed to force Washington back to the negotiating table. Secretary Rice called the launch preparations a provocation that would be met with increased sanctions and international isolation.[12] Pyongyang was not impressed and continued to steadily increase its missile and nuclear capabilities. Resumed missile launches were the next logical step.

Former Secretary of Defense William Perry and his colleague (and future Secretary of Defense) Ashton Carter were alarmed by the potential dangers of these next North Korean moves. In a *Washington Post* op-ed they argued that the United States should plan to target and destroy the long-range missile on the launch pad, citing the dramatic escalation in the North's capabilities that this missile could portend—the potential ability to strike the U.S. mainland with nuclear weapons.[13] It is ironic that Perry and Carter, both former Clinton administration officials, would call for a

12. Glenn Kessler, "N. Korea Warned on Testing Missile; Act Would Spur Penalties, Rice Says," *Washington Post* (June 20, 2006), https://www.washingtonpost.com/archive/politics/2006/06/20/n-korea-warned-on-testing-missile-span-classbankheadact-would-spur-penalties-rice-saysspan/963a6cce-05d5-4040-abb3-8689b0f1e0bf/

13. Ashton B. Carter and William J. Perry, "If Necessary, Strike and Destroy; North Korea Cannot Be Allowed to Test This Missile," *Washington Post* (June 22, 2006), https://www.washingtonpost.com/archive/opinions/2006/06/22/if-necessary-strike-and-destroy-span-classbankheadnorth-korea-cannot-be-allowed-to-test-this-missilespan/acofccd7-014d-4bc1-8dd5-37e038665b3f/

muscular response to North Korea's actions, whereas Bush administration officials, including Vice President Cheney and national security advisor Stephen Hadley, responded by publicly downplaying the risk posed by what they called the North's "fairly rudimentary" missile capabilities.[14] Indeed, there was little concern that the missile could reach the U.S. mainland, but it would be a step in that direction. On June 30, President Bush reiterated, "Launching the missile is unacceptable," but threatened Pyongyang only with continued international isolation, not a military response.[15] If North Korea continued to stay diplomatically involved during this time of intense technical preparations, primarily to assess how much they could get away with in terms of missile and nuclear advances, the Bush administration pretty much gave them a green light to proceed.

Indeed, on July 5, North Korea launched the first of seven missiles before the break of dawn. Six were of the short-range variety and judged successful. One was the intermediate-range Taepodong-2, which failed a few minutes after launch and fell into the Sea of Japan. Unlike the 1998 launch of the Taepodong-1, which the North had called a space launch, this Taepodong-2 launch was portrayed as part of routine military exercises staged by the KPA to "increase the nation's military capacity for self-defence . . . "[16] This long-range missile was meant to appear menacing to Washington. Indeed, Defense Secretary Donald Rumsfeld later stated in his memoir that U.S. missile interceptors had been put on high alert.

Hadley called the missile launches "provocative behavior," but downplayed the severity of the threat posed. President Bush rejected any consideration of bilateral talks with North Korea in the wake of the missile test, but the United States also quickly ruled out a military response. The prevailing sense was that there was no acceptable military option—or at least, at a risk anyone was willing to take. Bush tried to rally the international community

14. Glenn Kessler, "U.S. Rejects Suggestion to Strike N. Korea Before It Fires Missile," *Washington Post* (June 23, 2006), https://www.washingtonpost.com/archive/politics/2006/06/23/us-rejects-suggestion-to-strike-n-korea-before-it-fires-missile/45e6ec7c-71d4-4dab-bc81-d7a2f96ba33d/

15. Peter Baker, "Japan and U.S. Warn N. Korea on Missile," *Washington Post* (June 30, 2006), https://www.washingtonpost.com/wp-dyn/content/article/2006/06/29/AR2006062901918.html

16. DPRK Foreign Ministry Spokesman, "DPRK Foreign Ministry Spokesman on Its Missile Launches," *KCNA* (July 6, 2006).

to take strong punitive measures at the United Nations. John Bolton, who was U.S. ambassador at the UN by this time, argued forcefully for UN Security Council sanctions, stating, "We want a resolution. It should be

that's clear. The level of provocation engaged in by these North Korean missile launches warrants that."[17]

On July 16, the UN Security Council passed a resolution that demanded North Korea end its ballistic missile program and called on states to curb the import and export of the North's ballistic missile technology. The resolution was weakened to avoid a veto from China, preventing the invocation of Chapter VII and the possibility of the UN sanctioning a military intervention into North Korea. Oberdorfer and Carlin point out that no one seemed to realize that the most important result of the UN sanctions was to lock Washington into an escalating series of responses after subsequent missile launches. The U.S. felt obliged to ratchet up the pressure based on the precedent it had set, which in turn sparked new North Korean countermoves.[18]

WARNING SIGNS

The first such countermove to the sanctions was a big one: a nuclear test less than three months later. Pyongyang had planned the timetable for the test long before these diplomatic spats. It began publicly laying the groundwork as early as July 16, with a long blistering DPRK Foreign Ministry pronouncement condemning the UN Security Council resolution and accusing it of creating

> an extremely dangerous situation on the Korean Peninsula where the sovereignty of the Korean nation and the security of the state have been seriously infringed. . . . Our Republic will bolster its war deterrent for self-defense in every way by all means and methods now that the situation has reached the worst phase due to the extremely hostile act of the U.S.[19]

17. Warren Hoge and Norimitsu Onishi, "China Fights Sanctions to Punish North Korea," *New York Times* (July 8, 2006), https://www.nytimes.com/2006/07/08/world/asia/china-fights-sanctions-to-punish-north-korea.html

18. Oberdorfer and Carlin, *The Two Koreas*, 415.

19. DPRK Foreign Ministry, "DPRK Foreign Ministry Refutes Resolution of UN Security Council," *KCNA* (July 16, 2006).

Shortly thereafter, in August, the first signs appeared of preparations for an imminent nuclear test at the Punggye-ri site in the northeast. In late September, Kim Gye Gwan gave visiting Selig Harrison, a frequent U.S. interlocutor with the North, another forewarning. Kim told him that the North intended to unload the next batch of fuel rods from the 5 MWe reactor. Kim said they would continue to press Washington to drop the financial sanctions so the two sides could resume negotiations. Most importantly, he told Harrison that a nuclear test should be viewed as opening up new diplomatic opportunities and should not be viewed solely as a military challenge. Kim said that the North was still committed to completely and finally dismantling their nuclear weapons program but that this was going to take some time. While that was happening, "you must learn to coexist with a North Korea that has nuclear weapons."[20] At the time of Harrison's visit, almost everything had been put in place at Punggye-ri to carry out the nuclear test.

Indeed, on October 4, 2006, North Korea announced that it intended to conduct a nuclear test, though without giving a specific date. The DPRK Foreign Ministry made the usual claims that hostile daily U.S. threats forced the North to bolster its war deterrent. For good measure it added that "the Korean nation stands at the crossroads of life and death. . . . The DPRK will in the future conduct a nuclear test under the condition where safety is firmly guaranteed." The statement added that the North had manufactured "up-to-date" (likely meaning modern) nuclear weapons. A nuclear test, the ministry asserted, was "an essential process of bolstering the nuclear deterrent."[21]

Compared to the Bush administration's disjointed pronouncements and actions, this statement was the essence of clarity. The North made the case as to why it would conduct a nuclear test. The Foreign Ministry stated, "nuclear weapons will serve as reliable war deterrent for protecting the

20. Selig S. Harrison, "In a Test, a Reason to Talk Bilateral Diplomacy Could Still Roll Back North Korea's Nuclear Arms Effort," *Washington Post* (October 10, 2006), https://www.washingtonpost.com/archive/opinions/2006/10/10/in-a-test-a-reason-to-talk-span-classbankheadbilateral-diplomacy-could-still-roll-back-north-koreas-nuclear-arms-effortspan/6ae9d54b-dc76-496d-a45b-0798e9541311/
21. DPRK Foreign Ministry, "DPRK Foreign Ministry Clarifies Stand on New Measure to Bolster War Deterrent," *KCNA* (October 4, 2006).

supreme interests of the state." It added that the DPRK would, "never use nuclear weapons first," and it "will always sincerely implement its international commitment in the field of nuclear non-proliferation as a responsible

At the same time the Foreign Ministry was making these noble claims, North Korean technical and military workers were busily trying to finish up the construction of a Yongbyon reactor clone at al-Kibar on the Euphrates River in Syria, a reactor that was, as we shall see later, designed strictly for the purpose of plutonium production.

The North Korean announcement came amid a new internal administration process led by Secretary Rice designed to change the U.S. approach one more time, in coordination with South Korea. In her memoir, Secretary Rice traces this "strategic leap" back to the meeting President Bush had with China's president, Hu Jintao, during a visit to Washington in April. The process was jumpstarted after President Bush met with South Korean President Roh in mid-September. Rice had hoped to use the crucial six-week period to develop ideas and test them on a trip to Northeast Asia—but Pyongyang's announcement about a test seemed to close the door on any new negotiations when it concluded there is "no benefit in reaching a deal."[23]

On October 5, Hill delivered a direct U.S. response to the DPRK UN mission, and stated publicly, "We are not going to live with a nuclear North Korea, we are not going to accept it. . . . It can have a future, or it can have these weapons. It cannot have both." The White House delivered a hawkish response to the North's possible nuclear test, settling on a robust list of sanctions that would be implemented as a "signal that there would be no going back, that the long-running debate about engagement vs. pressure would be over, with a decisive victory for pressure."[24]

22. Ibid.

23. Glenn Kessler, "N. Korean Move Comes Amid Bid for Talks; With Plan to Conduct Nuclear Test, Pyongyang Again Dismisses U.S. Peace Feelers," *Washington Post* (October 4, 2006), https://www.washingtonpost.com/archive/politics/2006/10/04/n-korean-move-comes-amid-bid-for-talks-span-classbankheadwith-plan-to-conduct-nuclear-test-pyongyang-again-dismisses-us-peace-feelersspan/d97e4e8a-4fac-4341-b7ef-87a510f2d2ce/

24. Ibid.

THE FIRST NUCLEAR TEST

On October 9, in the wee hours of the morning, Pyongyang took the unprecedented step of notifying Beijing as to the time, location, and expected yield of the upcoming test. No other country has ever given such notice for its first nuclear test. Shortly thereafter, seismic stations around the world registered weak but clear signals emanating from the general location of Punggye-ri in northeast North Korea. Although the weak signals implied a low explosion yield, North Korea had clearly arrived as the eighth self-declared nuclear state. Condemnation from around the world was swift, but none of it could hide the realization that all efforts to keep the North from going nuclear had failed.

Secretary Rice warned that the North would now face the prospect of sanctions from the international community "unlike anything that they have faced before." She added, however, that the U.S. had no plans to attack or invade North Korea.[25] South Korea's President Roh characterized the nuclear test as a grave threat and warned that South Korea would sternly deal with Pyongyang's announcement, lamenting the fact that because of this test, South Korea had lost ground in arguing for dialogue and for its engagement policy. The Chinese government announced that it resolutely opposed the nuclear test by the DPRK and strongly condemned the test as flagrant and brazen. It expressed its displeasure to Pyongyang and sent emissaries out to key capitals around the world to underscore how unhappy it was.

By October 15, Ambassador John Bolton had managed to orchestrate new UN Security Council sanctions on North Korea in response to the nuclear test. Resolution 1718 passed after watering down some provision to gain the support of China and Russia. The resolution banned trade in items related to the North's WMD program, ballistic missile program, conventional weapons, and luxury goods. This resolution, unlike the most recent one adopted in July, was passed under Chapter VII authority, which authorized the use of force.

25. Thom Shanker and Warren Hoge, "Rice Asserts U.S. Plans No Attack on North Korea," *New York Times* (October 11, 2006), https://www.nytimes.com/2006/10/11/washington/11diplo.html

However, the united hawkish front the White House displayed before the test evaporated almost overnight. Stressing punishment, the hard-liners got the UN resolution, but to the president and Secretary Rice it must have

in office had not worked. They quickly pivoted to hunting for a diplomatic solution. The threats from South Korea and China also faded. President Roh remained firmly committed to his engagement policy. He resisted U.S. demands to take more stringent measures. He also informed President Bush that the South would not participate fully in a plan to intercept possible North Korean nuclear shipments, fearing the provocative potential of that activity. China also stated that it would ignore the provision that sought the inspection of goods entering and leaving North Korea.[26]

Of all the parties, Kim Jong Il was best prepared to deal with the political consequences of the test. The Foreign Ministry called the UN Security Council action a "declaration of a war." It argued "the DPRK had exerted every possible effort to settle the nuclear issue through dialogue and negotiations" but that the United States "responded to our patient and sincere efforts and magnanimity with the policy of sanctions and blockade." As a result, it said, "The DPRK was compelled to substantially prove its possession of nukes to protect its sovereignty and right to existence."[27] It pushed back further with a warning: "The DPRK wants peace but is not afraid of war. It wants dialogue but is always ready for confrontation. . . . The DPRK will closely follow the future U.S. attitude and take corresponding measures."[28]

In retrospect, I find it remarkable that the Bush administration was unprepared to deal with the consequences if its decision to issue a set of impossible demands in its unilateral statement at the September 19, 2005, Six-Party Talks. It should have realized that the North would take the steps necessary for a nuclear arsenal—namely, continue to produce more fissile materials, go back to missile testing, and conduct a nuclear test. It apparently learned

26. Colum Lynch and Glenn Kessler, "U.N. Votes to Impose Sanctions on N. Korea; Council Demands End to Nuclear Program," *Washington Post* (October 15, 2006): A1.

27. DPRK Foreign Ministry Spokesman, "DPRK Foreign Ministry Spokesman on U.S. Moves Concerning Its Nuclear Test," *KCNA* (October 11, 2006).

28. DPRK Foreign Ministry Spokesman, "DPRK Foreign Ministry Spokesman Totally Refutes UNSC Resolution," *KCNA* (October 17, 2006).

nothing from having made the same mistake after walking away from the Agreed Framework. Although administration officials were engaged in a constant flurry of activity and allegations related to the North's nuclear program between September 2005 and the nuclear test in October 2006, this crucial period gets little coverage in the memoirs of the key players, namely Ambassador Hill and Secretary Rice. Hill spends less than two pages of *Outpost* on this period. Either Bush administration officials did not expect the North to proceed with these next obvious steps in their nuclear program or they didn't understand that the nuclear test would change everything.

In late October, barely two weeks after the test, I was on my way to North Korea for the third time. I was anxious to hear directly from the North Koreans what the nuclear test meant to them.

8 "Tell America It Worked. DPRK Is Filled with Pride"

On October 31, 2006, John Lewis, Jack Pritchard, Robert Carlin, and I stepped off the Air Koryo flight from Beijing into a warm and smoggy Pyongyang afternoon. The wait for our bags was sufficiently long that I began to wonder what they may have found of interest in our luggage. For my part, as before, I made sure not to take anything that might arouse suspicion. Our hosts, the Foreign Ministry's Song Il Hyok and Kim Hyon Chol, met us in the customs area and accompanied us into town for what was by now, on my third trip, a familiar sight—wide boulevards lined with lots of pedestrians and bikes on the roadsides and soldiers tending goats on the nearby hills. Our destination this time was the Koryo Hotel in the middle of town, a step up and more convenient from our previous hotel, the Potanggang. My room on the 17th floor had not only the standard two North Korean TV channels, but some channels in Chinese, Russian, Japanese, and the BBC. In the basement, the hotel sported a fitness room with bikes, steppers, and weights that I was able to use for one euro a day.

I had not expected to be allowed back into the country at this time. But surprisingly, in late September, Lewis had gotten approval through the DPRK UN mission for an October visit. I say surprisingly because by the time they invited us, Pyongyang must have already made the decision and was well into preparations for the October 9 nuclear test.

Immediately after the test, most Western analysts concluded the test had fizzled with little nuclear yield, but they missed the overarching significance. Despite the size of the blast, North Korea proclaimed its arrival on the global scene as a nuclear power. What I found most surprising was how deftly North Korea was able to stare down the international community and manage the political consequences. After the expected condemnations from the United States, South Korea, Japan, and even China, all of them returned quickly to coax North Korea back to the negotiating table, and Pyongyang was perfectly willing to show up.

For the group, it was a fascinating time to be back in North Korea—both to explore the myriad technical questions I had about the test and the status of the North's nuclear program, as well as the political implications for the North of this new step toward proving itself a state with nuclear weapons. In the leadup to the missile and nuclear tests, Pyongyang engaged in diplomacy to buy time to pull these off. What now? Would it continue to try to buy time to conduct a second test successfully to demonstrate more convincingly its nuclear status to the world and to its own leadership, or would it turn seriously to diplomacy because a successful nuclear path looked more dubious? We were eager to hear the views of the North's political and technical leaders firsthand.

MEETING WITH AMBASSADOR RI GUN

During the agenda-setting session with the Foreign Ministry's Song and Kim, we were told that Vice Minister Kim Gye Gwan would not be able to meet us. There would also be no visit to Yongbyon, but Director Ri Hong Sop would meet us in Pyongyang, as would General Ri Chan Bok and a high-level representative from the Supreme People's Assembly. The rest of the agenda was heavy on cultural stops and some of John Lewis's typical visits and discussions. With access to BBC News on the TV in my room, I learned that North Korea had agreed to return to the Six-Party Talks and that Vice Minister Kim Gye Gwan was in Beijing. We found out later he had departed Pyongyang on the morning flight to Beijing, the same plane that then turned around and brought us in on Tuesday afternoon.

Ambassador Ri Gun, whom others in the group had known for many years and whom I had met on both of my previous trips, welcomed us at the Foreign Ministry the next morning. Ri said that our previous

understand the DPRK nuclear deterrent. Then, before we could ask, he answered the big question on our minds—why did they let us in so soon after the nuclear test? "You have arrived at a time of great celebration," Ri said. "The reason for allowing you in was to let the American people know that the people in the DPRK are living with confidence and pride." Ri's comments and his relaxed body language, even in the formal, stiff atmosphere of the ministry's conference room, clearly conveyed how important the North Korean leadership considered their contacts with our group. And based on their comments about my first two visits, the leadership regarded my technical findings and assessments to be beneficial to its purposes as well.

Ri explained that they carried out the test because of U.S. political pressure and said we should not have been surprised since it was quite natural for a country with nuclear weapons to conduct nuclear tests. With his trademark grin, he said, "You know very well that a country that has nuclear weapons has protection." Ri quickly added that despite the nuclear test, they still believed in the denuclearization of the Korean Peninsula. Although they would return to the Six-Party Talks, Ri warned, "We will make stronger, tougher demands for the U.S. to live up to its own commitments."

I took that as a major message they wanted conveyed to Washington: "Live up to your commitments." This was alien to the policy types in Washington, particularly to the Bush administration. They had taken what they considered the higher moral ground by claiming that it was Pyongyang that had cheated on every agreement it ever made—that it clearly could not be trusted and so must give up its nuclear program before any new deal could be achieved. Ri's statement was, in effect, the mirror image of that. In the North's view, it was the Americans who had reneged on their commitments. Pressed on this point, the North Koreans always had ready answers. What happened to the promise to normalize relations in the Agreed Framework? What happened to the promised schedule for LWR construction? And how could the Americans almost immediately walk back from the promises of the September 19 joint statement?

Wherever the fault lay, I felt it was important to understand where the North Koreans were coming from. That was particularly important if we were to better understand the tension and interplay between the two prongs of their strategy—nuclearization and diplomacy—and which way the North would turn next. Ambassador Ri's goal, I thought, was to try to convince us of the success of the country's first nuclear test despite Western press reports that the test was a failure or a partial success at best.

What we couldn't be sure of at the time, and still don't know, is why the North turned back to diplomacy—namely, Vice Minister Kim in Beijing for Six-Party Talks and Ri Gun exploring diplomatic options with our group— so soon after the test. Was it because they really believed the test bought them credibility and greater diplomatic leverage, as Ri Gun implied, or were they afraid that the test results showed a real nuclear deterrent was still a long way off, and thus diplomacy was still essential? Seeking relief from the BDA sanctions may also have been an important factor.

One of the benefits of being in North Korea with experienced diplomatic hands like Pritchard and Carlin was that they were able to cut through the North's prepared talking points with pointed, provocative questions. Pritchard bluntly asked Ri if DPRK came back to the Six-Party Talks because the nuclear test was not successful. Ri dismissed that idea with a laugh. "The test was successful," he replied without giving an inch. "We don't care what others say. We are confident that the test achieved our goals." Of course, it all depended on what their goals were. In my view, if they were trying to suggest they now had a viable nuclear deterrent, they were years from achieving that.

Pritchard continued to play devil's advocate. "Your nuclear test was not completely successful, your missile test was not, yet the pressure from the U.S. was successful." Ri wasn't fazed. Pritchard's statement, he said, was very different from reality. "It was a nuclear test," he repeated, "not a conventional test, and the U.S. found samples to prove it was nuclear." As for the small size, Ri repeated they didn't care what others said. They were used to such criticism. He admitted he didn't have the specific information, but North Korean experts confidently said it was powerful.

Carlin and Pritchard engaged Ri in a spirited discussion of what de-nuclearization and normalization mean and how they are to be achieved. Ri told them that the first step at the Six-Party Talks would have to be a

resolution of the BDA sanctions. He added that Ambassador Hill had signaled U.S. readiness to do so. Full normalization, Ri said, means securing
the political right for the DPRK to exist. It means normalizing intellectual,

out an overall strategy for denuclearization that would begin with suspension followed by dismantlement. Ri said the DPRK would stop production
and testing of weapons and not transfer them. There must be a monitoring
system in place, perhaps within the six-party process or by other means. Ri
invoked President Reagan's "trust but verify" pronouncement at the Cold
War's end. The parties should build trust and confidence. Whereas all the
DPRK does must be done in a verifiable way, the United States should take
actions in a verifiable way also, Ri continued.

One of Ri's most telling comments was during the discussion on the role
of China. Ri said that though some U.S. observers believed that China forced
the North back to the negotiating table, that wasn't true. It was, he said, a
DPRK decision. Besides, it was the Americans who had the "longer-term
strategic interest" in the Korean Peninsula. In the context of a discussion
on China, this seemed a veiled reference to the North's position that it understood the big game was between China and the United States and that
the North could be helpful to Washington in that game.

DISCUSSIONS WITH GENERAL RI CHAN BOK

General Ri Chan Bok received us graciously at the stately Palace of Culture as he had done during the previous two visits. He opened with a few
grace notes, asking Jack Pritchard about his family and telling me I looked
younger this time, despite my gray hair. We touched on many of the same
issues we covered with Ambassador Ri Gun. Although the general's comments were scripted along the party line, the dialogue was still useful. He
claimed that the North had anticipated all possible consequences of U.S.
actions in response to the test including military actions, and they were
fully prepared.

Jack Pritchard told General Ri, as he had told Ambassador Ri Gun, that
he would play the devil's advocate about the "successful" nuclear test. Jack
said, "Yes, you tested, but the test did not go well. You don't have a deterrent
and you'll need to do more testing." Ri didn't miss a beat, not even half a
beat. "We know some people have claimed failure, some have claimed a

partial success. Dr. Hecker is well aware that it is easier to do a large test than a small one." He said they considered the test to be a complete success. The nuclear explosion, he said, "was scaled to mount the device on means of delivery."

I mentioned to General Ri that I found it peculiar that North Korea announced its test ahead of time—no other country had done so. Also, the first tests of all other countries were considerable larger than theirs. He was eager to respond: "We weighed not telling the world against carrying out the test in a safe and secure manner. Which do you consider more beneficial and reasonable?"

General Ri was prepared to knock down any suggestions that the test had failed or was only partially successful. He was smart enough to say he didn't have the details of the test, which he knew was the reason for my questions. And if I thought I might get those from Director Ri Hong Sop later in the day, I was to be equally disappointed.

TECHNICAL DISCUSSIONS WITH
DIRECTOR RI HONG SOP

We met with Ri Hong Sop at the Koryo Hotel. He was accompanied by two officials from the General Department of Atomic Energy and a no-tetaker. Director Ri extended warm greetings and said he was ready to answer my questions, within authorization, of course. As we found out, he was not authorized to talk about the nuclear test but never said that in so many words. Instead, he dodged by telling us the test was outside his purview. Given his subsequent assignment a few years later to head what was called the Nuclear Weapon Institute, that hardly seems likely.

I asked Director Ri for an update on Yongbyon. He said not much had changed since we were there a bit more than a year ago. Ri reminded us that when we visited the previous August, they were in the middle of a reprocessing campaign precluding a visit to the site. At this visit, they had just completed some nuclear waste disposal activities associated with the 2005 reprocessing campaign, and "the level of radioactivity is higher than ever in the facility." Hence, no visit to Yongbyon this time either.

Director Ri said the 5 MWe reactor was operating now at full power and without problems. I had seen open source reports that the reactor apparently was cycling on and off, potentially indicating they had operational problems.

Ri said that wasn't the case. They had shut down the reactor to make some minor repairs, but only during planned inspections. I asked him how the latest load of fresh fuel rods had performed. I was curious because these

said these fuel rods were in good shape; only a few of them had corroded during the long storage time. Ri told me that they had decided to lower the operating temperature of the reactor from 350 to 300 C because that caused less cladding failure. He said the lower temperature was less desirable for electricity production, but it was better for plutonium production. This was one of several sharp jabs meant to drive home that they were fully committed to plutonium production for weapons and that they knew what they are doing.

Ri said they were almost done with the Fuel Fabrication Facility refurbishment plan to make new fuel in 2007. Once completed, they could produce one reactor load of fuel rods (8,000 rods) per year. They were not in a hurry now, he said, because they still had spare rods from the old inventory. There were not enough for an entire load, but they had enough to replace rods as necessary or do a partial reload. He said that by the next time they shut the reactor down, they would have enough rods for the entire core. As we will see later, the reactor was shut down in 2007, but it was not restarted until August 2013 for reasons other than lack of fresh fuel.

During my previous visit, Director Ri had explained the changes they made in the Radiochemical Laboratory. I told him I was still puzzled about those changes. Replacing what are called "mixer-settlers" with pulsed columns, he said, increased the efficiency of reprocessing by 30 percent, which I thought would not be of much benefit considering they had excess capacity in that facility. I told Ri that such an efficiency increase is likely not worth the risks in the intense hot-cell radiation environment and said we would be very reluctant to make such a change in the United States. Ri chuckled. "Yes," he replied, "it was difficult, but we did it. Maybe it shows that our technicians may be more advanced than yours." It was one of several comments he made to let me know that they were not a nuclear backwater. Then, turning serious, he added it was worth taking the risk to produce the plutonium for the nuclear test because of the nuclear threat from the United States. The mixer-settlers in the co-precipitation line were replaced with pulsed columns not to increase the throughput, but because clogging problems with the mixer-settlers produced plutonium production losses. Now that, I thought, made good sense.

I asked if all materials and equipment for fuel fabrication and reprocessing were indigenously produced. Ri replied that they were now able to do so, including corrosion-resistant stainless steel required for many of the operations. The same was true for all the chemicals required. I asked about the prospects of completing construction of the larger 50 MWe reactor. Ri said they were not in full swing but were rather trying to recover the original state of the equipment of the reactor, which was only a few years from completion when construction stopped in 1994. Interestingly, he blamed the problem on industries outside of Yongbyon. They were not able to provide the components needed, he said. He added that they must do everything themselves now because it is difficult to import anything. At this point, he said, the decision as to whether to proceed was in the hands of people at a higher level.

I tried to get more details about what I had learned about the plutonium production during the 2004 visit, when they allowed me to hold a piece of cast plutonium. Ri was reluctant to add much. When pressed a bit, he indicated that they knew how to electro-refine plutonium to make high purity material, and that they had done a lot of casting research to produce high-purity, sound castings. He said they were not doing much research on the properties of plutonium because most of that was already available in the literature. He would not say if the plutonium core for the nuclear test device was made in Yongbyon but indicated that they only made the metal there. As he had done previously, he was implying that the final casting and machining of the parts happened outside Yongbyon and were not within his jurisdiction.

Ri deflected most of my questions on the nuclear test by saying that was not his responsibility. His job and that of Yongbyon, he said, was to make the plutonium metal. I asked if he was present at the site during the test. He said he was not. Interestingly, he noted that the security situation for the nuclear program was very tight. There were no links between the different technical sectors for security reasons. I tried one more time by talking about the best way to measure the yield of a nuclear test. It was well known, I said, that the best method was to conduct a drill-back into the test cavity, take samples of the test debris, and perform radiochemical analysis (it turns out the nature of the fission products provides the most accurate measure of the explosion that took place). Ri agreed that this was the best method, but again emphasized that this was not his responsibility. I probed further by

to do the radiochemical analysis, no? He implied that was the case, but again said it was not under his jurisdiction. Though Ri was clearly uneasy discussing anything about the test, I thought it was important to get an idea of how they measured the yield. What I took away from this conversation was that they did conduct drill-back operations, which must have told them that the device was of low yield. It also most likely gave them good clues about what may have gone wrong.

It was clear that Director Ri had instructions to stay away from discussing the test. I had previously asked Ambassador Ri Gun if I could talk to the technical people who had responsibility for the rest of the nuclear program and the nuclear test. Ri told me earlier in the week, "We heard your request." In the West, that might imply something was being seriously considered. In North Korea, it's a nice way of saying no. In fact, Ambassador Ri never delivered.

Returning to more comfortable ground for Director Ri, I turned to get more information about the IRT-2000 research reactor. Ri said they operated it in a very limited mode and made some iodine-131 radiopharmaceuticals for thyroid cancer treatment. I told him that Vice Minister Kim Gye Gwan was still asking for an LWR in the diplomatic negotiations, although the KEDO project had now been formally terminated. I was curious as to what role Director Ri would see for the Yongbyon nuclear center. He was very guarded in his answers. Carlin pointed out that the end of the KEDO project left about a hundred young North Korea technical people out of a job. Had any of them found jobs at Yongbyon? Ri said, no, we have enough workers here. He reiterated what he had told us during the previous trip: The Yongbyon complex had nothing to do with KEDO.

I inquired about what Yongbyon might do to support an indigenous LWR program. Would the facility continue to convert yellowcake uranium in its huge chemical facility on site and then make its own fuel—which now would have to be uranium oxide, rather than metal as it is for the 5 MWe reactor. Or would the yellowcake or oxide be sent to another country, such as Russia, to enrich and make fuel rods? Ri said that depended on the "price balance"—in other words, the economics—before they could decide how much North Korea would do itself. Would they be able to make the oxide fuel themselves as well as the cladding? And would that be stainless steel or zircaloy cladding? Ri said they could use some of their buildings for oxide fabrication but would have to install new equipment. As for the cladding, he said stainless steel would be better for them. I asked about reprocessing in case they were able to get an LWR. Would they do it in-house or send the spent fuel back to the country of fuel origin? Ri said that all depended on the nature of the purchase agreement. He indicated that these questions were all too hypothetical. The DPRK didn't have enrichment capabilities, he said, so they hadn't given any thought to indigenous LWRs. I found out later that these questions had been quite pertinent because four years later they showed us the initial construction of their indigenous LWR.

I concluded my questions by asking Director Ri how his people at Yongbyon were doing. He said, "There is more work, thus better for our people." What I hadn't appreciated at the time was that Ri was likely referring not only to the plutonium operations for their nuclear weapons program, but the work to complete preparations for the Yongbyon-like reactor they were building in Syria. That reactor was not discovered until 2007, at which point the Israelis destroyed it. The expertise for building such reactors resided in Yongbyon, although fabrication of components and equipment was likely done elsewhere in North Korea, perhaps at the same industrial sites Director Ri was blaming for not getting the 50 MWe reactor at Yongbyon completed.

In addition, by this time in 2006, the North was likely moving its uranium centrifuge program to the pilot production stage. The centrifuge facility existed outside of Yongbyon, but the chemical conversion facilities in Yongbyon may well have provided some of the precursor uranium tetrafluoride and hexafluoride compounds for the operation.

Despite the rather stiff atmosphere of our meeting in the hotel, the discussions with Ri were informative. The technical details helped me make a better estimate of plutonium production rates and inventories. I was able to conclude that Yongbyon was running at full speed—the reactor was operating, and the Radiochemical Laboratory was standing by to separate the next load of weapon-grade plutonium when the spent fuel was unloaded. The Fuel Fabrication Facility was just about fully refurbished to make the next load of fuel. The future of the 50 MWe reactor was still uncertain.

Restarting construction looked less and less plausible. Instead, I would have expected them to rebuild from scratch—they had the design, the requisite infrastructure, and some components that could have been used. They gave

BACK TO DIPLOMACY

In Pyongyang, the Kim regime publicly touted the North's possession of nuclear weapons. In mid-October, the leadership staged a mass rally in central Pyongyang to "welcome the historical successful nuclear test." Since the regime tightly controlled all information and limited contact of its people with the outside world, the regime was able to declare the test a success, much like the satellite beacon that was orbiting in the Three Revolutions Exhibition in Pyongyang.

During dinner, Ambassador Ri Gun asked surprisingly detailed technical questions about bombs. He was curious about plutonium production in the 5 MWe reactor. He asked if it made any difference as to whether it is loaded with fresh fuel or running on partially used fuel. I explained that it didn't really matter, either way it can produce a maximum of about 6 kilograms per year. He wanted to know what the relationship was between the yield of a device and the amount of plutonium it contained. After noting, "Nagasaki contained 6 kilograms of plutonium and produced 20 kilotons," Ri asked, "How much plutonium do you need for a 1 kiloton explosion?" He seemed to think it scaled directly with the amount of plutonium. Without getting into design details, I told Ri that it doesn't scale that way. At some point, I said, you simply don't have enough plutonium to produce a nuclear explosion at all. It seemed to me that Ri was asking these questions to get a sense of the veracity of the information he was being given about the nuclear test. He undoubtedly had read the Western news reports about what was called a failed nuclear test, and he had sparred with Jack Pritchard on that very point.

I asked Ri if it was true that the DPRK gave notice to China and Russia ahead of the nuclear test and had told them it would be a 4-kiloton explosion. Ri said they had given both Beijing and Moscow two-hours warning, but he was adamant that the notice did not mention the expected explosion yield.[1]

---

1. Our Foreign Ministry escort had told us the same thing earlier.

I pointed out that safety and security become a demanding responsibility for a state that possesses nuclear weapons. In addition, keeping fissile materials secure is paramount. Ambassador Ri asked me how other countries handle such responsibilities. I explained the work American nuclear scientists did with Russian nuclear scientists and engineers right after the dissolution of the Soviet Union when Russia faced immense safety and security challenges. Ri seemed to take some satisfaction that this work followed, not preceded, the Soviet Union's demise.

A BROADER PERSPECTIVE

The rather light nuclear agenda during this trip allowed John Lewis to schedule more cultural stops as part of his unyielding desire to look at the North Korean issue from a full 360-degree perspective—that is, looking at the economy, the educational system, health issues, and cultural aspects. John explored opportunities for the North to cooperate with American institutions, particularly with Stanford University. We met with representatives of the Committee on the Promotion of International Trade, the Peoples' National Economic University, and the Ministry of Education. Bob Carlin was especially interested in the North's economy and what effect Kim Jong Il's 2002 economic reforms had. Based on his many years of working on North Korea within the U.S. government, Carlin was convinced that rather than a singular focus on denuclearization, a much more holistic approach in dealing with the DPRK was required. He asked Dean So Jae Yong of the Economic University if there was room for a market economy in their socialist system. How were resources allocated within their Songun (military-first) policy? Do military needs come first, or does a strong economy bolster the military? Dean So said the economy was doing reasonably well due to the new economic reforms. The university's job, he told us, was to develop economic relations with foreign countries because without foreign trade, a country can't survive. But that was being made more difficult by increased U.S. sanctions, especially those restricting international financial transactions. However, since its founding, he said, defense has consistently been the number one priority for North Korea. First is the defense industry, second are those industries that support defense, and then come the light industries.

I found the visit with the Ministry of Education enlightening. Like so many of the Soviet and Eastern Bloc communist countries, education was a high priority. The ministry's dean of the faculty of Industrial Management,

and by 1958 middle school was compulsory. The entire educational system, including universities, was free. The literacy rate in the DPRK was close to 100 percent. The priority now was to improve the quality of education. They had 300 universities and colleges, with 100 of them being PhD-granting institutions. When asked if they had sufficient resources, Kim replied "No, but the sovereignty of the state comes first." They did wish they had more equipment to study areas such as nanotechnology and biotechnology. They had rather few foreign students, mostly those who wanted to study the Korean language. About 500 North Korean students were attending foreign universities. Lewis again explored collaboration with Stanford University and got a familiar reply: "Yes, we are interested, but it will depend on our governments."

We also got a firsthand look at the education system with a visit to Middle School No. 1, housed in a big six-story building with 1,500 students ages 10–11 to 16–17. It was a wonderful visit—ranging from students performing physics experiments to study magnetism and the thermoelectric effect, to chemistry and biology labs, to art classes and a music performance. My favorite stop was in an English-language class, in which we were told the students were writing essays about the West. I walked down the aisle and leaned over a student's notebook to see that her essay was about the American inventor, Thomas Alva Edison. It not only looked very well composed but was written in a beautiful calligraphy-style English.

We also visited the Three Revolutions Exhibition housed in a huge planetarium-shaped building. The exhibition celebrates the accomplishments of the country's leaders and glorifies the Juche ideology of self-reliance and independence. We were guided by a lively, smart young woman, who spoke impeccable English (with an American accent) and knew every detail about each exhibit. She explained that the little blinking red object circulating the Earth in the planetarium was the Kwangmyŏngsŏng satellite North Korea launched in 1998. Either she was unaware that the rocket had failed before it reached orbit, or she had to stick to the party script. The most entertaining part of the visit was the guide's explanation of the North Korean electrical grid. Standing in front of a huge map of the North, she lit up the various parts of the grid, powered either by hydropower or coal, and showed how much of the system supplies electricity around the country, particularly to Pyongyang. As she completed her tour de force explanation, our Ministry of Foreign Affairs minder stopped her dead in her tracks. "Why then do our lights keep going out all the time in Pyongyang?" he asked. We were happy to see he was still our minder the next morning.

We visited the Pyongyang Embroidery Institute close to the Ryugyong Hotel, the unfinished 105-story pyramid-shaped skyscraper, to look at the exquisite artwork. We also returned to the Tong-il Street Market. I was again impressed by the selection of goods, including meats, fruits, nuts, Nescafé instant coffee, small electrical appliances, batteries, and shoes—most goods made in China. We were told that the market opened in 2003 and was now pretty much at capacity, hosting 100,000 to 150,000 shoppers per day.

One of my favorite stops—and one many foreign visitors enjoy—was the stamp store around the corner from the hotel. North Korea, much like other former Soviet Bloc countries, put a lot of effort into commemorating historical, cultural, and technological accomplishments with postage stamps. I was able to buy stamps celebrating the 1998 satellite launch—the one that failed before it reached orbit. The kiosks across the street from the hotel were also busy—fried donuts, bananas, pineapples, Chinese pears, pepperoni pizzas, and rotisserie chickens. The chicken sold for 10,000 Korean won, which I was told by one of our minders was about four-months wage for the average worker.

COMPARING NOTES WITH THE CHINESE

Saturday morning, it was back on Air Koryo, destination Beijing, where I had arranged a meeting and a dinner with my Chinese nuclear colleagues. They were keenly interested in what we learned about the nuclear test. I asked Dr. Hu Side if the North Koreans gave China advance notice of the test. He said that the Chinese embassy in Pyongyang received notice two hours before the test. It was told the location, the time, and that the anticipated yield would be 4 kilotons. Hu claimed that the Russians were given similar information except for the expected yield. That pretty much mirrored what we had been told in Pyongyang, except the Chinese apparently did have information about the expected 4 kiloton yield.

Dr. Hu and his colleagues were well aware of the firestorm of reports in the Western media that the test was a fizzle. He said that based on the seismic signals of 4.1 to 4.2 on the Richter scale that China picked up—reminding us ~~the closest to the Punggye-ri test site~~—and their own assessment of the geological structure there, they believed the test was about 1 kiloton, not the several hundred tons estimated by most Western analysts. Hu's bottom line was that at 1 kiloton, it was a nuclear test. "They aimed for 4 kilotons," he said, "but they got 1 kiloton. I'd call it successful, but not perfect." After all, he said, a first nuclear test is not so easy.

Our discussion was quite speculative because it was difficult to come to definitive conclusions about the test only weeks after it was conducted. After the second test in 2009, North Korea revealed a lot more information about its test site and its efforts to safely contain the nuclear blasts. Based on that information and our detailed analysis of the test site topography and seismic signals, my colleague Frank Pabian and I concluded that the first test was conducted in a tunnel accessed by the east portal.[2] All subsequent tests were conducted in a series of tunnels accessed through the west portal. Another portal, the south portal, is not known to have been the site of nuclear tests to date. Our analysis pinpointed the exact location of the 2006 test and pegged it at just about 1 kiloton, very much in line with what we heard from the Chinese during this visit.

As Hu Side pointed out, a first test is not easy. There were many possible reasons that the North Korean test did not reach the 4-kiloton design yield. Implosion devices require perfect geometries as well as simultaneous detonation and precise neutron initiation. What was a greater puzzle was why they chose a design that would yield 4 kilotons, compared to the first U.S. test at 20 kilotons. Was the test designed to simply demonstrate nuclear capability or to develop a deliverable nuclear warhead? Hu thought they may have decided to test at a low yield of 4 kilotons to ensure safety—that is, containment of the blast in the underground tunnel. I pointed out that the general test experience shows that larger tests (on the order of tens of kilotons) are easier to fully contain because the larger blast does a better job

2. Frank V. Pabian and Siegfried S. Hecker, "Contemplating a Third Nuclear Test in North Korea," *Bulletin of the Atomic Scientists* (August 6, 2012), https://thebulletin.org/2012/08/contemplating-a-third-nuclear-test-in-north-korea

of sealing the test cavity. We concurred that although that information was available in the literature, the North Korean engineers may not have known it. Besides there was also the question of different containment experience for tunnels (such as the North Korean case) and vertical shafts (like most American tests).

We concluded that they contained the blast adequately. There was no blowout of bomb debris that resulted in massive radioactive contamination. To the Chinese, that was most important since Punggye-ri is less than 80 kilometers from the Chinese border. Despite extensive underground testing experience, the U.S. program suffered a massive blowout in the 1970 Baneberry event at the Nevada Test Site. It produced a radioactive cloud similar to a small atmospheric test and spewed contamination into neighboring states. I believe that North Korea was determined to avoid such a blowout, particularly because of the backlash it would receive from China. In our discussions in Pyongyang, General Ri Chan Bok had stressed the importance of having conducted the test safely.

A week after the test, the U.S. Office of the Director of National Intelligence reported that radioactive gaseous fission products were detected off-site on October 11, confirming that the blast was a nuclear test.[3] Our Chinese colleagues strongly disputed some U.S. news reports that the leaked radioactive gases indicated the device used plutonium. They were correct because by the time the samples were believed to have been collected, crucial data would have been lost on the xenon isotopic ratios, which are required to differentiate between a plutonium and a uranium bomb. In other words, the off-site monitoring did not tell us anything about the status of the North's uranium enrichment activities because it was not possible to distinguish between an HEU and plutonium device. In Pyongyang, however, Director Ri Hong Sop had told us that the first test was a plutonium device. The slight leakage of radioactive gases is not surprising because xenon is a noble gas, meaning it does not chemically interact with either the geologic surroundings or have much solubility in water. Hence, it can easily escape through rock fissures or porosity. The level of leakage from the North Korean test did

3. Joseph DeTrani, "Statement on North Korea Nuclear Test," *Office of the Director of National Intelligence* (October 13, 2006), https://www.odni.gov/files/documents/Newsroom/Press%20Releases/2006%20Press%20Releases/20061013_release.pdf

not represent a health hazard. Our Chinese colleagues told us that China did not pick up any radioactive signals in its air sampling because at that time of the year, the winds blow east, away from the Chinese border.

could detonate a nuclear device, I would have expected the North to choose a robust design, perhaps something along the lines of the Trinity test the United States conducted in 1945 and the Nagasaki nuclear device. That is precisely what the Soviet Union did in 1949. When I met Yuli B. Khariton, the Russian scientific leader of its nuclear weapons program, during my first visit to Russia in 1992, he told me they tested a Trinity look-alike in the first test. However, he added quickly, that by the time of the test, they had designed a bomb with twice the yield and half of the mass. When I asked why they didn't test their advanced design, Khariton said, "You have heard of Lavrenti Beria [Stalin's notorious henchman who had been put in charge of the overall bomb effort]? Well, we knew yours worked, and we wanted to live."

My first guess was that the North Koreans would choose a design like the Trinity device with sufficient plutonium that was known to work. In retrospect, they were not quite that cautious. After all, it was sixty years after Trinity, and the North may have had some assistance from Pakistan's A. Q. Khan. When Libya's Gaddafi relinquished his nuclear weapons program in 2003, he also turned over design information he had purchased from Kahn of a missile-capable HEU implosion device, a design that originated in China and was generally believed to be the CHIC-4, the fourth Chinese test device. Given Khan's uranium centrifuge cooperation with North Korea, it is likely that he also sold the nuclear bomb details to the North. Although that design was an HEU implosion device, it still would have been of great help to the North Koreans in calibrating their computer codes for a plutonium device. This is particularly true if Khan also gave North Korea access to the Pakistani nuclear test results.

It is, therefore, more likely that the North Korean nuclear scientists detonated a design that was much closer to a missile-capable device than the nearly 10,000-pound Trinity test model. When I asked the Chinese nuclear specialists if they thought the North Koreans tested a small, sophisticated (meaning missile-capable) device, they said it was likely small, but not sophisticated. At that time, there were also reports in the news media that the North Koreans may have used as little as 2 kilograms of plutonium in the test device. My Chinese colleagues and I concurred that such a low quantity of plutonium was simply not credible. Some Western analysts suggested that perhaps Kim Jong Il overruled his scientists and insisted on a riskier design with less plutonium. My Chinese colleagues told us that Mao Zedong had respected the opinions of the scientists. They expected a similar situation in North Korea.

Our meetings with Chinese DPRK scholars at the China Reform Forum and with Foreign Ministry officials, including Cui Tiankai, assistant minister of the Ministry of Foreign Affairs and later China's ambassador to the United States, underscored what we had heard in previous trips. Although China was unhappy with the North Korean nuclear test, it placed the burden directly on the Bush administration's shoulders for its hostile policy toward Pyongyang and its sanctions regime. North Korea, they said, developed nuclear weapons to protect itself from the United States. They believed the test had most likely united the North Korean people and strengthened the role of the military and hard-liners. It was likely, they said, that the lesson North Korea learned from the nuclear tests by India and Pakistan in 1998 was that the initial condemnation would be followed by acceptance of its nuclear status. They stressed that China had limited influence on North Korea, and it was time for the United States to make concessions to Pyongyang.

Upon our return to the United States, John Lewis provided a short summary of our trip to Secretary Condoleezza Rice. He reported that at Yongbyon, operations were in full swing. The North had now fully mastered the entire plutonium fuel cycle and was producing high-purity, weapons-grade plutonium. North Korean diplomats were fully aware of the criticism that missile and nuclear tests were less than successful and that U.S. pressure was seen as working—however, this did not appear to bother them. They believed the nuclear test provided deterrence, equal footing, and the ability to return to the Six-Party Talks. I prepared a written summary and presented it at a public meeting at the National Press Club in Washington, DC,[4] where the U.S. government viewed the North's nuclear test with not much more than some handwringing.

4. Siegfried S. Hecker, "Report on North Korean Nuclear Program" (November 15, 2006), https://fas.org/nuke/guide/dprk/nuke/hecker1106.pdf

9   2007: Back to the Negotiating Table

By early November 2006, the North's nuclear test was history. North Korean nuclear specialists successfully limited the radioactive fallout to a small seep-age of fission gases from the underground tunnel. Pyongyang was equally successful in limiting the political fallout despite having flaunted the inter-national nuclear nonproliferation regime. It became only the eighth nation to conduct an underground nuclear test and declare itself a nuclear weapon state. It was weathering immediate condemnation from around the globe including UN Security Council Resolution 1718 on October 15.

North Korea's strategy had succeeded. After the Bush administration derailed the September 2005 agreement with its unilateral statement, Pyong-yang had continued its dual-track approach. It was full speed ahead with its nuclearization efforts, while keeping diplomacy alive to buy time for the missile and nuclear tests. The American reaction to the tests was strangely passive. The price Pyongyang had to pay for the tests was to agree to return to the Six-Party Talks and put up with watered-down UN sanctions (thanks to Chinese and Russian insistence). The White House had its hands full with the deteriorating situation in Iraq and the Middle East. It also had just lost Republican majorities in both houses of Congress in the mid-term elections, and it was revamping the administration's national security team. Over the next few months, several of the most ardent hard-liners, including

Secretary of Defense Donald Rumsfeld, UN Ambassador John Bolton, and Assistant Secretary of State Robert Joseph left their government positions, although they continued to voice their opposition to talking with North Korea from the sidelines.

Secretary Rice found a silver lining in that the test gave a boost to the new policy toward North Korea that had been conceived in April but had been blocked by the hard-line elements of the administration that now had less influence in the White House. Instead of punishing North Korea, the administration now tried a more conciliatory approach that primarily entailed giving Ambassador Chris Hill more running room to make a deal with the North. At the Asia-Pacific Economic Cooperation Forum on November 19, President Bush and his team signaled that they were willing to "dangle a new set of incentives" for North Korea, but in return they would need the North to come to the next round of the Six-Party Talks in December prepared to take concrete steps to immediately begin dismantling and disarming the nuclear program.[1] Hill followed up in Beijing with specific proposals to Vice Minister Kim Gye Gwan and Chinese officials at the end of November. Kim and his team returned to the Six-Party Talks in late December. Although the parties made little headway, the North Koreans did get something they had been denied through the first six years of the Bush administration—direct bilateral dialogue with American counterparts.

As the new year dawned, Kim Jong Il must have been pleasantly surprised as he reflected on the events of 2006. The nuclear test had served to shore up domestic support, and although it was initially condemned by the international community, it also surely afforded North Korea a new sense of pride and some measure of prestige on the international stage. North Korea was now one of a small number of countries that claimed nuclear power status. The half-life of the prestige far exceeded that of the condemnation.

Whereas Pyongyang gained domestic and international benefits from the nuclear test, the third and most important reason to possess nuclear weapons—namely, enhanced security—was not accomplished because

1. Helene Cooper and David E. Sanger, "U.S. Signals New Incentives for North Korea," *New York Times* (November 19, 2006), https://www.nytimes.com/2006/11/19/world/asia/us-signals-new-incentives-for-north-korea.html

of the test's limited success.[2] From a security perspective, conducting a less-than-successful test left Pyongyang worse off than before. North Korea's claims to a nuclear deterrent would have been more credible and persuasive

actual capabilities. The test undoubtedly gave the North's nuclear specialists valuable technical insight into how to remedy the problem, but it meant that North Korea would have to test again because it had conclusively demonstrated that it could not field a viable nuclear device. Fortunately for the North, the technical path to a second nuclear test was quite straightforward. The North's designers and engineers likely got to work the day after the first device was detonated. The political path was much less certain.

THE DUAL TRACK CONTINUES WITH REJUVENATED DIPLOMACY

Pyongyang remained on its dual-track path—nuclearization and diplomacy. On the nuclear front, the Stanford delegation was told in October 2006 that operations at Yongbyon were proceeding rapidly. The weapons designers were surely working to refine their design to incorporate the lessons from the first test. In parallel, Vice Minister Kim Gye Gwan was working the diplomatic levers on multiple fronts, although it was not clear how seriously North Korea would pursue the diplomatic path. During the next two years, the last of the Bush administration, Kim Jong Il appears to have given Vice Minister Kim room to make a deal, much as Washington did for Ambassador Hill. They both fell short.

Diplomacy got an important boost during the moribund December Six-Party Talks in Beijing as the parties were preparing to adjourn for the holidays. A quiet bilateral meeting between Vice Minister Kim's staff and part of Ambassador Hill's delegation led to a meeting between Hill and Kim in Berlin in mid-January 2007 that sketched out the essence of a new deal.[3] The key to getting the North Koreans to come back to the Six-Party Talks and engage on denuclearization was that Hill committed the United

2. Siegfried S. Hecker, "Lessons Learned from the North Korean Nuclear Crises," *Daedalus* 139, no.1 (Winter 2010): 44–56.

3. Christopher Hill, *Outpost: Life on the Frontlines of American Diplomacy: A Memoir* (New York: Simon & Schuster, 2014), 253.

States to a process leading to the release of $25 million of North Korean assets frozen in its BDA accounts. It was somewhat puzzling that Pyongyang appeared to prioritize resolving the BDA sanctions when it looked like they used these mostly as a pretext to buy time. Perhaps they just wanted to see Washington wriggle to find a solution, especially since, as Hill admitted in his memoir, nobody had quite yet figured out how to resolve the sanctions problem.[4] Others believe that Pyongyang's concern about being shut out of the international financial system had them place high priority on resolving the BDA issue.[5]

The next session of the Six-Party Talks, in mid-February, quickly produced the "Initial Actions for the Implementation of the Joint Statement."[6] On the surface, it seemed to signal that the North was done buying time and was about to get serious again about diplomacy. The actions-for-actions list included the DPRK agreement to shut down and seal the Yongbyon nuclear center, for the purpose of eventual abandonment, including the reprocessing facility, and to invite back IAEA personnel to conduct all necessary monitoring and verifications as agreed between IAEA and the DPRK. In addition, the DPRK would discuss with other parties a list of "all its nuclear programs as described in the [September 2005] Joint Statement, including plutonium extracted from used fuel rods, that would be abandoned pursuant to the Joint Statement." The qualifying language—as described in the joint statement—unfortunately gave the North room to avoid answering for its HEU program. Hill had to return to this in subsequent discussions with Kim Gye Gwan.

The list of "initial actions" included the DPRK and the United States starting "bilateral talks aimed at resolving pending bilateral issues and moving toward full diplomatic relations." And the parties agreed to cooperate in economic, energy, and humanitarian assistance to the DPRK. On the sidelines, Hill promised to resolve the BDA sanctions issue, which eventually happened. Importantly, unlike in September 2005, the United States did

---

4. Ibid., 255.

5. S. Haggard and M. Nolad, *Hard Target: Sanctions, Inducements, and the Case of North Korea* (Stanford: Stanford University Press, 2017).

6. "North Korea–Denuclearization Action Plan," *U.S. Department of State Archive* (February 13, 2007), https://2001-2009.state.gov/r/pa/prs/ps/2007/february/80479.htm

not add deal-breaking additions in a unilateral statement. It appeared that Hill was given a chance to make the 2005 joint statement work this time.

To resolve the BDA sanctions, Washington struggled to extract itself

tion. It wasn't until June that the Federal Reserve, with the assistance of an obscure Siberian bank, was able to get the bulk of the $25 million returned to the DPRK. In the meantime, Kim Gye Gwan vigorously pursued diplomatic initiatives to implement a deal to Pyongyang's liking.

One of Kim's more unusual stops along the diplomatic whirlwind was meeting with John Lewis and our Stanford team in California at the Inn at Saratoga. During his trips to North Korea, John Lewis had extended a standing invitation for Kim to visit Stanford University. In late February, the UN mission asked Lewis if he could arrange for a visit by Kim in one week's time. Kim was coming to the United States to meet with Ambassador Hill in New York City in early March and thought this would be a good time to come to Stanford and meet with our team. Remarkably, Lewis was able to get State Department approval in time. Concerned about the potential of having a news media mob on the open Stanford campus, John arranged the meeting at the quiet inn in nearby Saratoga. I provide greater detail about the Saratoga discussions in the next chapter.

From the west coast, Kim and his entourage flew to New York City for two days of talks with Hill. Discussions focused on how to finally resolve the BDA sanctions issue, what it would take to get North Korea removed from the U.S. list of State Sponsors of Terrorism, and how to get them off the old (1917) Trading with the Enemies Act. Hill pressed Kim for disclosure of all the North's nuclear programs, including highly enriched uranium.[7] On April 14, the Banco Delta Asia sanctions were lifted after the U.S. Treasury Department announced that had ended its investigation. It would take another two months, including another round of Six-Party Talks, to resolve the technical issues to release the money.

The administration remained steadfast in working toward a deal, but Washington hard-liners were unrelenting in their opposition. Although John Bolton had left the administration, he continued to use the op-ed

7. David E. Sanger, "U.S. to Offer North Korea Face-Saving Nuclear Plan," *New York Times* (March 5, 2007), https://www.nytimes.com/2007/03/05/world/asia/05korea.html

pages of various news outlets to voice his displeasure. Before the February statement, he wrote, "Any deal that they [North Korea] would agree to now is no good. It is inconceivable that they will agree to the intrusive inspection regime that we need to have any confidence they would live up to the terms of the deal."[8] Bob Joseph, who also had departed the administration, weighed in after the parties came close to a deal, saying, "The deal would perpetuate the rule of a government that holds political prisoners in gulags and trades in drugs and counterfeits American currency, using the profits to build its nuclear arsenal."[9] There were no hints of remorse that both had failed when they were in government. Bolton's hammer gave us the North's bombs. Joseph's pen, authoring the U.S. unilateral statement that unraveled the September 19 deal, gave us the North's first nuclear test.

Astute North Korea watchers like Bob Carlin and John Lewis viewed the situation differently from Bolton and Joseph. In a January *Washington Post* op-ed, they argued that above all, and what North Korea had pursued steadily since 1991, was

> a long-term, strategic relationship with the United States, which is derived from a cold, hard calculation based on history and the realities of geopolitics as perceived in Pyongyang, where North Koreans believe in their gut that they must buffer the heavy influence their neighbors already have, or could soon gain, over their small, weak country.[10]

This is why, they said, the North has been "doggedly" seeking bilateral talks with the United States, and why the six-party process had not been productive.[11]

On June 25, most of the $25 million in the BDA accounts was finally released to North Korea's bank accounts. IAEA inspectors, led by the superbly knowledgeable Deputy Director General Olli Heinonen, were back

8. Glenn Kessler, "N. Korea May Accept Deal in Nuclear Talks," *Washington Post* (January 31, 2007): A12.

9. David E. Sanger, "Money Shift Could Clear Way to Shut North Korea Reactor," *New York Times* (April 7, 2007), https://www.nytimes.com/2007/04/07/world/asia/07korea.html

10. Robert Carlin and John W. Lewis, "What North Korea Really Wants," *Washington Post* (January 27, 2007). https://cisac.fsi.stanford.edu/news/what_north_korea_really_wants_20070127

11. Ibid.

in North Korea the next day. On July 15, North Korea announced it had shut down the 5 MWe reactor and supporting facilities at Yongbyon, which was confirmed two days later by the IAEA. The Six-Party Talks reconvened

Yongbyon facilities and have North Korea submit a complete declaration of its nuclear program.

A MODICUM OF PROGRESS ON THE NUCLEAR FRONT

Shutting down the Yongbyon complex again, and agreeing to take disablement steps toward eventual dismantlement in 2007, appeared to be strong signals that Pyongyang was, indeed, again pursuing diplomacy seriously, rather than just buying time for the nuclear program. But concurrently, as we learned later, North Korea was still moving along the nuclear path, preparing for its second nuclear test. Work also continued on a long-range rocket system to rectify the problems that sent their last attempt, in July 2006, crashing into the sea after forty-two seconds. By this time, the uranium centrifuge program must have been at a prototype testing stage. And, as would be revealed in two months' time, the North was close to completing construction of the reactor in Syria.

Nevertheless, shutting down Yongbyon was not a minor step. It would completely stop the North's plutonium production, at that point still the country's only source of fissile material for nuclear weapons. The fuel rods in the reactor since summer of 2005 were estimated to contain 10 to 12 kilograms of plutonium. The disablement agreement would allow unloading the fuel rods, but they were to be stored rather than reprocessed. Considering that at that time North Korea was believed to have a meager plutonium inventory of 24 to 42 kilograms, shutting down the reactor would seriously limit the program.[12]

Consequently, I believe that once Kim Jong Il realized that the first nuclear test appeared to have garnered diplomatic leverage rather than ostracization (or worse, a military response), he gave Kim Gye Gwan and the diplomats another chance to see if they could reach a deal to move them toward normalization with Washington. But he also instructed the nuclear

12. S. S. Hecker, "Report on North Korean Nuclear Program," National Press Club, Washington, DC, November 15, 2006.

and missile teams to proceed in case diplomacy did not work out. In other words, both paths of the dual-track strategy were given the green light, unlike what had happened from 2002 to 2006, when diplomacy was merely buying time for developing the nuclear program.

For example, in 2007, Vice Minister Kim was moving aggressively on several engagement fronts. Pyongyang accepted John Lewis's invitation for a medical team to visit Stanford University to consult with the Bay Area Tuberculosis Consortium to explore collaboration to help North Korea deal with multiple-drug-resistant TB, which had reached alarming levels. During meetings with Ambassador Hill, Kim dropped hints about the North's desire for broader cultural exchanges, including a visit to Pyongyang by the New York Philharmonic—an invitation that was extended directly to the orchestra in August. Also in August, the Stanford delegation was invited back to Yongbyon to witness some of the disablement actions and to see previously undisclosed laboratories. IAEA inspectors were given access to the Yongbyon facilities they had inspected during the Agreed Framework. To top things off, in August the two Koreas announced a summit meeting for later that month between Chairman Kim and South Korean President Roh Moo Hyun to explore steps toward reconciliation. The summit ended up having to be postponed until October because of torrential rains in the North.

A SURPRISE IN SYRIA

On September 6, 2007, the world was abuzz with reports of a daring Israeli airstrike inside of Syria. The Bush administration had already been alerted by the head of Israeli intelligence in mid-April about the Syrian reactor and the North's involvement. It chose to remain silent on the strike, as did Israel for reasons explained in the next chapter. For now, suffice it to say that key Bush administration officials, particularly Ambassador Hill, who was one of the very few in the U.S. government read into the secret existence of the reactor and its destruction, did not want the Syria issue to derail negotiations with North Korea. Yet, the event and how it was handled by the administration made a difficult job of negotiating a deal with North Korea essentially impossible. Whatever little support existed in Washington for the administration's current strategy to engage the North Koreans began to evaporate as more and more information came to light about the Syria incident. Hill was in the awkward position of knowing, but not being allowed to talk. He generally gave non-answers in response to inquiries about North Korea's attempt to pull off one of the most daring

> "We've always been concerned about the issue of proliferation. To me, this simply is an important reminder of the need to accelerate the process which we've already engaged in, to achieve denuclearization of the Korean Peninsula, and the issue does not change the goal of what we're aiming for."[13]

These words did not dissuade critics such as John Bolton, who warned, "They are rushing to finish this [that is, to end the discussion] and declare victory, which could be a catastrophe for the president."[14] In his memoir *Outpost*, Hill recounts that after having received CIA permission to share photographs of North Korea's complicity in the Syrian reactor with Vice Foreign Minister Kim, the response was that they were photoshopped. Until the following April when the United States made public the details behind the Syrian reactor and its destruction, the U.S. government appeared to sweep this open secret under the rug.

TAKING DISABLEMENT STEPS

The North Koreans in the meantime continued their diplomatic outreach. A week after the Syrian air strikes, American technical specialists were in Yongbyon along with Russian and Chinese specialists to get a better sense of how the disablement steps should proceed. By the end of September, President Bush authorized the first shipment in five years of U.S. heavy fuel oil to North Korea, meant to be seen as a concrete U.S. step in support of the "action for action" bargain. The diplomats also reconvened the Six-Party Talks in Beijing. These concluded with very specific recommendations of how the disablement process and the rest of the steps to achieve the objectives of the September 2005 joint statement should proceed.

13. Glenn Kessler, "N. Korea, Syria May Be at Work on Nuclear Facility," *Washington Post* (September 13, 2007), https://www.washingtonpost.com/wp-dyn/content/article/2007/09/12/AR2007091202430.html

14. Mark Mazzetti and Helene Cooper, "U.S. Official Says Syria May Have Nuclear Ties," *New York Times* (September 15, 2007), https://www.nytimes.com/2007/09/15/world/middleeast/15intel.html

The resulting October 3 second-phase actions statement called on North Korea to provide a "complete and correct" declaration of all its nuclear programs—including clarification regarding the enrichment issue—by the end of the year.[15] That didn't shut the barn door completely, but it was at least a step beyond the February statement, which had been silent on enrichment. Pyongyang also agreed to disable Yongbyon facilities, and it repeated a pledge not to transfer nuclear materials, technology, and know-how. This latter commitment was certainly brazen on the North's part, so soon after the Syrian episode, and it was hard to fathom on Washington's part. Even though none of those involved—the Israelis, the Syrians, the North Koreans, or the Americans—had yet to officially acknowledge what had happened, there was already plenty of public reporting and speculation.

Although the administration had kicked the Syria reckoning down the road, it would run up against the insurmountable difficulty of getting North Korea to produce a "complete and correct" declaration up front. Washington insisted that the declaration must encompass the plutonium program, the uranium enrichment issue, and (per private discussion between Hill and Kim Gye Gwan) North Korea's nuclear cooperation with Syria. Over the next nine months, North Korea took serious steps to disable the Yongbyon nuclear facilities and made some surprising attempts to pacify Washington's demands for declaration of its plutonium program, but it continued to stonewall the uranium enrichment and Syria questions. North Korea's stalling may have proved an insurmountable barrier in the long run, but what immediately precipitated the demise of the negotiations was the administration's abrupt insistence on intrusive verification measures before the negotiations had produced the necessary trust, compounded by a medical emergency in Pyongyang.

15. "Six Parties October 3, 2007 Agreement on 'Second-Phase Actions for Implementation of the Joint Statement,'" *U.S. Department of State Archive*, https://2001-2009.state.gov/r/pa/prs/ps/2007/oct/93223.htm

10 2007 and 2008 Visits:
Back to Yongbyon to Confirm Disablement

John Lewis did not waste much time after we returned from our November 2006 trip to press the DPRK UN mission in New York for a return visit. In addition to tackling the nuclear issues, he also continued to press for broader educational, medical, and cultural exchanges. Lewis's efforts brought me back to North Korea in 2007 and 2008 during a time of active diplomatic engagement—when the first serious steps were taken that could have led to rolling back the nuclear program in Yongbyon.

NORTH KOREAN DELEGATION STOPS IN SARATOGA
Vice Minister Kim Gye Gwan was equally eager to reengage. Through the DPRK UN mission, he had arranged for the aforementioned visit to Lewis and our Stanford team in Saratoga, California. John Lewis was out on the tarmac with FBI agents at the San Francisco airport on the morning of March 1 to whisk Vice Minister Kim and his delegation away to avoid facing reporters in the airport. However, South Korean reporters had already gotten wind of Kim's trip and booked tickets in business class not far from Kim. From the San Francisco airport to Saratoga, Kim and his team were escorted by California Highway Patrol cars and motorcycles that blocked

the highway entrances along the way. Some of the news media, however, had staked things out well enough that when Vice Minister Kim, his entourage, John Lewis, and the FBI escorts arrived at the sleepy little Inn at Saratoga, they were right behind them. Fortunately, the FBI was able to keep them off the premises so that the inn provided an ideal place for relaxed, candid dialogue for our Stanford group with the seven-member Kim delegation. Kim was accompanied by Ms. Choe Son Hui and several other familiar faces from the North American Bureau. In addition to Bob Carlin and several Stanford University faculty members, John Lewis had also invited John Merrill, an experienced North Korea hand from the State Department's Bureau of Intelligence and Research.

This visit was part of Vice Minister Kim's multipronged diplomacy campaign that would soon take him to New York to meet with Ambassador Hill for in-depth discussions on moving forward with the February action plan, including finally resolving the BDA sanctions issue. After a short rest, in the comfortable and quiet atmosphere of the inn, Kim told us that he wanted our Stanford delegation to understand how Pyongyang was planning to carry out the steps of the February action plan. He was upbeat about the plan, saying, "The agreement is not based on the collapse of my government—this time it recognizes our sovereignty and pledges co-existence." Kim told us that Pyongyang was prepared to denuclearize in accordance with the September 2005 joint statement, but that it would have to be done step by step in concert with progress toward normalization of U.S.–DPRK relations. Since Pyongyang questioned the Bush administration's commitment to the agreement, he said the North would keep two safety nets—the weapons for now and reversible disablement steps in its nuclear facilities. Kim told us if the proper steps were taken, "Pyongyang sees no need to keep nuclear weapons and is committed to rejoining the NPT and admitting IAEA inspectors." When asked why the nuclear test hadn't changed that long-term commitment, Kim replied that it was just a small science test, unlike the first tests of other nations that had gone nuclear. It sounded as if Kim was still trying to come to terms with the fact their first test hadn't worked so well.

Kim made another impassioned pitch for a light water reactor, a position that had been pushed to the background during the prior six-party session. He reiterated what he had told us in August 2005 that an LWR was important politically and symbolically, as well as economically. He noted that it had been an important factor in the North's willingness to give up the graphite-moderated reactors. Besides, as he had stressed before, by providing the North with an LWR, which would take years to construct, it would symbolize U.S.

of the potential of developing a cooperative threat reduction program as North Korea denuclearized—something along the lines of what the United States did with Russia at the end of the Cold War. I described my experience working hand in hand with the Russian nuclear scientists to help some of them transition from military work to civilian work, as well as to secure and safeguard the fissile materials we each had produced over the years. Kim professed to show some interest but said that at this point the LWR was more important.

Some of the most spirited discussion centered on the question of uranium enrichment. Kim recounted his previous explanations of what happened during the fateful visit to Pyongyang by Ambassador Kelly in October 2002. When I reminded him again that every nuclear country has explored both paths to the bomb, he told me, "You don't understand everything about our country. We chose to pursue a civilian nuclear program with reactors." I didn't say, as I might I have, that those reactors were turned to bomb building. When I pressed, he said that they were prepared to clarify the uranium enrichment issue to the United States. At dinner in a little Italian restaurant that evening, he mentioned that when this enrichment question first came up in October 2002, he had asked a lot of their people, but nobody gave him answers. He said, "This issue remains one of my biggest headaches." We thought it was quite possible that in October 2002, Vice Minister Kim had not been told of the North's enrichment efforts. But, even considering the North Korean stove-piped information system, it was inconceivable that he didn't know it in 2007.

At one point when discussing the motivations of the different players on the Korean Peninsula, Kim lauded the *Washington Post* op-ed piece that Carlin and Lewis had recently written in which they stated that what Pyongyang really wanted a long-term, strategic relationship with the United States to buffer the heavy influence their neighbors already had, or would soon gain, over their small, weak country.[1] Kim said that was "exactly right."

1. Robert Carlin and John W. Lewis, "What North Korea Really Wants," *Washington Post* (January 27, 2007), https://cisac.fsi.stanford.edu/news/what_north_korea_really_wants_20070127

I thought this was more than just a nice gesture to Carlin and Lewis—it sounded genuine.

At dinner, I alerted Kim that I was about to publish an article presenting my best estimates of the North's nuclear program.[2] In it, I assessed the plutonium program based on my visits to Yongbyon and said that the evidence pointed to the North having a centrifuge program. I also described what I considered to be one of the most dangerous aspects of the North's nuclear program—namely, potential nuclear cooperation with Iran. Kim didn't push back but said that he knew the greatest concern in Washington right now was to have North Korea stop making more plutonium and to make sure that plutonium was not exported. We knew Kim was always fast on his feet, but what came next surprised us. The vice minister raised his glass of wine and said, "This is the most important issue—one must keep these materials out of the hands of terrorists." For reasons explained below, I doubted the sincerity of this comment.

In the article I mentioned to Kim, I expressed concern about a potential marriage made in hell if North Korea and Iran collaborated on nuclear programs. I thought the probability that Pyongyang would sell plutonium to Iran was low, unless it had been able to complete the larger reactors and greatly expand plutonium production. The likelihood of cooperating on nuclear technologies was much greater. Iran was pursuing the uranium path to the bomb covertly. North Korea had developed the requisite know-how and technologies to produce metallic uranium components for its reactor fuel, knowledge that could help Iran build metallic uranium components for bombs. Iran, on the other hand, after having received assistance from North Korea to build its first liquid-fueled missiles, had moved ahead of North Korea with solid-fueled missile technologies that were critical to the North's missile ambitions. Politically, it wasn't clear if the two would forge such nuclear bonds since relations were not as close between North Korea and Iran as they were for North Korea with several other Middle East countries such as Egypt and Syria. As of March 2007, we had no idea that North Korea was deeply involved in building a plutonium production reactor in Syria. I was not made aware of that until the Fourth of July holiday.

2. Siegfried S. Hecker and William Liou, "Dangerous Dealings: North Korea's Nuclear Capabilities and the Threat of Export to Iran," *Arms Control Today* 37, no. 2 (March 2007): 1.

As I learned later, after the White House was alerted by Israeli intelligence that the Syrian reactor was nearing completion, Prime Minister Ehud Olmert asked President Bush to destroy the reactor. Vice President

Bush mounted a closely held investigation to assess the intelligence. He did not want to repeat the mistakes of 2003 when the administration launched an invasion of Iraq to eliminate Saddam Hussein's nuclear weapons that didn't exist. During the 2007 summer holiday break, I returned to Los Alamos from Stanford University. I received a visit from a U.S. government official who laid out the Syria evidence. I was asked to come back to CIA headquarters to assess the rest of the information that the U.S. team had expertly assembled. I was convinced that the structure in question was, indeed, a nuclear reactor close to becoming operational and that North Korea had a major role in its construction.

President Bush accepted the intelligence community's assessment that Syria was building a nuclear reactor, but he decided it was not sufficient cause for the United States to take preemptive military action. He left it to the Israelis, but with the understanding that the U.S. government would remain silent, which it did until the following April. I was also bound by secrecy, but I viewed this as North Korea's most audacious nuclear transgression.

AUGUST 2007 VISIT TO PYONGYANG AND YONGBYON

On August 7, John Lewis, Bob Carlin, the State Department's John Merrill, and I were back in Pyongyang. We had followed our typical route through Beijing, meeting again with our Chinese colleagues prior to and after the North Korea trip. We were not expecting to return to North Korea so soon because we had hosted Vice Minister Kim Gye Gwan in California just five months earlier. But John Lewis had received a call from the DPRK UN mission in late July, requesting that we return to Pyongyang during this week in August because the vice minister had only a short time window before his next six-party commitments. Kim had previously told Lewis that he wanted me along on future visits because my technical knowledge "would provide greater transparency of the DPRK nuclear program." Although I realized that they practice "selective" transparency, I was still ready to see the Yongbyon facilities again firsthand since we had not visited in 2005 or 2006.

At the Koryo Hotel, we were hosted for dinner by Vice Minister Kim, Ms. Choe Son Hui, and other representatives of the ministry's North American Bureau. Kim thanked us for the hospitality we extended him and his team in Saratoga. He was upbeat about the status of negotiations. He lauded the benefits of bilateral discussions with Americans now that Ambassador Hill had been given the okay to talk by the administration. He told us that we would visit the Yongbyon nuclear complex and assess the disablement actions they had taken. Kim was eager to get my views on the disablement actions, but not before he described disablement as a complicated process that involved numerous issues—technical, political, and environmental. He said that it would have to be done in stages. He demonstrated detailed knowledge of what would be involved in disabling the facilities and wanted to get concurrence from me that to do it safely, it would take time.

Although Kim was correct, he was clearly looking to use the disablement time clock to the North's diplomatic advantage. It appeared to me they had worked out multiple fallback positions to preserve maximum tactical flexibility in the negotiating process. Initial disablement steps would be reversible. Irreversible dismantlement steps would come only at the end, and only in conjunction with the provision of an LWR. Kim made it clear that "if the U.S. doesn't want to give us LWRs, then we can't go to irreversibility."

The entire focus of the disablement discussion was on the Yongbyon nuclear complex and the production of fissile material. We got the impression that discussing what would happen to their nuclear weapons was off the table as anything but a rhetorical "eventual" goal. When I asked about the rest of the nuclear weapons enterprise, Kim said I should "tell the people at Yongbyon to show you the process of weaponizing." I did not understand that comment until later, when during the Yongbyon visit they showed me the plutonium glovebox labs. It is in these labs that the plutonium product from the reprocessed spent fuel is refined to metallic, weapon-grade plutonium. When I asked Kim about seeing the weapons themselves, Kim smiled, "Not yet; we are still belligerent parties."

The issue of enrichment came up only briefly. At one point, Kim said he was speaking "off the record," implying that he was taking us into his confidence. I have no doubt that his remarks were carefully scripted to further enable the North to maneuver on the enrichment issue. Kim said that North Korea would deal with enrichment "completely" at the time of its declaration. We found it interesting that Kim had gradually softened

delegations since January 2004. At that time, he insisted that the DPRK had no uranium enrichment program—no facilities, no equipment, and no technical people trained in uranium enrichment. By March 2007, he told us at dinner in Saratoga that in October 2002 he couldn't get answers on enrichment from his own people. And now he would not say definitively that the North did not have an enrichment program—only that it would be dealt with in the declaration.

The next day, Ambassador Ri Gun, whose approach was well coordinated with his vice minister's, elaborated on the disablement theme. He said that stages of disablement of their facilities should correspond with stages in construction of LWRs. He acknowledged that disablement followed by dismantlement would, of course, present serious challenges for what to do with the nuclear workers. Kim had told us that the director at Yongbyon was not happy with the current shutdown. He said that we would be able to judge their progress and their mood ourselves when we visited Yongbyon the next day.

MOVING BEYOND THE NUCLEAR ISSUE

Our delegation was interested in promoting the theme of U.S.–DPRK "normalization." Lewis and Carlin believed that if normalization were to be sustained and truly significant, it had to be broadened and deepened across the spectrum, beyond the nuclear issues and formal diplomatic steps. With Vice Minister Kim's help, Lewis was able to arrange meetings with officials from the education and health ministries. These visits and discussions revealed a significant, and very positive, shift in the North's approach on the overall question of nonofficial engagement with the United States.

A visit to Pyongyang No. 3 Tuberculosis Hospital, headed by Hospital Chief Dr. Li Jong Chan, explored cooperation to combat multiple-drug-resistant tuberculosis. I must confess to being on edge as we walked through the hospital's TB research wing. I know how to judge nuclear risk and how to monitor for nuclear radiation but felt quite helpless in the TB labs. We

2007 and 2008 Visits   175

survived the visit, and Lewis was able to set in motion the visit from a North Korean medical team to Stanford University and the Bay Area Tuberculosis Consortium the following January. The visit to the Ministry of Education started off quite slowly, but Lewis was also able to bring that into positive territory. Promises of follow up, however, never materialized from the North Korean side. Our delegation also got an audience with Kim Yong Dae, the vice president of the Supreme People's Assembly. Much like during our 2006 visit, this was strictly a pro forma courtesy call.

We visited the small cyclotron laboratory in which the North Korean scientists conducted nuclear physics research. It was a small, dated facility, although I enjoyed the enthusiasm of the elderly director who showed us around in the sweltering heat without electricity in the building. He told us that power outages were sufficiently common to greatly limit their research programs. At one point the power failed, and the small room went dark. The director laughed and said he was grateful to the United States for cutting off the heavy fuel oil shipments because now his technicians were accomplished at completely taking apart and putting the machine back together in the dark. The facility and discussions confirmed my belief that North Korea had very limited nuclear science capabilities, but as witnessed at Yongbyon, good engineering know-how.

RETURN TO YONGBYON

On August 10, we traveled to Yongbyon in Toyota Land Cruisers, through light traffic but heavy rain. We were greeted by the new director general, Ri Sang Gun, Assistant Director Choi Kil Man, and Li Yong Ho, the affable head of the safeguards section, who accompanied us during our 2004 visit. I was surprised not to see former Director Ri Hong Sop, who was our host in 2004 and who met us in Pyongyang in 2005 and 2006. I was told that he was no longer director and now resided in Pyongyang. The implication was that he had retired, but as we found out several years later when he appeared in the North Korean media showing Kim Jong Un their nuclear devices, he was anything but retired.

We confirmed that operations at the three primary facilities—the 5 MWe reactor complex, the reprocessing complex, and the fuel fabrication complex—had been halted. At the reactor, we were limited to only those rooms with windows providing access to daylight because the overnight storms had caused a major power outage. We did see IAEA seals and cameras back in place to prevent clandestine restarting of operations. The fuel rods that contained an estimated 10 to 12 kilograms of plutonium remained in the

dioxide coolant, although we were told the operators were prepared to restart the two blowers at low speed if the temperatures rose. The new chief engineer, Yu Sun Chol, said that the fuel could remain there for years if necessary, so that the best technical and political decisions could be made for the disposition of the fuel rods. Yu told us that the reactor could be restarted and operated for another two years with the current load of fuel. Director General Ri Sang Gun said it would require 200 days to remove the fuel rods if the decision was made to do so. They were clearly setting up the possibility that they could drag out the reactor unloading because the last time they removed the fuel (to extract the plutonium), they did it in only two months. They also acknowledged that they had been operating the reactor at lower power and at reduced temperature. This contrasted with 2004, when then-Director Ri Hong Sop proudly stated that they were able to restore reactor operations after the Agreed Framework at the full design power of 25 MWth. The lower power operation may have been a harbinger of the difficulties they would have in restarting operations in the future.

On the way to the Radiochemical Laboratory, we drove by the abandoned 50 MWe reactor. It was even in worse shape than when we saw it in 2004. Most likely it was now not salvageable. However, the graphite blocks for the reactor core fabricated prior to 1994 and stored in Yongbyon (now under IAEA watch) would have to be destroyed to make it more difficult to build such a reactor at a different site. To our knowledge, that was not done.

The power was still out as we got to the Radiochemical Laboratory, but they were determined to take us through the facility to demonstrate that it had been shut down and cameras and seals had been put in place to monitor the status. It was a surreal experience to walk through the corridors and peer into the hot cells using flashlights. I was looking forward to the promised visit to the laboratory in which the plutonium metal was produced. During my 2004 visit, I was shown the plutonium metal product but was not taken to those labs. The plutonium production labs were housed in a two-story annex to the Radiochemical Laboratory and had not been accessed by IAEA inspectors or the U.S. technical teams. In June, Olli Heinonen,

IAEA's Deputy Director General, was shown the labs for the first time. I was hoping to see the labs to give me a better sense of how sophisticated their plutonium operations were, how large the facilities were, and what sort of safety practices they had in place. The safety question was answered immediately when we were told that the power just came back on, and we could enter the labs.

To get the nod to go into a plutonium glovebox facility minutes after power was restored was unusual to say the least. The last time I faced such a situation was in September 1993 at Los Alamos, the first day at my new job as division director of CMB (Chemistry-Metallurgy-Baker) Division, which had responsibility for all plutonium facilities. In the afternoon, severe thunderstorms knocked the power out in the Chemistry-Metallurgy Research building. I did not go home until 6 the next the morning because balancing the complex ventilation systems in plutonium labs is crucial to prevent radiation leakage from the gloveboxes. The pressure in the gloveboxes must remain more negative than in the lab, which in turn must be more negative than the hallways and offices in the building. The idea is to keep the plutonium confined in the gloveboxes. At Los Alamos, I thought it was necessary for me to stay to oversee the safe restoration of the ventilation system.

When Director Ri Sang Gun gave us a big smile and said let's go, I decided that I would go with them but advised my American colleagues to sit this one out. I had two criteria to decide if I would enter the labs. First, if the director doesn't go in, I don't go. Apparently, he was planning to because he was putting on the requisite smocks and booties. The second criterion was to look which way the gloves were pointing when we entered the glovebox laboratories. If the pressure in the boxes was lower than in the lab, as it should be, the gloves would point inwards. If they pointed outwards, you run like hell. Fortunately, they pointed in.

We had time to see three of the four laboratories in which plutonium metal was produced, purified, and alloyed (a step in which gallium is added to molten plutonium to obtain the desired engineering properties). The glovebox labs were quite primitive, but functional, and the interiors of the boxes were remarkably clean considering they did not have sophisticated glovebox atmosphere controls. The lack of radiation monitors at the gloveboxes and general layout of the labs indicated they had only the most basic safety practices in place—similar to the plutonium laboratories that I visited in Russia in the 1990s.

The size of the labs and the equipment I saw indicated a limited through-of a meager plutonium inventory of less than 50 kilograms. The labs did not contain sufficiently large furnaces for casting plutonium weapon components or the requisite capabilities to machine the final parts. They confirmed what I was told in 2004—namely that these operations were conducted outside the Yongbyon complex. That is likely true because once the plutonium is produced in the reactor, extracted during reprocessing, and then reduced to metal, the rest of the operations can be done in gloveboxes in industrial laboratories, hidden in tunnels or warehouses, which have small footprints and would be difficult to detect.

Although the plutonium laboratories were in the annex of the Radiochemical Laboratory, we were told they were operated by a different organization—although not stated, likely still within the Yongbyon complex. That made sense because the technologies for working with metallic plutonium are very different from those for reprocessing operations used to extract plutonium from the spent fuel. As for the rest of the Radiochemical Laboratory, we were told that the only activity during our visit was waste reprocessing. The technical specialists indicated that disabling the facilities would take at least one year and possibly as long as four or five, depending on the path chosen for the disposition of the spent fuel currently in the reactor. To complete dismantlement, they said decommissioning and cleanup would take more than a decade. These were sensible estimates in my opinion.

We discussed the best method of dealing with the spent fuel currently in the reactor with what I estimated to be 10 to 12 kilograms of plutonium. Unsurprisingly, the Yongbyon staff did not confirm the amount of plutonium. For Washington, the preferred political solution was to send the spent fuel out of the country to store or reprocess after it was allowed to cool, both radioactively and thermally. That was to have been the path for the spent fuel during the Agreed Framework. Then, the parties got only as far as repackaging the fuel to store it safely in the spent fuel pool, but the rods were never shipped out because the Agreed Framework was terminated, allowing the North to extract some 25 to 30 kilograms of plutonium. My concern, both then and now, was that even if the agreement was brought to the point of shipping out the spent fuel, the transport of 50 tons of radioactive spent fuel halfway around the world to the UK or France (the only countries with the facilities to reprocess this type of spent fuel) was a nightmare. The best solution, in my opinion, was to reprocess the spent fuel at Yongbyon under IAEA monitoring and then send the resulting 10 to 12 kilograms of plutonium out for internationally monitored storage in Russia or China. Such a sensible technical solution was strongly opposed by both Clinton and Bush administration skeptics because they believed North Korea could not be trusted to give up reprocessed plutonium. I disagreed because shipping out 50 tons of spent fuel compared to a dozen kilograms of plutonium metal was an enormous safety challenge and a huge financial burden.

We visited the Fuel Fabrication Facility for the first time. These facilities were huge and in poor shape—they showed the effects of being shut down for eight years and not fully restored over the past four. We checked out the six-story uranium conversion building, which turns yellowcake uranium received from the mining complex to uranium oxide, which in turn becomes the feed material for either reactor fuel or centrifuge operations. We walked up the five flights of steps on this hot and rainy August afternoon and then followed the chemical processing steps downward through rusted equipment and foul chemical odors. It was much like the rest of Yongbyon—not pretty, but functional. On the ground floor, they had packaged five tons of uranium oxide ready to move on to the next stage of processing. It wasn't clear what the next stage would be or where it would go. It is possible that the uranium oxide was to be shipped off site to serve as feed material for uranium tetrafluoride (UF_4) and uranium hexafluoride (UF_6) for a clandestine centrifuge program. Or it could be stored for the time when UF_4 would be used to produce fresh metallic reactor fuel rods to produce more plutonium.

The building designed to process uranium oxide by a hydrofluorination process into UF_4 was not accessible because much of the internal structure and piping had corroded and collapsed. Thus, no UF_4 was produced at Yongbyon during the Agreed Framework and for several years thereafter. We were told that they were now working to correct the problem by developing an alternate process to produce UF_4, one that used a dry rather than aqueous process. That would allow them to make fresh uranium metallic fuel to keep the 5 MWe reactor operating. What they didn't say was that UF_4 is also a necessary precursor to produce UF_6, which is the feed material for enrichment in centrifuges. Yet, they had produced UF_6 at least for several years for the covert centrifuge program and had produced UF_6 that they sold to Libya earlier in the decade. Consequently, North Korea must have had another bulk fluorination facility somewhere outside of Yongbyon along with a fluorination facility that allowed them to produce UF_6. The capacities of these facilities were unknown.

We saw the storage racks with the fresh uranium metal fuel rods in a dilapidated warehouse building with no atmosphere or temperature control. The rods were kept in what looked like wooden wine racks, enclosed only in plastic sleeves. We were told they had 98 metric tons of fresh uranium metal fuel produced before the 1994 signing of the Agreed Framework. No new fuel had been produced since. There were about 2,000 unclad fuel rods for the 5 MWe reactor, although we were told about 30 percent had corroded during storage. There were 12,500 rods that had been intended for the now crumbling 50 MWe reactor. It was not clear at the time, but I heard subsequently from the American technical team that these were of the same diameter as the rods for the 5 MWe reactor but were 10 percent longer. The American team believed that nine of these longer rods could be stacked in the reactor core instead of the typical ten. For disablement, it was desirable to make these fuel rods unusable, which could be done quite simply by severely bending them. As an alternative, the rods could be sold for their uranium content. South Korea showed interest in buying the rods as feed material to make uranium oxide fuel pellets for their power reactors. The uranium in these fuel rods was valued at about $25 million at the time. Unfortunately, the North and South could not agree on terms of sale, leaving the rods available for the North to make a full load of 8,000 when the reactor was restarted, which did not occur until August 2013.

We wrapped up the visit at the guesthouse with a discussion of the potential avenues for worker reorientation after the Yongbyon facilities were disabled and dismantled. There was not much interest in this topic. Our hosts viewed that prospect as being too far in the future. They did point out, however, that the IRT-2000 reactor, which we did not visit, could be used for producing medical isotopes, but it was lacking fresh fuel.

As we departed Yongbyon in late afternoon, it struck me that the facilities seemed to be more primitive and dilapidated than I remembered. Partly, that was because we visited the Fuel Fabrication Facility with a large variety of chemical processes in which the labs and equipment had decayed more than in the rest of Yongbyon. The driving rainstorm during the day likely also contributed to the rather gloomy overall outlook, as did trekking through some of the facilities in the morning with flashlights. However, I also knew not to underestimate the North's ability to reconstitute all its operations once it decided to do so. Our departure was delayed because of news that the road along the river had been damaged by the heavy rains. The idea that we might have to stay much longer at the guesthouse under these conditions was a little unsettling. As it happened, the delay was a short one.

As we pulled out of the complex, the road on the guesthouse side of the river was shored up with special woven sandbags that were holding back a torrential creek. As we crossed the river on the concrete bridge, the road became treacherous. The sight at the bridge was astounding. People were working a conveyer system from the river to the uphill side of the road. They were passing along rocks—either held one at a time by hand or in plastic dish pans. It looked like the villagers were out in force—adults and lots of kids working in squads of about twenty or thirty. The river was flowing fast and brown. It had washed away much of the roadway on both sides. The roadbed on the other side, which we needed to get back to the town of Yongbyon and then to Pyongyang, had been filled in with rocks and sand where it was washed out during the day. People were soaking wet—some wearing rain ponchos, but most simply their street clothes. The adults had grim looks, but the kids had big smiles on their faces, seemingly enjoying the adventure. Many people were already walking back to Yongbyon, which was still several miles away. There was an occasional truck on the road, but no cars besides ours.

As we drove back, we could see considerable damage from the storm—trees had toppled, the corn had been battered down, and low-lying fields were flooded. People were out with axes chopping up the trees. On the way back, I saw old-fashioned lumberjack saws that require two people used to cut up the bigger downed trees. I hadn't seen such saws since my childhood in the Austrian Alps where spring used to bring similarly devastating floods and downed trees. We found out later the enormous extent of the damage from the torrential rains. Over 20 inches of rain left 200 people dead across North Korea and 200,000 to 300,000 homeless. An estimated 450,000 tons of crops were lost, including 10 percent of the corn and rice.[3] In addition to the human tragedy of being so unprepared for Mother Nature, I couldn't help but think how unprepared they would be for a nuclear accident emergency.

WRAPPING UP THE VISIT

We concluded the day with dinner at the Arirang Restaurant at the hotel hosted by Ambassador Ri Gun. Having our team confirm the disablement steps at Yongbyon was apparently an important part of their diplomatic outreach. I still found it surprising that our visit mattered to them considering they had allowed the IAEA inspectors back in. They had given Deputy Director General Olli Heinonen the same access we received and were about to have a steady flow of American technical teams throughout Yongbyon. I had found the visit useful because it gave us access to the Fuel Fabrication Facility for the first time and an updated status on the rest. During dinner, we also got the sense from Ambassador Ri, as we had earlier from Vice Minister Kim, that they viewed our visit to be a good opportunity to disseminate and test their positions at the upcoming Six-Party Talks. We found out later in Beijing that Kim had done the same with Chinese government officials a few days before our arrival. It also seemed clear to us that the Foreign Ministry was interested in seriously exploring broadening academic, medical, and cultural engagement with Americans.

On Saturday morning, it rained sheets of water. Surprisingly, Air Koryo boarded on time but sat at the end of the runway for about 30 minutes—rain coming down so hard it was impossible to see anything from the plane's windows. When the weather lifted enough, the Russian Tupolev-154 rolled down the runway and lifted off without problems. We felt relieved to be heading back to a safe haven, namely Beijing. Foolishly, this time we didn't expect the throng of more than fifty reporters that awaited us on the other side of the baggage claim. Our Chinese colleagues were able to quickly get us free after we made a few anodyne comments about being pleased with North Korea's progress in shutting down the Yongbyon nuclear complex.

3. Burt Herman, Associated Press, "Fatal Floods Endanger N. Korea's Food Supply," *Arkansas Democrat Gazette* (August 15, 2007), https://www.arkansasonline.com/news/2007/aug/15/fatal-floods-endanger-n-koreas-food-suppl-20070815/

While in Beijing, we again met with colleagues from the Chinese nuclear weapons program, and John Lewis had arranged dinner with officials from the Ministry of Foreign Affairs. Discussions focused on both the technical and political aspects of dismantlement. We sensed a great relief from our Chinese colleagues that diplomacy appeared to be on the upswing and the plutonium facilities were halted.

Upon our return to the United States, we briefed numerous Washington officials, including Ambassador Hill, on our findings, particularly on what the next steps should be in the Yongbyon disablement process. The technical steps would be quite straightforward to begin to disable, not just to halt, operations, as had been done up to that time. I indicated that it would be difficult to get anything close to an accurate declaration before moving on to dismantlement. In view of what I knew about Syria but thought I couldn't share, I expressed only a general concern about the transfer of nuclear technologies. At the time, I didn't realize that Hill had been briefed on the Syrian reactor.

FEBRUARY 2008 VISIT TO PYONGYANG AND YONGBYON

Both Washington and Pyongyang remained silent about the Syria bombing and carried on with specific steps to begin disabling the Yongbyon facilities and moving toward normalization of relations with the North. Early in the new year, we were informed that Pyongyang was prepared to have us return to Yongbyon. John Lewis and Bob Carlin were unavailable at the time, but I was fortunate to have Keith Luse, the senior staffer on the Senate Foreign Relations Committee, join me. Luse had joined up with our Stanford delegation for the 2004 visit. He enlisted Joel Wit, a former State Department official who had helped to negotiate and implement the Agreed Framework in the 1990s and was now senior fellow at the Johns Hopkins University School of Advanced International Studies U.S.–Korea Institute. I made visit arrangements with Minister Kim Myong Gil at the DPRK New York mission.

We were back in Pyongyang on February 12, 2008. In contrast with the wet, steamy visit the previous August, Pyongyang was clear and very cold. We were greeted by Ingrid Johanssen of the Swedish embassy and by Pat O'Brian, who was the logistics coordinator for the U.S. technical team in Pyongyang. Johanssen arranged a meeting later in the week with ambassadors from most European countries represented in Pyongyang. These meetings always provided important assessments of the state of affairs in North Korea.

visit. Our principal host was, as usual, Ambassador Ri Gun. He was joined at the policy discussions and dinners by Choe Son Hui from the American Bureau. She had been promoted from the interpreter role she had served during our previous visits. We asked to see Vice Minister Kim Gye Gwan, but we were told he was not available this time. Ambassador Ri stressed that the main reason for our visit was to verify the seriousness of their disablement actions at the Yongbyon nuclear center.

On Thursday, we traveled the familiar route along the deserted highway until we turned off onto the dirt road toward the town of Yongbyon. There were many people on foot and on bikes, dressed quite warmly on a bright, cold morning. At the Yongbyon nuclear complex, we received extraordinary permission to use our own cameras inside the complex, an indication of how serious they were about having us confirm the disablement steps. I have never been allowed to use my own camera inside of foreign nuclear weapons program facilities. They did caution us to point the cameras only at the disablement actions, although they did nothing to verify.

Our Yongbyon hosts explained that in their view the disablement activities were meant to make it more difficult, but not impossible, to bring the facilities back into operation. Disablement included four actions at each of the three key facilities—the Fuel Fabrication Facility, the 5 MWe reactor, and the Radiochemical Laboratory. We would see ten of the twelve disablement actions that had been completed. The eleventh, the discharge of the reactor fuel rods from the 5 MWe reactor, was intentionally slowed by the DPRK to prod the other five parties to catch up with their commitments, such as delivery of heavy fuel oil, under the 2007 agreement. They told us the twelfth, the removal of the control rod drive mechanisms, would be completed once all fuel rods were discharged. Our tour through these facilities, which took me into some buildings and rooms that I had not seen before, confirmed that the disablement actions were serious and would require significant time and effort to restart, though as they pointed out, it would not be impossible.

At the 5 MWe reactor, we were shown specific disablement steps such as the secondary cooling pipes outside the reactor having been cut and laid on the ground. They seemed to be most proud of showing us that the internal wooden structure of the cooling tower had been taken down and disposed of—some 240 cubic meters of wood. They claimed it would take one year to rebuild this structure. My estimate was more like three or four months, and if they decided not to rebuild it, they could use an alternative means for cooling, such as going to the river. The American side tried to get Pyongyang to level the entire tower, but the North refused. We don't know if they were putting that off as part of negotiating tactics or there really was opposition within the regime to moving that fast. By June, however, the North had reversed course and did, indeed, blow up the cooling tower with great fanfare in front of foreign news media. The North rejected suggestions for more permanent disablement actions—such as removing the two big carbon dioxide blowers (at 10 to 15 tons apiece) or pouring gadolinium oxide into the reactor core to poison it. Our hosts reminded us that for now, disablement steps were designed to be reversible in case the United States failed to do its part. This was entirely consistent and shed more light on the dual-track approach the North was following: Never overcommit to one path, always keep the alternative open.

At the Radiochemical Laboratory, they had only taken disablement steps on the front end of the process, where the spent fuel rods are introduced. For example, we witnessed that the cable for the trolley that brings the spent nuclear fuel into the facility was cut and the actuator removed. The receiving cell cranes and motors were removed. They told us that the rest of the facility had to remain operable to treat the waste from previous campaigns, which from a safety and practical point of view was not unreasonable. They told us they had about 100 tons of uranium waste left over from the 2003 and 2005 reprocessing campaigns.

The Fuel Fabrication Facility appeared to be the most seriously disabled. As we saw in 2007, the building that housed the hydrofluorination facility had so badly deteriorated during the freeze (1994 to 2003) that the building had been abandoned. In the six-story uranium conversion building, three uranium dissolver tanks were disabled. The disassembly of seven conversion furnaces with thousands of refractory bricks constituted serious disablement. The removal of the casting furnaces and machining lathes could be more easily reversed, but the interior of Building 4 was pretty much gutted. I was impressed by how far they had gone to disable the uranium metal fabrication capabilities. Little did we know at the time that two years later this building would be completely renovated and house a modern centrifuge facility. One wonders how much of that had already been planned even as

changed since our 2007 visit. At least one more reactor core load of fuel was available but would need a Magnox cladding. We did not see the facilities required for that operation.

The most striking difference we saw at all facilities compared to our previous visits was the dramatic improvement in health and safety practices. In previous visits, dress code in the facilities was casual, and radiation monitors were essentially nonexistent. This time, smocks and booties were worn in most labs and full anti-contamination suits in several. Portable radiation monitors were everywhere. The U.S. technical team had supplied a large amount of equipment, including full face masks, half masks, HEPA (air filter) units, safety equipment, electrical generators, heavy equipment, and winter clothes. They also supplied 1,000 tons of winter-use diesel fuel. The supplies were designed to allow the DPRK to disable the facilities expeditiously and safely. The money for this came from the U.S. State Department's Nonproliferation and Disarmament Fund, the only permitted source for such funds while sanctions were still in place. Ambassador Hill was also able to convince the U.S. government to compensate Yongbyon for the labor during disablement, paying on the order of $100 per man per day for the North Korean workers. I was told by some of the American participants that the overall U.S. assistance for disablement was estimated to cost $19.3 million, with $15 to $17 million having been spent by the end of 2007.

During this period, the United States had a constant presence in Yongbyon and an office in Pyongyang. The level of access to Yongbyon facilities by the U.S. technical teams, and the cooperation from the Yongbyon hosts, were extraordinary. Two U.S. teams alternated every two weeks at Yongbyon, stayed at the guesthouse, and had excellent rapport with the Yongbyon technical staff. When I asked the ever-present and friendly safeguard section head, Li Yong Ho, what he thought of one of my young technical colleagues on the U.S. team, Li smiled and said, "He is very good, he never makes mistakes." The IAEA also got a much more cooperative reception this time than they had in the past. They had two to three people constantly present at Yongbyon to verify compliance. The access afforded the U.S.

technical team, the IAEA inspectors, and our nongovernmental delegation underscored that having feet on the ground is crucial for getting critical insights into Yongbyon's operations.

POTENTIAL YONGBYON WORKER REDIRECTION

We were greeted for the out-brief at the guesthouse by former director Dr. Ri Hong Sop. We were surprised to see him, since in 2007 we had been told he now lived in Pyongyang. I briefly summarized our impressions and gave my assessment of the disablement actions. Dr. Ri was pleased and said that he hoped we could contribute to an acceptable resolution, which I took as a reference to the 2007 agreements. I told Ri that I was particularly interested to discuss options for the future of the Yongbyon nuclear workers now that they had taken such serious disablement steps. I had hoped to at least get an idea of how many people worked in the nuclear program overall. Although I didn't venture to guess in front of Ri, I thought they had perhaps 2,000 at Yongbyon and 10,000 in the entire nuclear sector, including mining. Ri said he had concerns about the future of their workers, but for now their focus was on disablement. If the provisions of the 2007 agreement were carried through to completion, then perhaps the technical people could talk about the future.

Despite his expressed reluctance to discuss redirection of the Yongbyon workforce, Dr. Ri was willing to discuss alternatives when I asked him about what the future holds. He said the Yongbyon complex should be focused on peaceful nuclear energy. They expected that an LWR would be introduced. They could train their technicians and engineers for light water reactor technologies and power plants. They were exploring how to train their nuclear engineers to engage in non-nuclear areas. He was interested in my ideas about cooperation and wanted to know how to keep a scientific base for the future. He thought that cooperation on the future of nuclear workers could be implemented after the 2007 agreement was fulfilled. To date, Ri said, they were still only thinking about these things; they were not ready to do anything. I thought it was enough that he was ready to listen. That gave me an opening to present some of my specific ideas.

I noted that in the near future, dismantling the Yongbyon facilities would involve a lot of work. The decontamination and decommissioning of facilities would require a large workforce for some time. I believed they

188 2007 and 2008 Visits

required considerable assistance in radiation health physics and environment remediation. Their facilities contained a lot of radioactive materials,
and there was heavy contamination throughout the facilities and to some

could develop collaboration in radiation monitoring and assessment of
health effects. I pointed out that in these areas, the United States had sixty
years of experience; the same for environmental issues. Dr. Ri nodded,
"Yes, these are good areas. We have been thinking along these lines as well."

I then presented some ideas for consideration that I had discussed with
Dr. Bekhzod Yuldashev, former director general of the Institute for Nuclear
Physics in Tashkent, Uzbekistan, who was a visiting scientist at Stanford.
Yuldashev faced a similar challenge when the Soviet Union dissolved. His
institute had to reorient to fully peaceful activities that required financial
support. They had a Soviet-supplied reactor like the IRT-2000 research reactor at Yongbyon. I told Ri that Yuldashev had done nuclear research at the
Dubna facility outside of Moscow during Soviet days when Uzbekistan was
part of the USSR. Ri said that he had also visited Dubna several times during
the Soviet days, something he had not mentioned to me previously. We went
through Yuldashev's extensive list of suggestions for the IRT-2000. Ri was
impressed and pleased. He said the key to the IRT reactor was the fuel. They
had not been able to get delivery of new fuel from Russia—in other words,
none since 1992. They had experience in the production of medical and industrial isotopes. The Isotope Production Laboratory (IPL) in the IRT-2000
reactor complex had channels that allowed them to irradiate targets and
extract the radioisotopes of interest. They had not done cancer treatments,
but Ri said it would be helpful to have exchanges in these areas. They have
people with thyroid cancer but don't have the radioisotopes to treat them.

Ri lamented the fact that before the nuclear crisis they had access to
everything, and now it was all gone.[4] When I asked him when the nuclear
crisis began, Ri then went off into a rare diatribe against the United States
and in the process dated the beginning of the nuclear crisis long before
when Americans would generally assume. He said the crisis began when

4. I took that to mean that they had a robust nuclear research program and radioisotope
production in a fully functional IRT reactor with HEU fuel supplied by the Soviet Union.

the United States deployed Honest John missiles in the South. These, he said carried the W-31 warhead designed at Los Alamos. He went on to talk about the W-33 bomb that he said was also deployed in the South and mentioned the deployment of American nuclear artillery shells and neutron bombs. Ri said he read all of this in a U.S. publication, what he called the "Handbook for Nuclear Weapons." I found it remarkable that Ri would know so much about U.S. nuclear weapons when he had told me previously that his responsibility at Yongbyon was to make the plutonium and that it then went "somewhere else." As noted earlier, we later found out that Ri eventually headed the Nuclear Weapons Institute, which I believe had the responsibility for all nuclear programs.

I tried to get Ri back into a cooperative mood by focusing specifically on what could be done with the IRT-2000 reactor in the future. I had detailed technical discussions with him and Chief Engineer Yu Sun Chol about the reactor's design characteristics and operational history. Such details are important to assess what civilian activities could be effectively conducted at the reactor complex. In addition, they helped me to understand the facility's HEU inventory at the time. I summarize the main points here.

The IRT reactor was originally supplied with 10 percent LEU (low-enriched uranium) bar-type fuel by the Soviet Union in the late 1960s. The North Koreans upgraded the reactor to use 36 percent and 80 percent enriched fuel, also supplied by the Soviets. Yu said if the only new fuel they could purchase was LEU (because of proliferation concerns), they could re-convert the reactor. Yu described the vertical and horizontal irradiation channels the reactor contained. These allowed irradiation experiments, such as the production of medical isotopes. Though Yu didn't say so, it would also be possible to produce limited quantities of plutonium and/or tritium. The casks holding the irradiated products were transferred in air-pressure pipes to the Isotope Production Laboratory where they had a full team of radiochemists who could handle the separation of the isotopes. They had hot cells with manipulators provided by the Soviet Union. These were operational. They had handled the packaging and shipping of radioisotopes in the past. As mentioned previously, they were eager to get back into the production and supply of medical isotopes, but they needed new fuel.

Yu presented a detailed inventory of all fuel, its isotopic composition, and the burnup level. Based on his description, they had very little fuel left for operations. At that time, the reactor could be operated only sporadically. They had an inventory of about 15 kilograms of irradiated HEU (highly enriched uranium) at the facility. The reactor core could be converted back

as cooling and control systems, would need to be replaced, but if so, Dr. Ri told us that they could operate the forty-year-old reactor for another thirty to forty years. He said their ancillary capabilities such as radiochemistry and analytical chemistry were modern and in good shape.

Dr. Ri seemed very pleased with our suggestions on what to do with the IRT. "When the time comes," he said, "we will be able to use these ideas." I asked for his views on LWRs. He had previously told me that his people had nothing to do with the KEDO LWR project. Was there a role for his engineers in LWR projects if the plutonium operations were shut down? Ri said that they had no LWR experience at Yongbyon, but they would look at the best ways to retrain their engineers. I also asked if they would be able to produce the ceramic oxide fuel required for LWRs. He said they had not thought about this. They would likely have to get the fuel from the outside first and in the meantime learn how to do it themselves. In retrospect, it seems highly unlikely that Ri and his Yongbyon colleagues had thought so little about possible LWRs when a bit more than two years later they showed me their own experimental LWR under construction at Yongbyon.

Joel Wit and Keith Luse joined the conversation to explore worker redirection ideas. Wit mentioned he was involved in a project on worker redirection with Russia sponsored by the U.S. National Academy of Sciences. He said there was substantial interest in cooperating on these issues with the Yongbyon workforce, including in possible collaboration in radiation health physics and what could be done in non-nuclear industries. Luse told Dr. Ri that Senators Richard Lugar and Joe Biden of the Senate Foreign Relations Committee favored supporting worker redirection. On behalf of Senator Lugar, Luse raised the question of nuclear materials security. Ri replied that they had strict regulations and standards for storage of nuclear materials. He said that even the General Department of Atomic Energy officials cannot get into these facilities without the permission from Yongbyon. Ri said at Yongbyon they had a small amount of nuclear material, and this was stored under strict control. Luse asked Ri if nuclear specialists from Myanmar had visited Yongbyon, an issue on which there had been speculation in the news media recently, to which Ri replied that he had no idea. Then he quickly added that he believed that no foreigners had come here to Yongbyon for training.

BEYOND NUCLEAR

During the remainder of the week in Pyongyang, we visited the education and health ministries. We met with Dr. Choe Dok Hun, the deputy director general of International Department, Ministry of Education, on Wednesday. As in past discussions, we found an innate desire to collaborate and exchange academic personnel, but also reluctance because "the U.S. has not fully given up its hostile policy." It was a pity since back at Stanford several faculty members had expressed great interest in developing educational ties with North Korean universities.

We also met with Dr. Ri Hyon Chol and other officials of the Ministry of Health to follow up on the TB project. Kim said that their visit in January 2008 to Stanford was their first to the United States. They greatly appreciated the hospitality that Professor Lewis extended and the cooperation from the Bay Area Tuberculosis Consortium. He said they learned a lot that they would be able to use in North Korea. My discussions with the health officials gave me an opportunity to see how American NGOs helped the North Koreans deal with such serious health crises. Dr. Steve Linton, founder and chairman of the Eugene Bell Foundation, was instrumental in providing medical humanitarian assistance to rural North Korea, particularly for multiple-drug-resistant tuberculosis. Ms. Heidi Linton (no relation), executive director of Christian Friends of Korea, also supported North Korea's treatment and capacity building for tuberculosis and hepatitis care. For my part, I conveyed the interest of the Stanford University team to continue collaborating with them on treating multiple-drug-resistant TB. Lewis was scheduled to visit in about a month's time to help move the cooperation along. Ms. Linton worked with the Stanford University School of Medicine to jointly establish a National TB Reference Laboratory in the DPRK beginning in 2009. These efforts were strongly supported within the United States until later in 2009 when the political relations between the two nations collapsed once again.

At Keith Luse's request, we visited the School of Foreign Languages and the Pyongyang University of Foreign Studies next door. We got a warm reception, especially in the English class, in a bitterly cold classroom. Students around 13 years old were at their little wooden desks taking an English lesson with headphones. I was asked to address them. They were very

which students spoke remarkably good American English. At the university, from which our Foreign Ministry escort, Mr. Hwang, had graduated, it was similarly cold inside. As we walked in, the class was looking at their computer monitors that displayed the question of the moment: "Where and when was Wolfgang Amadeus Mozart born?" In an instant I answered the question, "Salzburg, Austria, on January 27, 1756," much to the amazement of the students. It turns out that when I was growing up in Austria, every kid knew that by heart. I had also memorized the names of all the emperors and the dates that they had ruled the Habsburg empire.

We wrapped up our visit with a dinner—as usual with Ambassador Ri Gun, Ms. Choe Son Hui, and colleagues—to review what we found and to look at the road ahead. We said that the visit to Yongbyon convinced us that they were seriously pursuing disablement. The steps taken were impressive but reversible. Ambassador Ri acknowledged that and explained again their plan was to disable and then move toward dismantlement in the second phase in concert with the other parties meeting their obligations. I mentioned that the declaration phase would be particularly challenging. Ri claimed that they met their declaration responsibilities in November 2007. When pushed about a "complete and correct" declaration, Ri stated that they were not prepared to provide such a list until the five parties completed their corresponding measures according to the October 3, 2007, agreement.

We discussed what I considered to be the three principal components of a complete and correct declaration: (1) plutonium and weaponization, (2) uranium enrichment, and (3) nuclear cooperation and export. Ri said they had made a plutonium declaration of 30 kilograms. They had no plans to declare weapons until much later in the negotiations process. On the question of uranium enrichment, Ri said they had already resolved this issue with the Americans by giving U.S. experts access to the aluminum tubes in question at a missile factory and demonstrating that these were not used for enrichment purposes. On exports, they stuck to the road ahead, stating "We will not export nuclear technologies in the future." I did not raise the Syria reactor issue because it was not yet public knowledge. We left on positive terms, both sides agreeing that we had an opportunity to move on from disablement to the final elimination of the North's nuclear weapons, but that much work remained to be done.

On Saturday morning, we returned to Beijing. The plane was not very full, but as was Air Koryo's custom, they squeezed us all in the front rows and left the back empty. I wound up being seated next to Ewald Haas from an Austrian mining and minerals company. Their team of about six people had been in North Korea for a week exploring mining of magnesite for use in refractories in the Austrian steel industry. Haas said his team had gone far north where it was bitterly cold, about -30 C (-22 F). Most places had little electricity and no heat. His company was headquartered in Leoben, Austria. It turns out that one of its factories was located less than 10 kilometers from my hometown of Rottenmann. He said he loved to ski and promised to take me to his favorite ski area in Donnersbachwald, also close to my hometown. I had never skied there; it was far beyond our financial means when I was growing up.

Back in the United States, I presented my observations to government officials in Washington, DC, and to the public. I concluded that the DPRK leadership had made the decision to permanently shut down plutonium production if the United States and the other four parties lived up to their October 2007 commitments. However, the North had retained a hedge to be able to restart the facilities if the agreement fell through. We verified that the disablement actions taken would effectively delay a potential restart of plutonium production. I estimated that it would take several months to get some of the facilities back up and about one year to get all facilities restarted. I reported that the diplomatic efforts had put a permanent shutdown of the Yongbyon plutonium production complex within reach. To do so, highest priority would have to be placed on completing the disablement (discharging the reactor fuel and disabling or selling the existing fresh fuel rods) and proceeding to the dismantlement stage. If this were accomplished, the DPRK would not be able to make more bombs because at that point, it had only plutonium production capabilities. The HEU program, I believed, was not yet at a production scale. And, without additional nuclear tests, the North would not be able to make better bombs.

11   2008: Almost There, but It All Falls Apart

On April 24, 2008, two months after the Stanford delegation returned from Pyongyang, CIA Director General Michael Hayden went public with the intelligence that North Korea had helped Syria build a plutonium production reactor.[1] It had been nearly eight months since Israel conducted a covert, midnight airstrike against a mysterious facility in the Syrian desert. Now the U.S. government was breaking its official silence on the matter by releasing photos and videos of the construction and destruction of a gas-cooled, graphite-moderated reactor. The timing of the announcement couldn't have been worse for Ambassador Chris Hill, who was desperately trying to push North Korea through the diplomatic doors the two sides had reopened in 2007. After my February 2008 visit to Yongbyon, I had told Hill that the North had taken serious but reversible disablement steps at the nuclear complex. He had appeared to be optimistic that continued progress was possible.

But however significant the North Korean disablement actions in Yongbyon were, they paled in comparison to the scale of North Korea's complicity in Syria's nuclear reactor construction that General Hayden and CIA analysts described. Their evidence of North Korea's involvement

---

1. "CIA: North Korea Helping Syria Build Nuke Reactor," *National Public Radio* (April 24, 2008), https://www.npr.org/templates/story/story.php?storyId=90115722

followed painstaking open source imagery analysis by David Albright and colleagues at the Institute of Science and International Security. They located the bombed site a little more than one month after the bombing, and their technical analysis tied the reactor directly to North Korea's 5 MWe reactor. But Hayden did not go public for another six months after Albright's report. It took the IAEA another three years before it announced that it had come to the same conclusions as Albright and the CIA.[2]

The Syrians—and their North Korean partners—were able to keep such a huge construction project secret for so long thanks to a masterful job of obfuscation. They masked the site by modifying the terrain around the reactor and designed the reactor without the usual telltale signatures, such as a cooling tower.[3] How the Syrians were able to import the materials and equipment for the reactor—considering the Bush administration's vaunted Proliferation Security Initiative designed to interdict shipments related to weapons of mass destruction—remains a mystery.

The evidence also pointed to the reactor being near operational capability just before its destruction. However, no signs were found of a reprocessing facility that would be required to extract weapon-grade plutonium from the spent reactor fuel. Such a facility could have been in the planning stage at that point because the reactor would have to operate for a few years before spent fuel required reprocessing. The puzzling question that remains unanswered to this day is: Who was the customer for the reactor's plutonium? Hans Ruehle, a former German defense official, who had worked on these issues before retirement, provided an initial, intriguing answer in a Swiss newspaper in 2009. He speculated that the deal stipulated that "Iran would provide the money, Syria the territory, and North Korea the nuclear hardware."[4] Syria likely did not have the financial means to fund such a project at the time. It is inconceivable that North Korea would pay to have

2. "Implementation of the NPT Safeguards Agreement in the Syrian Arab Republic," Report by the Director General, IAEA (May 24, 2011), https://www.iaea.org/sites/default/files/gov2011-30.pdf

3. Constructing the Syrian reactor without a cooling tower may have given the North the confidence to blow up their cooling tower in Yongbyon, since they had developed a viable alternative that could provide cooling directly from the river.

4. Hans Ruehle, "Wie Iran Syriens Nuklearbewaffnung vorangetrieben hat: Hintergründe der Israelischen Aktion gegen den Reaktor von al-Kibar," *Neue Zuericher Zeitung* (March 19, 2009), http://jer-zentrum.org/ViewNews.aspx? ArticleId=1196 ("How Iran

a reactor built elsewhere for its own program. Instead, such a project would have been a likely source of badly needed foreign currency. Iran, which had apparently scaled back an enriched uranium-based nuclear weapon

its weapons ambitions. The Syrians could have involved several parties and developed options for determining the final recipient of the plutonium. It all remains speculation some fifteen years later.

Nevertheless, what we do know about the reactor's development tells us a lot about North Korea's technical proficiency and tolerance for risk. It pursued the reactor development while its nuclear activity at Yongbyon was under strict international scrutiny. It did so in blatant disregard for the nonproliferation standards and responsible nuclear stewardship principles it professed to uphold. Ruehle put it best in his article, writing that "one should not forget the North Koreans' chutzpah, on the one hand, to conduct negotiations on nuclear disarmament and, at the same time, to upgrade Syria to nuclear power." Contact between North Korean nuclear specialists and high-level Syrian officials possibly began as early as 1997. The first serious discussions apparently took place with Bashar al-Assad when the North Koreans attended the funeral of his father, Hafez al-Assad, in Damascus in June 2000 and, per Ruehle, the plan was agreed upon when Syria, Iran, and North Korea convened a meeting in July 2002. Consistent with this timeline, U.S. intelligence detected North Korean ship deliveries of construction supplies to Syria starting in 2002, and American satellites spotted the construction at the site as early as 2001, but U.S. intelligence assessments at the time regarded the work as nothing unusual.[5]

In mid-September 2007, shortly after the attack, the Syrians began a massive effort to raze the bombed reactor building and to remove all potentially incriminating nuclear-related materials, equipment, and structures. Syria's effort to destroy the evidence briefly revealed internal elements of the building to U.S. satellites and corroborated much of what the United States had concluded about the reactor previously.

Pushed Forward Syria's Nuclear Armament: Background of the Israeli Action Against the Reactor of Al-Kibar.")

5. David E. Sanger, *The Inheritance: The World Obama Confronts and the Challenges to American Power* (New York: Harmony Books, 2009), 273.

The Israeli government did not admit having destroyed Syria's reactor until March 2018. Numerous articles and books have speculated on how Israelis were able to get the treasure trove of photos and documents on the reactor project. The most detailed and credible is the recent book *Shadow Strike* by Israeli investigative journalist Yaakov Katz.[6] He describes how the Mossad, Israel's intelligence agency, entered the hotel room in Vienna of the visiting head of the Syrian Atomic Energy Agency, Ibrahim Othman, while he was out. He had carelessly left his laptop with the details of the reactor, including photos of the project. Not only were there photos of the reactor, but there was a photo of a North Korean Yongbyon engineer posing with Othman. The Israelis downloaded all his files and also left a Trojan Horse on his computer to continue to provide updated information.

NEGOTIATING THROUGH THE NORTH KOREA–SYRIA REVELATIONS

The lack of a forceful response by Washington to the North Korea–Syria nuclear connection appears puzzling at first glance. It is inconsistent with the White House's hard-line attitude during Bush's first term. For many U.S. officials, North Korea's Syria venture confirmed their worst assumptions about North Korea's credibility as a diplomatic partner. Indeed, behind the scenes, some of these officials, particularly General Hayden and Vice President Cheney, favored an American effort to take out the reactor. But Hill's diplomacy was in full swing and ultimately those favoring a U.S. military strike, or even early public acknowledgment of the North's activities, were overruled by President Bush. In his memoir, Hayden laments that the United States never took decisive action to punish the North for its behavior, citing the prioritization of the diplomatic process above all else. He notes that Hill was "negotiating a deal with a country that had just been caught red handed in the single greatest act of nuclear proliferation in history. And they had not been called on it!"[7] Instead, Hill sought to subtly tailor the U.S. response to get the North to acknowledge

6. Yaakov Katz, *Shadow Strike: Inside Israel's Secret Mission to Eliminate Syrian Nuclear Power* (New York: St. Martin's Press, 2019).

7. Michael V. Hayden, *Playing to the Edge: American Intelligence in the Age of Terror* (New York: Penguin Press, 2016), 266.

its activities in Syria (which it has never done) without letting the issue
derail the entire diplomatic process, as had happened with the uranium
enrichment revelations in 2002.

threatened to impede negotiations over the implementation of the September 2005 joint statement, other developments looked encouraging for diplomacy. On October 2, 2007, South Korean President Roh Moo Hyun crossed the Korean demilitarized zone and proceeded to Pyongyang for talks with Kim Jong Il, the second North–South summit. It ended with an ambitious agenda including important military cooperation to deal with troubled West Sea disputes and promises of economic cooperation. The agenda was moribund, however, once Lee Myung Bak won the presidential election in December. President Lee ushered in a much more conservative government opposed to the "Sunshine Policy" of the previous two administrations.

Another development in early 2008 looked promising for boosting Hill's diplomatic efforts, but it also fell short when Washington missed an opportunity to take advantage of a historic feat of musical diplomacy. On February 26, the New York Philharmonic, led by Musical Director Lorin Maazel, received a five-minute standing ovation in Pyongyang's 2,500-seat East Pyongyang Grand Theater when it concluded its performance with the traditional Korean folk song, "Arirang." Among the collection of works performed were Dvořák's Symphony No. 9 (New World Symphony), Wagner's Prelude to Act 3 of *Lohengrin,* and Gershwin's "An American in Paris." The Philharmonic also received permission to play the "Star-Spangled Banner," with the American flag displayed on stage.

Although the live audience was primarily Pyongyang's elites, the Philharmonic had insisted on allowing foreign journalists to attend and for the concert to be broadcast live throughout North Korea. A bigger broadcast audience of 200 million people around the world saw a North Korea that was very different from the typical goose-stepping soldiers in a military parade. The 400-person U.S. delegation of journalists, orchestra members, and invited guests included former Secretary of Defense William Perry. But Ambassador Hill was nowhere to be seen. After initially encouraging the visit as part of what he saw as a long-term process of developing better understanding and relations, he was told by the administration to stay away. Secretary Rice, an accomplished concert pianist, also opted not to attend even though she was next door in Seoul the day before for President Lee Myung Bak's inauguration. The Bush administration had decided that the concert should be disconnected from the broader policy of engagement, rather than attempting to build on the goodwill that the concert would generate.

Washington's decision to have senior-level officials like Hill and Rice forgo attendance at the concert was a missed opportunity to continue building momentum toward improved relations and implementation of the 2005 joint statement. The atmosphere at the conclusion of the performance was magical. As John Deak, the orchestra's principal bassist described it,

> "Half of the orchestra burst into tears . . . and suddenly there was this kind of artistic bond that is just a miracle. I'm not going to make any statements about what's going to change . . . things happen slowly. But I do know that the most profound connection was made with the Korean people tonight."[8]

William Perry, an ardent classical music fan, sitting next to Ambassador Ri Gun, remarked after the concert that this was, "a historic moment. This might just have pushed us over the top." Perry added, "I hope so. . . . You cannot demonize people when you're sitting there listening to their music. You don't go to war with people unless you demonize them first."[9]

Perhaps the most disappointing part of this special moment (that had clearly been blessed by Kim Jong Il) was Secretary Rice's dismissive comments about the event. She stressed that North Korea had not changed, and "we shouldn't get carried away with what listening to Dvořák is going to do in North Korea."[10] White House Press Secretary Dana Perino concurred: "I think at the end of the day, we consider this concert to be a concert, and it's not a diplomatic, you know, coup."[11] Although Rice continued to fight off

8. Cynthia P. Schneider, "The Sound of Music in Pyongyang," *Brookings Institution* (February 28, 2008), https://www.brookings.edu/opinions/the-sound-of-music-in-pyong-yang/

9. "N.Y. Philharmonic Plays Concert in North Korea," *NBC News* (February 26, 2008), https://www.nbcnews.com/id/wbna23347082

10. Bill Powell, "A Gershwin Offensive in North Korea," *Time* 171, no. 8 (February 25, 2008), http://content.time.com/time/world/article/0,8599,1717019,00.html

11. "U.S. Anthem Gets Orchestral Airing in Pyongyang," *The Chosun Ilbo* (February 27, 2008), https://web.archive.org/web/20080301220150/http://english.chosun.com/w21data/html/news/200802/200802270015.html

hard-liners such as Vice President Cheney and to support engagement with
the North, when push came to shove, she returned to her basic instincts of
mistrust for this regime. As Hill pointed out, she had a "two-track policy,"

continuing to "talk" with it.[12] Unfortunately, these two tracks competed
with each other rather than being orchestrated in a strategic manner to
pull North Korea in the right direction. Ultimately, the concert turned out
to be blip on the radar rather than a momentum-building piece to further
the U.S. drive to successfully implement a deal.

DIPLOMACY STALLS OVER ACTION FOR ACTION
Over the winter, as the public news and internal deliberations about Syria
and the New York Philharmonic played on in the background, the diplomatic process itself was grinding to a halt. The declaration process agreed
upon in October ran into obstacles, and the North missed the December 31, 2007, date for its nuclear declaration. The two parties continued
to bicker about which was not meeting its obligations. Pyongyang complained about the lack of movement on sanctions relief while Washington remained concerned that North Korea was slow rolling the nuclear
declaration, even as it engaged in ongoing disablement activity at Yongbyon. The Bush administration was running out of time, and the North
continued to dismiss allegations about its Syrian and uranium enrichment
activities.[13] Following another round of talks in early 2008, Hill publicly
expressed frustration with North Korea's "foot-dragging," lamenting that
the North Koreans "seem to think I have nothing better to do in my time
or in my life than to keep asking them questions."[14]

Hill and Kim Gye Gwan met in Geneva in March, followed by another
meeting in Singapore in early April, where Hill decided to take matters into
his own hands without consultation with the interagency process. This independent maneuvering had become his modus operandi in navigating the

12. Mike Chinoy, *Meltdown: The Inside Story of the North Korean Nuclear Crisis* (New York: St. Martin's Griffin, 2009), 306.

13. Glenn Kessler, "Kim's Realm Shows Signs of a Rift," *Washington Post* (March 27, 2008): A11.

14. David Ignatius, "A Ticking Clock on N. Korea," *Washington Post* (March 23, 2008): B7.

bitterly divided and dysfunctional atmosphere in Washington. Hill reached an agreement with North Korea on a path forward. The core purpose of the agreement, from the U.S. standpoint, was to clear the way for North Korea to finish the disablement of the 5 MWe reactor and provide a full account of its plutonium stockpile. In response, President Bush would take actions to remove North Korea from the State Sponsors of Terrorism list and exempt it from the Trading with the Enemy Act. To facilitate the deal, Hill made a significant concession. He softened the U.S. position, which had previously called for the North to provide hard details of its uranium enrichment program and its proliferation activity in Syria before the United States would move ahead. Instead, the North would merely have to acknowledge the allegations without needing to publicly confirm or admit them.

To many observers, Hill's actions on this front fell far short of what was needed to enforce strong nonproliferation norms and hold North Korea to account, particularly over Syria. At the time, he certainly paid a price for how the issue played out. The Syria revelations and Hill's handling of them in the context of the disablement negotiations hurt his standing within the Bush administration through the spring and into the summer. It left Hill politically damaged, further eroding his credibility with Congress.[15] The reaction in much of Washington was swift and devastating. Hill was seen to have sold out to the North Koreans, and he came under fire from much of Washington's foreign policy establishment. John Bolton, now opining from outside the government, derisively called Hill's moves "like something out of Bill Clinton or Jimmy Carter's playbook."[16] Hill's adversaries, who had been growing in number because of his increasingly "Lone Ranger" mode of operation seized this opportunity to get the Syria story into the public spotlight. Hill sought to counter this opposition by doubling down on his independent approach in a frantic effort to get a deal before the end of the Bush administration.[17]

15. Chinoy, *Meltdown*, 366.

16. Helene Cooper, "Past Deals by N. Korea May Face Less Study," *New York Times* (April 18, 2008), https://www.nytimes.com/2008/04/18/washington/18diplo.html

17. Chinoy, *Meltdown*, 366.

HILL'S EFFORTS—PROMISING, BUT
POLITICALLY UNTENABLE

I viewed Hill's efforts in 2008 to be a pragmatic risk management ap-
Framework over the uranium enrichment issue, which had resulted in
North Korea restarting the plutonium complex. Hill viewed the declaration and surrender of the North's weapons-grade plutonium—enough for
perhaps half a dozen weapons—as most important to reducing the proliferation risk. He considered it worth the cost of having to finesse the uranium enrichment and Syria issues for the time being. In Hill's own words,
the United States was "trying to focus on the plutonium," as that posed
the most immediate proliferation risk and concern, since "[t]hat's where
the bombs are. We don't have suspicions about plutonium; we have cold,
hard facts about plutonium."[18] For the first time, the Bush administration
showed an appropriate willingness to trade immediate gains on the plutonium front by managing and temporarily sidestepping the less urgent
questions about uranium enrichment. Hill also realized that this was the
best he could get from the North Koreans for the time being. Having decided that getting the plutonium program shut down was better than getting nothing at all, Hill and Rice had accepted the fact that the North was
not going to provide a "full confession."[19] They did not want to risk the
collapse of the entire negotiation process over these issues.

In return for softening the U.S. position, Hill was able to obtain several
important concessions from North Korea. In early May, the North Koreans
handed Sung Kim, the director of the State Department's Korea Office,
copies of more than 18,000 pages of operating records of Yongbyon facilities
dating back to 1986, the start of operations of the 5 MWe reactor. Kim Gye
Gwan also promised Hill that they would blow up the reactor's cooling
tower as soon as they were removed from the terrorism list. The previous
November, North Korea had taken the unusual step of giving U.S. diplomats
and technical specialists access to a military factory to demonstrate that aluminum tubes suspected of having been purchased for a centrifuge program

18. Glenn Kessler, "U.S. Ready to Ease Sanctions on N. Korea; Pyongyang Would Have
to Acknowledge Evidence About Nuclear Activities," *Washington Post* (April 11, 2008): A15.

19. Cooper, "Past Deals."

were instead used for rocket launchers.[20] These were surprising actions by the typically secretive North Koreans. Strangely, and still not understood today, upon analysis back in the United States, both the aluminum tubes and the copies of operating records were found to be contaminated with traces of highly enriched uranium.[21] This was at a time when North Korea was still denying having any enrichment capabilities, and they considered handing over sections of the aluminum tubes as proof of not having a centrifuge program, likely not realizing they were contaminated.

Despite the criticism the administration and Hill received following the April revelations about North Korea's role in the Syrian reactor project, Hill was able to keep the dialogue moving. For their part, the North Koreans were content to simply deny or ignore the accusations of their involvement in Syria and with uranium enrichment if the denial was not going to prevent a deal from moving forward. On May 28, Hill and Kim met in Beijing to work out final details of the declaration of the North's nuclear materials. Hill needed a bit more from Kim before he could convince Washington to move forward with implementation. He told Kim that they would need to work out an acceptable verification protocol. Somewhat surprisingly, Kim agreed in principle—details to be worked out later. Hill believed he now had enough from the North to convince Secretary Rice and the president to delist North Korea from the terrorism list.

THE AMERICANS MOVE THE GOALPOSTS

But Hill underestimated the widespread opposition that his tentative agreement would generate. Japan and South Korea, with its conservative President Lee Myung Bak, were both opposed to delisting the North and urged Washington to toe the hard line. In Washington, the reception was not much better.

---

20. Chinoy, *Meltdown*, 366. North Korea gave Americans access to aluminum tubes it had acquired from abroad. These were suspected of being used for rotors for the clandestine centrifuge program. Americans were allowed to visit the missile factory and remarkably were even given samples of the aluminum (delivered to their hotel late at night). As cooperative as this appeared to be at the time, it was inconsequential because, as I found out in a subsequent visit, North Korea used high-strength steel, rather than aluminum, for rotors of its centrifuge program.

21. Glenn Kessler, "Uranium Traces Found on N. Korean Tubes: Discovery Appears to Clash with Pyongyang's Denial of Secret Nuclear Program," *Washington Post* (December 21, 2007): A25.

Hill's most significant backer within the administration, Secretary Rice—who had given him top-level cover to conduct his recent spate of relatively independent deal-making—now seemed to be pulling back. Although Rice indi-

favored negotiating a deal, she laid out a much tougher line on delisting by insisting first on rigorous verification by the North. She later acknowledged that she was moving the goalposts on the North Koreans by shifting the verification parts up in the sequence of actions.[22] In addition, she asked Paula De-Sutter, of the State Department's Bureau of Verification and Compliance and a hard-line proponent of lock-tight verification measures, to develop a plan. DeSutter developed a four-page maximalist, intrusive verification plan that was bound to be rejected by the North. Ultimately, Hill's risk management approach would not survive Washington's deep suspicions of Pyongyang.

Notwithstanding the apparent shifting winds in Washington, North Korea continued to meet part of its obligations. On June 26, it delivered a sixty-page declaration to China, the chair of the Six-Party Talks. The declaration indicated that North Korea had separated about 30 kilograms of plutonium and claimed to have used about 2 kilograms for its 2006 nuclear test. The declaration fell short of the level of completeness insisted upon by the administration, but even so, within hours President Bush announced that he had lifted the provisions of the Trading with the Enemy Act with respect to North Korea. He also announced that he was informing Congress that at the end of the formal forty-five-day notification he intended to take North Korea off the terrorism list. At that point, the president implied vaguely that the final removal of the North from the terrorism list depended on its working with the United States during the forty-five days "to develop a comprehensive and rigorous verification protocol."[23] The issue was further muddied when soon after the speech, U.S. officials warned that the process of removing North Korea from the terrorism list could be stopped if North Korea proved uncooperative. A DPRK Foreign Ministry spokesman responded quickly and positively to Bush's proclamation, expressing the

22. Chinoy, *Meltdown*, 367.

23. George W. Bush, "President Bush Discusses North Korea," *The White House* (June 26, 2008), https://georgewbush-whitehouse.archives.gov/news/releases/2008/06/20080626-9.html

expectation that the sanctions removal would now be completed pursuant to the October 3, 2007, agreement. The statement did not mention the president's reference to a verification protocol.[24]

The next day, as previously agreed, North Korea staged a made-for-TV spectacle—blowing up the 5 MWe reactor's cooling tower. It was a great symbolic move but made little actual difference since the interior had already been gutted as part of the North's disabling actions. By this time, the major sticking point was not disablement activity at Yongbyon but rather the content of the North's nuclear declaration and the sequence of the delisting and verification steps that would follow.

Hill went to the next Six-Party Talks in Beijing during the second week in July with DeSutter's maximalist verification protocol and with no choice but to present it, despite his misgivings, since his support in Washington was crumbling. The verification protocol specified that North Korea must grant full access to all materials at any site the United States suspected; that inspectors be allowed to remove samples for analysis outside the country; and that the North provide records of all imports and exports of nuclear materials and nuclear-related equipment.[25] Upon hearing the hard-line demands, Kim Gye Gwan was furious. These verification requirements must have struck him as reminiscent of the poison pill unilateral U.S. signing statement that Hill presented in September 2005. After nearly three years of intensive negotiations, the United States and North Korea were no closer to resolving the nuclear impasse. Whereas Kim Gye Gwan had indicated that Pyongyang was prepared to take some verification measures, these U.S. demands were over the top.

When President Bush followed up with additional tough demands in response to a question in a speech in Bangkok—not only stating that verification measures must include uranium enrichment and proliferation activities but also that North Korea must "end its harsh rule and respect the dignity and human rights of its people"[26]—it indicated that Hill had

24. DPRK Foreign Ministry Spokesman, "DPRK Foreign Ministry's Spokesman on U.S. Lifting of Major Economic Sanctions Against DPRK," *KCNA* (June 27, 2008).

25. Glenn Kessler, "Far-Reaching U.S. Plan Impaired N. Korea Deal; Demands Began to Undo Nuclear Accord," *Washington Post* (September 26, 2008): A20.

26. Office of the Press Secretary, "President Bush Visits Bangkok, Thailand," *The White House* (August 7, 2008), https://georgewbush-whitehouse.archives.gov/news/releases/2008/08/20080807-8.html

questionable support in the White House for moving forward at all with the North. Hill had not only lost most of the policy community in Washington, because they believed he was selling them a bill of goods, but he

administration was sticking to a different, tougher line. From the North's perspective, Hill was no longer a credible negotiating partner; they could not be sure that he spoke with authority for the U.S. government.

The forty-five days expired on August 11, but the president did not remove North Korea from the terrorism list. Washington told Pyongyang that it would not do so until there was a strong verification regime in place. In a sign that the tentative deal had truly collapsed, on August 26 Pyongyang announced it would suspend the disablement of its key nuclear facilities at Yongbyon and consider taking steps to restore them "to their original state."

A MEDICAL SCARE CHANGES THE CALCULUS

When Kim Jong Il missed the big September 9 parade, commemorating the sixtieth anniversary of the founding of the DPRK, rumors began to circulate that he was either seriously ill or had died. He had been most recently seen in public on August 14 (reported by North Korean media the next day). It was not long before it became clear that Kim Jong Il had suffered a serious stroke around that time. The combination of the Americans failing to deliver once again and Chairman Kim's life apparently in danger was the death knell for diplomacy. Hill did not let up on trying to salvage a deal. He met again with Kim Gye Gwan in Pyongyang in early October. Hill promised to back off from DeSutter's intrusive verification regime. Kim accepted that verbally but not in writing. That was enough for Hill to convince President Bush and Secretary Rice to delist North Korea because it was going to be the best deal they could get with time running out for the administration.

But it was all too late. Domestic political imperatives were now driving North Korea's decision-making, and these imperatives did not provide for further rapprochement with the United States. Kim's stroke opened the need for succession planning. Concern that outsiders would try to take advantage of the North at such a vulnerable time apparently triggered a decision that the moment for reconciliation had passed and that the North must now proceed quickly with its nuclear program. At the top of their priorities must have been a second nuclear test to demonstrate that North Korea had a working nuclear device and would be able to field a deterrent to the United States. But for the remainder of 2008, the moment was not right to pull out all together. The North continued to string the Americans along, opting to slow down the disablement process rather than restart Yongbyon immediately as threatened in August.

Don Oberdorfer and Bob Carlin in *The Two Koreas* and Anna Fifield in *The Great Successor* describe what is known about succession planning during this time.[27] Both indicate that French brain specialist, Dr. Francois-Xavier Roux, who had treated Kim after an accident some fifteen years prior, was summoned to Pyongyang to treat Kim. Kim's sister, Kim Kyong Hui, was brought into the ruling elite, including appointment to the party's ruling Political Bureau and as a four-star general. Fifield reports that on January 8, 2009, Kim informed top Workers' Party officials that he had chosen his youngest son, Kim Jong Un, as his successor. It was his 25th birthday. The roll out to the populace was slow but determined. To understand the political developments on the nuclear front, we must take into consideration this dramatic domestic transition. This was not a time for the Kim family to show weakness either to the international community or to the folks back home.

It is curious that in his memoir *Outpost*, Hill makes no mention of Kim Jong Il's stroke or succession planning and the resulting complications he may have had to handle. It is possible that, at the time, Hill did not realize he was simply fighting a battle he could not win. After Barack Obama was elected president on November 4, 2008, Hill managed to hold one more round of Six-Party Talks in December with the support of the Chinese. But those talks ended in acrimony, particularly because Hill was getting pressure again from others in the administration to press for the extreme verification measures. And the North was not prepared to engage seriously at this time regardless. The last of the Six-Party Talks went out with a whimper on December 11, 2008, much as the North had wanted.

27. Don Oberdorfer and Robert Carlin, *The Two Koreas: A Contemporary History*, 3rd ed. (New York: Basic Books, 2014), 426; Anna Fifield, *The Great Successor: The Divinely Perfect Destiny of Brilliant Comrade Kim Jong Un* (New York: PublicAffairs, 2019), 67.

Prospects that the North would gladly welcome President Obama and a new administration were dashed in private meetings in New York the day after the elections. Ambassador Ri Gun heard from several experienced North

Department official and at that point president of the Korea Society), three former American ambassadors to South Korea, and others—that Pyongyang should expect a new administration committed to diplomacy, eager to move ahead with negotiations.[28] Ri told them that now everything had changed. He upped the ante of what it would take for the North to give up its weapons, seemingly to make it clear that they were no longer interested.

Condoleezza Rice reflected in *No Higher Honor* that the administration's push for multilateral diplomacy, particularly to enlist China, produced results. She wrote, "As a result, North Korea remained isolated in the region and the incoming president was not confronted with a crisis on the peninsula on day one of his term."[29] She added, "At least in giving the diplomatic track its best shot, the U.S. can't be blamed for what North Korea has done."

In reality, the North Korean regime took advantage of early missteps by the administration, built the bomb, tested it, and even assisted Syria with the construction of a plutonium production reactor. Then, when the administration could have taken advantage of Kim Jong Il's exploring serious steps to give up his nuclear weapons program in 2007 and early 2008, it again missed the mark. Even though it gave Ambassador Hill, a deal maker, some room to negotiate, the administration and, for that matter, Washington overall continued to be divided. The administration was not able to overcome internal divisions or the president's aversion to dealing with a regime he didn't like. Once Kim Jong Il suffered a stroke in the summer of 2008, the game was over. North Korea now needed to establish the credibility of its nuclear deterrent in a newly uncertain future. The next U.S. president would indeed be confronted with a crisis. Kim Jong Il was no longer willing to deal because he was determined to conduct a second nuclear test and put succession planning on a solid track, as I describe in the next chapter.

28. Chinoy, *Meltdown*, 372.

29. Condoleezza Rice, *No Higher Honor: A Memoir of My Years in Washington* (New York: Crown, 2011), 743.

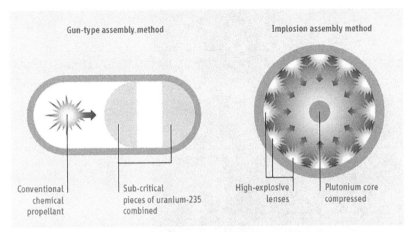

Gun-type assembly method

Implosion assembly method

Conventional chemical propellant

Sub-critical pieces of uranium-235 combined

High-explosive lenses

Plutonium core compressed

FIGURE 1. Two fission bomb designs. In the technically less sophisticated "gun-type" method used in the Hiroshima bomb (*left*), a subcritical projectile of HEU is propelled towards a subcritical target of HEU. This assembly process is too slow for plutonium. In the faster "implosion" method used in the Nagasaki bomb, plutonium is compressed beyond its normal metallic density to achieve a supercritical mass. The gun-type assembly works only with U-235, the implosion assembly works for either U-235 or Pu-239. (Eighth annual report of the International Panel on Fissile Materials, Global Fissile Material Report 2015: Nuclear Weapon and Fissile Material Stockpiles and Production, 2015 International Panel on Fissile Materials.)

FIGURE 2. Tour of 5 MWe reactor control room showed the reactor was operating at full power. 2004.

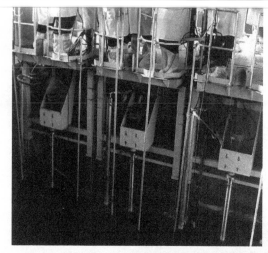

FIGURE 3. At the spent fuel pool observation platform, North Korean technicians convinced me the spent fuel had been removed. 2004.

FIGURE 4. At the Radiochemical Laboratory, Yongbyon technical staff demonstrated the ability to reprocess plutonium from spent nuclear fuel. 2004.

FIGURE 5. Toasting the visit to Yongbyon with water and juice after an informative visit. Ambassador Ri Gun: "We have shown you our deterrent." 2004.

FIGURE 6. Meeting with Korean People's Army Colonel General Ri Chan Bok (*center*) and staff with John Lewis (*left*) and Jack Pritchard. 2004.

FIGURE 7. Friendly reception by Yang Hyong Sop, vice president of the Presidium of the Supreme People's Assembly (*left to right*: Hecker, Lewis, Yang, Pritchard, and Kim Gye Gwan). 2005.

FIGURE 8. "We are not able to have you come to Yongbyon this time . . . because it's not safe for you to visit." Yongbyon Director Ri Hong Sop (*center*) meeting in Pyongyang. 2005.

FIGURE 9. Cultural visits included a stellar performance by young girls on a Kayagŭm, a 12-stringed zither, at the Mangyongdae Students' and Children's Palace. 2006.

FIGURE 10. During a visit to a Pyongyang Middle School English class, I leaned over the notebook of a young lady to see that her essay was about the American inventor Thomas Alva Edison. It was not only very well composed but was written in a beautiful calligraphy style English. 2006.

FIGURE 11. Hecker with Director Ri Hong Sop in Pyongyang a few weeks after North Korea's first nuclear test. 2006.

FIGURE 12. John and Jackie Lewis with Vice Minister Kim Gye Gwan and Ms. Choe Son Hui from the DPRK North American Bureau. She was present during each of my visits to North Korea and later became Minister of Foreign Affairs. 2007.

FIGURE 13. Hecker (*third from right*) in plutonium glovebox laboratory. I was told this was where the plutonium was prepared for the first nuclear test. It looked clean and functional for that job. 2007.

FIGURE 14. Yongbyon technical staff guided our Stanford group (*Hecker on left*) through the Radiochemical Laboratory to verify that North Korea had taken serious disablement steps in the summer of 2007.

FIGURE 15. The Stanford delegation's departure from the Yongbyon nuclear center was delayed by torrential floods. The nearby townspeople were repairing the road and bridge over the flooded Kuryong River. 2007.

FIGURE 16. First Vice Minister Ri Yong Ho, an experienced DPRK diplomat, had taken over from Kim Gye Gwan and hosted our Stanford delegation in Pyongyang. 2010.

12   2009 Visit: "You Don't Know How Bad It Will Get"

During the latter half of 2008, Professor John Lewis pressed the DPRK UN mission for another visit to North Korea. I was surprised when he got the green light for us to come in early 2009. On February 24, roughly a month after President Obama's inauguration, we were back in Pyongyang. Although the diplomatic endeavors during the last two years of the Bush administration had not brought the nuclear issue closer to resolution, our hope was that President Obama's stated commitment to dialogue and negotiations would be received positively by the North. Instead, Pyongyang greeted President Obama with a satellite launch. And it set in motion a series of events that would lead to its second nuclear test, shaping the president's distrust of the North's regime for his entire time in office.

The Lewis delegation included Bob Carlin and me, along with Marjorie Kiewit and Paul Carroll, who represented two foundations that supported Lewis's North Korea work, and David Straub, a very knowledgeable Korea analyst who had recently joined Stanford University after many years in the State Department, including as director of the Korea Desk.

AMBASSADOR RI GUN TAKES A TOUGH STANCE

Greeting us at the Foreign Ministry, Ambassador Ri Gun read a prepared statement. As usual in such a formal setting, Ri spoke in Korean. To Ri's obvious irritation, his Korean interpreter did not have as good a command of English as Ri did. He broke in with corrections where he thought the interpretation missed the point.

in the past month.[1] He said that he was aware of rumors that the DPRK was not willing to denuclearize but claimed that was not true. It was the "life-long wish" of Kim Il Sung, repeating an oft-stated North Korean position. According to Ri, the DPRK was prepared to denuclearize according to the September 2005 joint statement in a verifiable way.

Having checked off the obligatory verbal commitment to denuclear-ization, Ri turned to business. He claimed that the DPRK had met its obligations during the disablement process with the Bush administration, but unless the other parties did the same, there would be "difficult times ahead." Ri laid out Pyongyang's position on the current state of play for the three phases of the joint statement's implementation. The first involved shutting down Yongbyon after Washington released the Banco Delta Asia funds. The second involved the North's disablement of the Yongbyon nuclear facilities in return for economic and political compensation—that is, normalization steps—from Washington. Pyongyang was now prepared to move to the third phase—the *dismantlement* of Yongbyon facilities—but that had run into stumbling blocks because Japan and South Korea had fallen behind in their second-phase commitments of supplying heavy fuel oil.

The North had done its part, Ri said, in the second phase, including providing the requisite verification when it handed over copies of more than 18,000 pages of Yongbyon operating records to American officials. But, he continued, "Washington turned the verification issue upside down" (seemingly a reference to the Bush administration having moved the veri-fication goalposts in 2008). Ri stressed that verification of nuclear weapons was something that held for the entire peninsula. The North had to not only verify South Korea's claim that it had no nuclear weapons but also, somehow,

1. Selig Harrison (journalist and scholar), January 2009; Stephen Bosworth and Mor-ton Abramowitz (diplomats), February 2009; Susan Shirk (academic political expert), Feb-ruary 2009.

continue to verify U.S. claims that it would not reintroduce nuclear weapons to the Korean Peninsula.

Ri's comments became increasingly harsh. As for the Obama administration and its interest in dialogue, Ri said that all signs so far had been negative. President Obama began by sanctioning DPRK companies, and the U.S.-ROK military exercises were scheduled to take place in a few weeks. Ri reserved the harshest criticism for Secretary Hillary Clinton, whom he called "Secretary Hillary." He complained that the previous week, during her first trip to Northeast Asia, she referred to the DPRK as a tyranny and had mentioned the succession issue. Such comments, he said, are "beyond common sense that shocked the international community." The DPRK perception was that nothing had changed from the hostile policies of the Bush administration. Ri said that this meant that there would not be a "favorable atmosphere in the near future to discuss the abandonment of nuclear weapons," so the United States "must get used to fact that North Korea is a nuclear weapon state." He charged that "the Obama administration is still insisting that the DPRK denuclearize first, then the U.S. will follow with normalization, peace treaty, and other benefits. We don't agree." Bob Carlin remarked that the current situation reminded him of the dynamic in the spring of 1994. To that Ri said, somewhat wearily, "You don't know how bad it is going to get."

Given that this was an official, cleared presentation, the complaints were not unexpected. Normally, the follow-up discussion would lack such a sharp edge. The less formal atmosphere would permit a fuller exploration of views, even if no fundamental concessions were identified. That turned out to be the case here, with one notable exception. "Washington should be realistic and pragmatic," Ri said as he laid aside the formal presentation. "Denuclearization must come little by little. We must build trust step by step. Only when we have normalization and trust, then we won't need a single nuclear weapon." Ri also reminded us that Pyongyang still expected the United States to provide a light water reactor. If not, they would have no choice but to build their own. That turned out to be a hint of things to come.

Dinner with Ri was still more relaxed, but all conversations came to the same bottom line: Times have changed, and the DPRK is not going to denuclearize anytime soon. Much to my dismay, Ambassador Ri told me that I would not be able to visit Yongbyon, nor meet with its former director, Dr.

Ri Hong Sop. He told me there was nothing new to see at Yongbyon, and besides the technical people were preparing to stop the disablement actions for reasons he had cited—South Korea and Japan not keeping their end of the Septe... ...agreement. When I asked Ri rhetorically why I had been invited to the North if I couldn't go to ... Ri replied blithely, "You can tell the news media you were not allowed to visit because we are p... ...to suspend disablement." I told Ri that this was a long way to come to make a press statement. "I won't do so," I told him. "You can do this yourself."

During dinner discussions, we got a bit more insight into the DPRK's view on the current status of the multilateral negotiations and about its plans for the future. Ambassador Ri and the other interlocutors from the ministry expressed their distaste for the Six-Party Talks and the entire negotiation format. Ri was especially incensed that in the six-party format, Japan and South Korea had apparent veto rights over three full UN Security Council members—the United States, Russia, and China. Ri also said, "the Bush administration left a real mess for the Obama administration" in how it mishandled the nuclear verification issue. He complained that President Bush had personally approved the initial agreement on verification protocols that the North had negotiated with Ambassador Hill, only to allow others in the administration to change them and make them unacceptable to the DPRK.

Ri also informed us that the North would further slow the process of unloading the spent fuel rods from the 5 MWe reactor in the next month, then stop all disablement actions at Yongbyon. They would then bring the facilities back into operation, including extracting the plutonium in the spent fuel rods. Moreover, Ri said the DPRK was preparing to conduct a satellite launch. Our delegation was particularly critical of the planned launch. We told Ri that the situation reminded us of the North's missile launch attempt in July 2006, which greatly exacerbated the nuclear crisis and led to the North's first nuclear test. We told Ri that proceeding with the launch would surely move the Obama administration to stop dialogue and push for more UN Security Council sanctions. It would see a space launch as a long-range missile test in disguise. But the die was cast; North Korea was moving ahead with its nuclear and missile programs and preparing for a negative response from the Obama administration. I told Ri that instead of unclenching their fist, they were planning to punch the Obama administration right between the eyes.

When asked if the KCNA announcement of the launch had been cleared through the Foreign Ministry, Ri replied that the ministry "had been informed" about the announcement. He rather boldly added that the reference in the announcement to the "Korean Committee of Space Technology" was the first time he had heard of such an organization. He mused that now the North had a public channel for going through the formalities of space launch notifications. Ri's admission that the ministry had only been "informed" of the launch told us—as it was probably meant to—that the ministry was much less plugged into the North's missile and space programs than to their nuclear program. That is most likely because the nuclear program had been front and center of official negotiations with Washington. It also reflected the fact that the United States had little knowledge or contact with experts from the missile and space programs.

We did not get to see Vice Minister Kim Gye Gwan, who had hosted us for most of our previous trips and visited us in California in 2007. We were told that he was hospitalized. As usual, John Lewis had arranged several additional visits unrelated to the nuclear issues. These, as always, provided me with a better sense of the country. This time we were able to visit the city of Sariwon, south of Pyongyang, to tour a model farm.

COMPARING NOTES IN BEIJING

We departed Pyongyang on Saturday morning with the sinking feeling that more difficult times were ahead on the Korean Peninsula. The trip had borne out our assessment that the game had changed in the latter half of 2008. Pyongyang had decided to move the nuclear track to the front burner and to put diplomacy, if even necessary, into a supporting role to buy time. It appeared that Pyongyang had set a trap for the Obama administration. We anticipated a scenario in which North Korea would conduct a satellite launch, which would force the administration to argue for strong UN Security Council sanctions, following the precedent set by the response to the 2006 launch. That, in turn, would give Pyongyang justification to conduct the second nuclear test, which was required to convince itself and the world it had functional nuclear weapons. It seemed like a replay of the events of 2006 when the North's July missile launch attempt was used by the Bush administration to garner support for UN Security

Council sanctions, which the DPRK countered with its first nuclear test in October.

Back in Beijing, John Lewis, Bob Carlin, and I made our usual stops with

program to compare notes on the North's nuclear program with some of China's experts. The Chinese nuclear weapon specialists shared my view that the North would likely soon conduct a second nuclear test. They were very skeptical that North Korea could return the Yongbyon nuclear complex to full operations. They believed that the nuclear reactor and the plutonium reprocessing facility had sat idle for too long, especially considering that they were completely shut down during the Agreed Framework. They also believed that North Korea did not have the industrial capacity to build a new 5 MWe reactor to replace the one shut down (seemingly ignoring the North's ability to construct such a reactor in Syria, which was public knowledge by that time). Resuming construction of the two larger reactors abandoned during the Agreed Framework was far beyond their capabilities now, they added. I also asked them what they thought of North Korea's declaration in 2008 that it used only 2 kilograms of plutonium in its first test. They considered that not credible and offered a sensible explanation: The North announced the low plutonium amount to mask the fact that the test fell far below its expected explosion yield.

The Chinese policy experts were dismayed that the North was insisting on a rocket launch, realizing that Washington would feel compelled to punish Pyongyang. They stressed that although China did not want North Korea to have nuclear weapons, it took a very different view from the Americans in how to deal with Pyongyang. They claimed that what Pyongyang disliked most is to be ignored. Beijing believed that it was best not to respond to the North's provocative acts. Our Chinese colleagues believed that Pyongyang was willing to take some denuclearization actions to get economic concessions, use those to improve its economy, and then declare themselves a nuclear weapon state. Pyongyang, they said, would not give up its nuclear weapons. They believed it best to have the other five parties work together to make life difficult for Pyongyang—that is, to keep Pyongyang in check—so as not to entice Japan or South Korea to develop nuclear weapons.

THE POTENTIAL RAMIFICATIONS
OF A SATELLITE LAUNCH

Once I returned to the United States, I analyzed the threat posed by the actions North Korea telegraphed during our visit—a satellite launch, likely followed by a nuclear test, and a restart of the Yongbyon nuclear facilities. A successful satellite launch would yield some important information that could aid a long-range missile program, but it did not pose an imminent threat. Washington should stay focused on preventing a second nuclear test. The North needed a successful test both for technical and political reasons. It had been working on fixing the problems it encountered in its first test in 2006. Halting activity at Yongbyon in 2007 and 2008 hadn't been an obstacle to preparing for a second test because it already had a sufficient inventory of plutonium for a test device. Director Ri had explained during my first visit that once plutonium was reprocessed from the spent nuclear fuel, it was moved outside of Yongbyon—indicating plutonium weapon components were not manufactured in Yongbyon. These activities had undoubtedly continued because the 2007 disablement agreements were limited to Yongbyon. Work surely continued at the Punggye-ri test site to prepare for a second nuclear test tunnel. The test site had also not been covered by the disablement agreement. Once the order was given to go ahead, North Korea was able to take all the necessary steps to conduct a nuclear test in short order.

I reported to the U.S. government and mentioned in public that the Yongbyon facilities were in rather poor shape, but that North Korea had carefully orchestrated the disablement actions to allow relatively rapid reconstitution should it decide to do so. For example, it could quickly bring the facility back into operation to reprocess the spent fuel being unloaded at the time to add another 7 to 8 kilograms, more than enough for one bomb, of weapon-grade plutonium to its inventory. The 5 MWe reactor would be somewhat more difficult to restart. Disablement actions there had included blowing up the reactor's cooling tower. To restart the reactor, the North would have to reconstruct the cooling tower or find an alternate way to use the river water for cooling. Either path, I believed, would require less than a year. The Fuel Fabrication Facility was seriously disabled and would take some time to reconstitute. However, during our previous visits, we learned that the North had an inventory of previously fabricated fuel rods it could use for one more reactor load. Overall, I believed that all key operations in Yongbyon could be resumed in a year's time, or less. These actions would constitute a much greater threat than a planned satellite launch.

elsewhere. For example, at that time, the North's uranium enrichment effort must have been outside of Yongbyon. IAEA inspectors had not found uranium centrifuge facilities in the Yongbyon complex during the time they had access in 2007 and 2008. They had also not found facilities that could produce uranium hexafluoride, the feed material for centrifuges. Pyongyang had continued to deny having an enrichment program. Indeed, there was little information available on the location, size, and maturity of the enrichment program, but the circumstantial evidence—including the history of the North's procurement efforts and the traces of highly enriched uranium on the materials it provided to the United States in 2008—overwhelmingly suggested that the North was pursuing such a capability.

Uranium was mined at the Pyongsan mine, which had operated with little interruption during the previous two decades. The huge, six-story uranium conversion building in the Yongbyon fuel fabrication complex had also continued to refine the yellowcake from the mining complex to uranium oxide even during the Yongbyon disablement period. It is likely that this material was then shipped to an undisclosed location to produce uranium tetrafluoride, which could be used to make metallic fuel elements for the reactor it was building for Syria or to make the hexafluoride sold to Libya. These facilities were also used to provide feed material for the covert centrifuge facilities located somewhere outside of Yongbyon. Consequently, whereas the disablement actions in Yongbyon stopped additional production of plutonium, the uranium enrichment program was proceeding elsewhere. I believed it was, at most, at a pilot centrifuge cascade stage, not an industrial-scale centrifuge facility.

It now appears that although Pyongyang pursued both the diplomatic and nuclear prongs of its dual-track strategy in 2007 and into early 2008, by the fall it had decided to push the nuclear program ahead months before the Obama administration took office. By Inauguration Day on January 20, 2009, the North was poised to greet the Obama administration with a satellite launch.

13 2009 and 2010: Clenching the Fist, Not Reaching for Obama's Outstretched Hand

Not long after Ambassador Ri Gun's warning to our Stanford group, the Foreign Ministry announced the planned satellite launch would take place in early April. The announcement stressed that the launch was civilian in nature, unrelated to the military program. The ministry issued multiple statements in March, emphasizing the right to use space for peaceful purposes and insisting the upcoming launch was a valid exercise of its sovereignty. It was also well known to North Korea watchers that the North was keenly interested in besting the South's space program, which until then was built on foreign assistance. Pyongyang sought to legitimize and normalize the action by providing formal notice of the expected satellite launch dates to the International Civil Aviation Organization and the International Maritime Organization.[1] Pyongyang warned that if sanctioned for its peaceful satellite launch, it would put an end to the Six-Party Talks and its adherence to the September 2005 joint statement.[2] As I pointed out in the previous chapter, the stage was set for Pyongyang to take its

1. DPRK Foreign Ministry Spokesman, "Spokesman for DPRK Foreign Ministry Slams Anti-DPRK Campaign over Its Projected Satellite Launch," *KCNA* (March 24, 2009).
2. Ibid.

nuclear program to the next level, not by conducting the satellite launch, but rather by using the expected condemnation and sanctions as a pretext to end the disablement of the Yongbyon nuclear complex and conduct a

President Obama entered the presidency committed to dialogue and negotiations as advertised in his presidential campaign. Almost immediately after he was inaugurated, he sent public and private messages to the North Korean leadership that he was sincere in his desire for negotiations.[3] But once the North announced its intention to launch a satellite, the president turned quickly to telling his staff to get tough with North Korea. Concerned that the U.S. alliances had frayed during the Bush administration, Obama was also intent on closely coordinating his North Korea policies with Seoul and Tokyo, as underscored by Secretary Hillary Clinton's first overseas visit to the region in February. The appointment of Ambassador Stephen Bosworth—at the time dean of the Fletcher School of Law and Diplomacy at Tufts University—as the Special Representative for North Korea Policy (albeit only part time at his request while he remained at Fletcher) was a promising sign early in the Obama administration. Bosworth was an experienced diplomat with deep knowledge of Northeast Asia, including having served as first executive director of KEDO from 1995 to 1997 where he dealt directly with DPRK officials, and as ambassador to South Korea from December 1997 to February 2001. Sung Kim, a veteran State Department diplomat with extensive experience on the Korean Peninsula, was named the new lead negotiator for the failing Six-Party Talks.

Bosworth's appointment was also a bit of a relief for the two Koreas in that his personality and style were in stark contrast with those of his predecessor, Ambassador Chris Hill. Whereas Hill was a wheeler and dealer who loved the public spotlight, Bosworth was a quiet academic and diplomat who preferred to work the tough issues behind the scenes. Bosworth had previously articulated his views on how to deal with the Korean Peninsula conundrum. Following a visit to the DPRK in 2008, he and Morton Abramowitz wrote that the fundamental issues in North Korea went beyond

3. David Straub, "North Korea Policy: Why the Obama Administration Is Right and the Critics Are Wrong." Talk presented at Stanford University (May 13, 2016), https://aparc.fsi. stanford.edu/events/north-korea-policy-why-obama-administration-right-and-critics-are-wrong

Washington's singular focus on denuclearization.[4] Pyongyang, they stated, had both short- and long-term policies toward the United States:

> It is willing to bargain away its nuclear-weapons programs piece by piece starting now, but only in return for a new, non-hostile relationship with Washington and more help for its economy. It falls to the next administration, one hopes, to devise a strategy toward Pyongyang that addresses both the nuclear program and the long-term question of how to deal with the weak but dangerous nation.[5]

Now, Bosworth was part of that administration; unfortunately, his deep experience and counsel were never fully utilized. To some extent, his influence may have been short-circuited from the start by Pyongyang's decision to demonstrate progress in its nuclear program and shore up the leadership succession from an ailing Kim Jong Il to his son.

WITH THE SATELLITE LAUNCH, THINGS GET WORSE

True to its word, in late morning on April 5, 2009, North Korea attempted the advertised satellite launch from the Tonghae east coast launch station. The first stage of the Unha-2 rocket fell into the Sea of Japan. The other stages fell into the Pacific Ocean. And the payload on the rocket—the Kwangmyŏngsŏng-2 communications satellite—never made it into orbit. Nevertheless, the DRPK government portrayed the launch a success. Washington's response was predictable and exactly what Pyongyang had anticipated.

President Obama called the rocket launch a provocative act and a clear violation of UN Security Council Resolution 1718. It was an action, he said, that would further isolate Pyongyang from the community of nations. Obama considered this an early test of his leadership. The United States, he said, would hold private discussions to bring about a UN resolution that would "tighten enforcement of existing sanctions and take appropriate steps to let North Korea know that it can't threaten the safety and security of

---

4. Morton Abramowitz and Stephen Bosworth, "Reaching Out to Pyongyang," *Newsweek* (May 12, 2008), https://www.newsweek.com/reaching-out-pyongyang-89613

5. Ibid.

other countries with impunity."[6] Secretary Clinton followed with language reminiscent of the early years of the Bush administration: The United States would not be blackmailed by Pyongyang, but instead it would bring together

The administration was able to orchestrate a UN Security Council statement on April 12 that condemned the North Korean launch, demanding that North Korea comply with Resolution 1718 and cease missile testing. It also threatened financial and travel sanctions on North Korean officials and organizations with ties to the missile program. Susan Rice, the new U.S. ambassador to the United Nations, said the statement sent a clear message that the North's violation of international law would have consequences.[8] The watered-down UN Security Council statement, however, was not a legally binding resolution. It avoided tough new punishments as a result of Chinese and Russian objections and, hence, wound up playing into the hands of the North Koreans.

The DPRK Foreign Ministry called the UN Security Council statement an "intolerable mockery" and went on to say that it would not be denied its right to the use of outer space. Pyongyang would also cancel its participation in the six-party process and not recognize any past agreements because of Washington's response. The Foreign Ministry outlined the North's predetermined course of action. It stated that the DPRK would boost its nuclear deterrent for self-defense "in every way," examine the construction of a light water reactor, and restore the facilities disabled during 2007 and 2008 "to their original state." Moreover, it would fully reprocess the spent fuel rods from the 5 MWe reactor.[9] A few days later, the IAEA's inspectors were put on a plane out of North Korea. They have not returned since.

6. Blaine Harden, "Defiant N. Korea Launches Missile; Neighbors Express Dismay; U.S. Decries 'Provocative Act,'" *Washington Post* (April 5, 2009): A1.

7. Choe Sang-Hun, "Citing U.N. Penalties, North Korea Threatens Uranium Enrichment and Missile Tests," *New York Times* (April 30, 2009): A10.

8. Colum Lynch, "Key U.N. Powers Agree on N. Korea Statement," *Washington Post* (April 12, 2009): A12.

9. DPRK Foreign Ministry, "DPRK Foreign Ministry Vehemently Refutes UNSC's 'Presidential Statement,'" *KCNA* (April 14, 2009).

THE SECOND NUCLEAR TEST AND
ITS POLITICAL FALLOUT

Despite having failed its technical mission to put a satellite into orbit, Pyongyang achieved its political objective: to use the UN Security Council condemnation as thin cover to end all agreements and expel U.S. and international inspectors from Yongbyon and the entire country. Most importantly, the U.S. response paved the way six weeks later for Pyongyang to conduct its second nuclear test on May 25, 2009. Estimates based on the seismic signals monitored around the world indicated an explosion yield of 2 to 7 kilotons. Although this second explosion was smaller than the first explosions of other nuclear countries, I judged it a success.[10] KCNA bluntly declared the test to be a step toward improving the North's nuclear deterrent for self-defense "as requested by its scientists and technicians" and claimed that the test "helped satisfactorily settle the scientific and technological problems arising in further increasing the power of nuclear weapons and steadily developing nuclear technology."[11] In other words, the nuclear scientists needed a second test to correct the deficiencies in design or manufacture of the first device. The KCNA report noted further that the test "was safely conducted on a new higher level in terms of its explosive power"—a theme the North was to repeat after all the nuclear tests it conducted over the next eight years to blunt Beijing's expressions of concern about potential radiation danger to the population in neighboring northeast China.

The administration's response was not surprising. The Bush administration had orchestrated sanction resolutions following the North's 2006 missile and nuclear tests, which essentially banned the North from conducting any such tests in the future. Responding to subsequent, perhaps inevitable, violations of these initial UN Security Council resolutions with a push for even more UN sanctions and more pressure became the modus operandi after that. As Don Oberdorfer and Bob Carlin point out, the United States felt obliged to ratchet up the pressure in the form of new sanctions

10. Frank V. Pabian and Siegfried S. Hecker, "Contemplating a Third Nuclear Test in North Korea," *Bulletin of the Atomic Scientists* (August 6, 2012), http://www.thebulletin.org/web-edition/features/contemplating-third-nuclear-test-north-korea

11. "KCNA Report on Successful 3rd Underground Nuclear Test," *KCNA* (May 25, 2009), https://www.ncnk.org/resources/publications/KCNA_3rd_Nuke_Test.pdf

resolutions, which, in turn, sparked new North Korean countermoves.[12] Pyongyang's response to what was supposed to deter future violations was instead to take the next steps to advance its nuclear and missile programs.

minted Obama administration to harsh criticism from Bush hard-liners like John Bolton and Robert Joseph, who were blasting every conciliatory move toward Pyongyang from their current nongovernmental positions without owning up to their own dismal record on North Korea while in office. Moreover, current administration officials like Defense Secretary Robert Gates also voiced sentiments about the need for punishment. At the Shangri-La Dialogue in May, he called for increased worldwide pressure on the North:

> "We will not stand idly by as North Korea builds the capability to wreak destruction on any target in the region—or on us. . . . [President Obama] is hopeful, but he is not naïve. Likewise, the United States and our allies are open to dialogue, but we will not bend to pressure or provocation."[13]

Such language was in line with President Obama's basic instincts. During his seminal Prague speech, Obama singled out North Korea:

> "Rules must be binding. Violations must be punished. Words must mean something. The world must stand together to prevent the spread of these weapons. Now is the time for a strong international response, and North Korea must know that the path to security and respect will never come through threats and illegal weapons."[14]

Obama wrote in his autobiography *A Promised Land* that part of the motivation for the speech, was to "ramp up international pressure on both countries (referring to North Korea and Iran), including with enforceable economic sanctions."[15] The robust sanctions, which he credits Susan Rice

---

12. Don Oberdorfer and Robert Carlin, *The Two Koreas: A Contemporary History*, 3rd ed. (New York: Basic Books, 2014), 415.

13. Elisabeth Bumiller, "North Korea Is Warned by Gates on Testing," *New York Times* (May 29, 2009), https://www.nytimes.com/2009/05/30/world/asia/30military.html

14. President Barack Obama, "Remarks by President Barack Obama in Prague as Delivered," *The White House* (April 5, 2009), https://obamawhitehouse.archives.gov/the-press-office/remarks-president-barack-obama-prague-delivered

15. Barack Obama, *A Promised Land* (New York: Crown, 2020), 348.

for having successfully maneuvered through the UN Security Council after the North Korean nuclear test, were considered an effective response.

But, if this was effective, the question might be asked, how so? Pyongyang's response to the sanctions was an expansion of the nuclear program. It did not end the program or even, as far as can be determined, slow it down. The sanctions did not induce any positive behavioral change by North Korea. A response more along the lines of President Clinton's after the North's August 1998 launch attempt, to engage North Korea on missile talks while insisting on a continued presence in Yongbyon, would have been more effective. The sanctions action the United States orchestrated at the UN backed Washington into a corner and simply perpetuated a pattern of pressure and condemnation that worked to the benefit of Pyongyang's nuclear ambitions.

After the nuclear test, there was little chance of getting the White House to step into negotiations. President Obama seemed to consider the North's actions almost as a personal affront and maintained that the primary U.S. objective should be to change the North's behavior by, in part, breaking the cycle of "provocation and reward," which would mean not having the United States participate in a dialogue.[16] Although some members of the Obama administration later suggested they were ready to carry on the six-party process if Pyongyang had been willing, the Obama administration decided to focus the president's attention and political capital on other issues that, unlike North Korea in their judgment, he "could not avoid or he had a fair chance of winning." They concluded that the Bush administration's experience demonstrated that there was no basis for a deal with Pyongyang. Thus, there was no reason to expend high-level time or effort trying to achieve one.[17] Moreover, the president's attention was needed to deal with the collapse of the U.S. financial system and its international implications. The early assessment that not much could be gained from dealing with North Korea remained relatively fixed for the remainder of Obama's presidency, even as conditions changed on the ground that sometimes opened new opportunities.

Notwithstanding high-level ambivalence to any kind of engagement with the North, Ambassador Bosworth continued to do his job as best he could

16. Oberdorfer and Carlin, *The Two Koreas*, 430.

17. Ibid., 434.

and struck a more conciliatory tone in testimony before the Senate Foreign Relations Committee on June 11.[18] He laid out a pragmatic strategy of diplomatic engagement to negotiate a path to denuclearization that included

and appropriate defensive measures. He stressed that a central tenet of the Obama administration's foreign policy approach to date had been a willingness to engage in dialogue with countries with which the United States had differences. Bosworth lamented the fact that North Korea greeted the open hand with preparations to launch a ballistic missile, and it had not accepted his proposal to visit Pyongyang. Unfortunately, Bosworth's views were not widely accepted within his own government, and the North did not invite him to visit until December.

BILL CLINTON GOES TO PYONGYANG

In July, Pyongyang gave several signals through state media that it would be interested in dialogue, but it was finished with the Six-Party Talks. In August, former President Clinton visited Pyongyang on a mission to free two American journalists detained in March for crossing into the North from China. Kim Jong Il used Clinton's visit to probe Washington's thinking and to suggest he was open to resuming engagement, exactly what the Obama administration feared he would do. Oberdorfer and Carlin pointed out that the extraordinary dialogue between Kim Jong Il and Bill Clinton "might have provided an early opening for a thaw with North Korea, a chance to convince Kim to 'unclench' his fist . . . but Washington was not in a frame of mind to probe." The administration gave Clinton strict instructions to "go, come back with the journalists, and do not under any circumstances smile."[19]

Since at least mid-summer 2008, amid internal concerns over Kim Jong Il's stroke and a perceived need to present a tough posture externally, Pyongyang had put the nuclear program first, while using diplomacy to keep external powers—including both the United States and China—at bay.

18. "North Korea: Back at the Brink?" Testimony of Ambassador Stephen W. Bosworth, Special Representative for North Korea Policy, U.S. Department of State, Before the Senate Foreign Relations Committee (June 11, 2009), https://2009-2017.state.gov/p/eap/rls/rm/2009/06/124657.htm

19. Oberdorfer and Carlin, *The Two Koreas*, 436–437.

Now, Kim sought to use the meeting with Clinton to explore the diplomatic track again after the second nuclear test had succeeded and Kim's health had improved.[20] Warmly welcoming Clinton, Kim Jong Il appeared in much better shape than foreign media reports had suggested. He was clearly in command, knew his brief, and more than held his own in the back and forth. Kim reminisced about the good relations that the two countries had developed during Clinton's presidency. However, he said the relationship under Bush "returned to square one due to the neoconservatives in the United States." The nuclear issue, he said, worsened after Bush affixed the "axis of evil" label on the DPRK, and the world situation deteriorated after the U.S. invasion of Iraq. Kim added that he believed if the Democrats had won the 2000 election, all agreements between the two countries would have been implemented, the DPRK would have light water reactors, and the United States "would have a new friend in Northeast Asia in a complex world." It is easy to dismiss Kim's approach to Clinton as so much smoke to hide the nuclear program, but that ignores Kim's need for a propitious external security environment for the succession, as well as his long-term effort to continue his father's strategic policy of seeking normalization with the United States.

Kim complained that the Obama administration had not made a good first impression with the DPRK. He said that Obama publicly expressed willingness to talk even with hostile countries, but he would not even permit the DPRK to exercise its right to send satellites into orbit. Kim stressed that he had no intention of seeing the United States as a sworn eternal enemy.[21] If the bilateral U.S.–DPRK relationship developed, he said, it would lead to better relationships with many others in Northeast Asia. The North Korean leader also reminded Clinton that during his time in office the DPRK had unilaterally respected a missile moratorium, one it continued into the Bush administration for a total of seven years. Kim told Clinton, "If the Obama

20. The Kim–Clinton dialogue is captured in notes of the meeting taken by David Straub, former director of the State Department's Korea Desk, who had accompanied President Clinton. "Memorandum of Conversation: President Clinton and Chairman Kim Jong Il, 5:05–6:05 P.M., Tuesday, August 4, 2009."

21. According to Bob Carlin, this was a powerfully important theme Kim Jong Il had first used in the late 1990s. It was used subsequently by North Korean diplomats at key moments to signal Pyongyang's desire to move back to engagement.

administration took a sincere and constructive attitude, the DPRK could make such a promise again."

President Clinton was not able to pursue this extraordinary offer as his

He told Kim that he was not negotiating for the United States, but simply offering his personal observations. He reiterated the Obama administration's desire to get the DPRK back to the Six-Party Talks, which he said President Obama desired. He also encouraged Kim to give Ambassador Bosworth permission to visit North Korea, as he had not received replies to his requests to come. Kim politely parried that he would have to think about ways to save the Six-Party Talks while pursuing bilateral talks with the United States.

The Clinton visit played out in complex domestic and regional circumstances. Domestically, the Kim regime's focus was on creating favorable conditions for the succession. Improving the economy would be the biggest challenge especially since Kim made a disastrous reevaluation of the North Korean currency late in 2009. In the region, the North was not on particularly good terms with any of its neighbors. Relations between the North and South had deteriorated since Lee Myung Bak became president in February 2008. Although Lee was not so much of a hard-liner himself, many in his cabinet strongly opposed what they called the hopeless vision of his predecessors' Sunshine Policies. In August 2009, Kim began exploring better relations with the South and a potential inter-Korean meeting with Lee when he sent a delegation to the funeral of former president, Kim Dae Jung. Lee entertained the possibility of a summit, including holding secret talks with the North later in the year. Yet, as Lee stated in his memoir, *President's Time,* he rejected the overture from Kim because the North insisted on a huge compensation package and, echoing the rhetoric from Washington, "he wanted to break the pattern of rewarding the recalcitrant government in Pyongyang . . . simply for agreeing to talk."[22] Tokyo was deep into its own hard-line policy toward Pyongyang, focusing on the abductee

22. Lee Myung Bak, *President's Time* (2015), https://book.naver.com/bookdb/book_detail.nhn?bid=8736461 This book is not translated into English. See Choe Sang-Hun, "North Korea Sought Talks and Attached a Hefty Price Tag, South's Ex-Leader Says," *New York Times* (January 29, 2015), https://www.nytimes.com/2015/01/30/world/asia/north-korea-sought-talks-and-attached-a-hefty-price-tag-souths-ex-leader-says.html

issue.[23] With Beijing, Kim had some fence mending to do. Relations had once again deteriorated, this time because of Beijing's unhappiness over the North's nuclear testing. Kim couldn't afford vulnerability on that front, and besides, he needed Chinese economic help.

NORTH KOREA CONTINUES TO
MAKE TECHNICAL STRIDES

Although Kim Jong Il's attempts for a thaw in relationships with Washington and Seoul appeared genuine, he pressed forward with the North's nuclear program at the same time. Without the burden of having international inspectors and American technical teams at Yongbyon in the latter half of 2009, the North reprocessed the spent fuel from the 5 MWe reactor to separate another roughly 8 kilograms of weapon-grade plutonium. Unbeknownst to the United States at the time, it continued to reconstruct some of the disabled plutonium facilities in Yongbyon to house centrifuges for uranium enrichment. And, since Pyongyang announced it would pursue a light water reactor, its nuclear scientists and engineers were undoubtedly already working on an indigenous LWR design. An LWR would also require uranium enrichment for its fuel. By September, the North for the first time acknowledged the existence of a uranium enrichment program in its state media, announcing that "experimental uranium enrichment has successfully been conducted to enter into completion phase."[24]

In addition to the attempted satellite launch, North Korea stepped up operational exercises for its short- and medium-range missiles with fourteen launches between May and October. Their engineers must also have been modernizing the designs for their missile fleet, including working on

23. Between 1977 and 1983, DPRK government agents abducted Japanese citizens from coastal areas in Japan. The Japanese government has officially identified seventeen abductees, five of whom were returned in 2002 after the North admitted to and apologized for the abductions. Japan has continued to press for the return of the remaining abductees, maintaining that it won't be able to normalize relations with North Korea without a satisfactory resolution to the abductee issue. See "Japan–North Korea Relations: Abductions of Japanese Citizens by North Korea," Ministry of Foreign Affairs of Japan (August 6, 2021), https://www.mofa.go.jp/region/asia-paci/n_korea/abduction/index.html

24. Jonathan Thatcher, "N. Korea Says in Last Stage of Enriching Uranium," *Reuters* (September 3, 2009), https://www.reuters.com/article/us-korea-north/n-korea-says-in-last-stage-of-enriching-uranium-idUSTRE5826IG20090903

intermediate- and intercontinental-range missiles. Pyongyang apparently felt no need to hide its ambitions. On September 4, KCNA reported that the North's permanent UN representative warned the Security Council, "The

... Reprocessing of spent fuel rods is at its final phase and extracted plutonium is being weaponized." His statement concluded with the standard formulation, "We are prepared for both dialogue and sanctions."[25]

In early October, Chinese Premier Wen Jiabao flew to Pyongyang accompanied by several Chinese businessmen. Kim Jong Il was waiting for him as he descended the plane's stairs. Clearly this was going to be an important visit for China–DPRK relations. Kim told his visitors what Beijing wanted to hear: Pyongyang would return to the Six-Party Talks if "it sees progress in bilateral talks with the United States." It appeared that if the North continued to provide some semblance of interest in engagement with the United States, Beijing would not punish it for its nuclear development. In return for the pledge to pursue diplomacy, and with Kim Jong Il lining up his son to succeed him, China signed a series of agreements on aid and economic exchange, reflecting "China's foremost concern . . . to secure stability in North Korea."[26] Over the next few years, China increased its annual trade with North Korea from $3 billion to $6 billion.

In December, North Korea at last hosted a visit by Special Representative Bosworth. Although the North demonstrated it was willing to keep the diplomatic track alive, the visit did not plough much new ground. The Foreign Ministry statement declared that they "reached a series of common understandings of the need to resume the Six-Party Talks and of the importance of implementing the 19 September Joint Statement."[27] Bosworth issued a cautious statement echoing the same sentiment but added "there was no decision on the timing of talks, as it remains to be seen when and how the North would return to negotiations."[28] The North had no interest

25. DPRK Permanent Representative of the DPRK to the United Nations, "DPRK Permanent Representative Sends Letter to President of UNSC," *KCNA* (September 4, 2009).

26. Choe Sang-Hun, "China Aims to Steady North Korea," *New York Times* (October 6, 2009), https://www.nytimes.com/2009/10/07/world/asia/07korea.html

27. DPRK Foreign Ministry Spokesman, "DPRK on US Envoy's Pyongyang Visit," *KCNA* (December 11, 2009).

28. Choe Sang-Hun, "North Korea Says Differences with U.S. Narrowed During Visit by

in returning to the six-party format, but the United States would not agree to bilateral talks outside of the multilateral framework. In other words, putative disagreements over process allowed both sides to avoid substantive engagement on the real issues.

WASHINGTON MOVES TO "STRATEGIC PATIENCE"

By this time, the administration was settling into what Secretary Clinton called "strategic patience," a label that the administration tried to disavow for the rest of its tenure. Clinton used that term in answering a news media query while visiting Croatia as Bosworth was wrapping up his North Korea trip. She explained that Bosworth's meeting in Pyongyang was quite positive for a preliminary visit. She said that the trip was able to:

> reaffirm the commitment of the United States to the Six-Party process, to the denuclearization of the Korean Peninsula; and to discuss with the North Koreans their reactions to what we are asking them to do to move forward. . . . The approach that our administration is taking is of strategic patience in close coordination with our Six-Party allies.[29]

"Strategic patience" centered on a stated aversion to "rewarding bad behavior" on the part of North Korea, coupled with a conditional willingness to return to high-level talks if North Korea showed a serious commitment to negotiating an end to its nuclear program. It also entailed the gradual escalation of economic and diplomatic pressure on Pyongyang in response to provocations.[30] Its end result was that the Obama administration engaged only episodically in talks with Pyongyang.

North Korea's relations with South Korea and the United States turned particularly tense when on March 26, 2010, the North sunk the South Korean warship *Cheonan* while it was on patrol in the West Sea, killing forty-six sailors. Pyongyang denied responsibility. In May, a report from a

Obama's Envoy," *New York Times* (December 11, 2009): A6.

29. Hillary Rodham Clinton, Secretary of State, "Remarks with Croatian Foreign Minister Gordan Jandrokovic After Their Meeting," *U.S. Department of State Archive* (December 10, 2009), https://2009-2017.state.gov/secretary/20092013clinton/rm/2009a/12/133416.htm

30. Daniel Wertz, "The U.S., North Korea, and Nuclear Diplomacy," National Committee on North Korea, Issue Brief (October 2018), https://www.ncnk.org/sites/default/files/issue-briefs/US_DPRK_Relations.pdf

team of international investigators squarely put the blame on North Korea. President Lee announced that the South would cut almost all trade with North Korea: "We have always tolerated North Korea's brutality, time and again. . . . ~~~~~~~~ things are different. North Korea will pay a price corresponding to its provocative acts. Trade ~~~~~~~~~~~~~ between South and North Korea will be suspended." That amounted to the most serious action the South could take short of an armed retaliation.[31] Responding to the South's move, the North announced that it was severing all relations with the South.[32] It was not clear what possessed Pyongyang to initiate the sinking of the warship, but some suspect that the North wanted to teach Lee Myung Bak a lesson for the excessive military actions South Korea had taken the previous fall when a North Korean ship wandered across the Northern Limit Line and for the generally uncompromising stance his administration was taking against the North.[33]

In April, tensions rose even higher as the Obama administration released its Nuclear Posture Review. North Korea and Iran were identified as "outliers," that is, exceptional states that could be targeted by U.S. nuclear weapons. It was also clear that the designation was part of a broader administration strategy of putting more pressure on North Korea. Pyongyang responded,

> This proves that the present U.S. policy towards the DPRK is nothing different from the hostile policy pursued by the Bush administration. . . . As long as the U.S. nuclear threat persists, the DPRK will increase and update various type nuclear weapons, as its deterrent in such a manner as it deems necessary in the days ahead.[34]

The fact that Seoul had rejected Kim's attempts to hold inter-Korean talks was likely also a contributor to the North's displeasure.

---

31. Choe Sang-Hun, "Korean Tensions Grow as South Curbs Trade with North," *New York Times* (May 23, 2010), https://www.nytimes.com/2010/05/24/world/asia/24korea.html

32. Blaine Harden, "North Korea Severs All Ties with South; Move Follows Sanctions Imposed by Seoul over Sinking of Warship," *Washington Post* (May 26, 2010): A1.

33. Oberdorfer and Carlin, *The Two Koreas*, 444.

34. DPRK Foreign Ministry Spokesman, "Foreign Ministry Dismisses US Nuclear Plan," *KCNA* (April 9, 2010).

Not long after the *Cheonan* incident, the DPRK Foreign Ministry laid out a detailed justification for the North's nuclear program. It claimed that the Bush administration's nuclear threats forced it to lift a ten-year moratorium on nuclear weapon development. It was necessary to resume building nuclear weapons and testing devices (in 2006 and 2009) so that it had an effective deterrent. It added that the North was prepared to "join the international nuclear disarmament efforts with an equal stand with other nuclear weapons states."[35] Pyongyang was flexing its political muscle, while repeating the claim that it would be a responsible nuclear power.

On the technical side, North Korea may have had sufficient plutonium to fuel five or six bombs, but with limited nuclear testing and missile testing experience, it most likely was not yet able to field a militarily useful nuclear-tipped missile. However, on several occasions during the year, Pyongyang made statements to make its nuclear and missile programs appear more daunting than they were. For example, in May the North announced the successful achievement of nuclear fusion. Although the reference was to energy rather than bombs, it raised the specter that North Korea was working on a hydrogen bomb.

By the summer, Secretary Clinton concluded that the administration's policy toward North Korea was not working. She convened a group of North Korea specialists, both governmental and nongovernmental, to solicit advice. The meeting, which I attended, was evenly split between those favoring engagement with Pyongyang and those favoring a hard line. It was the consensus judgment of the group that the United States needed to resume some form of contact with Kim Jong Il. Ambassador Bosworth was also supportive of a "fresh overture," though the administration maintained a tough and unflinching public posture. According to the NSC's Jeffrey Bader, "We don't want to go down the old road and repeat the experiences of the past. . . . We are looking for behavior change by the North Koreans."[36]

At the sixty-fifth anniversary of the ruling Workers' Party on October 10, North Korea invited international media to witness its military

35. DPRK Foreign Ministry, "Foreign Ministry Issues Memorandum on N-Issue," *KCNA* (April 21, 2010).

36. Mark Landler, "U.S. Considers Possibility of Engaging North Korea," *New York Times* (August 27, 2010), https://www.nytimes.com/2010/08/28/world/asia/28diplo.html

parade. Pyongyang displayed three never-before-seen missile systems: the intermediate-range Musudan, a new medium-range Nodong variant, and a new surface-to-air missile system that resembled the Russian S-300 and

hardware was the prominent presence of Kim Jung Un, who two weeks before had been made a four-star general and vice chairman of the Central Military Commission of the Workers' Party.

Although the Obama administration's response to the North's attempted space launch in 2009 was understandable from one perspective—and there were many defenders of that course—it turned out to be a hinge point. The administration did not adequately evaluate the risk of imposing sanctions to those of taking an alternate approach. The launch, even if it would have been successful, would have done little to advance the North's nuclear/ missile program. On the other hand, once the administration walked away from the agreements, the North restarted its nuclear facilities and conducted a successful nuclear test, thereby greatly advancing its nuclear program. Although it's not clear that any decision in Washington could have stopped the progression from a satellite launch to a nuclear test, the administration's decision to organize UN Security Council measures against the North seemed to leave it few alternatives.

At the same time, Kim Jong Il could have taken a different path and avoided this hinge point altogether by not launching the satellite, or at least delaying it. Although internal pressures on Kim, both from the Workers' Party and the military, to conduct the salvo of a satellite launch and a nuclear test must have been great, proceeding with this course poisoned the relationship with the administration for the rest of Obama's term in office.

In November 2010, Pyongyang was ready to spring its next big surprise. It chose our Stanford delegation to be on the receiving end.

---

37. The Musudan, with a range of 2,500 to 4,000 kilometers, had been in development for at least a decade but would not be tested until years later in 2015. When it was, it failed catastrophically over a series of test launches and never entered the arsenal.

14   2010 Visit: "Tomorrow, You Will Have a Bigger Surprise"

In 2009, after negotiations had broken down and Pyongyang had announced advances in its nuclear program, John Lewis requested the North approve another visit in 2010. His first inquiry in January was politely turned down on the grounds that it was not a good time. After Lewis made several more attempts, in August the DPRK mission extended an invitation for us to visit within the next few months. The dates slipped until we finally got the green light for a visit in early November. We informed Ambassador Stephen Bosworth and his team. They voiced no objections.

John Lewis, Bob Carlin, and I had prepared for a broad spectrum of possibilities for what we would find during our trip, but nothing we imagined came close to what we saw. This was to be my seventh visit to North Korea and my fourth to Yongbyon. I was expecting to be shown their successful uranium enrichment, which North Korean had announced in September 2009. Based on my previous estimates of the North's progress with uranium centrifuges, I thought it was possible that they may have a few hundred centrifuges working in "cascades."[1] These, I thought, would include the two

---

1. To process sufficient material, centrifuges, sometimes hundreds, are operated in parallel. To get the necessary degree of enrichment, the enriched output of one set of centri-

dozen they received from Pakistan's A. Q. Khan and others they had fabricated from materials they imported through the black market. Some of my
technical colleagues also told me to be on the lookout for chemical isotope

their open literature journals. Although chemical separation for uranium
isotopes was possible on a laboratory scale, no country had developed it
commercially. Chemical enrichment was much less effective than centrifuge enrichment. As for the North's announcement that it was building its
own LWR, I thought this was a long shot at best. The technologies are very
different and are more demanding than the gas-graphite reactor the North
already possessed. Although some North Korean technical specialists were
involved in the KEDO project, those LWR reactors were designed by, and
their components were manufactured primarily by, South Koreans and
Japanese. We had also not seen any sign of construction of a new reactor
in open source satellite images of the Yongbyon complex.

On the way to North Korea, our team met with our Chinese nuclear
colleagues in Beijing to compare notes on what to expect when we landed.
They viewed the construction of an LWR to be beyond the North's reach
and thought the claim of enrichment success not credible. When asked if
the North Koreans had requested assistance with an LWR from China,
they gave a definitive no. We reviewed what was known about the North's
second nuclear test. I viewed it to have been a successful detonation, but
believed North Korea was not yet able to miniaturize a warhead to put on a
missile. My Chinese colleagues told me not to be so certain. After all, they
(the Chinese) were able to mount a nuclear warhead on a missile—albeit a
short-range missile—early in their program. One of the Chinese specialists
pointed out that their device (the same CHIC-4 mentioned in Chapter 8)
used highly enriched uranium (HEU). He said the North Koreans would
have to modify the design to accommodate plutonium, which has different nuclear and physical properties, but they may have succeeded. Before

fuges will be fed in as input to another set of centrifuges for further enrichment. Each set of
centrifuges enriches the uranium a bit more than the previous set until the desired enrichment is achieved. Such a collection of centrifuges is called a cascade. See Ivan Oelrich and
Ivanka Barzashka, "How a Centrifuge Works," *Federation of American Scientists*, https://
fas.org/programs/ssp/nukes/fuelcycle/centrifuges/centrifuge.html (accessed November 26,
2021).

departing for Pyongyang, we received a phone call from Jack Pritchard, who told us that he was just leaving Pyongyang after a short Track 2 visit during which the North Koreans showed him the start of construction of a 100 MW light water reactor at Yongbyon. I got the impression that it was a 100 megawatt-electric, but we found out later it was 100 megawatt-thermal—in other words, three to four times smaller than I thought.

THE FINAL TRIP TO NORTH KOREA

On Tuesday November 9, 2010, we were back on Air Koryo. However, this time we flew on a new Tu-204 (Tupolev) plane, which foreshadowed the improved economy we were to see in Pyongyang. Ambassador Ri Gun greeted us the next morning at the Foreign Ministry. Although he initially read in Korean from a prepared statement, he was friendly and added extemporaneous comments along the way. He told us that much had changed since our visit the previous year when relations were tense and confrontational. Although the situation continued to be tense, the mood had begun to change after former President Clinton's visit in August 2009. Ri said he had been recently granted permission to attend meetings with private scholars in New York and San Diego. Ambassador Bosworth had visited Pyongyang in December. The two sides, he said, confirmed their willingness to implement the September 2005 joint statement and return to the Six-Party Talks.

All of that was interrupted, Ri said, by the *Cheonan* incident in March 2010. But, he said, a UN Security Council presidential statement in July put a formal end to the incident. Ri told us that the U.S. side contacted Pyongyang and indicated it was ready "to turn the page" and restart dialogue. A South Korean report claimed it was a North Korean torpedo that sunk the *Cheonan*, which Ri denied. He went on at great length to complain how South Korea intervened and poisoned the restart of U.S.–DPRK talks. He complained that the Obama administration had strengthened relations with Seoul and now relied blindly on South Korea. Looking at North Korea through the eyes of the South will not help the United States, he said.

Ri was critical of the Obama administration's "strategic patience" policy. He defined it as "demanding that we give up our system, our ideology and our principles, which our people have chosen." Ri said with some irony, "What's happened is that while Obama has waited, we have realized the miniaturization of the nuclear weapon and have developed a deterrent." He added, "If the Obama administration keeps relying on a strategy of patience, we can concentrate on our economy without worries."

During ~~~~~~~~~ discussion following Ri's prepared statement, we asked what could be done to return to the ~~~~~ ~~~~~~~ ~~~~~~~ agreements. Ri claimed the agreements got off track when Japan and South Korea did not follow through on their obligation for heavy fuel oil delivery. He said Lee Myung Bak stopped after completing 70 percent of the South's commitment, and Japan never supplied "one gram." On the other hand, Ri said that North Korea had done its part: It had disabled Yongbyon facilities and even destroyed the reactor's cooling tower. Ri also complained about the sanctions imposed after their satellite and nuclear tests. "We cannot talk about denuclearization while we are under sanctions," he said.

I told Ri what I would like to see in Yongbyon on Friday. That list included the construction site for the LWR that Jack Pritchard had just told us about, as well as the Fuel Fabrication Facility in which they planned to make the fuel for the LWR. I also wanted to visit the 5 MWe reactor again to find out why it had not been restarted as announced in 2009. I requested to see the IRT-2000 research reactor, which had been mostly dormant for the past twenty years but could be resurrected. I told Ri I would like to see the facilities where they achieved nuclear fusion as they announced earlier. Then, just to shoot for the moon, I told him I was interested in seeing any facilities related to weaponization and mating warheads to delivery vehicles, particularly since the North had claimed to have miniaturized nuclear warheads. Ri said Jack Pritchard made big news with his visit. "Tomorrow, you will have a bigger surprise. I will relay your requests to the relevant agency." As we found out, they had already decided to limit our visit to the two places they wanted us to see.

A RETURN TO YONGBYON

We arrived on a crisp, clear morning in Yongbyon. We were surprised by the amount of residential building construction in the town just outside the nuclear complex. We saw at least sixteen seven-story apartment-style buildings going up. In the nuclear complex, we were greeted at a new guesthouse by Li Yong Ho, the safeguards section chief, who said he was happy to welcome us for the fourth time. He was accompanied by officials from the General Department of Atomic Energy. I was impressed by the new, modern three-story guesthouse and asked Li what it was used for. Li told us that they started construction during the six-party process when they were expecting a lot of visitors, but that turned out not to be the case.

During our previous visits, Section Chief Li was the most talkative and friendly of the Yongbyon nuclear specialists. This time, he was all business, although still with a pleasant demeanor. Li gave us a concise technical synopsis of how Yongbyon got to its current state as a prelude to what we were about to see. Li said that in the 1990s, the DPRK agreed to give up their (gas-graphite) reactors for two LWRs to be provided by the United States and its allies. They had begun construction on a 50 MWe and a 200 MWe reactor to complement their operating 5 MWe reactor. Now, Li said, "they have become ruined concrete structures and iron scrap." He explained that since their nuclear program had not proceeded as expected, it had not delivered electricity, and that had impacted the North's economy. Given that reality, Li said, "we decided to make a new start. We will convert our center to an LWR and pilot enrichment facility." Uranium enrichment, he said, has become a high priority. He acknowledged that they knew there would be some difficulties with this, but the decision was made to go ahead with the LWR fuel cycle. The enrichment facility was the most urgent, so they were proceeding with that. Li told us the construction was completed, and the facility was operational. "You will be the first to see it."[2] Li said that the delegation from the Korea Economic Institute, headed by Jack Pritchard, had just visited and was shown the LWR construction site, but not the enrichment facility. Li also told us that they had completed the discharge of the 5 MWe reactor's spent fuel, reprocessed it, and delivered it to the military for weaponization. Following his script, he said they were still willing to proceed with the Six-Party Talks and the September 2005 agreement but weren't going to wait forever.

Li accompanied us to the nuclear complex. In contrast to my previous visits to Yongbyon, the technical team clearly had instructions to show us only the basics at two facilities and only to answer a minimum number of

2. It turns out that as of this writing, in April 2022, we were also the last to see it since both the Obama and Trump administrations passed on opportunities to return to Yongbyon.

questions. We were hurried along at every stage. On the way to the LWR construction site, we passed the 5 MWe reactor, which appeared dormant. We stopped by the foundation of the round containment structure being

---

had taken this new post after having served as chief engineer at the 5 MWe reactor for a several years. I was puzzled, I said, that they had not restarted the 5 MWe reactor, which was their only source of additional plutonium and tritium. When Yu hesitated in his reply, I added that there are many in the West who claimed the reactor was too old and couldn't be restarted. At that Yu smiled, "Yes, I know, but that's also what they said in 2003. We proved them wrong then and will again."

The construction site for the LWR turned out to be near the destroyed cooling tower. This area had been identified a couple of months earlier from satellite imagery as a place of new activity, but for an unknown purpose.[3] Chief Engineer Yu gave us a canned briefing on the basic design information. The reactor was designed for a power level of 100 MW (thermal). He wouldn't specify the electrical power but agreed with me that the conversion efficiency from thermal to electric is typically 30 percent. Therefore, I estimated the electrical power to be roughly 25 to 30 MWe. This is much smaller than the two 1,000 MWe LWRs that had been under construction by KEDO at the Kumho site. Yu explained that they were building a prototype LWR first because the technology was very different from their experience base with gas-graphite reactors. Once they had mastered this technology, they planned to build a bigger LWR.[4] Yu told us it was a pressurized light water reactor with the steam generator outside the pressure vessel. The reinforced concrete containment structure just emerging from a large concrete pad, Yu said, was 22 meters diameter, 0.9 meters thick, and would be 40 meters high when complete. They would build two electrical generators to supply electricity to the local communities and would be hooked into the national grid.

3. David Albright and Paul Brannan, "What Is North Korea Building in the Area of the Destroyed Cooling Tower? It Bears Watching," *Institute for Science and International Security* (September 30, 2010), https://isis-online.org/isis-reports/detail/what-is-north-korean-building-in-the-area-of-the-destroyed-cooling-tower-it/10

4. Hereafter I refer to the reactor that I saw under construction as the experimental light water reactor, or ELWR.

The construction, Yu went on, started on July 31, 2010, with the target date for operations of April 2012. When I remarked that this was unrealistically optimistic, he replied, again with a smile, "You don't understand Dr. Hecker, April 15, 2012, is centenary of Kim Il Sung's birth, and everything in our country is targeted to be completed by that time." It was hard to tell if he was being ironic or serious. Yu volunteered little else about the reactor; the rest I had to pry from him. I was curious about the reactor's designers and inquired about details such as the specifications for reactor fuel, cladding, pressure vessel materials, and manufacture. Yu said a new, young team, one without reactor design experience, had done the work. The experienced gas-graphite reactor designers were mentoring them. The new designers were in their 40s, had graduated from North Korean universities, and had spent their careers at Yongbyon. They had not yet brought any of the North Korean KEDO LWR team members to Yongbyon but might do so for the operational phase. What was most striking was that during our discussion, we got the impression of an unusually ad hoc approach for such a complex engineering project. It seemed that they were finishing the design of the reactor as they went along.

Yu said the pressure vessel would be fabricated out of high-strength steel, possibly with a stainless steel liner. The pressure vessel, pumps, and other reactor components would be produced domestically. He assured us that they had the requisite welding experience, which is one of the most demanding skills required from a quality control and safety standpoint. The reactor would be fueled with uranium dioxide fuel enriched to a nominal 3.5 percent uranium-235, typical of LWR fuel. They understood that ceramic oxide fuel elements use fabrication technologies substantially different from the metallic uranium alloy fuel rods used in the gas-graphite reactor. Yu said a full load of fuel would be comprised of 4 metric tons of uranium. I found out later that the North had ample domestic uranium ore resources. I asked whether the cladding material for the oxide fuel pellets would be zircaloy or stainless steel. Zircaloy is typically used in modern LWRs because of its superior nuclear properties, but the DPRK was not known to have experience with these zirconium alloys. Yu said they have yet to decide. When I indicated that this choice was fundamental to the reactor design, Yu told us that although the reactor design had been completed, they were still working on many of the details. He said that I had to understand, "The reactor is like a fetus, like a baby. We are working closely with the designers. They are first-time designers." I also inquired if they would have adequate cooling for the reactor. Yu said they would build a dam on the nearby Kuryong River,

cooling continued to be problematic for the experimental LWR (ELWR) as well as for continuing operation of the 5 MWe reactor.

As we surveyed the reactor construction site, it struck us that it looked more like construction of an apartment building. We saw one small Hitachi EX200 excavator and a cement mixer that would have been just the right size for a garage floor. Our immediate reaction was that this was no way to build a nuclear reactor. For example, international standards for reactor-grade concrete work requires continuous pours of concrete to make certain it cures evenly. That is not possible with a small cement mixer. The foundations for the containment structure must also extend down to the bedrock to provide proper earthquake protection. We saw no signs of blasting to indicate this foundation was deep enough. When we asked if they had excavated down to the bedrock and performed seismic analysis of the site, Yu assured us that they had, but we were not convinced. I asked if they had a nuclear regulatory agency to license and oversee the project. Yu said that the National Nuclear Safety Commission had oversight; they had submitted their plans to that commission, and the commission had inspectors on site. I found it difficult to imagine that an independent regulator would approve construction of a reactor with so many key design parameters still undecided.

THE BIG SURPRISE: THE URANIUM ENRICHMENT WORKSHOP

We drove next to the Fuel Fabrication Facility. Unlike the previous visits to this complex of buildings, now it had heightened security. Security guards checked our passports at the entrance. We stopped in front of what appeared to be a new two-story gray stucco building with white trim, about the length of a football (or soccer) field. It was, in fact, the refurbished Building 4, the former uranium metal fuel rod workshop. In 2008 I had visited Building 4 to confirm that the DPRK had gutted it as part of its disablement actions. Safeguards Chief Li introduced us to Son Nam Hyon, whom he identified as the chief process engineer. Son called the building the uranium enrichment workshop, for which he said construction had begun in April 2009. He said the facility had been completed several days prior to our visit.

The "workshop" consisted of a cascade hall, control room, supply and recovery stations, and power supply. As we were about to enter, Son said, "We did not want to show you this facility, but our superiors told us to do so." That was not surprising since centrifuge technologies and operations are typically considered proprietary. He took us up polished marble steps to the second-floor control room and observation windows. The tour through the facility was intentionally hurried by Section Chief Li. He repeatedly cut us off and moved us along. It was exceedingly difficult to get a good look and to get answers to our questions. Clearly, they were meeting their obligations to take us through, but they wanted us to see as little as possible. All of this was very different from my previous trips to Yongbyon, during which the technical specialists were proud to show off their facilities and to display deep knowledge of their operations.

The first look through the windows of the observation deck down to first-floor operations was mind-boggling. My jaw must have dropped wide open. I was expecting to see a few small cascades of centrifuges, but instead we looked at a modern, clean centrifuge plant of more than a thousand centrifuges all neatly aligned and plumbed below us. There were two high-bay areas, one on each side of the central island. The high-bay areas were two stories high, 50 meters long each, and 12 to 15 meters wide: about the length of a football field and roughly one-third as wide. The central island bridge contained control and monitoring equipment—very neatly plumbed with stainless steel tubes and flanges. Each hall contained pairs of centrifuges on either side of overhead plumbing lines. There were three lines of centrifuge pairs, closely spaced, for the entire length of each hall. I estimated the centrifuges to be about 8 inches in diameter and less than 6 feet high. The exterior of the centrifuges looked like smooth aluminum casings, with no heating coils visible.

In response to my question, Son said there were 2,000 centrifuges total in six cascades, three in each hall. He did not want to give me specific centrifuge dimensions, saying that I would also not reveal such proprietary details about U.S. centrifuges. On the way back to Pyongyang, I made a quick calculation of how many centrifuges we might have seen. Based on our estimates of dimensions of the halls and the centrifuges, the estimates spanned from 1,500 to 2,500, so the 2,000 number seemed reasonable. I asked Son if the rotors were made of aluminum or steel. High-strength steel rotors can spin much faster and have separation efficiencies four to five times ~~~~~~~~~~~~~~~~~~~~ aluminum alloys. He replied it was an alloy that contained iron. Although he didn't specify, that mo~~~~~ ~~~~~~~~~~~~ were made of maraging steel—a specialty high-strength steel with good corrosion resistance to protect against chemical attack from the uranium hexafluoride gas. When asked, Son confirmed that the casings (the outer shells of the centrifuges, which were the only parts we could see besides the plumbing lines and base flanges) were made of an aluminum alloy. He also told us later that the rotors have one bellows, a technique typically used to increase the length of the rotor for improved separation capacity. Son told us the centrifuges were manufactured domestically—in fact, he said, "everything you see was done domestically." John Lewis asked if these were like P-1 centrifuges, referring to the Pakistani version of a German centrifuge design that used aluminum rotors. Son said they were not—they were domestic but modeled after ones at Almelo (the European centrifuge consortium Urenco located in Almelo, Netherlands) and Rokkasho-mura (the Japanese centrifuge facility). I asked about the SWU (separative work units) capacity of the facility. SWU provides the most direct measure of enrichment capacity of centrifuges. Son replied that it was 8,000 kg SWU per year. He said the enrichment level was 3.5 percent, and the tails (the depleted product) were 0.27 percent. Son said the reactor designers told him to target 2.2 to 4 percent enrichment levels.

We got a hurried look at the control room. It was astonishingly modern, unlike those at the old reactor and reprocessing facility. Five large panels were mounted in the back with numerous LED displays of operating parameters. Computers and four flat-screen monitors were tended by operators who were watching the flow diagrams on the screens. I did not get a close enough look to decipher these or to see if they were real time displays. Son rushed us through the control room for a quick look at the recovery room. It also had two flat panel displays and lots of tanks and plumbing. There was a set of steps leading down to the feed room on the ground floor.

Section Chief Li, who had been with us the whole time, ushered us outside to take us to lunch and to stop us from asking more questions, but I had many more, much to Li's annoyance. In response to my questions, he claimed to have all critical components and materials for the centrifuges—such as bearings, ring magnets, and specialty oils—on hand and that all were produced domestically. I asked if they had flow forming machines, which are necessary to produce the precision rotors, but did not get a response. Li did tell us that they produced uranium hexafluoride right there in the fuel fabrication complex, pointing across the street to the six-story processing building.

I asked Li if the centrifuge facility was running and enriching uranium. I was not able to confirm that from our quick look, although everything we saw was consistent with it running. Li said yes. I told him that Americans would be concerned that the DPRK was now producing highly enriched uranium (HEU) in that facility. Li said that anyone could have been able to tell by looking at the monitors in the control room that the cascades were configured for low-enriched uranium (LEU). Besides, he said with typical North Korean verve, people can think what they want. I didn't reply that reading the monitors had been impossible because they had rushed us through. In any case, the captions were also primarily in Korean.

Li was unhappy that we were late to the guesthouse. In parting, I asked him how former director Ri Hong Sop was doing. Li replied that he was fine, but he couldn't meet with me because the UN sanctions had him on the banned list. This was likely just pique on their part since being listed shouldn't have prevented Ri from traveling in his own country to meet with me. From my perspective it was a pity to lose access to the person who had been our best conduit to Yongbyon. The tight timing of our visit to Yongbyon was obviously planned by Pyongyang. The schedule called for us to leave Yongbyon and drive to the huge Daedonggang Fruit Farm, an orchard with over 1 million apple trees imported from Italy. We would have been happy to skip that, but they insisted we go.

Our itinerary throughout our stay—the orchard, a textile mill, a modern wire factory, lunch with European embassy staff, an evening celebration of Polish independence, and our travels through Pyongyang and environs—showed that North Korea was not on the verge of collapse. A visit to Kim Il Sung University was particularly impressive. There, they showed off the new e-library as well as the new pool building with an Olympic-size swimming pool, diving areas, and saunas. Every place we visited demonstrated that economic activity had picked up compared to our previous visits. Central

Pyongyang was loaded with flashing neon signs, fully lighted streets, and well-lit government buildings. Most of the women directing traffic at intersections had been replaced with traffic lights. The exterior glass façade of

and a large increase in the number of taxis, including several Ford Focus cabs. Cell phones were everywhere, with people talking on them while walking the streets of Pyongyang. The European diplomats told us that upwards of three-quarters of the country might now have cell coverage. Computers and flat-screen monitors were ubiquitous at the university. The bottom line was if the sanctions were biting, we saw few signs of it among the elite in Pyongyang.

I especially enjoyed the evening celebration of Polish Independence Day hosted by Ambassador Edward Pietrzyk. The concert featured performances by Polish musicians and by North Korea's Jong Kyong Hui, in exquisite piano renditions of Frédéric Chopin's compositions. During the Cold War, Poland was a close Eastern Bloc ally of North Korea. It kept its contacts afterwards through an active embassy in Pyongyang. In fact, some years later, Ambassador Ri Gun, who had been our steady interface with the Foreign Ministry, was made North Korea's ambassador to Poland. It turns out I have a special interest in Poland as well. It is where I was born in late 1943 while my father was stationed there working in a German military factory.

READOUT WITH THE MINISTRY OF FOREIGN AFFAIRS

On Friday evening over dinner, we reported on the Yongbyon visit to the new vice minister of foreign affairs, Ri Yong Ho. Bob Carlin had met Ri during the Agreed Framework negotiations and several times thereafter. A former ministry official told us that Ri was one of the architects of the Agreed Framework. Ri also accompanied Vice Marshal Jo Myong Rok to Washington to meet President Clinton in 2000. He served as ambassador to the United Kingdom from 2003 to 2007 and later participated in the six-party negotiations. He was a consummate diplomat, fluent in English, smart, calm, precise, and insightful.

I presented a summary of the technical findings at the LWR reactor site and the uranium centrifuge workshop. Carlin expressed his concerns about the negative political fallout once we reported this news back in Washington and lamented the bad timing of all of this. He said the Obama administration had just begun to look for ways to engage with Pyongyang, but now it seemed this initial reevaluation would be crushed by the weight of these new developments. Ri said that when he first heard of the plans for the LWR and enrichment, he also expressed concerns about the political fallout. But he said that the DPRK had reached the conclusion that even with the new Obama administration, America's North Korea policy would not change. "We had to find a way out," he added. He said that if the Americans were really concerned, they must first think and then act in ways that make the DPRK feel safe. He repeated a North Korean refrain: "Every time the administration changes in Washington, everything changes." He asked rhetorically, what would make the DPRK feel safe? His answer: "If the administration would reaffirm the October 2000 Joint Communiqué and demonstrate that it was serious, that would be quite helpful."

Lewis asked what they had hoped to accomplish by letting us see the two facilities. Ri said they announced in 2009 that their nuclear program would proceed this way, but no one believed them. He added, "That includes you, Dr. Hecker. We wanted to show that we are serious." We asked about possible Chinese reaction to the news. Ri said they had already informed Beijing. "We told them that the official statement of April 2009 was not a lie, but the truth." Ri said he was sure the Chinese would be more understanding than the Americans. Then he touched on a sensitive point. "The LWR and enrichment are peaceful at the moment, but we [apparently referring to the Foreign Ministry] don't know if one day the military people will ask the Yongbyon people to take the technology for their use. I'm doing my best to see it doesn't happen." His not-so-subtle hint of differences between the North Korean military and diplomats seemed genuine. In the past, he said, Pyongyang had argued that they could get an LWR from the outside, but that hope had vanished. Now, the scientists said they would do it on their own.

Ri laid out what he considered a central problem: The Obama administration didn't think of the DRPK as a country but only as an enemy to collapse. The United States had diplomatic relations with 188 out of 192 countries of the world, he noted, but no relations with Iran, Cuba, Bhutan, and the DPRK. It was, he said, not possible to have a normal dialogue when the United States sees the DPRK that way. Moreover, the Obama administration's so-called strategic patience policy reflected Washington's inability to figure out how to deal with the DPRK. He said that in Pyongyang, many people thought that strategic patience was not bad for the North. "It gives us time to finish the LWR and produce the [low-enriched uranium] fuel for it. We can wait. Time is what we need."

Ri emphasized that the DRPK's nuclear weapons would be around as long as the United States continued to be hostile to the DPRK. The reason for having nuclear weapons hadn't diminished, it had increased, he told us. He pointed out, "You have an aircraft carrier in the West Sea." Carlin asked Ri if relations were reestablished, could the DPRK adopt what Hecker called the "three no's"—that is, no more bombs, no better bombs, and no exports. I added that this must, of course, be accompanied by "one yes": the U.S. side addressing the DPRK's security concerns. Ri said that they understood the "three no's" and the "one yes." He added that it didn't matter, however, if that proposal came from me. What mattered was if the U.S. government asked that question. If so, Ri said, "I will answer it," though he wouldn't go on to say what his answer would be. He explained that Pyongyang refers to these as no horizontal and no vertical proliferation and said that they are prepared to discuss these ideas with the United States.

Ri ended the dinner conversation with the tantalizing comment that building the LWR and uranium enrichment facility was not the North's preference. Rather, it had been forced to do so. Therefore, we (seemingly meaning North Korea and the United States) can do something about it, but he said, "We must make the results benefit both countries." It certainly seemed as if he was pointing to a way out of the current impasse, even if his explanation for why the two countries had reached this point left something to be desired.

RETURN TO THE UNITED STATES

On Saturday morning, we were again on the flight to Beijing. We were met at the airport by a throng of reporters. We said little about our trip, wanting to get back to the United States first. We did, however, call and send e-mails to Ambassador Bosworth and his team to give them the heads-up for the blockbuster news to follow. We planned to present a full report of our findings on November 23rd at a meeting at the National Press Club in Washington, DC, organized by Jack Pritchard. At this point, we had only acknowledged publicly that we visited the construction site for an

LWR, which had also been shown to Pritchard. That was not to be, because the Friday before, I received a call from Gary Samore, the U.S. nonproliferation czar at the National Security Council, asking me to brief David Sanger of the *New York Times*, one of the most influential national security reporters in Washington. Samore said the administration decided to go public with our findings because they were about to brief the other countries involved in the six-party process.

I gave Sanger a brief review and then hurried to complete my full report to have it ready when he would make headlines on Sunday morning.[5] The lead paragraph in Sanger's article read:

> North Korea showed a visiting American nuclear scientist earlier this month a vast new facility it secretly and rapidly built to enrich uranium, confronting the Obama administration with the prospect that the country is preparing to expand its nuclear arsenal or build a far more powerful type of atomic bomb.[6]

Fortunately, I had my report ready for the deluge of requests for comments from around the world. I wanted to be sure to provide proper context for what we saw and what it meant. At the National Press Club event the following Tuesday, Bob Carlin and I made headlines around the world, despite David Sanger having already given away the punch line in his article.

I spent time with nuclear technical experts in various government agencies describing the technical details of what we saw. I also addressed what many in government and in the public called a U.S. intelligence failure—that is, how could North Korea build a modern centrifuge facility in the most-watched place on Earth without being detected. Ironically, I found out after the visit that the refurbished building that housed the centrifuges was covered with a bright blue metal roof that stood out like a sore thumb in satellite images of Yongbyon's fuel fabrication complex. It is true that

5. "North Korea's Yongbyon Nuclear Complex: A Report by Siegfried S. Hecker," *Center for International Security and Cooperation (CISAC)* (November 20, 2010), https://cisac.fsi.stanford.edu/publications/north_koreas_yongbyon_nuclear_complex_a_report_by_siegfried_s_hecker; David E. Sanger, "North Koreans Unveil Vast New Plant for Nuclear Use," *New York Times* (November 20, 2010), https://www.nytimes.com/2010/11/21/world/asia/21intel.html?ref=todayspaper

6. Sanger, "North Koreans Unveil Vast New Plant for Nuclear Use."

unlike nuclear reactors, centrifuge facilities are easy to hide, but how the North could bring a couple of thousand centrifuges into a closely watched Yongbyon nuclear complex and not get noticed by the U.S. intelligence community was (and is) alarming. If a centrifuge facility can be completed under the watchful eye of the U.S. government, then it's no wonder that Washington still is not certain how many additional centrifuge facilities North Korea has nor where they might be located.

Carlin and I gave a private briefing to Secretary Hillary Clinton. I had prepared a set of charts that summarized our findings and provided a brief historical timeline of the North's nuclear program. I explained that North Korea's desire for LWR reactors has a long history, going back to requests to the Soviet Union in the mid-1980s and continuing through the Clinton, Bush, and Obama administrations. Their claim during our visit that they had decided to do it on their own and had turned the Yongbyon complex into an LWR and uranium enrichment facility was credible and consistent with what we saw. If they were just interested in the bomb program, the quickest way to enhance it would have been to restart the 5 MWe plutonium production reactor or to build a larger gas-graphite reactor like the ones that atrophied during the Agreed Framework. Nevertheless, it was true that the facilities we were shown could also be used to advance the North's nuclear weapons program, particularly if the United States or international inspectors did not gain access to Yongbyon. I also expressed my concern that once they produced HEU, it would increase the risk of nuclear export because they could produce more HEU than plutonium and HEU is more difficult to detect. I raised that concern with Secretary Clinton because I knew that the security and potential export of nuclear materials were high on President Obama's list of concerns. The first of his nuclear security summits, one of his signature nuclear initiatives, was held in Washington, DC, in April 2010.

We concluded the briefing by stressing that it was most important to stop things from getting worse. We restated the Perry Process recommendation to deal with North Korea the way it is, not the way we would like it to be. We advised that the United States should stay the course on denuclear-ization for the long term, but in the short term, it should focus U.S. policy on containing the threat with the "three no's," along with addressing the fundamentals of the North's insecurity. We believed that the revelation of a modern centrifuge facility and construction of an indigenous LWR underscored how badly U.S. policies had failed. Secretary Clinton was an attentive listener and very engaged, much as she had been when she met with Korea experts the summer before. The principal concern she expressed was how the South Korean government would view our recommendations.

We hoped that our findings and our recommendations would convince the administration to reengage seriously with the North to address the mounting threat from its nuclear program. North Korea, however, did not make it easy. The same day we briefed Secretary Clinton, November 23, North Korea shelled Yeonpyeong Island, one of several South Korean held islands in the disputed waters of the West Sea, killing two South Korean marines, two construction workers, and injuring numerous others. Pyongyang claimed that it had warned the South ahead of time, and when it was ignored, it responded to a live-fire exercise in which the South dropped artillery shells into the North's waters. The shelling became an international incident that temporarily sank stock markets.

I didn't know at the time that this would be my last visit to North Korea. In the years that followed, I continued to track North Korea's nuclear developments closely, but was only able to learn about those in Yongbyon from a distance with the help of satellite imagery analysis. What I learned during my visits, both from the facilities I saw and the technical and political specialists and officials I met, greatly aided my interpretation of satellite images and of North Korea's public display of hardware and test results. I followed the political developments through publicly available sources and by conferring with officials and experts in Washington, South Korea, China, and Russia. In the remaining chapters, I detail key technical and political developments to demonstrate even more clearly how North Korea's nuclear policy evolved and how the Obama and Trump administrations failed to respond effectively, each making the wrong calls at critical hinge points.

15 November 2010 to April 2012:
Deal Blows Up, Along with Rocket

Obama administration officials sought to substantiate and frame the narrative surrounding the uranium enrichment revelations. Public analysis of commercial satellite imagery corroborated the presence of the blue-roofed centrifuge hall at Yongbyon. U.S. officials sought to downplay the news and defend against accusations that the administration was caught off guard. The South Korean government also reacted with outward calm to the news, echoing the claims of the Obama administration. For Washington, the news was seen as yet another confirmation that North Korea could not be trusted, that it has never honored an agreement. The timing was unfortunate. Together with the shelling of Yeonpyeong Island, the enrichment revelations scuttled what has been a nascent U.S. effort to re-engage. Although the North claimed that the uranium enrichment effort was part of its civilian nuclear power program, the underlying weapons potential was undeniable. The news served to remind Washington that it would have much to lose by not coming to the negotiation table.

All indications were that the North was prepared to meet. The Foreign Ministry expressed the North's interest in dialogue to American Lee Sigal, a frequent nongovernmental visitor to North Korea, in Pyongyang a few days after the *New York Times* story broke about the Stanford delegation's visit to Yongbyon. Sigal was told that the North was prepared to stop the uranium enrichment program and reverse course if the United States would recommit to the October 2007 six-party agreement and to energy help.[1]

The prevailing mood in Washington, however, was skepticism about the North's offer. Obama administration officials echoed the Bush administration's mantra that it did not want to reward North Korea for bad behavior. Although the administration viewed the uranium enrichment development as an issue of concern, it did not consider it a crisis. The administration decided to consult with its allies to develop a unified response. Both South Korean and Japanese governments were run by conservative leaders, so it was no surprise they did not advocate more engagement. Washington also turned to China to have it take a tougher stance with increased pressure on North Korea. In Washington, China was seen as an enabler for Pyongyang's transgressions, often calling for peace but failing to condemn the North's behavior.[2] During an early December phone call with President Hu Jintao, President Obama implored Hu to tighten the leash on North Korea after their provocations in the West Sea and cited the uranium enrichment program as a violation of the North's commitments under the six-party process.[3]

But China's support for North Korea had grown in the years since Pyongyang had decided to end its disengagement with Beijing, and Kim Jong Il had traveled to China in 2000. Kim took seven trips to China between 2000 and 2011, during which time economic ties picked up steadily. The Lee Myung Bak administration's hard-line policies and pull-back on North/South economic activities only helped to push Pyongyang further into China's corner. Although Kim was concerned about continuing to move farther under Beijing's shadow, after his stroke in the summer of 2008 the China connection was critical for establishing a secure external environment to pave the way for the succession. In August 2010, Kim had taken his son to China for formal introductions and likely to connect him with the

1. John Pomfret, "N. Korea Suggests Discarding One of Its Nuclear Arms Programs," *Washington Post* (November 23, 2010): A10.

2. Chico Harlan, "China Affirms N. Korea Ties with 'Candid' Official Visit," *Washington Post* (December 10, 2010), www.washingtonpost.com/wp-dyn/content/article/2010/12/09/AR2010120901782.html

3. Mark Landler, "Obama Urges China to Check North Koreans," *New York Times* (December 6, 2010), https://www.nytimes.com/2010/12/07/world/asia/07diplo.html

history and legitimacy of North Korea's revolutionary activities, including those of his grandfather, in the Chinese northeast.[4] Kim Jong Il returned to China in May 2011 to continue to cement the relationship with Beijing.

In addition to relations with China, the second crucial requirement for a stable external environment for the Kim succession was to put relations with Washington on a better track. That was the message conveyed to Lee Sigal in late November 2010. It was repeated to Bill Richardson, New Mexico governor and former U.S. ambassador to the United Nations, during his visit to Pyongyang in late December. Richardson was told that the North would permit the IAEA to visit its newly unveiled uranium enrichment facility.[5] The successful nuclear test in 2009, planning for which was likely finalized after Kim Jong Il's stroke in the summer of 2008, left little question that the North had a workable plutonium bomb. Revealing a modern uranium enrichment facility demonstrated it had the second path to the bomb. The North must have believed it was now able to deal with Washington from a position of strength. It signaled to Washington it was serious about negotiations by offering to halt the enrichment operations and allow inspections.

Although Obama administration officials showed some willingness to engage in a diplomatic dialogue in early 2011 after the Yeonpyeong Island shelling scare—which had for a few days looked to be building toward a serious escalation of tensions—little ground was gained. The spring of 2011 was an unusually turbulent time in the world that required attention from the highest levels of the administration. The Arab Spring was unfolding from Tunisia, to Oman, Yemen, Egypt, Syria, and Morocco, and Libya was falling into chaos. Pyongyang, however, continued to signal its interest in negotiations. In March, the Foreign Ministry told Russian Deputy Foreign Minister Aleksei Borodavkin that the DRPK was not opposed to discussing a moratorium on nuclear tests and ballistic missile launches—giving access to IAEA experts to uranium enrichment facilities in the Yongbyon area and discussing the issue of uranium enrichment.[6]

4. Anna Fifield, *The Great Successor: The Divinely Perfect Destiny of Brilliant Comrade Kim Jong Un* (New York: PublicAffairs, 2019), 76.

5. John Pomfret and Chico Harlan, "North Korea Makes Gestures Toward Calm After South's Drills," *Washington Post* (December 21, 2010), https://www.washingtonpost.com/wp-dyn/content/article/2010/12/20/AR2010122005890.html

6. Don Oberdorfer and Robert Carlin, *The Two Koreas: A Contemporary History*, 3rd ed. (New York: Basic Books, 2014), 454.

THE PLANNED SUCCESSION BECOMES A REALITY

As spring turned to summer, Washington supported reengagement with Pyongyang by having Seoul lead the way. A positive bilateral meeting between North and South Korea's nuclear envoys at a foreign ministers' summit in Indonesia resulted in an agreement to resume the Six-Party Talks as soon as possible.[7] Stephen Bosworth and Vice Minister Kim Gye Gwan met in New York in late July for the first high-level diplomatic talks since Bosworth's three-day trip to Pyongyang in December 2009. The readout from both sides was positive but cautious. The meeting set the two sides on a path toward negotiations, but it took until late October for them to engage in a serious pattern of diplomacy. By this time, Glyn Davies, another seasoned diplomat, had been appointed to replace Bosworth. Davies joined Bosworth to get up to speed in a meeting with Kim Gye Gwan on October 25 in Geneva. The U.S. and North Korean officials agreed they had narrowed their differences, with Kim sounding rather optimistic.

In mid-December, Davies and Robert King, the U.S. special envoy for North Korean human rights issues, met with Ambassador Ri Gun and his team in Beijing to discuss the resumption of humanitarian aid to North Korea. They moved toward the United States providing assistance in return for nuclear concessions by the DPRK, including suspending its uranium enrichment program and its nuclear and ballistic missile testing, in addition to readmitting nuclear inspectors expelled in 2009. They also agreed to resume dialogue between North and South Korea.[8] Just as Washington and Pyongyang appeared to have reached a diplomatic breakthrough, Kim Jong Il died of a sudden heart attack on December 17. One line in the KCNA announcement of his death touted his significant nuclear achievement as having made the country "emerge a nuclear weapons state and an invincible military power which no enemy can ever provoke."[9]

7. Chico Harlan, "U.S. Invites North Korea Official to N.Y. for Talks," *Washington Post* (July 24, 2011), https://www.washingtonpost.com/world/asia-pacific/us-invites-n-korean-official-to-new-york-for-talks/2011/07/24/gIQATQKeWI_story.html

8. Jean H. Lee, "U.S. Set to Pledge Food Aid to North Korea," *Washington Post* (December 19, 2011): A14.

9. The Central Committee and the Central Military Commission of the Workers' Party of Korea, National Defense Commission of the DPRK, the Presidium of the Supreme People's Assembly and the Cabinet of the DPRK, "Notice to All Party Members,

The Obama administration remained in a holding pattern to see what emerged in terms of North Korean leadership after the mourning period, having little knowledge of and virtually no leverage over what would happen there. In Pyongyang, Kim Jong Un was suddenly thrust into the role of the Supreme Leader. On December 30, the day after Kim Jong Il's memorial service, the government announced that on October 8, Kim Jong Un had assumed the supreme command of the Korean People's Army at the bequest of Kim Jong Il, which sounded suspiciously like back dating the appointment. Kim Jong Un moved quickly to consolidate power. He displayed a hands-on management style and was willing to mix more easily with the public than his father. A lack of explicit, direct denouncement of the United States in the New Year's editorial signaled a desire to keep diplomacy on the table. Indeed, on January 12, 2012, a DPRK Foreign Ministry statement was explicit: "We will wait and see if the United States has a willingness to establish confidence by increasing the amount of food aid it would offer."[10]

THE LEAP DAY DEAL

On February 23 and 24, Glyn Davies and Clifford (Ford) Hart, special envoy for the Six-Party Talks, met in Beijing with Vice Minister Kim Gye Gwan for what Washington termed "bilateral exploratory talks," but turned out to be much more than that. The two sides apparently put the finishing touches on the deal almost reached in December. Keeping expectations low, in response to a reporter's question upon departing Beijing, Davies claimed no "breakthrough" was achieved. Yet, on February 29, the United States and North Korea almost simultaneously issued separate press statements outlining what has been called the Leap Day Deal. How well those pronouncements were coordinated beforehand is not clear. The statements indicated that the North's year-long efforts to resume dialogue had paid off. Yet, they also contained the seeds of self-destruction.

First, the announcements differed in tone and emphasis. The North Korean version gave a sense of reporting on a joint agreement, stating

Servicepersons and People," *KCNA* (December 19, 2011), https://kcnawatch.org/new-stream/1451890638-677103435/notice-to-all-party-members-servicepersons-and-people/

10. Choe Sang-Hun, "North Korea Suggests That It Is Open to More Nuclear Talks," *New York Times* (January 12, 2012): A11.

numerous times that the DPRK and the United States had agreed to or affirmed specific provisions. Pyongyang stressed U.S. commitments to improve bilateral relations in the spirit of mutual respect for sovereignty and equality.[11] The State Department press statement focused primarily on the need for the DPRK to demonstrate its commitment to denuclearization.[12] U.S. commitments were couched mostly in terms of reaffirmations listed as points that had "flowed" from the discussions in Beijing. There was no hint of a joint agreement.

On the technical side, the DPRK stated that upon request by the United States and to maintain a positive atmosphere for DPRK–U.S. high-level talks, it agreed to a moratorium on nuclear tests, long-range missile launches, and uranium enrichment activity at Yongbyon and to allow the IAEA to monitor the moratorium on uranium enrichment while productive dialogues continue. The American statement said the moratorium included nuclear activities at Yongbyon (implying everything else in addition to uranium enrichment) and that the IAEA inspectors would not only verify and monitor uranium enrichment activities but also confirm the disablement of the 5 MWe reactor and associated facilities. There was also no mention of the North's proviso that the deal would move forward "while productive dialogues continue."

The two sides agreed to move forward with the proposed U.S. package of 240,000 metric tons of what the United States called "nutritional assistance" to the DPRK. Negotiators had crafted a new standard for North Korean food aid—one that would give U.S. aid workers unprecedented access to the closed-off country and set new monitoring benchmarks to ensure that help reached North Koreans suffering from malnutrition and would not be diverted into military hands. Additional provisions included the United States declaring it had no hostile intent toward the DPRK, reaffirming its commitment to the September 2005 joint statement, recognizing the 1953 Armistice Agreement as the cornerstone for peace and stability on the Korean Peninsula, and stating that U.S. sanctions were not targeted against the

11. "Comment on US-DPRK Talks," *KCNA* (February 29, 2012), https://www.ncnk.org/sites/default/files/content/resources/publications/KCNA_February_29_2012.pdf

12. Victoria Nuland, "U.S.-DPRK Bilateral Discussions," *U.S. Department of State Archive* (February 29, 2012), https://2009-2017.state.gov/r/pa/prs/ps/2012/02/184869.htm

livelihood of the DPRK people. The North Korean statement also revived the issue of LWRs, noting, "Once the Six-Party Talks are resumed, priority will be given to the discussion of issues concerning the lifting of sanctions on the DPRK and provision of light water reactors."

The Obama administration appeared to deliberately keep public expectations low, describing the deal as "important, if limited," perhaps because President Obama was up for reelection. Stephen Bosworth, by now out of the government, signaled its importance by remarking that the deal was "what we had been trying to do for the last year. . . . It's a sign that the North Koreans want to have continuity. . . . First, they need the food aid, and I think they probably want a relatively quiet political environment to carry on the transition."[13]

But on March 16, a Korean Committee for Space Technology spokesman announced North Korea's intent to launch the Kwangmyŏngsŏng-3 polar-orbiting Earth observation satellite to mark the centenary of the birth of Kim Il Sung on April 15. The State Department issued a rejoinder stating that the Leap Day Deal explicitly forbade missile tests and satellite launches. A satellite launch would be seen as a potential cover for developing (long-range) missiles, and it would violate UN Security Council resolutions prohibiting the launch of rockets with ICBM technology.[14] The State Department also announced that it would suspend food aid discussions, although it still claimed that the food aid was not directly linked to the deal. It warned that if the launch occurred, the administration would find it "very hard to imagine how we would be able to move forward with a regime whose word we have no confidence in and who has egregiously violated its international commitment."[15]

A few days later, a DPRK Foreign Ministry spokesman provided a more authoritative account of the North's plans to launch a peaceful satellite by

13. William Wan, "N. Korea Agrees to Suspend Uranium Enrichment, Nuclear Tests," *Washington Post* (March 1, 2012), https://www.washingtonpost.com/world/national-security/n-korea-agrees-to-suspend-uranium-enrichment-nuclear-tests/2012/02/29/gIQAsxwAiR_story.html

14. Choe Sang-Hun and Steven Lee Myers, "North Korea Says It Will Launch Satellite into Orbit," *New York Times* (March 16, 2012), https://www.nytimes.com/2012/03/17/world/asia/north-korea-satellite-launch-missile-test.html

15. Chico Harlan and William Wan, "N. Korea Rebuked for Plan to Fire Rocket," *Washington Post* (March 17, 2012): A1.

pointing to the space treaty for authority to conduct the launch. The North also said that it had chosen a safe flight orbit (heading south from the west coast Sohae Satellite Launching Station) so that carrier rocket debris would not impact neighboring countries. The Foreign Ministry spokesman asserted further that the satellite launch did not contradict the Leap Day Deal, stating that "the DPRK had already consistently clarified at the three rounds of the DPRK–U.S. high-level talks that the satellite launch was not included in the long-range missile launch moratorium." Pyongyang asserted that it remained committed to implementing the DPRK–U.S. agreement and that it had already invited IAEA inspectors to "discuss the procedures to verify the moratorium on uranium enrichment."[16]

The greatest failing of the Leap Day Deal turned out to be that the two sides had different understandings of what the moratorium on long-range missile launches included. The agreement was the product of constructive ambiguity, allowing the parties to agree at a general level to overcome substantive disagreements about terms in order to advance broader political objectives. Both sides understood these differences over the test moratorium but decided to proceed with what they had. The other discrepancies in their statements were never put to the test because the North proceeded with its space launch on April 13. It did so despite what Ambassador Davies called an intensive four weeks of public and private calls from the other five members of the six-party process urging Pyongyang not to proceed.[17] The rocket disintegrated shortly after launch in front of an international cadre of journalists invited to Sohae and the control center in Pyongyang. As a sign that Pyongyang was under a new style of leadership, North Korea publicly acknowledged for the first time a satellite launch failure. The announcement stated that the rocket "failed to enter its preset orbit" and that North Korean scientists and technicians were looking into the cause of the malfunction.[18]

16. DPRK Foreign Ministry Spokesman, "DPRK Foreign Ministry Spokesman on Launch of Working Satellite," *KCNA* (March 23, 2012), https://kcnawatch.org/new-stream/1451900316-518734172/dprk-foreign-ministry-spokesman-on-launch-of-working-satellite/

17. "Ambassador Davies Provides Students with Firsthand Lesson in Diplomacy," *Graduate School of Public and International Affairs, University of Pittsburgh* (February 6, 2013).

18. Choe Sang-Hun and Rick Gladstone, "North Korea, Defiant, Fails in Rocket Test," *New York Times* (April 13, 2012): A1.

The launch failed, but it succeeded in scuttling any hope that the Leap Day Deal had longevity. Pyongyang would follow that failed attempt with its first successful launch of a satellite in December 2012.

Kim Jong Un proceeded with the April satellite launch despite heavy international pressure not to launch. The decision to launch a satellite to commemorate the centenary of his grandfather's birth was made by his father long before his death. It was not for the new leader to change these plans. Moreover, access to space had long been touted by the North as being an important economic asset. The space rivalry with South Korea also likely played a role as it did in previous satellite launch attempts. In fact, with the successful launch in December 2012, North Korea beat South Korea into space with an indigenously built rocket, which the South did not manage until the following spring. The decision to launch almost certainly was not part of a new strategy to go all out to enhance the country's missile and nuclear programs since a satellite launch would represent only a small step in the direction of functional ICBMs. It might have been that Kim misjudged what the U.S. reaction would be since the DPRK appeared prepared to follow through with the deal right up to the launch.

The Obama administration had put on a full court press for nearly a month to try to stop North Korea from proceeding with the launch. President Obama personally ratcheted up the pressure on Pyongyang in a visit to the DMZ while in Seoul for the second Nuclear Security Summit in late March. He warned North Korea using language remarkably similar to how the Bush administration framed the nature of diplomatic negotiations—warning that "they need to understand that bad behavior will not be rewarded."[19] At the summit, Obama held a ninety-minute bilateral meeting with Hu Jintao that was dominated by talk of how to deal with Pyongyang's belligerence.[20]

Having boxed itself into a corner, after the launch attempt the White House predictably and as promised announced that the food aid would be

19. Mark Landler and Choe Sang-Hun, "Obama Warns North Korea to End 'Bad Behavior,'" *New York Times* (March 26, 2012): A8.

20. David Nakamura and Chico Harlan, "Obama Urges China to Add to Global Pressure on N. Korea," *Washington Post* (March 26, 2012), https://www.washingtonpost.com/politics/obama-urges-china-to-add-to-global-pressure-on-north-korea/2012/03/26/gIQA8T-7vbS_story.html

suspended.[21] The Obama administration did not plan to pursue additional sanctions or other punishment through the UN Security Council but rather planned to push for stepped-up enforcement of existing UN resolutions. The administration did not show much interest in further dialogue. It issued a White House statement that North Korea was further isolating itself, and Obama would only be prepared to engage with the North if it again met the U.S. "pre-steps"—that is, satisfy its existing international obligations, including the ones it signed up for in the Leap Day Deal.[22] The White House was able to trigger unanimous censure of North Korea's actions at the UN Security Council.

Kim Jong Un delivered his maiden speech at the military parade on April 15. Given the massive display of military equipment, Kim's tone was quite measured with no anti-U.S. or anti-ROK rhetoric. He expressed the party's determination not to make people "tighten their belts again." He foreshadowed the desire to establish a stable external security environment to enable a shift of resources from the military to the civilian economy,[23] an early indication that the new leader recognized that improving the North's economy was paramount. Yet, on April 18, 2012, following repeated U.S. statements that the Leap Day Deal had been abrogated because of the North's satellite launch, the DPRK Foreign Ministry released a statement that it was abandoning the deal, freeing the North to move the nuclear track ahead of diplomacy again.

21. Choe and Gladstone, "North Korea, Defiant."

22. Chico Harlan and William Wan, "North Korea Signals Rocket Launch Does Not Flout Deal with US," *Washington Post* (April 13, 2012), https://www.washingtonpost.com/world/asia_pacific/north-korea-signals-rocket-launch-does-not-flout-deal-with-us/2012/04/12/gIQAXSgNCT_story.html

23. James Church, "Keep Your Eye on the Duck," *38 North* (June 19, 2012), https://www.38north.org/2012/06/jchurch061912/

16 "Does the U.S. Blow This Up Over One Stupid Rocket Launch?"

North Korea found itself in a good place at the end of November 2010. By letting our Stanford team view the new enrichment facility at Yongbyon, it had served notice to Washington that it had the capacity to significantly expand its nuclear weapon program and pursue nuclear electricity on its own. Yet, Kim Jong Il chose to reengage the Americans diplomatically to make a deal and was on the verge of doing so when he died in December 2011. His son, Kim Jong Un, picked up the negotiations and followed through to complete the deal in February 2012.

This should have been a good opportunity: a new, untried leader looking to stabilize the external situation to give himself time to consolidate his rule. Instead, it turned into a hinge point—a bad decision by the Obama administration leading to bad consequences. In this case, the bad decision was Washington's choice to blow up the Leap Day Deal because of North Korea's attempt to launch a satellite.[1]

---

1. In colorful language typical of his informative and entertaining blog, Jeffrey Lewis—director of the East Asia Nonproliferation Program at the Center for Nonproliferation Studies at the Middlebury Institute in Monterey— asked the question in the chapter title: "Does the U.S. blow up this deal over one stupid rocket launch?" See Jeffrey Lewis, "Rockets and the Leap Day Deal," *Arms Control Wonk* (March 23, 2012), https://www.armscontrolwonk.com/archive/205098/rockets-and-the-leap-day-deal/

The demise of the Leap Day Deal was yet another example of how U.S. policy and technical assessments were decoupled. By abandoning the Leap Day Deal over the North's attempt to put a satellite in orbit, the Obama administration sacrificed getting observers back on the ground at the Yongbyon nuclear complex, stopping the centrifuges from spinning there, and achieving a moratorium on nuclear and long-range missile tests. All of this would have been achieved for the promise of a couple of hundred thousand tons of U.S. nutritional aid (worth roughly $240 million).

In contrast, North Korea coupled diplomacy and technical assessments in its dual-track strategy. Whenever one of these was put in the lead, the other was closely coordinated to provide a hedge or to create new opportunities. Washington, on the other hand, reacted solely from a political perspective, one driven primarily by ideology in the Bush administration and by a complete lack of trust in the Kim regimes by the Obama administration. President Obama apparently decided to walk away from the Leap Day Deal because Pyongyang once again, as he said numerous times during his tenure, tried to follow the cycle of "provocation, extortion and reward."

During the runup to the Leap Day Deal, there was a lot we knew about the North's nuclear program, much of which resulted from our trips to North Korea and particularly from the visits and discussions at the Yongbyon nuclear complex. But there was much we didn't know, and that was why returning to Yongbyon was crucial to make a better assessment of the status of the North's nuclear program and its future direction. From a technical point of view, the benefits of the suspensions and access that the North offered in the Leap Day Deal greatly exceeded the additional risks posed by a satellite launch, even if it had succeeded. But the Obama administration used the launch as a litmus test to see if Pyongyang could be trusted to keep its word. Such a test was bound to end up with a failing grade by Washington's standards, given that the North Koreans had insisted all along that they considered satellite launches their sovereign right, regardless of what the United States or the UN Security Council might say. Setting up such a litmus test would only confirm for the president his belief that Pyongyang was following its familiar cycle.

I had hoped that sharing what we had learned from our visits to North Korea with two U.S. administrations would help Washington make better technically informed risk/benefit decisions on North Korea. It didn't. For example, when Bob Carlin and I briefed Secretary Clinton after our return from the November 2010 trip to North Korea, we emphasized that Pyongyang had been able to advance its nuclear program on several fronts. Our advice to the Obama administration was for Washington to take steps to stop matters from getting worse, for example, with the "three no's"—no more bombs, no better bombs, and no exports. We advised that diplomatic initiatives should first focus on preventing plutonium and tritium production by keeping the 5 MWe reactor shut down. The ELWR (experimental or prototype LWR) was of lesser concern because it would take several years before it could become operational. We urged Washington to get Pyongyang to agree in writing to a nuclear testing and missile launch moratorium. Though difficult, we said Washington should also try to constrain the centrifuge program. And it should reiterate the warning to Pyongyang that export of nuclear technologies and materials would result in stark measures from the other five parties of the six-party process.

I believed Washington should get Pyongyang back to the diplomatic table and explore every opportunity to stop operations at Yongbyon. I also urged getting U.S. technical people back on the ground to learn more about how far North Korea had progressed in its centrifuge program and in building an LWR. I did not anticipate that almost immediately after revealing the centrifuge facility to us in 2010, Pyongyang would engage in a year-long diplomatic effort offering to halt uranium enrichment. The North would have allowed IAEA inspectors back to Yongbyon and into the enrichment facility to monitor and verify the moratorium on uranium enrichment. I was also surprised that Pyongyang agreed to a nuclear test and long-range missile launch moratorium in the Leap Day Deal. I considered the technical concessions the North offered sufficiently attractive that Washington should have been willing to accept greater political risk in its policy decisions, but that was not to be the case.

At this point, after seven visits to North Korea and the Leap Day Deal having fallen apart, let me pause and take stock of the status of the North's nuclear program. This is where it was in April 2012 when the Obama administration decided to scupper the deal and thus forgo access to Yongbyon and a freeze on DPRK nuclear and long-range missile tests, as well as where the North might have been heading.

PLUTONIUM AND TRITIUM PRODUCTION

Plutonium remained crucial to the North's nuclear weapons program in 2012. Plutonium had been produced since the 5 MWe reactor began operations in 1986. The reactor was quickly restarted in 2003 with fresh fuel despite an eight-year freeze once the Agreed Framework collapsed. The reactor was in operation from early 2003. It was refueled once in 2005 at which time the spent fuel was reprocessed to extract plutonium. As part of the February 2007 disablement agreement, it was shut down in June.

Pyongyang's public version of the Leap Day Deal was silent on the fate of the 5 MWe reactor, whereas the American statement claimed that IAEA inspectors would confirm the disablement of the reactor and associated facilities. At the time, it didn't matter because the reactor was not operating, but since the United States walked away from the deal, it opened the door to allowing the North Koreans to fix whatever was ailing the reactor. They did restart it, making more plutonium and, likely, some tritium, beginning in August 2013. Completing the Leap Day Deal could have closed that route to plutonium and tritium production.

WHY AN INDIGENOUS LWR?

During our 2010 visit, Vice Minister Ri Yong Ho told us that Pyongyang finally gave up on Washington and decided in April 2009 to build its own LWR. I believe that the ELWR represented a legitimate attempt by North Korea to learn how to produce electricity with light water reactors. However, Pyongyang likely also had intentions of using the ELWR as a backup to the 5 MWe reactor to produce plutonium and tritium for the weapons program. Normal operation of the ELWR to produce electricity would produce a mix of plutonium isotopes that is less than ideal for bombs. However, the reactor could be run on very short operation (or burn) cycles to remove spent fuel before the undesirable plutonium isotopes make it less useful for weapons. Such operation requires frequent reactor fueling and defueling that could be detected by overhead satellites. However, it is also possible to produce plutonium by inserting natural uranium judiciously into the reactor's neutron flux to absorb neutrons and transmute to plutonium. A similar process but using lithium-6 instead of natural uranium could be used to produce tritium. Depending on how the North chose to use the ELWR to produce plutonium, it could possibly add as much as 10 to 15 kilograms per year. But even if the ELWR were to be used only to produce electricity, we had serious concerns about the reactor's safety based on the construction practices we saw and what we were told about the reactor design during our 2010 visit.

Without regaining access to Yongbyon for its technical team or the IAEA, the United States could only watch from afar as North Korea completed the exterior of the ELWR, including construction of the pumphouse for its cooling system. That pumphouse was used initially to provide cooling to enable the restart of the 5 MWe reactor to produce more plutonium and, probably, tritium. The young team of LWR designers and engineers must have encountered technical problems since the ELWR has not begun operation as of this writing.

URANIUM ENRICHMENT

Once the Bush administration terminated the Agreed Framework, Pyongyang was able to ramp up the centrifuge program that it had begun clandestinely during the last few years of the framework. It was puzzling that the North located the enrichment facility in Yongbyon rather than at a hidden location. Perhaps doing so served an important diplomatic purpose. As Vice Minister Ri Yong Ho told us at dinner in 2010, no one believed them when they announced success with uranium enrichment the previous September. He said we were invited to see the centrifuge facility to show that the DPRK was serious. Well, that worked—the report of our visit made international news.

Pyongyang also demonstrated that the United States would not know how many centrifuge facilities it had, where they were located, and how much enriched uranium the North could produce.[2] Our visit also left some uncertainty that the centrifuges we saw were of the P-2 type. If they were of the P-1 type, with aluminum instead of steel rotors, our estimates would be four times too high. Although the Yongbyon facility was likely producing low-enriched uranium (LEU), it had everything required to produce highly

---

2. A North Korean diplomat warned a former U.S. official at a conference in Europe on April 1, 2012, that the Leap Day Deal was perhaps the last chance for the United States to limit the North's program to Yongbyon. Bob Carlin, personal communication with author (November 11, 2021).

enriched uranium (HEU). The cascades of centrifuges at Yongbyon could be readily replumbed to increase enrichment levels from the nominal 3.5 percent uranium-235 for reactors to 90 percent for bombs. In that case, it could produce as much as 40 kilograms of HEU annually (assuming P-2 centrifuges), sufficient for one to two bombs per year. However, rather than replumbing the Yongbyon facilities from LEU to HEU production, I considered it more likely that the Yongbyon facility was dedicated to produce LEU. Some of the LEU product could then serve as feed material for a different centrifuge facility that could easily increase the enrichment in stages, first to 20, then 60, and finally 90 percent. That could be done off site at a covert facility. The bottom line, however, was that we just didn't know.

A moratorium on centrifuge operations at Yongbyon would have resulted in at least a slowdown of potential HEU production. It would not have closed all avenues for producing HEU since the North must have had other covert centrifuge sites. But gaining access to the Yongbyon centrifuge facility would have provided a better assessment of just how sophisticated the North's centrifuge program was and how well it was operating. The covert facilities almost certainly used the same technologies and likely also depended heavily on the massive chemical conversion facilities at Yongbyon, which would have been halted during an enrichment moratorium. Instead of slowing the program and learning critical technical details, the United States was left watching from satellites as the North doubled the size of the centrifuge facility during the next couple of years. That is why one of the most important objectives of U.S. diplomatic overtures with the North should have been to get the U.S. teams, and/or the IAEA inspectors, back into the Yongbyon facilities.

STATUS OF MISSILES

In addition to the attempted satellite launch in 2009, North Korea launched fourteen short- and medium-range missiles, a combination of test launches and operational field exercises, between May and October that same year. No missile tests were conducted in 2010, but at the October 10 parade, Pyongyang displayed the intermediate-range Musudan (Hwasong-10), a new medium-range Nodong variant, and a new surface-to-air missile system. North Korea was also completing the new Sohae Satellite Launching Station on the west coast. This was the facility from which the satellite launch took place in April 2012. There were no missile launches in 2011 but without a new moratorium, the missile program would surely resume, which it did. North Korea test-launched over sixty missiles during President Obama's second term.

NUCLEAR WEAPONS

Without the constraints of a nuclear test moratorium, the North proceeded to prepare for another nuclear test, which it conducted a little less than a year from the time the United States walked away from the deal. After successfully detonating a plutonium device in 2009, it might have been preparing to test an HEU device to demonstrate it had mastered both paths to the bomb. By the time of the 2013 test, it likely had produced sufficient HEU to allow it to expend some in a nuclear test. And, if the North had the CHIC-4 design in hand (possibly along with its nuclear test data from A. Q. Khan), it might have been possible to test an HEU device sufficiently miniaturized to fit on Scud and Nodong missiles. Without the 2013 nuclear test, I considered it unlikely that the North could have fielded a militarily useful nuclear-tipped missile fueled either with plutonium or HEU.

In sum, the United States paid a heavy price by walking away from the Leap Day Deal. The nuclear track moved back on top. There are no signs that the U.S. government appreciated the risk or did a risk/benefit analysis. By not shutting down Yongbyon, the North was able to continue a torrid pace of renovation and new construction in the Yongbyon nuclear complex and further advanced the sophistication and range of its missiles.

17   From Strategic Patience to Benign Neglect

The rest of 2012 brought no diplomatic openings. A Foreign Ministry memorandum at the end of August issued the usual refrain that U.S. hostile policy was the main obstacle in resolving the nuclear matters, and the DPRK would therefore "completely reexamine the nuclear issue."[1] The Foreign Ministry cited the derailment of the Leap Day Deal following its satellite launch as an indication of U.S. double standards. The statement continued, "If the U.S. does not make a right choice, the DPRK's nuclear possession will inevitably be prolonged, modernizing and expanding its nuclear deterrent capability beyond the U.S. imagination."

Following a successful North Korean satellite launch on December 12, the UN Security Council unanimously adopted Resolution 2087 on January 22, 2013, citing the launch as a violation of two previous resolutions that prohibited any further development of technology applicable to North Korea's ballistic missile programs. The Foreign Ministry responded the next day: "The DPRK drew a final conclusion that the denuclearization of the Korean

---

1. DPRK Foreign Ministry, "DPRK FM Memorandum Terms U.S. Hostile Policy Towards DPRK Main Obstacle in Resolving Nuclear Issue," *KCNA* (August 31, 2012), https://kcnawatch.org/newstream/1451899878-39520168/dprk-fm-memorandum-terms-u-s-hostile-policy-towards-dprk-main-obstacle-in-resolving-nuclear-issue/

Peninsula is impossible."[2] The statement added, "The DPRK has already risen to be a full-fledged nuclear state and the day was gone when the U.S. threatened the former with nukes." And in what was likely a warning of an upcoming nuclear test, the Foreign Ministry stated:

> Now that the hostile acts toward the DPRK have gone beyond the limit of universally accepted understanding and norms of the international community, the DPRK's option in reaction to it will also go beyond the imagination of the hostile forces.[3]

THE NORTH'S THIRD NUCLEAR TEST

On February 12, 2013, shortly after President Obama began his second term, he was greeted with another rumble at Punggye-ri, North Korea's third nuclear test. The test was successful, producing a nuclear yield of 7 to 14 kilotons—larger than the second test and on the order of the Hiroshima blast. Pyongyang announced the test had met design goals, thus demonstrating that its nuclear deterrent had become "diversified."[4] What did that word "diversified" signify? A good guess, even at the time, was that it meant the North had used HEU for the test, confirming it now had a second path to the bomb. The announcement also stated that the test was of "a smaller and lighter A-bomb unlike the previous ones, yet with great explosive power," a formulation that may have signified that the North had taken a critical step toward bombs small enough to fit on its existing arsenal of short- and medium-range missiles.

Kim Jong Un was on a roll. The satellite launch and the nuclear test were, in effect, the first fruits of the United States walking away from the Leap Day Deal. While this third test was an exclamation mark punctuating the administration's first-term North Korea policy failure, it did not prompt Washington to reexamine its strategy. Unfortunately, to administration officials it seemed only to reinforce the view that negotiations with North Korea would not work. For most of the second term, they continued to

---

2. "Korean Peninsula's Denuclearization Comes to End," *KCNA* (January 25, 2013).

3. "DPRK's Choice Will Be Beyond Imagination of Hostile Forces," *KCNA* (February 5, 2013).

4. "KCNA Report on Successful 3rd Underground Nuclear Test," *KCNK* (February 12, 2013), https://www.ncnk.org/resources/publications/KCNA_3rd_Nuke_Test.pdf

pass up opportunities to begin slowing the program in favor of looking for evidence that Pyongyang was sufficiently "serious" about denuclearization to warrant even sitting down at the table. At every turn, they harbored deep suspicions that diplomatic outreach by Kim Jong Un was designed to trap the administration into talks that were destined to fail. Pyongyang's pattern was viewed as one to leverage threats for political and economic gain.

The first term had put the Obama administration into a diplomatic cul-de-sac. It showed no interest or aptitude at extricating itself in the second term. As the administration closed out its first term, John Delury, professor at Yonsei University in Seoul and an astute Korea watcher, provided a good summary of what had gone wrong and what might get worse if not fixed. The conventional wisdom, Delury wrote, was that the North's provocative and irresponsible behavior early in the administration left Obama no choice but to punish North Korea. Yet, he noted, by the spring of 2009 the administration had already decided on a policy that amounted to containment and watchful waiting—later dubbed "strategic patience." Delury listed numerous factors that led the administration down the path of strategic patience and what he called "disengagement." Obama officials believed Pyongyang would never give up its nuclear weapons, making negotiations to that end a fool's errand. There was an aversion to investing political capital for limited returns, along with a belief that the Kim regime would soon collapse. The administration continued to believe in the efficacy of sanctions and that Washington was now in a better position because it was aligned with the new, more conservative South Korean administration.[5]

By the summer of 2013, President Obama became even less engaged from the North Korean problem when he saw a potential opening in his overtures to Iran. In August, Hassan Rouhani, a more moderate politician in Iran especially when compared to the firebrand Mahmoud Ahmadinejad, won Iran's presidential election. As Obama points out in *A Promised Land*, the secret letter offering to talk he had sent to Ayatollah Khamenei within weeks after his inauguration in 2009 was essentially rebuffed with a middle

5. John Delury, "The Disappointments of Disengagement: Assessing Obama's North Korea Policy," *Asian Perspective* 37, no. 2 (April–June 2013), https://www.jstor.org/stable/42704824

finger from Iran.[6] This time Obama placed a phone call to the newly elected Rouhani during the UN General Assembly meeting in September. Obama had high hopes for Rouhani and placed great emphasis on reengagement with Iran.

THE ONSET OF BENIGN NEGLECT

Some years later, after they had left office, Kurt Campbell and Jake Sullivan, two of Obama's key national security officials, described strategic patience in *Foreign Affairs* as reflecting "uncertainty about what to do and when."[7] Although the article was primarily about China, that definition is an apt description of how the Obama administration formulated its North Korea policy as it entered its second term.

Patience was not the watchword for Kim Jong Un. He was a man in a hurry. Kim saw himself under pressure from the United States and South Korea, challenged by those outside—and inside—to show he had the right stuff to take control and last. Tensions on the peninsula heightened through the winter with a series of highly provocative North Korean statements, until at a March 2013 Korean Workers' Party meeting Kim announced the *byungjin* policy for the simultaneous development of nuclear weapons and the economy. The announcement broke the immediate tension, signaling that Kim was not preparing to make good on the threats thrown around in the preceding weeks. But it made official the long-term priority on the nuclear weapons program and followed through on the January Foreign Ministry declaration that denuclearization was explicitly off the table. This was a half-step back from his earlier focus on the economy, and a half-step back, as well, from the "military first" policy of his father that was still, formally, in effect. Kim may well have realized that the nuclear deterrent he inherited was not as robust as he had thought. In April, Pyongyang announced that it would restart all Yongbyon nuclear facilities including the 5 MWe reactor, which had been shut down since mid-2007.

6. Barack Obama, *A Promised Land* (New York: Crown, 2020), 454.

7. Kurt M. Campbell and Jake Sullivan, "Competition Without Catastrophe: How America Can Both Challenge and Coexist with China," *Foreign Affairs* 98, no. 5 (September–October 2019), https://www.foreignaffairs.com/articles/china/competition-with-china-without-catastrophe

Faced with this new status of the North's nuclear program, the Obama administration returned to a familiar, comfortable, and ultimately entirely ineffective policy of passing the burden onto Beijing. The administration in late March and early April sought to push Beijing to take a stronger stance toward the North and communicated this choice to Xi Jinping, the newly appointed president: Crack down on the North or face greater American military presence in Northeast Asia. This warning was transmitted through a flurry of exchanges, including a direct phone call between Obama and Xi.[8] Obama informed Xi of his administration's plans to upgrade its missile defense and to take other defensive steps to counter the threats from North Korea—surely intended as an oblique threat to Chinese interests in the region, unless Beijing acted in line with U.S. interests toward the North.

In mid-June, the North's National Defense Commission (chaired by Kim Jong Un) issued a crucial statement reversing the January announcement that denuclearization was off the table. It proposed senior-level talks between the authorities of the DPRK and the United States, calling for broad and in-depth discussions on defusing military tensions, replacing the armistice system with peace mechanisms, and other issues of mutual concern including the building of a world without nuclear weapons proposed by the United States.[9] The following month, at a Track 1.5 meeting (involving government and nongovernmental participants) in Europe, a DPRK official expressed exasperation and profound puzzlement to his American interlocutor that Washington had not seemed to grasp the importance of the offer, especially in view of its source. It came, he implied, directly from Kim Jong Un.[10]

Instead of pulling on this thread for a bilateral effort, Washington continued to lean on China to rein in North Korea. In early December, Vice President Biden visited with President Xi in Beijing. He asked Xi to exert more economic and financial pressure on North Korea, citing the effectiveness of concerted international sanctions in getting Iran to agree to the

8. Mark Landler, "Detecting Shift, U.S. Makes Case to China on North Korea," *New York Times* (April 5, 2013), https://www.nytimes.com/2013/04/06/world/asia/us-sees-china-as-lever-to-press-north-korea.html

9. "DPRK Proposes Official Talks with U.S.," *KCNA* (June 16, 2013).

10. Bob Carlin, personal communication with author (November 11, 2021).

preliminary Iran deal.[11] The new secretary of state, John Kerry, followed suit with a visit to Asia in February 2014 with a priority goal of enlisting China's "help to try to pressure North Korea" to move toward denuclearization,[12] but with little success. In December, DPRK–China relations nosedived when Kim Jong Un executed his uncle, Jang Song Thaek. Jang, always a problem in the leadership, may or may not have been plotting against Kim. In any case, he was considered much too close to China. For the next couple of years, Pyongyang's relations with Beijing—never as close as sometimes portrayed—were uglier than they had been for many years. Xi and Kim had no use for each other, all of which made the administration's efforts to rely on China a feckless exercise.

Throughout the year, Washington seemed to waffle on engaging Pyongyang. In late April 2014, as President Obama departed for a visit to Seoul and Tokyo, there were some rumblings in Washington that the United States may be willing to soften some of the preconditions that Pyongyang had to meet in order to return to the dialogue. However, after meeting with President Park Geun Hye, who succeeded Lee Myung Bak the previous year, Obama told the press that the United States, South Korea, and their allies might increase the sanctions on the North, giving them even more bite.

In November, Secretary Kerry and special envoy Syd Seiler proposed that the Six-Party Talks be resumed and suggested discussing human rights issues with the North. A few days later, on November 9, two Americans held by North Korea for actions to "subvert the state," Matthew Miller and Kenneth Bae, were returned to the United States via Director of National Intelligence James Clapper, who had traveled to North Korea to secure their release.[13] But, the U.S. focus on human rights issues in North Korea raised hackles in Pyongyang. The Foreign Ministry admonished the United States for, in recent months,

11. Mark Landler, "Biden Looks into North Korea at Border," *New York Times* (December 7, 2013), https://www.nytimes.com/2013/12/08/world/asia/biden-peers-into-north-korea-at-tense-border.html

12. Michael R. Gordon, "North Korea a Priority as Kerry Begins Asia Tour," *New York Times* (February 12, 2014), https://www.nytimes.com/2014/02/13/world/asia/north-korea-a-priority-as-kerry-begins-asia-tour.html

13. DNI Clapper's visit to North Korea was one of a series of U.S.–DPRK contacts in the intelligence channel during the Obama administration.

seeking to politicize and internationalize the human rights issue of an individual country and use it for toppling its social system. . . . Now the U.S. hostile policy toward the DPRK compels the latter not to exercise restraint any longer in conducting a new nuclear test.[14]

A tough warning, yet there was not to be another test for over a year. There is no way of knowing whether the warning was meant to set the stage for two attempts by Pyongyang to engage Washington in 2015, one in January and then again in the autumn, and whether these two efforts at engagement were attempts by some in Pyongyang to head off the next nuclear test.

First, though, and aside from the diplomatic and political gestures, things deteriorated even more when Sony Pictures released a movie—a comedy titled *The Interview*—in December 2014 that contained a scene portraying the assassination of Kim Jong Un. The North warned that the movie was a supreme insult, threatening that no country should countenance the portrayal of an assassination of the sitting head of state. American officials shrugged off the warnings and told Sony not to worry. But soon after the Clapper visit, North Korean hackers conducted a devastating cyberattack against Sony. The United States accused North Korea of orchestrating the attack.[15] Barack Obama said he would "review" whether North Korea should return to the State Sponsors of Terrorism list, pledging that the United States would "respond proportionately." He added, "I think it was an act of cybervandalism that was very costly, very expensive. We take it very seriously."[16]

A LAST CHANCE AT ENGAGEMENT?

Barely into 2015, on January 10, KCNA announced that the day before, the DPRK had passed to Washington a proposal that the United States would

14. DPRK Foreign Ministry Spokesman, "FM Spokesman Rejects UN 'Human Rights Resolution' Against DPRK," *KCNA* (November 20, 2104).

15. Ellen Nakashima, "U.S. Accuses N. Korea of Cyberattack on Sony," *Washington Post* (December 20, 2014), https://www.washingtonpost.com/world/national-security/us-attributes-sony-attack-to-north-korea/2014/12/19/fc3aec60-8790-11e4-a702-fa31ff4ae98e_story.html

16. Amy Chozick, "Obama to See If North Korea Should Return to Terror List," *New York Times* (December 21, 2014), https://www.nytimes.com/2014/12/22/us/politics/obama-cuba-north-korea-cyberattack.html

"temporarily suspend joint military exercises in South Korea and its vicinity this year" in return for which the North "was ready to take such a responsive step as temporarily suspending the nuclear test over which the U.S. is concerned." The message further proposed to sit with the United States at any time to discuss the issue.[17] This had the earmarks of a serious offer. Rather than simply make the proposal in a public statement, the North had first passed it to the U.S. government, and then reported they'd done so. The idea of such a trade had been floated months before by a senior DPRK official overseas. It had obviously been in the works in Pyongyang for some time when it surfaced in January. It was consciously based on the precedent of 1992, when the United States had suspended a major U.S.–ROK exercise, and the North had taken a step on the nuclear issue that the United States had wanted. But the Obama administration immediately rebuffed the current proposal. In a monumental misreading of the offer, State Department Spokeswoman Jen Psaki told reporters while traveling with Secretary John Kerry in Europe, "The DPRK statement that inappropriately links routine U.S.–ROK exercises to the possibility of a nuclear test by North Korea is an implicit threat."[18] Rather than a threat, the North was concretely offering to put its nuclear program on the table.

For the proposal to be rejected out of hand, literally the next day, was a slap in the face to Kim Jong Un. Daniel Russel, who had moved from the National Security Council (NSC) to be assistant secretary of state for East Asian and Pacific Affairs in mid-2013, made the decision to dismiss Pyongyang's overture.[19] Russel said he didn't think the North was serious. He believed that the North was not prepared to do another nuclear test at the time and, hence, they were asking the United States to give them something in exchange for what they couldn't do anyway. But as it turned out, the

17. Choe Sang-Hun, "North Korea Offers U.S. Deal to Halt Nuclear Test," *New York Times* (January 10, 2015), https://www.nytimes.com/2015/01/11/world/asia/north-korea-offers-us-deal-to-halt-nuclear-test-.html

18. Reuters Staff, "North Korea Offers to Suspend Nuclear Tests If U.S. Suspends Military Drills," *Reuters* (January 10, 2015), https://www.reuters.com/article/us-northkorea-usa-drills/north-korea-offers-to-suspend-nuclear-tests-if-u-s-suspends-military-drills-idUSKBN0KJ09F20150110

19. Daniel Russel, personal communication with author, Stanford University (April 21, 2016).

deep distrust of the North resulted in yet another missed opportunity—a mini-hinge point.

In the autumn, Pyongyang made another run at engaging Washington. In October, the North opened a new campaign implicitly linking discussions of a peace treaty to replace the 1953 Armistice Agreement with discussion of its nuclear weapons program. The focus was on timing and sequence, and, significantly, putting the nuclear program on the table was not ruled out. Exactly how far Pyongyang might have been prepared to go with this initiative is anyone's guess because no one seriously probed what Pyongyang might have been prepared to do. As usual, there was enormous suspicion in Washington and Seoul that this was nothing but a propaganda ploy. Yet, the consistency and mode of the DPRK messaging suggests it reflected a high-level decision about concrete policy. Still pressing the case, on November 13, a Foreign Ministry spokesman asserted that, "If a peace treaty is concluded and there exists confidence that the U.S. is no longer the enemy of the DPRK, it will be possible solve all other problems."[20] By December, after weeks of back and forth behind the scenes between the North and U.S. officials from the NSC, Kim Jong Un lost patience and likely gave the final approval for the long-threatened nuclear test, preparations for which had been in the works for some time.

THE FOURTH AND FIFTH NUCLEAR TESTS

The explosive force of this fourth test on January 6, 2016, was in the range of 7 to 14 kilotons, like the third nuclear test in 2013. The DPRK government announced that it had successfully tested a hydrogen bomb and that the test "scientifically verified the power of [a] smaller H-bomb." It praised the symbolic value of the hydrogen bomb, a sign that the North "proudly joined the advanced ranks of nuclear weapons states." It also promulgated some details regarding the North's nuclear doctrine, claiming that as a responsible nuclear weapons state, the North would "neither be the first to use nuclear weapons nor transfer relevant means and technology under any circumstances . . . as long as the hostile forces for aggression do not

---

20. DPRK Foreign Ministry Spokesman, "FM Spokesman Accuses the US of Shunning Conclusion of Peace Treaty," *KCNA* (November 13, 2015).

encroach upon its sovereignty."[21] This was very much in line with what I had heard from the Foreign Ministry officials during my visits to Pyong-yang.

The yield as measured by seismic stations around the world was much too low for a typical hydrogen bomb blast. Yet, I have learned not to dismiss the North's claims out of hand. They often contain hints as to what it is trying to accomplish. In this case, I did not believe the hydrogen bomb claim at the time, but after the huge blast a year later, I realized that this earlier test may well have been a clever proof-of-principle test of a hydrogen bomb. In other words, the North could possibly have detonated a boosted fission device using the fusion fuels deuterium and tritium to "boost" the explosive yield of a fission "primary," the front end of a two-stage hydrogen bomb. It is not clear what they may have had in the back end, the "second-ary," but with the right diagnostics, the test may have given them sufficient information for what appeared to be a successful hydrogen bomb test, its sixth, in September 2017.

On September 9, 2016, North Korea announced that it had conducted its fifth nuclear test. The DPRK Nuclear Weapons Institute (NWI) issued a statement that explained that the test "finally examined and confirmed the structure and specific features of movement of nuclear warhead that has been standardized to be able to be mounted on strategic ballistic rockets of the Hwasong artillery units." It again reiterated, in a nod to Chinese concerns, that there was "no radioactive materials leakage" and "no adverse impact on the ecological environment of the surroundings."[22] It praised the "standardization" of the warhead in that it would "enable the DPRK to pro-duce as many as it requires [of] a variety of smaller, lighter and diversified nuclear warheads of higher strike power with a firm hold on the technology for producing and using various fissile materials."

Based on the seismic signals, I estimated an explosive yield of 15 to 25 kilotons, the North's largest at the time. The NWI announcement made two claims that may have provided important hints about the test. It pointed to

21. DPRK Government, "DPRK Proves Successful in H-bomb Test," *KCNA* (January 6, 2016).

22. DPRK Nuclear Weapons Institute, "DPRK Succeeds in Nuclear Warhead Explosion Test," *KCNA* (September 9, 2016), https://www.cnbc.com/2016/09/09/heres-the-full-state-ment-from-north-korea-on-nuclear-test.html

smaller, lighter, and standardized warheads, crucial to being able to mount them on North Korea's missiles. In early March, North Korea had publicized Kim Jong Un's visit to what is believed to be the Tae-sung Machine Factory, the North's main missile production facility outside of Pyongyang, in which he inspected what they termed a "miniaturized nuclear warhead."[23] It was a mock-up, but it was sufficiently small that it could be fit inside some of North Korea's missiles. In fact, they wanted to make sure that was appreciated around the world by showing Kim in a place that had missile mock-ups and sketches of missiles that could house such a warhead. Missile experts pointed out that there were many inconsistencies in the types of missiles shown and in their dimensions. Kim was also featured at one of the North's test facilities witnessing an apparent test of a nose cone to demonstrate that their missiles could withstand the enormous temperatures during atmospheric reentry on the way to their targets. Although none of these demonstrations were convincing evidence that the North had mastered the production of nuclear warheads small enough to mount in its missiles and that the warheads could survive reentry, the North made its point. This was the direction in which they were heading, and the September nuclear test was yet another important step.

The other claim in the NWI statement following the fifth nuclear test concerned the use of "various" fissile materials for the test. The only other fissile material besides plutonium that works for bombs is highly enriched uranium. I believe it was first used in the third test and then again in the fifth. If so, this test may have given Pyongyang the confidence it needed to mount a warhead with a destructive power of Hiroshima or Nagasaki on its Scud and Nodong missiles to be able to destroy cities in South Korea and most of Japan. The ability to mount a nuclear warhead on an intercontinental ballistic missile (ICBM) and deliver it to target, I believe, was still out of reach. However, the North also sent several messages that it was working on that objective. On April 9, it publicized photos from an engine test for solid-fueled rockets at the Sohae launch facility.[24]

23. Jeffrey Lewis, "Five Things You Need to Know About Kim Jong Un's Photo Op with the Bomb," 38 North (March 11, 2016), https://www.38north.org/2016/03/jlewis031116/

24. John Schilling, "North Korea's Large Rocket Engine Test: A Significant Step Forward for Pyongyang's ICBM Program," 38 North (April 11, 2016), https://www.38north.org/2016/04/schilling041116/

278 From Strategic Patience to Benign Neglect

Looking back, it's clear that the Obama administration rejected out of hand a nuclear test moratorium at what would wind up to be the halfway point of the North's nuclear testing. In other words, at least half of the knowledge that the North has learned from its nuclear tests has been acquired since the 2015 offer for the testing moratorium was rejected by the administration.

Moreover, if the nuclear test moratorium had been accepted and, as Pyongyang suggested, talks had resumed, it may well have led to broader restraints by the North on its nuclear program along the line of what had been offered in the 2012 Leap Day Deal. Such restrictions would have been crucial because, by this time, operations at Yongbyon were in full gear. The 5 MWe reactor was producing roughly 6 kilograms of plutonium per year. The centrifuge facility appeared to have been doubled in size by 2013, most likely leading to 4,000 centrifuges spinning with the potential of increasing the North's highly enriched uranium inventory to 80 kilograms every year.[25] Other buildings were being constructed at Yongbyon, including what appeared to be new extraction facilities for tritium, which possibly was being produced in the 5 MWe reactor at that time. But the administration's suspicions and deep mistrust of North Korea resulted in yet more "patience," which allowed the North to run its nuclear program at full speed.

With no agreements in place and no serious dialogue in progress, the North also greatly geared up its missile test program. North Korea changed its testing patterns, moving launch locations over much of its territory, launching more frequently, at all hours of the day, and using the occasions to publicize Kim Jong Un's ubiquitous presence at launch sites, control rooms, and on the factory floor. In 2015, North Korea launched eighteen missiles as it had in 2014, when it began ramping up missile tests.[26] The 2014 and

25. The 80-kg HEU estimate was for the Yongbyon facility if it were dedicated to HEU production. Instead, I believed that that facility was used in combination with one or two covert facilities, which together could produce up to 150 kg HEU per year. This analysis was published in an article I co-authored with Stanford University colleagues: John E. Bistline, David M. Blum, Chris Rinaldi, Gabriel Shields-Estrada, Siegfried S. Hecker, and M. Elisabeth Paté-Cornell, "A Bayesian Model to Assess the Size of North Korea's Uranium Enrichment Program," *Science & Global Security* 23, no. 2 (2015): 71–100.

26. North Korea's missile testing history is provided in great detail by the Center for Strategic and International Studies, "Missiles of North Korea," https://missilethreat.csis.org/country/dprk/ (last updated March 24, 2022) and the James Martin Center for Nonproliferation Studies (CNS), "The CNS North Korea Missile Test Database," https://www.nti.org/analysis/articles/cns-north-korea-missile-test-database/ (last accessed April 30 2022).

2015 launches were predominantly of short- and medium-range missiles, but by midyear, Pyongyang began to show an interest in submarine-launched ballistic missiles (SLBMs), what it called the Pukguksong-1. Most of these were launched from undersea platforms and even then were photoshopped by the North Koreans to hide failures and disappointing performance. The SLBM program would suffer through several more failures, but it reached important initial milestones in August 2016 when a missile launched from a submarine traveled 500 kilometers before splashing down in the East Sea.

The year 2016 was notable mostly for the persistent launch failures of the Musudan missile. Seven of eight launch attempts failed catastrophically. The Musudan had been displayed in the October 2010 missile parade. It was also believed to have been shared with Iran before being test-launched in North Korea in 2016. It was a single-stage missile of intermediate range, apparently based on the Soviet R-27 missile. Pyongyang decided to terminate the Musudan program, changing directions with its intermediate-range missile program and moving on to ICBMs, with spectacular success in 2017.

While Pyongyang was making rapid advances in its nuclear and missile programs during Obama's final two years, the administration stayed its course, responding to what it called North Korea's "provocations" with the same broken playbook—though by 2016 there was growing unease that North Korea policy was failing and would leave the Obama administration with a blot on its legacy. Assistant Secretary Daniel Russel, who handled much of the administration's communications with Congress and the public, described the administration's policy as grounded in three tracks: diplomacy, pressure, and deterrence.[27] Deterrence, he said, was derived from what he called Washington's "ironclad" alliances with South Korea and Japan. The Obama administration did make a concerted effort working with the conservative administrations of South Korea and Japan to strengthen the alliances and their confidence in America's extended nuclear deterrent.

The administration continued to turn to the idea of pressure, rather than diplomacy, along with broader and better enforcement of UN sanctions. Washington leaned even more heavily on Beijing to punish Pyongyang for

27. Daniel R. Russel, "The Persistent Threat of North Korea and Developing an Effective U.S. Response," *U.S. Department of State Archive* (September 28, 2016), https://2009-2017.state.gov/p/eap/rls/rm/2016/09/262528.htm

its lack of progress to denuclearize. President Obama made personal appeals to President Xi. Deputy Secretary Antony Blinken was particularly blunt with his Chinese counterparts. He alerted China that the United States would have to take additional steps to defend itself and its allies if North Korea didn't change its behavior. In other words, the United States would take regional actions to defend against the North that would be inimical to Chinese interests, such as the deployment of the THAAD (Terminal High Altitude Area Defense) missile system. Blinken explained that everything was on the table, including secondary sanctions on Chinese institutions.[28]

Despite its public claims that it had gone the extra mile to reach out to North Korea's government and encourage it to engage in an "authentic and credible" negotiating process, the Obama administration never mounted a sustained, concerted process to engage Pyongyang to eliminate its nuclear weapons program. Instead, it continued to push for Pyongyang to demonstrate that it was serious about denuclearization and "to agree to complete, verifiable, and irreversible denuclearization."[29] All along, it harbored deep suspicions that every diplomatic outreach by Kim Jong Un was designed to trap the administration.

The Obama administration's level of mistrust was too great to test whether Kim Jong Un, like his father and grandfather, was interested in reaching strategic accommodation with the United States. As a result of the U.S.-led sanctions, which had cut off the North from its legitimate trade with the rest of the world, North Korea had become increasingly dependent on China. The Obama administration was not willing to test Kim's intentions. There were few advocates for North Korea in Congress and little sympathy among the American public.

President Obama toed a tough line from the beginning of his tenure to the end. He vowed in 2009 not to let the North Koreans continue the cycle of "provocation, extortion, and reward." As late as May 2016 during a trip to Japan, he lambasted Kim Jong Un's regime as unstable and isolated, flouting international norms and rules and being "hellbent on getting

28. Choe Sang-Hun, "After Nuclear Test, South Korea Urges China to Rein in North," *New York Times* (January 13, 2016), https://www.nytimes.com/2016/01/14/world/asia/south-korea-china-north-nuclear.html

29. Russel, "The Persistent Threat of North Korea."

nuclear weapons that they can fire long distances."[30] In July, consistent with prior efforts, the administration announced new sanctions—this time on Kim Jong Un personally and North Korea's senior leadership, blacklisting them in response to alleged human rights abuses documented in a State Department report.[31]

Nothing much changed in the administration's handling of North Korea through the rest of President Obama's term. The view from inside the administration was captured well in remarks Russel had made in April 2016. He mocked Kim Jong Un's nuclear weapons program and said that Pyongyang's strategic posture had been weakened. He asked rhetorically, "What has it [the nuclear program] gotten Kim Jong Un?" To which he replied, "He has made splashes in the ocean with missiles and detonated nuclear devices underground . . . but it has gotten him exactly nothing in terms of respect, security, economic support, or diplomatic recognition." Russel added, "We've united the world so that the North is more isolated than any country has ever been."[32]

Despite the administration's unyielding public stance of confidence in its handling of North Korea, President Obama told President-elect Donald Trump in November during their one transition meeting that he saw North Korea as the top national security priority.[33] There was no glossing over the facts. President Obama came into office with North Korea having conducted one nuclear test, perhaps having amassed sufficient plutonium for five or so primitive nuclear weapons, yet with no capability to deliver these on missiles. He was leaving with North Korea having added four more nuclear tests, sufficient plutonium and highly enriched uranium for roughly

30. Gardiner Harris, "Obama, in Japan, Emphasizes Lingering Threat of Nuclear War," *New York Times* (May 26, 2016), https://www.nytimes.com/2016/05/27/world/asia/g7-summit-2016.html

31. Julie Hirschfeld Davis, "Obama Places Sanctions on North Korean Leaders for Human Rights Abuses," *New York Times* (July 6, 2016), https://www.nytimes.com/2016/07/07/world/asia/obama-puts-sanctions-on-north-korean-leaders-for-human-rights-abuse.html

32. Daniel R. Russel, "North Korea: How to Approach the Nuclear Threat," speaking at the Institute for Corean-American Studies, Washington, DC (April 4, 2016), https://2009-2017.state.gov/p/eap/rls/rm/2016/04/255492.htm

33. Gerald F. Seib, Jay Solomon, and Carol E. Lee, "Barack Obama Warns Donald Trump on North Korea Threat," *Wall Street Journal* (November 22, 2016), https://www.wsj.com/articles/trump-faces-north-korean-challenge-1479855286

twenty-five nuclear weapons, and impressive demonstrations of missile capabilities through dozens of successful missile tests. Unlike Russel's claim that Kim Jong Un got exactly nothing from his nuclear weapons, they got him a nuclear arsenal that threatened U.S. assets and allies in the region.

A POSTMORTEM ON THE OBAMA ADMINISTRATION

Whether it was strategic patience, deep mistrust, or benign neglect, the Obama administration never gave the North Korean threat the priority it required until it turned the issue over to Trump with the dire warning. Neither President Obama nor his top officials were fully engaged in coming to grips with the North's nuclear advances during his presidency. In fact, even after they left office and wrote memoirs of their time in the administration, one key official after another, starting with the former president, treated North Korea as an afterthought.

President Obama, in his highly acclaimed *A Promised Land* covering the first two and a half years in office, only mentions North Korea in passing. He lauded Susan Rice's efforts at the UN to get the Security Council to impose new sanctions on North Korea after the 2009 nuclear test. In contrast, he dedicated six pages to Persian and Iranian history, the reign of the shah, and the Islamic revolution. He displayed a good understanding of the status of Iran's nuclear program (although still making a crucial technical error in its assessment).[34] He states the intelligence community's assessment that Iran did not yet have nuclear weapons but that it may have been coming within reach. Yet, North Korea, which by the time he entered office did possess nuclear weapons and was steadily making progress toward a more menacing nuclear arsenal, gets only two short mentions—no discussion of the divided Korean Peninsula, of the tens of thousands of U.S. troops in South Korea, or of the continuing state of the armistice.

Secretary Hillary Clinton gives North Korea less coverage than Myanmar in *Hard Choices*. She describes the 2009 satellite launch mostly in terms

---

34. For example, President Obama states that "from 2003 to 2009, Iran boosted its capacity from a hundred to as many as five thousand, far more than any peaceful program could justify" (Obama, *A Promised Land*, 453). That is incorrect. Civilian nuclear energy programs require much greater uranium enrichment capacity than nuclear weapon programs. In fact, the original centrifuge facility at Natanz was designed for 50,000 to 60,000 centrifuges (of the P-1 type) for a civilian program.

of how successful she and Susan Rice were in orchestrating a unified UN Security Council sanctions response. She also makes several crucial errors in the book describing North Korea's nuclear program.[35] Secretary Kerry, in *Every Day Is Extra,* mentions North Korea once when he refers to President Bush using his 2002 State of the Union address to "excoriate an 'axis of evil' linking Iraq, Iran, and North Korea."[36]

William J. Burns, deputy secretary of state in the second Obama term, wrote in *Back Channel* that "[he] wasn't directly engaged in our fitful diplomacy with North Korea."[37] Susan Rice in *Tough Love* barely mentions North Korea during her terms as ambassador to the United Nations and as national security advisor. She touches primarily on her work on UN sanctions following North Korea's 2009 satellite launch and nuclear test. She does admit that the administration fell short on Syria, on stabilizing Libya, on addressing the Israel–Palestine conflict, and on "eliminating North Korea's nuclear and missile program."[38] Samantha Power, who served on the National Security Council before taking the UN ambassador role, also has rather little to say about North Korea in *Education of an Idealist.* She does discuss leading efforts to tighten sanctions on the North after its fourth and fifth nuclear tests. She also describes her efforts to bring attention to North Korea's brutal treatment of its own people. Yet, she offers no real insights into the administration's strategies for North Korea.[39] Even Secretary of Defense Robert Gates, who deals at great length with hot spots around the globe in his missive *Duty,* has little to say about the major issues on North Korea during his watch, other than providing some important details of North Korea's covert effort to build a plutonium production reactor in Syria during his time in the Bush administration.[40]

35. Hillary Rodham Clinton, *Hard Choices: A Memoir* (New York: Simon & Schuster, 2014).

36. John Kerry, *Every Day Is Extra* (New York: Simon & Schuster, 2018), 246.

37. William J. Burns, *The Back Channel: A Memoir of American Diplomacy and the Case for Its Renewal* (New York: Random House, 2019), 271.

38. Susan Rice, *Tough Love: My Story of the Things Worth Fighting For* (New York: Simon & Schuster, 2019), 450.

39. Samantha Power, *The Education of An Idealist: A Memoir* (New York: Dey St./William Morrow, 2019).

40. Robert Gates, *Duty: Memoirs of a Secretary at War* (New York: Alfred A. Knopf, 2014).

Kurt Campbell, one of the principal architects of Obama's approach to Asia, provides more detail on North Korea, including quite a bit of early history, in *The Pivot*. While each Asian country receives attention and is viewed from the opportunities/challenges perspective, Campbell calls North Korea a "vexing and compounding" issue, perhaps more so than any other in Asia. He states, "Virtually every aspect of my professional experience involving NK has been frustrating and counterintuitive. No country has played a bad hand more daringly, or more dangerously."[41] In his engaging *The World as It Is*, billed as a behind-the-scenes account of Barack Obama's presidency, Ben Rhodes—one of the president's closest national security advisors, early speech writer, and deputy national security advisor for strategic communications during the entire Obama presidency—never mentions North Korea.[42]

The two most glaring silences from the Obama administration regarding North Korea policy engagement are Wendy Sherman and Ernest Moniz. Wendy Sherman was undersecretary of state for political affairs from 2011 to 2015 (and acting deputy for a few months in late 2014). In that capacity, Sherman led the U.S. team during six negotiating rounds between Iran and six world powers on Tehran's nuclear program. She had been the Clinton administration's policy coordinator for North Korea. In *Not for the Faint of Heart*, she gives an insightful account of her time working with former Secretary of Defense William Perry and Secretary of State Madeleine Albright, trying to salvage the Agreed Framework as President Clinton's presidency drew to a close, but there is not a word about North Korea during the Obama administration. As demonstrated in her book's coverage on the Obama years, her insights and influence were sorely missed for North Korea.[43]

Ernest Moniz, secretary of energy during Obama's second term, told me he played little to no role in North Korean policy.[44] The Energy Department and its nuclear laboratories had long supported the intelligence agencies in

41. Kurt M. Campbell, *The Pivot: The Future of American Statecraft in Asia* (New York: Twelve, 2016), 170.

42. Ben Rhodes, *The World as It Is: A Memoir of the Obama White House* (New York: Random House, 2018).

43. Wendy R. Sherman, *Not for the Faint of Heart: Lessons in Courage, Power, and Persistence* (New York: PublicAffairs, 2018).

44. Ernest J. Moniz, personal communication with author (August 2021).

analysis of the North's nuclear developments. During the Clinton Agreed Framework and the Bush administration's disablement agreements, the department and technical specialists from the laboratories played an essential on-site role in monitoring and verification of the various agreements. However, the Obama administration passed up all opportunities to get back into the Yongbyon nuclear complex. Thus, that crucial role for the Energy Department was lost. And Secretary Moniz, technically competent and politically savvy, was never asked by the president to bring badly needed technically informed risk/benefit analysis to the table on North Korea. This oversight was in stark contrast to the Iran negotiations that President Obama asked Moniz to join. Moniz was able to marshal the nuclear assets of the Department of Energy laboratories to support the negotiations in addition to being a major force at the talks. His technical knowledge was crucial so that the United States could match Iran's technical expertise, presented at the negotiations by their team headed by Dr. Ali Akbar Salehi, chief of Iran's Atomic Energy Organization and a nuclear engineer trained at MIT. MIT also happened to be Moniz's home institution and where he had headed the nuclear physics department for years. Moniz was able to provide critical technically informed risk analysis of Iran's nuclear program directly to Secretary Kerry and the negotiating team.

President Obama's own involvement with the Iran negotiations was in stark contrast to his role with North Korea. He was intimately involved in all details of the Iran deal, to the point that some State Department officials in jest called the president the department's Iran desk officer. He pushed the Iran deal through despite objections from Israel and congressional opposition. It was the president's personal commitment and the engagement of his top political team that made diplomacy possible with Iran, as well as the looming threat of Israeli military action. That kind of commitment—or threat from another player in Asia—did not exist for North Korea.

Hopefully President Obama will give us better insights about his choices for Iran and North Korea in the second volume of his memoir. For now, we can only speculate. Perhaps he really did find the North Korean regimes so reprehensible that he felt it senseless to try. He said many times that he was determined to break their cycle of "provocation, extortion, and reward." But the ayatollah's Iran was no paragon of virtue. The "Iran Archive," obtained by a daring Israeli raid in Tehran, demonstrated Iran's duplicity.[45] Perhaps it was simply that nothing catastrophic was happening on the Korea Peninsula—the news headlines of another nuclear test or missile launch paled in comparison to the human catastrophes occurring daily in the greater Middle East. Maybe the president was looking at a grand strategy, hoping to solve the Iran problem to finally allow the United States to have a much lower profile in the Middle East so as to pivot toward China. Or perhaps he had planned to turn his attention to North Korea once he had a deal with Iran but couldn't because of the new turmoil on the Russian front in Crimea and eastern Ukraine. Whatever the reason, the consequences of his inaction on North Korea turned out to be one of his biggest foreign policy failures—one that made the world a much more dangerous place.

I was not sorry to see the Obama administration end from the standpoint of North Korea policy. During eight years of strategic patience and benign neglect, and several missed opportunities, the North's nuclear and missile arsenals had grown dramatically. The question was, what would come next?

45. David Albright with Sarah Burkhard and the Good ISIS Team, *Iran's Perilous Pursuit of Nuclear Weapons* (Washington, DC: Institute of Science and International Security, 2021).

18   The "Fire and Fury" of 2017

The year kicked off with Kim Jong Un's annual New Year's Day speech in which he announced that the North was in final preparation to test an intercontinental ballistic missile for the first time. In a Twitter post, President-elect Donald Trump replied, "It won't happen." Trump also expressed his displeasure with China, stating, "China has been taking out massive amounts of money & wealth from the U.S. in totally one-sided trade, but won't help with North Korea. Nice!"[1]

Those words were a harbinger of Trump's tumultuous first year in office. No one knew what he would say or do next. Trump was reported to "sit up and notice" during Obama's warning about the urgency of the North Korean threat during their meeting in November of 2016. As he departed the meeting, Trump reportedly remarked, "I will be judged by how I handle this [North Korea]."[2] But would he follow through on his prior offer

1. "Trump: North Korea Intercontinental Missile 'Won't Happen,'" *BBC News* (January 3, 2017), https://www.bbc.com/news/world-us-canada-38492947; Maggie Haberman and David E. Sanger, "'It Won't Happen,' Donald Trump Says of North Korean Missile Test," *New York Times* (January 2, 2017), https://www.nytimes.com/2017/01/02/world/asia/trump-twitter-north-korea-missiles-china.html

2. Evan Osnos, "The Risk of Nuclear War with North Korea," *New Yorker* (September 7, 2017), https://www.newyorker.com/magazine/2017/09/18/the-risk-of-nuclear-war-with-north-korea

to have a hamburger with Kim? Or to totally destroy North Korea, as he warned later at the United Nations? The first few months in office seemed to tilt the decision toward military action, especially after Trump ordered a strike of fifty-nine Tomahawk missiles in April at Syria's Shayrat Airfield as punishment for President Assad's use of chemical weapons in Syria.[3]

I was concerned that North Korea's young leader, with whom the Obama administration never established serious dialogue, would be tested by a president with an unpredictable temperament and little foreign policy experience. The United States knew little about the interests, motivations, or personality of Kim Jong Un, and it knew even less about the military. The risk was that the leadership in Pyongyang, as it prepared to take the significant technical steps outlined in Kim's speech, would be prone to overconfidence and miscalculation.

Just before Trump's inauguration, I wrote in the *New York Times*, "The crisis is here. The nuclear clock keeps ticking. Every six to seven weeks North Korea may be able to add another nuclear weapon to its arsenal."[4] I believed it was important for the Trump administration to break from the Obama administration's avoidant approach and reach out directly and immediately to establish critical lines of communication to avoid a nuclear catastrophe. I recommended that Trump send an envoy to Pyongyang. The outgoing administration, on the other hand, stuck to its failed policies right to the end. In his transition meeting, Obama encouraged then President-elect Trump to carry on a strategy of ratcheting up pressure both on North Korea and its ally China.[5]

THE PERSONNEL SHAPE THE POLICY

Lt. General Michael Flynn, who was to become Trump's national security advisor, had brought Matthew Pottinger on board during the transition to

3. Barbara Starr and Jeremy Diamond, "Trump Launches Military Strike Against Syria," *CNN* (April 7, 2017), https://www.cnn.com/2017/04/06/politics/donald-trump-syria-military/index.html

4. Siegfried S. Hecker, "The U.S. Must Talk to North Korea," *New York Times* (January 12, 2017), https://www.nytimes.com/2017/01/12/opinion/the-us-must-talk-to-north-korea.html

5. Jenny Lee, "Aide Says Obama Urged Trump to Press China on North Korea," *Voice of America* (February 22, 2017), https://www.voanews.com/a/aide-says-obama-urged-trump-to-press-china-on-north-korea/3736300.html

develop strategies for China and North Korea. Pottinger was a decorated Marine Corps officer and former reporter on China for the *Wall Street Journal*. He was fluent in Mandarin and conversant with Chinese history. He became Asia director at the National Security Council at the beginning of Trump's presidency. Flynn resigned after a tenure of twenty-two days amid accusations of foreign influence peddling and lying. He was convicted and later pardoned by Trump in 2020. Flynn's successor, Lt. General H. R. McMaster, describes in *Battlegrounds* how he and Pottinger formulated a range of options for the administration's North Korea strategy. Trump chose one aimed to "convince Pyongyang that its nuclear and missile programs were a danger rather than an asset." The United States would work with others "to apply unwavering, integrated, and multinational pressure on the Kim regime."[6]

That strategy was codified in the administration's policy review, approved by Trump in March, as the "maximum pressure strategy." I found it puzzling but not surprising that the administration thought it would get better results than Obama just by turning up the gain on the pressure knob. Ultimately, the Trump administration was able to significantly strengthen economic sanctions and diplomatic pressure on North Korea in 2017—resulting in Pyongyang making spectacular progress in advancing its nuclear weapons and missile programs.

In *Battlegrounds*, McMaster explains how what the scholar Hans Morgenthau called "strategic narcissism" must be replaced with "strategic empathy." Strategic narcissism is the failure to acknowledge the degree of agency and control of the "other" over the course of events. It is a mindset that McMaster says all too often leads presidents and their advisors to craft policies based on wishful thinking and to define problems as one might like them to be. The notion of strategic empathy, McMaster states, is seeking to understand what drives and constrains other states based on a "better understanding of their motivations, emotions, cultural biases and aspirations."[7]

McMaster is not only a decorated officer but also holds a doctorate in American history and was a professor at the United States Military

6. H. R. McMaster, *Battlegrounds: The Right to Defend the Free World* (New York: Harper, 2020), 351.

7. Ibid., 131.

Academy. He demonstrates some of his academic background in *Battlegrounds*, but he fails the strategic empathy test regarding North Korea. He doesn't come close to meeting the definition of empathy—the capacity to understand or feel what another is experiencing from within their frame of reference—as he vilifies North Korea at every turn. Moreover, it's ironic that McMaster wound up working for a president whose "America First" and "Make America Great Again" are the epitome of strategic narcissism, totally devoid of strategic empathy.

Throughout the two chapters McMaster dedicates to North Korea, he repeats a common hard-line American version of North Korea as an evil regime that constantly cheats and is determined to unify the Korean Peninsula under its dictatorial regime, rather than demonstrating an understanding of the North's history, culture, and emotions. The maximum pressure strategy fits his vision for much of the rest of the world in the spirit of his promotion of coercive diplomacy. McMaster writes, "Because of our flawed assumptions and misaligned policies, the NK regime had never felt diplomatic, economic, financial, or military pressure sufficient to convince its leaders that denuclearization was in their interest."[8] That is precisely how the Bush and Obama administrations explained their policies of tightening the noose around the Kims' necks.

KIM MAKES GOOD ON HIS MISSILE AMBITIONS

Kim Jong Un, for his part, was not waiting for Trump's policy review. He was on the path forecast in his New Year's address—moving steadfastly toward an ICBM capability, while diplomacy was relegated to the back seat. On February 11, North Korea launched a new medium-range missile, the Pukguksong-2, its first missile test of the Trump era and one of twenty-four in 2017. The missile—a modified version of the solid-fueled, sea-based Pukguksong-1—was launched on a lofted trajectory during Japanese Prime Minister Shinzo Abe's first summit with Trump at Mar-a-Lago. Abe and Trump were kindred spirits and, if anything, the timing of the launch gave Abe another justification for opposing all conciliatory gestures toward North Korea.

8. Ibid., 366.

In addition to striving for long-range missiles, Kim was determined to improve the operational capabilities and readiness of his short-range systems. The objective, as he later stated, was to be able to launch from anywhere at any time and be immune to U.S. missile defenses. In early March, North Korea launched a salvo of four extended-range Scud missiles that could reach all of South Korea and some of Japan. KCNA reported that the launches were timed to counter a joint U.S.–South Korean military exercise.[9] By firing the four missiles simultaneously, North Korea demonstrated that it could potentially launch a barrage capable of defeating advanced missile defenses in the region.

On March 18, Kim Jong Un witnessed a ground jet test of a newly developed high-thrust missile engine at the Sohae Satellite Launching Station. Kim Jong Un called it "a great event of historic significance that heralded a new birth of the country's rocket industry."[10] The new engine, it is believed, was the Russian RD250 rocket engine, likely imported from Russia or Ukraine, which would allow the North to move past the failures of its Musudan missiles. During the next six months, North Korea would launch six intermediate-range Hwasong-12 missiles and successfully launch two new Hwasong-14 ICBM-class missiles, all from mobile TEL (transporter-erector-launcher) platforms.[11]

Political tensions increased with each North Korean missile advance, but two of Trump's senior cabinet appointments took a reasoned approach. Secretary of Defense James Mattis, in his February visit to South Korea and Japan, issued levelheaded assurances affirming U.S. deterrence commitments.

9. Motoko Rich, "North Korea Launch Could Be Test of New Attack Strategy, Japan Analysts Say," *New York Times* (March 6, 2017), https://www.nytimes.com/2017/03/06/world/asia/north-korea-missiles-japan.html

10. Eric Talmadge, "North Korea Tests New Rocket Engine," *Associated Press* (March 19, 2017), https://www.usatoday.com/story/news/world/2017/03/19/north-korea-tests-new-rocket-engine/99380046/

11. A detailed account of North Korea's roll out and testing of missiles is presented in Ankit Panda, *Kim Jong Un and the Bomb: Survival and Deterrence in North Korea* (New York: Oxford University Press, 2020), 135–249. Tabulations of North Korea's missiles and test launches are given in Center for Strategic and International Studies, "Missiles of North Korea," https://missilethreat.csis.org/country/dprk/ (last updated March 24, 2022) and the James Martin Center for Nonproliferation Studies (CNS), "The CNS North Korea Missile Test Database," https://www.nti.org/analysis/articles/cns-north-korea-missile-test-database/ (last accessed April 30, 2022).

He stated that the North's use of nuclear weapons would be met with an overwhelming response in kind. He added that there was no need at this time for military maneuvers and that the dispute is "something that's best solved by the diplomats."[12] The Defense Department did, however, send a not-so-subtle message to Kim Jong Un when it authorized an overflight of the southern half of the Korean Peninsula by a nuclear-capable B-1B strategic bomber from the U.S. air base in Guam. KCNA warned that North Korea would "mount a resolute preemptive attack" if it thought the United States was about to strike.[13]

In mid-March, Secretary of State Rex Tillerson assured South Korea and Japan of Washington's defense commitments. In a stopover in Beijing, he expressed solidarity with Chinese Foreign Minister Wang Yi that the two nations were committed to preventing any type of conflict from breaking out.[14] In early April, when Trump met with President Xi at Mar-a-Lago, their first summit meeting, Trump pressed Xi on the trade imbalance and on doing his part for the denuclearization of North Korea. China did tighten up enforcement of sanctions on the North for a while. But relying on China to take care of North Korea, as Trump would find out, was not realistic.

In mid-April, there was public confusion about whether the Pacific Command's Admiral Harry Harris had ordered the deployment of the USS *Carl Vinson* aircraft carrier and warships to the Korean Peninsula, a potential escalatory move that occurred amid heightened tensions after the U.S. airstrikes on Syria.[15] Later, the *New York Times* reported that this was not the case; rather, the fleet was going to conduct military drills with Australian

12. Michael R. Gordon and Choe Sang-Hun, "Jim Mattis Seeks to Soothe Tensions in Japan and South Korea," *New York Times* (February 5, 2017), https://www.nytimes.com/2017/02/05/us/politics/jim-mattis-south-korea-japan.html

13. Anna Fifield, "North Korea May Be Preparing for Nuclear Test," *Washington Post* (March 31, 2017), https://www.washingtonpost.com/world/north-korea-might-be-preparing-for-another-nuclear-test-satellite-images-suggest/2017/03/29/f59bded6-14ed-11e7-924b-58851f3a675d_story.html

14. Simon Denyer, "China Tries to Calm U.S. on North Korea," *Washington Post* (March 19, 2017): A15.

15. Eric Schmitt, "U.S. Reroutes Warships Toward Korean Peninsula in Show of Force," *New York Times* (April 9, 2017), https://www.nytimes.com/2017/04/09/world/asia/korean-peninsula-us-aircraft-carrier-north-korea.html

forces.[16] I happened to be visiting the Pacific Command headquarters in Honolulu at the time, responding to a request to brief the leadership on my North Korea nuclear assessment. My Stanford colleagues and I were hosted for a lovely breakfast at the home of Admiral Harris. When I repeated the recommendation I had made previously to the Trump administration that the president send an envoy to Pyongyang, Admiral Harris said sarcastically, "He is, it's the *Carl Vinson*."

On May 14, after three failures, North Korea successfully launched the intermediate-range Hwasong-12 ballistic missile that flew for thirty minutes before landing in the East Sea. The missile could target key U.S. military bases in the Pacific, including those in Guam.[17] The missile used the engine that had been tested in March. KCNA said that the Hwasong-12 missile could carry a nuclear warhead and reported that the missile flew 787 kilometers with a maximum altitude of 2,100 kilometers. Kim Jong Un stated, "If the U.S. dares opt for a military provocation against the DPRK we are ready to counter it."[18] The test represented a level of performance never seen from a North Korean missile. The origin of the engines remains uncertain, although missile experts claim it occurred through massive technology and component transfer from Russia.[19] The turnaround from the massive failures of the Musudan missile to the success of the Hwasong-12 demonstrated North Korea's ability to navigate the challenges of missile technology, to circumvent export control regulations, and to manage internal decision-making to keep moving ahead with the program.

Missile analyst Markus Schiller made a convincing case that the North's missile programs relied heavily on foreign assistance and procurements. He showed how, over the years, North Korea's launch rates for its missiles were completely at odds with the experience of other missile development

16. Mark Landler and Eric Schmitt, "Aircraft Carrier Wasn't Sailing to Deter North Korea, as U.S. Suggested," *New York Times* (April 18, 2017), https://www.nytimes.com/2017/04/18/world/asia/aircraft-carrier-north-korea-carl-vinson.html

17. Choe Sang-Hun, "North Korea Says Missile It Tested Can Carry Nuclear Warhead," *New York Times* (May 14, 2017), https://www.nytimes.com/2017/05/14/world/asia/north-korea-missile-nuclear.html

18. Ibid.

19. Markus Schiller, "The Scope of Foreign Assistance to North Korea's Missile Program," *Science and Global Security* 27, no. 1 (2019), https://doi.org/10.1080/08929882.2019.1613805

countries—with far too few tests and too high a success rate. The exceptions are the satellite launches and the Musudan missiles, both of which experienced high failure rates and may be the most indigenous of the North's rockets.

The missile databases cited earlier also show how dramatically the missile testing program changed after 2014. Under Kim Jong Un, the North not only launched many more missiles, but their testing patterns changed, as launches were conducted all over North Korea rather than exclusively at conventional test sites. Analysts from the Nuclear Threat Initiative/Center for Nonproliferation Studies called this a strategic shift of immense importance. The North was now not just testing metal; it was "testing men."[20] In other words, the launch exercises were consistent with the regime's probable intent to deploy nuclear weapons to missile units throughout the country.

TENSIONS FLARE IN THE WAKE OF MISSILE TESTS

Following the rapid series of missile tests in May 2017, the rhetoric between Washington and Pyongyang became decidedly nastier. In early June the UN Security Council voted unanimously to add fifteen individuals and four entities linked to North Korea's nuclear and missile programs to a UN sanctions blacklist. Tougher sanctions, such as blocking critical oil deliveries, were opposed by China, although the resolution did include a global travel ban and freezing the assets of a range of North Koreans.

At the end of June, South Korean President Moon Jae In arrived in Washington for a two-day visit. In a statement in the Rose Garden, President Trump denounced the "reckless and brutal" regime in North Korea and demanded that Pyongyang choose a better path to deescalate tensions on the Korean Peninsula over its nuclear weapons program. Trump renewed calls for regional allies and powers to implement stronger economic sanctions on Pyongyang. McMaster reported that Trump and Moon agreed that the maximum pressure strategy was best for achieving denuclearization.[21] That was likely not what President Moon had in mind in his engagement strategy, but he didn't have much choice as Trump bullied the South Koreans,

20. Shea Cotton, "Understanding North Korea's Missile Tests," *NTI* (April 24, 2017), https://www.nti.org/analysis/articles/understanding-north-koreas-missile-tests/

21. McMaster, *Battlegrounds*, 365.

not only on North Korea but also on increasing their funding to support U.S. troops in the South. The tension between the Moon administration and Trump remained for the rest of Trump's presidency, as I witnessed in numerous visits to South Korea during this time.

Less than a week after Moon's visit, on July 4, North Korea successfully launched a Hwasong-14 intercontinental ballistic missile—a milestone for their nuclear and missile development. The missile took off from a mobile launch platform at the Banghyon Airfield in the northwest and flew 933 kilometers for thirty-seven minutes on a lofted trajectory before landing in the East Sea.[22] "The American bastards must be quite unhappy after closely watching our strategic decision," KCNA quoted Kim as saying after watching the missile test.[23] Though not immediately apparent to most observers, Kim also gave the first signal that he was prepared to put the missile and nuclear programs "on the table," using a formulation the North continued to repeat and build on in the coming months.

On July 28, North Korea conducted another successful test of its Hwasong-14 ICBM.[24] The missile flew almost straight up in its lofted trajectory for forty-five minutes and reached a height of about 3,700 kilometers before falling into the East Sea. In a stern warning to the United States, Kim boasted that the North was "capable of the surprise launching of an intercontinental ballistic missile at any time and from anywhere and that all of the mainland United States is within the range of our missiles." In response, Trump offered vague assurances before a cabinet meeting: "We'll handle North Korea. We're going to be able to handle them. It will be handled. We handle everything."[25]

22. "Kim Jong Un Supervises Test-Launch of Inter-Continental Ballistic Rocket Hwasong-14," *KCNA* (July 5, 2017), https://kcnawatch.org/newstream/276945/kim-jong-un-supervises-test-launch-of-intercontinental-ballistic-rocket-hwasong-14

23. Euan McKirdy, "North Korea State Media Celebrates 'Gift' to 'American Bastards,'" *CNN* (July 5, 2017). https://www.cnn.com/2017/07/05/asia/north-korea-missile-nuclear-gift/index.html

24. "Kim Jong Un Guides Second Test-Fire of ICBM Hwasong14," *KCNA* (July 29, 2017), https://exploredprk.com/press/kim-jong-un-guides-second-test-fire-of-icbm-hwasong-14/

25. White House, "Remarks by President Trump in Cabinet Meeting," *Newswires* (July 31, 2017), https://www.einnews.com/pr_news/395443397/remarks-by-president-trump-in-cabinet-meeting

TAKING STOCK IN MID-2017

These words were anything but reassuring. The demonstration of ICBM capability was a big deal, one that Trump himself had assured Americans "won't happen." As impressive as the success of the last Hwasong-12 and the two Hwasong-14 missile tests were, I thought it was important not to overstate the North's threat. In an interview with the *Bulletin of the Atomic Scientists* at the time, I said that the July missile tests demonstrated that the North had made substantial progress, much sooner than most analysts had predicted just a year or two before.[26] To get to this point, the North had been able to combine its prior progress in developing various missile stages and rocket engines. But to achieve a reliable, accurate ICBM, they would need additional tests, including testing on a normal rather than lofted trajectory. Such testing would be necessary to sufficiently master the engineering of its reentry vehicle, which would have to safely house the nuclear device to survive the mechanical stresses and extreme temperatures associated with launch, flight, and reentry.

On the nuclear side, the warhead remained the least developed part of North Korea's plans for nuclear ICBMs because of the extreme conditions that it must survive to detonate as intended at its target. The CIA made a preliminary assessment that the reentry vehicles on the Hwasong-14 would likely perform adequately if flown on a normal trajectory to continental U.S. targets, giving Kim "a minimally functional and credible ICBM system."[27] That may have represented a worst case scenario, for which the intelligence agencies and the Pentagon had to plan. But it was my judgment that, despite its rapid progress, North Korea was not able to confidently make a warhead small and light enough, and sufficiently robust, to survive an ICBM's journey to target. In other words, North Korea did not yet have a militarily useful ICBM. It needed more missile tests and more nuclear tests.

I was not making light of the North's nuclear threat, because all parts of its nuclear and missile programs were accelerating. Production of fissile materials and likely of tritium continued. The 5 MWe reactor was functioning

26. Elisabeth Eaves, "Talk to North Korea to Avert a Nuclear Disaster: An Interview with Siegfried Hecker," *Bulletin of the Atomic Scientists* (August 7, 2017), https://thebulletin.org/2017/08/talk-to-north-korea-to-avert-a-nuclear-disaster-an-interview-with-siegfried-hecker/

27. Panda, *Kim Jong Un and the Bomb*, 199.

for most of 2017, and the uranium enrichment facility at Yongbyon remained operational. At this point, North Korea probably had an inventory of 20 to 40 kilograms of plutonium, the preferred fissile material for constructing smaller warheads, while its highly enriched uranium inventory likely stood at 200 to 450 kilograms. This stockpile of fissile material was sufficient for about 20 to 25 nuclear weapons. I had previously assessed that the North would be able to reach all of South Korea and most of Japan with nuclear-tipped Scud and Nodong missiles.

The war of words accelerated. The risks of conflict continued to rise. My concern was that in the North's drive to reach the U.S. mainland to achieve a semblance of strategic parity with the United States, combined with an increasingly aggressive U.S. approach to ostensibly prevent him from doing so, one side or the other would miscalculate and trigger a response that could lead to war.[28] In an interview on MSNBC, McMaster explained that the United States was threatening preventive war if the North continued to rapidly accelerate its nuclear weapons program. He added, "I think it's impossible to overstate the danger associated with a rogue, brutal regime."[29] The U.S. military continued with its own more aggressive moves to send a message to the North. It was around this time that "South Korean and American militaries began actively practicing conducting 'decapitation strikes' on the North Korean leadership, including a dedicated decapitation unit established by South Korea."[30]

"FIRE AND FURY"

On August 6, the UN Security Council imposed the toughest sanctions yet on Pyongyang over its continued testing of missiles and nuclear weapons. Under the resolution's provisions, all exports of North Korean coal, iron, iron ore, lead, lead ore, and seafood would be prohibited. The resolution also imposed new restrictions on North Korea's Foreign Trade Bank and banned the country from increasing the number of workers it sent abroad.

28. Eaves, "Talk to North Korea: Interview with Hecker."

29. Jason Le Miere, "U.S. Prepared to Launch 'Preventive War' Against North Korea, Says H. R. McMaster," *Newsweek* (August 5, 2017), https://www.newsweek.com/us-north-korea-war-mcmaster-646942

30. Anna Fifield, *The Great Successor: The Divinely Perfect Destiny of Brilliant Comrade Kim Jong Un* (New York: PublicAffairs, 2019), 237.

Trump weighed in with off-the-cuff comments to reporters while on a trip to his golf club in Bedminster, New Jersey, on August 8. He told reporters, "North Korea best not make any more threats to the United States. They will be met with 'fire and fury' like the world has never seen."[31] Undaunted, several hours later, North Korea state media quoted a top general of the Strategic Rocket Force that it was considering a strike that would create "an enveloping fire" around Guam.[32] Some Trump administration officials sought to lower the heat in the weeks after the North's second Hwasong-14 test in late July. Secretary of State Tillerson weighed in on recent events to reporters: "We do not seek regime change. We are not your enemy, . . . but you are presenting an unacceptable threat to us, and we have to respond."[33] After Trump's "fire and fury" comment, Tillerson reassured the American public: "I think Americans should sleep well at night, have no concerns about this particular rhetoric of the last few days."

From his golf club in New Jersey, however, Trump doubled down on his "fire and fury" comments in the wake of Pyongyang's Guam announcement.[34] "Frankly, the people who were questioning that statement, was it too tough? Maybe it wasn't tough enough." After a phone consultation with President Xi, Trump continued the tough line on the North with a tweet that the U.S. military was "fully in place, locked and loaded" for an attack on North Korea. McMaster said that nearly a week of Trump's threats to rain down "fire, fury and frankly, power" on North Korea were an attempt to remove any ambiguity about what Pyongyang could expect if the threats against the United States continued.[35]

31. Jeff Zeleny, Dan Merica, and Kevin Lipton, "Trump's 'Fire and Fury' Remark Was Improvised but Familiar," *CNN* (August 9, 2017), https://www.cnn.com/2017/08/09/politics/trump-fire-fury-improvise-north-korea/index.html

32. Jonathan Cheng, "North Korea Threatens to Surround Guam with an 'Enveloping Fire,'" *Wall Street Journal* (August 9, 2017), https://www.wsj.com/articles/north-korea-threatens-to-surround-guam-with-an-enveloping-fire-1502325226

33. Peter Baker and Choe Sang-Hun, "Trump Threatens 'Fire and Fury' Against North Korea if It Endangers U.S," *New York Times* (August 8, 2017), https://www.nytimes.com/2017/08/08/world/asia/north-korea-un-sanctions-nuclear-missile-united-nations.html

34. Philip Rucker and Karen DeYoung, "More Threats from Trump," *Washington Post* (August 11, 2017): A1.

35. Carol Morello, "Officials Downplay Idea That Nuclear War with North Korea Is Imminent," *Washington Post* (August 13, 2017), https://www.washingtonpost.com/world/

On August 15, KCNA reported that while visiting the Command of the Strategic Force, Kim Jong Un inspected the plans for "enveloping fire at Guam" and determined that he would first give the United States the opportunity to step back from its threats. He would wait and see before acting on the Guam threat.[36] Bob Carlin wrote that this was a clear message from Kim that he was unilaterally claiming victory for the North while moving back from the cliff and signaling "a decisive break in the action."[37] Indeed, Carlin noted that one might have discerned that Pyongyang was not readying to carry out its Guam threat since it had not been taking any domestic actions in early August, including "no mobilization of the population in preparation for a military confrontation" and hardly a mention of Guam after the initial KCNA statement.

A few days prior to Kim's visit to KPA's Strategic Command, Tillerson and Mattis had authored an op-ed in the *Wall Street Journal* that sought to lower tensions with the North and may have contributed to Kim's decision to wait and watch.[38] The officials sought to tone down the unfiltered rhetoric from Trump and lower tensions by affirming that the United States was seeking denuclearization through a "peaceful pressure campaign" that did not aim for regime change, reunification, or to inflict harm on the North Korean people. They noticeably clarified messaging out of the White House, at least temporarily, but did not introduce any new elements that would make progress toward denuclearization, especially given that the North was not going to make any unilateral concessions before talks.[39]

national-security/officials-downplay-idea-that-nuclear-war-with-north-korea-is-imminent/2017/08/13/e64fd28c-fe74-47a3-afd2-937ee7987268_story.html

36. "Kim Jong Un Inspects KPA Strategic Force Command," *KCNA* (August 15, 2017), https://kcnawatch.org/newstream/1502749950-753062439/kim-jong-un-inspects-kpa-strategic-force-command/?mc_cid=e1e6830b06&mc_eid=8fc8089a7c

37. Robert Carlin, "Kim Jong Un Steps Back from the Nuclear Cliff," *38 North* (August 15, 2017), https://www.38north.org/2017/08/rcarlin081517/

38. Jim Mattis and Rex Tillerson, "We're Holding Pyongyang to Account," *Wall Street Journal* (August 13, 2017), https://www.wsj.com/articles/were-holding-pyongyang-to-account-1502660253

39. Siegfried Hecker, "If Nixon Went to China, Trump Can Talk to North Korea," *Politico* (August 23, 2017), https://www.politico.com/magazine/story/2017/08/23/north-korea-talk-nuclear-weapons-icbms-215523

Although dropping the Guam threat was a welcome diplomatic gesture, Pyongyang moved steadily ahead with its missile and nuclear programs. The North launched three short-range missiles on August 26 followed by another successful launch of the intermediate-range Hwasong-12.[40] This time the missile was not launched on a completely lofted trajectory but rather overflew Japanese territory. In its announcement of the test, the North made clear that such a missile could carry a "large-sized, heavy nuclear warhead." The test launch led to great confusion and fear in Japan, as public television programs were interrupted with a rare warning screen announcing the missile's flight over the country and citizens received a text alert. In an emergency session, the UN Security Council unanimously adopted a statement condemning the launch and three others on Saturday, calling them "not just a threat to the region but all U.N. member states."[41]

Trump responded to the test by rejecting diplomacy, admonishing both the international community as well as officials in his administration that "talking is not the answer!"[42] In a more formal statement earlier, Trump said,

> "The world has received North Korea's latest message loud and clear: this regime has signaled its contempt for its neighbors, for all members of the United Nations, and for minimum standards of acceptable international behavior. . . . All options are on the table."[43]

THE SIXTH NUCLEAR TEST

On September 3, North Korea followed with its sixth, and most audacious, nuclear test, which noticeably moved the side of Mount Mantap and sent Chinese citizens across the border scrambling in reaction to the tremors.

40. Choe Sang-Hun, "Route of Missile by North Korea Unnerves Japan," *New York Times* (August 29, 2017): A1.

41. Choe Sang-Hun, "U.N. Condemns North Korea's Latest Missile Tests, but Takes No Action," *New York Times* (August 29, 2017), https://www.nytimes.com/2017/08/29/world/asia/north-korea-japan-missile-us.html

42. Anne Gearan and Anna Fifield, "N. Korea's 'Perfectly Calibrated' Launch," *Washington Post* (August 30, 2017): A1.

43. White House, "Statement by President Donald J. Trump on North Korea," *Trump White House Archives* (August 29, 2017), https://trumpwhitehouse.archives.gov/briefings-statements/statement-president-donald-j-trump-north-korea/

Pyongyang claimed to have mastered hydrogen bomb technology.[44] KCNA added to the drama by publishing a photo of Kim inspecting what they called a two-stage thermonuclear bomb purportedly just hours before the detonation. The photos showed Dr. Ri Hong Sop—former director of the Yongbyon nuclear complex who had hosted me several times and was now the head of the Nuclear Weapons Institute—apparently explaining the device (unquestionably a model) to a very attentive Kim Jong Un. It is not known if the tested device mirrored the one being inspected in the photos, which was small enough to fit into the nose cone on the Hwasong-14, the ICBM test-launched in July, as indicated by a schematic visible behind Kim.[45]

At the time of the test, I stated in an interview in the *Bulletin* that the size of the blast was consistent with a hydrogen bomb, though it could also have been a large, boosted fission bomb, utilizing the deuterium and tritium isotopes of hydrogen, to increase the fission yield. Even if the September device wasn't a hydrogen bomb, I believed it was only a matter of time before the North reached thermonuclear capability. Initial estimates of the explosion yield were around 100 kilotons, but subsequent refinements put the explosion yield closer to 250 kilotons, more than ten times larger than the bomb that destroyed Nagasaki, indicating it was likely a hydrogen bomb. Much like the North's progress with ICBMs, bomb developments occurred on a much faster timescale than most analysts, including me, predicted.

The official KCNA statement quoted Kim as saying that "all components of the H-bomb were homemade . . . thus enabling the country to produce powerful nuclear weapons as many as it wants."[46] This was surely an exaggeration because the North was still very much constrained in its ability to produce these nuclear devices. It had a limited supply of plutonium as well as the tritium needed for boosted fission or fusion devices. The "homemade"

44. "DPRK Nuclear Weapons Institute on Successful Test of H-bomb for ICBM," *KCNA* (September 3, 2017). Full statement at https://www.cnbc.com/2017/09/03/north-korea-hydrogen-bomb-read-the-full-announcement-from-pyongyang.html

45. Elisabeth Eaves, "North Korean Nuclear Test Shows Steady Advance: Interview with Siegfried Hecker," *Bulletin of the Atomic Scientists* (September 7, 2017), https://thebulletin.org/2017/09/north-korean-nuclear-test-shows-steady-advance-interview-with-siegfried-hecker/

46. "DPRK Nuclear Weapons Institute on Successful Test of H-bomb for ICBM."

claim was also suspect. I was in Beijing shortly after the test to compare notes with my Chinese nuclear colleagues. They believed that Pyongyang must have had help if the device tested looked like the one shown in the North Korean photos. They claimed that the help must have come from Russia because it did not come from China. Based on my nearly twenty years of working with the Russian nuclear weapons enterprise, I believed that was not the case. However, I could not rule out that the North might have had some indirect help through information acquired from the Russian missile suppliers. It was also possible that the North had acquired design information through espionage, potentially even from the United States. North Korea, much like China, had likely pursued fission and fusion bomb designs concurrently from the beginning, because hydrogen bombs were known to exist, and the general physics principles were understood in the scientific community.

On September 9, the UN Security Council increased sanctions on the North, the ninth resolution since 2006, setting a further cap on oil exports to North Korea, but not going as far as U.S. representative Nikki Haley and other U.S. officials wanted. North Korea followed a week later with another launch of a Hwasong-12 ballistic missile, this time on a more standard trajectory of 3,700 kilometers over Japan, demonstrating for the first time an actual flight range capable of striking the U.S. territory of Guam.

Trump delivered his "Rocket Man" speech to the UN General Assembly on September 19, threatening, "We will have no choice but to totally destroy North Korea." He cast the North Korea issue in stark moral terms: "If the righteous many don't confront the wicked few, then evil will triumph." Referencing the North's nuclear development efforts, Trump said of Kim, "Rocket Man is on a suicide mission for himself."[47] Two days later, Kim responded with an angry and unusual first-person warning: "I will surely and definitely tame the mentally deranged U.S. dotard with fire."[48] Kim stated

---

47. "At U.N., Trump Singles Out 'Rogue' Nations North Korea and Iran," *New York Times* (September 19, 2017), https://www.nytimes.com/2017/09/19/world/americas/united-nations-general-assembly.html

48. "Statement of Chairman of State Affairs Commission of DPRK," *KCNA* (September 22, 2017), https://www.ncnk.org/resources/publications/kju_statement_to_trump.pdf/file_view

that Trump's speech had convinced him that the path he had chosen—that is, the development of a long-range nuclear deterrent—was correct.

In New York for the UN General Assembly session, Foreign Minister Ri Yong Ho told reporters that Kim might decide to conduct an atmospheric nuclear test over the Pacific. Ri also told reporters that the North was making progress on and had nearly completed the development of the "state nuclear force" and that the nuclear arsenal would serve as a war deterrent that would establish the balance of power with the United States. These comments were in line with what I considered the North's dual-track policy. They further suggested that following the completion of the military track with a deterrent in place, the North was prepared to pivot to a focus on economic development.

Trump responded to Kim's "dotard" remark with a tweet that Kim "is obviously a madman who doesn't mind starving or killing his people" and would now "be tested like never before!"[49] The next day, the Pentagon said the Air Force had sent B-1B bombers and F-15C fighters over waters north of the military demarcation line to demonstrate U.S. resolve and to send a clear message that the president has many military options to defeat any threat.[50] Minister Ri Yong Ho made some off-the-cuff remarks to reporters as he was leaving the UN after a week of General Assembly meetings in New York: "Since the United States declared war on our country, we will have every right to make countermeasures, including the right to shoot down United States strategic bombers even when they are not inside the airspace border of our country."[51]

MIXED MESSAGES AND A POTENTIAL WAY OUT

In reality, the North Koreans were not on a war footing. Rather, they, like much of the rest of the world, were trying to figure out Trump. They used

49. Choe Sang-Hun and Jane Perlez, "At U.N. and in the Air, North Korea and U.S. Trade Tough Messages," *New York Times* (September 23, 2017), https://www.nytimes.com/2017/09/23/world/asia/north-korea-us-china-south.html

50. Ibid.

51. Carol Morello, "North Korea Threatens to Shoot Down U.S. Warplanes," *Washington Post* (September 25, 2017), https://www.washingtonpost.com/world/national-security/north-korea-asserts-its-right-to-shoot-down-us-bombers/2017/09/25/74da66c4-a204-11e7-8cfe-d5b912fabc99_story.html

informal channels with U.S. interlocutors and people well connected to the administration to try to decipher Trump's tweets. They were also inquiring about U.S. "nuclear attack protocol" and whether Trump had sole authority to launch an attack.[52] North Korea's diplomats continued to participate in various conferences largely to get a better handle on what the Trump administration had in mind.

At the 2017 Moscow Nonproliferation Conference in late October, I met Ms. Choe Son Hui, whom I hadn't seen since my last visit to North Korea in 2010.[53] Participating on a panel on current global nuclear issues, she presented North Korea's case for its nuclear program, claiming that it was Washington's hostile policies that forced North Korea to develop a nuclear deterrent. When asked by Anton Khlopkov, the conference organizer and session moderator, what exactly she meant by hostile policies, Choe repeated Trump's words, "fire and fury, like the world has never seen," followed by "we will have no choice but to totally destroy North Korea," and "it's the calm before the storm." She then rested her case.

After the war of words unleashed at the UN, Secretary of State Tillerson acknowledged for the first time that the Trump administration was seeking direct communication with the government of North Korea over its missile and nuclear tests. He told news media, "We have lines of communications to Pyongyang—we're not in a dark situation, a blackout."[54] Trump was furious with Tillerson, bluntly contradicting him: "This is not a time to talk." To make his position clear, the president took to Twitter, "I told Rex Tillerson, our wonderful Secretary of State, that he is wasting his time trying to negotiate with Little Rocket Man. Save your energy Rex, we'll do what has to be done!" Trump tweeted again, "Being nice to Rocket Man hasn't worked in 25 years, why would it work now? Clinton failed, Bush failed, and Obama failed. I won't fail."

52. Fifield, *The Great Successor,* 239.

53. Center for Energy and Security Studies (CENESS) Moscow Nonproliferation Conference, October 21, 2017.

54. Emily Rauhala, "Tillerson: U.S. Is in Direct Contact with North Korea, Is 'Probing' Talks," *Washington Post* (September 30, 2017), https://www.washingtonpost.com/world/tillerson-us-is-in-direct-contact-with-north-korea/2017/09/30/eecb3ed2-a5c3-11e7-8c37-e1d99ad6aa22_story.html

McMaster notes in *Battlegrounds* that it was difficult to keep the entire U.S. government and international partners committed to the maximum pressure policy, especially after the September nuclear test. He criticized the State Department seeking several channels of communication with the North Koreans without first making them feel the consequences of their actions. Leaks appeared in the press of a "bloody nose" limited strike idea, to teach Kim Jong Un a lesson. The administration officially denied that such a strike was being considered due to its obvious risks, including that it could harden Kim's resolve to retain his nuclear forces at all costs and that it could initiate a nuclear war. Despite the obvious risks, analyst Ankit Panda points out that the United States had indeed developed some plans for preventive or preemptive strikes with nuclear weapons to eliminate North Korea's nuclear force, particularly in hardened or underground locations where these devices were presumably stored in North Korea's mountainous and rugged terrain.[55]

I was sufficiently concerned that I penned an op-ed in the *Bulletin* titled, "Time to Insert the Control Rods on North Korea." I likened the North Korea situation to a nuclear reactor that was about to go out of control and suffer a meltdown. To bring the reactor back under control, specially constructed control rods that absorb neutrons and slow down nuclear reactions are lowered into the reactor core. I viewed Mattis and Tillerson as the political equivalent of such control rods to temper a mercurial president and avoid a potential meltdown in North Korea.[56]

As Bob Woodward points out in *Rage,* Secretary Mattis was likewise concerned about a potential North Korean catastrophe. During the first year of Trump's presidency, Mattis lived "on permanent alert."[57] Only the president had the authority to launch nuclear weapons, but Mattis was sure he would play a role. What concerned Mattis was that Trump's "orders were so random, impulsive and unthoughtful." Woodward shares the stories about Mattis quietly slipping into the National Cathedral in Washington several times in late 2017 to pray and reflect. He also related that on many

55. Panda, *Kim Jong Un and the Bomb,* 291–292.

56. Siegfried S. Hecker, "Time to Insert the Control Rods on North Korea," *Bulletin of the Atomic Scientists* (October 17, 2017), https://thebulletin.org/time-insert-control-rods-north-korea11198

57. Bob Woodward, *Rage* (New York: Simon & Schuster, 2020), 71.

nights Mattis slept in his gym suit in the event of a late-night call about another North Korean missile launch when he would rush to join a top secret National Event Conference emergency session.

Trump kept up the unprecedented personal rhetorical assault on Kim during the rest of the fall, including during his Asian tour in early November. He delivered a well-received speech to the National Assembly in Seoul in which he said that "America does not seek conflict or confrontation, but we will never run from it." During his stay in Seoul, Trump's words were aimed to remind Kim that the United States had three aircraft carriers in the vicinity of the peninsula and nuclear submarines appropriately positioned. He pointed out that 24 miles to the north "the prison state of North Korea sadly begins. . . . An estimated 100,000 North Koreans suffer in gulags, toiling in forced labor, and enduring torture, starvation, rape, and murder on a constant basis." He also offered the North an alternative future and urged it to "come to the table and to make a deal." In reference to Kim, Trump said, "Despite every crime you have committed against God and man . . . we will offer a path to a much better future," one that requires total denuclearization.[58]

Back home, Trump continued to tighten the screws on North Korea. The administration officially redesignated North Korea as a state sponsor of terrorism, a diplomatic move the president said was aimed at drastically increasing pressure on the "rogue nation" to abandon its pursuit of nuclear weapons.[59] Former CIA analyst, Jung H. Pak, has suggested this move was also in response to the assassination of Kim's older half-brother, Kim Jong Nam, with the deadly chemical nerve agent VX at the Kuala Lumpur airport in Malaysia nine months earlier.[60] Although it is generally suspected that Pyongyang, and likely Kim Jong Un, had a role in the assassination, Kim Jong Nam was seen as not posing a threat to his brother's rule since he had been living a life of luxury in exile in Macao. However, unconfirmed reports

58. "Full Text of President Trump's Remarks to the South Korean National Assembly," *Voice of America* (November 8, 2017), https://www.voanews.com/a/text-of-trump-speech-to-south-korean-national-assembly-/4106294.html

59. Michael D. Shear and David E. Sanger, "Trump Revives Terrorist Label for Pyongyang," *New York Times* (November 21, 2017), https://www.nytimes.com/2017/11/20/us/politics/north-korea-trump-terror.html

60. Jung H. Pak, *Becoming Kim Jong Un* (New York: Ballantine Books, 2020), 153.

surfaced that he had been meeting and taking money from the CIA for some time, which Pyongyang would surely have known. Pak and others suggested that the very public airport execution was designed as a message to anyone harboring thoughts of dethroning Kim Jong Un. It was also a way for Kim to warn the world that he had a stockpile of chemical weapons (believed to be some 5,000 metric tons), along with a growing nuclear arsenal. In addition, North Korea is suspected to have produced biological weapon agents such as anthrax, cholera, plague, and others.[61]

Another event that reverberated in the White House and was said to particularly affect Trump was the tragic death of University of Virginia student, Otto Warmbier. He had been imprisoned in January 2016 during a tourist visit to North Korea for an alleged hostile act against the regime and had been sentenced to fifteen years of hard labor. After nearly seventeen months in captivity, in June 2017, U.S.–DPRK contacts in diplomatic channels secured Warmbier's release. In what was apparently a shock to the Foreign Ministry, Warmbier was in a coma, and had been for more than a year. He died six days after his return to the United States.

In early November, Congress backed new banking restrictions, named for Warmbier, against North Korea.[62] And when later that month Trump designated North Korea as a state sponsor of terrorism, he stated, "As we take this action today, our thoughts turn to Otto Warmbier." At the South Korean National Assembly, Trump had also said that Warmbier had been "tortured" to endorse the narrative that Otto was beaten, although whether he had been tortured remained in dispute. Andre Lankov, a Russian North Korea expert living in South Korea, suspected that the Trump administration was developing a rationale for justifying military action against the Kim regime. The White House allowed speculation about possible beatings to spread and gave people license to indulge their worst fears about Otto's fate and act accordingly.[63]

61. "North Korea Chemical Overview," *Nuclear Threat Initiative* (April 17, 2018), https://www.nti.org/analysis/articles/north-korea-chemical/; "North Korea Biological Overview," *Nuclear Threat Initiative* (July 13, 2018), https://www.nti.org/analysis/articles/north-korea-biological/

62. H.R. 4084: Otto Warmbier North Korea Nuclear Sanctions Act of 2019.

63. Doug Bok Clark, "The Untold Story of Otto Warmbier, American Hostage," *GQ*

Kim did not appear fazed by Trump's doubling down on measures to punish the North. On November 29, North Korea test-fired a new ICBM, the Hwasong-15. The enormous missile was launched on a lofted trajectory at night from a field launch site on a huge nine-axle TEL. It reached an apogee of almost 4,500 kilometers, flew 950 kilometers, and its thrust of 80 tons at ignition was double the Hwasong-14 missiles fired in July. Missile experts judged the Hwasong-15 to have a range of 13,000 kilometers, sufficient to reach the entire U.S. mainland if launched on a normal trajectory. The North issued its own proclamation that the missile could reach the entire United States, adding that it had now "completed the nuclear force."[64]

I viewed the proclamation to be aimed at Kim's domestic audience, as well as signaling his confidence to Washington, since it was the United States that would have to be convinced that Pyongyang's nuclear force now threatened the U.S. mainland. It didn't, in my opinion. As impressive as the North's three successful ICBM launches were, it left them a long way from an operational nuclear-capable ICBM force.[65] Besides, missile forces, both the hardware and the people, are never "complete." They are not simply stored on the shelf until needed. They must be constantly exercised. For example, just two days after the late July DPRK ICBM launch, the U.S. test-launched an unarmed Minuteman III ICBM from California's Vandenberg Air Force Base to a range near Kwajalein Atoll in the Pacific, nearly 7,000 kilometers away. According to Air Force Global Strike Command, "the purpose of the ICBM test launch program is to validate and verify the safety, security, effectiveness, and readiness of the weapon system."[66] It was the 299th test

(July 23, 2018), https://www.gq.com/story/otto-warmbier-north-korea-american-hostage-true-story

64. "Kim Jong Un Guides Test-fire of ICBM Hwasong-15," *KCNA* (November 29, 2017), http://www.uriminzokkiri.com/index.php?lang=eng&ptype=cfoson&page=1&mtype=view&no=7596

65. Siegfried S. Hecker, "What We Really Know About North Korea's Nuclear Weapons: And What We Don't Yet Know for Sure," *Foreign Affairs* (December 4, 2017), https://www.foreignaffairs.com/articles/north-korea/2017-12-04/what-we-really-know-about-north-koreas-nuclear-weapons

66. Vandenberg Space Force Base, "Unarmed Minuteman III Test Launch from Vandenberg" (August 11, 2021), https://www.vandenberg.spaceforce.mil/News/Article-Display/Article/2727025/unarmed-minuteman-iii-test-launch-from-vandenberg/

launch of the Minuteman III, the only land-based ICBM left in the U.S. nuclear arsenal.

The North believed the rapid advance of its nuclear force gave it a measure of "invulnerability," according to Bob Carlin. He voiced his concern that although this allowed Kim to edge toward diplomacy, the chance of miscalculation grew on both sides.[67] In addition to presenting my current estimates of the North's nuclear and missile programs in the December *Foreign Affairs* article,[68] I also advised the U.S. government to be receptive to Kim's offer to talk in case he was pivoting toward the economy—or if necessary, to initiate the discussion. Talking would not be a reward or concession but "instead be a first step toward reducing the risks of a nuclear catastrophe and developing a better understanding of the other side." Little did I know that's what Trump had in mind.

In early December, senior UN envoy Jeffrey Feltman, undersecretary for political affairs and a former senior U.S. diplomat, visited North Korea carrying a letter from UN Secretary-General António Guterres to Kim Jong Un.[69] On behalf of Guterres, Feltman requested that the North Koreans reopen military-to-military channels, be ready to engage the United States in talks, and implement Security Council resolutions. Feltman emphasized the seriousness of the situation to the North Koreans. The main message he was trying to convey was "that what they see as deterrence may provoke a war they think they are preventing." In Feltman's view, Pyongyang paid close attention to Trump's Twitter threats and to Republican hawks such as Senator Lindsey Graham, who had pegged the probability of Trump ordering a first strike on North Korea at 30 percent. Graham also boasted that there is no such thing as a surgical strike against the North: "you gotta be willing to take the regime completely down."[70]

67. Robert Carlin, "Death's Dusty Measure," *38 North* (November 7, 2017), https://www.38north.org/2017/11/rcarlin110717/

68. Hecker, "What We Really Know About North Korea's Nuclear Weapons." In this article in *Foreign Affairs*, I estimated North Korea possessed sufficient fissile materials for roughly twenty-five to thirty nuclear weapons and an annual production rate of six to seven. I expressed little doubt that its nuclear-tipped missiles could reach all of South Korea and most of Japan, but it did not yet have a militarily useful ICBM force.

69. David Ignatius, "Sleepwalkers in North Korea," *Washington Post* (December 20, 2017): A17.

70. Mick Krever and Joshua Berlinger, "UN Official Who Visited North Korea Sees

At a Tokyo news conference the week after Feltman's visit to Pyongyang, Guterres expressed his concerns, stating, "We all want to avoid that things get out of control and that misperceptions and mishandling of situations make us sleepwalk into a war that will have devastating consequences."[71] To dramatize this kind of message about the risk of unintended conflict, during his visit, Feltman gave Foreign Minister Ri Yong Ho a copy of historian Christopher Clark's study, *The Sleepwalkers: How Europe Went to War in 1914.*

Feltman's visit on behalf of the UN secretary-general was judged to have been important, but the secret, game-changing message he carried from President Trump was not publicly revealed until Feltman did so in a BBC program *Trump Takes on the World*, more than three years later.[72] Feltman described how he had been invited to visit Pyongyang in late 2017, but the U.S. State Department thought it was not a good idea for him to go. However, a few weeks later, Secretary-General Guterres visited the White House to discuss the North Korea situation. Guterres told Trump, "Jeff Feltman has this strange invitation to go to Pyongyang and lead a policy dialogue with the North Koreans." Feltman told the BBC that Trump leaned over toward Guterres and said, "Jeff Feltman should go to Pyongyang and Jeff Feltman should tell the North Koreans I'm willing to sit down with Kim Jong Un."[73]

I believe it was this offer that dramatically closed Trump's confrontational 2017 chapter with Kim and led to the about-face in 2018. Curiously, this crucial offer has not been mentioned by Trump in public. It is also not mentioned in Woodward's *Rage*, nor in Bolton's *The Room.*

'High Risk' of Miscalculation," *CNN* (December 15, 2017), https://www.cnn.com/2017/12/14/world/north-korea-jeffrey-feltman-amanpour/index.html

71. Ibid.

72. "The BBC Exclusively Revealed That the Hanoi Negotiations Broke, and Trump Invited Kim Jong Un to Go Home on the Air No. 1-International," *6PARK.News* (February 21, 2021), https://6park.news/en/the-bbc-exclusively-revealed-that-the-hanoi-negotiations-broke-and-trump-invited-kim-jong-un-to-go-home-on-the-air-no-1-international.html; Episode 3 of *Trump Takes on the World*, broadcast by the BBC in Great Britain (February 24, 2021), https://www.bbc.co.uk/iplayer/episode/moooslm7/trump-takes-on-the-world-series-1-episode-3

73. "The BBC Exclusively Revealed."

19 From the Olympics to Singapore

In late 2017, around the same time that President Trump extended an invitation to Kim Jong Un via Jeffrey Feltman, President Moon Jae In invited the North's athletes to participate in the February PyeongChang Winter Olympics. Pyongyang seemed to be interested in these overtures from Washington and Seoul. In his New Year's address, Kim Jong Un responded directly to the signals from the Blue House, noting that he would consider sending a delegation to the Winter Olympics and would prioritize a reduction in inter-Korean military tensions. But even as he sought to pivot toward engagement with the South, Kim did not immediately respond in the same manner to the United States.

Instead, Kim emphasized the results of the successful nuclear and missile tests in 2017 and their implications for the North's strategic relationship with the United States. Displaying a newfound confidence in the sophistication of the North's nuclear capabilities, Kim declared success in the completion of its nuclear deterrent—which he said now entailed the "mass production of nuclear warheads and missiles" whose "might and reliability are already firmly guaranteed." Kim also warned that the United States "should know that the button for nuclear weapons is on my table,"[1] alluding

---

1. "Kim Jong Un's 2018 New Year's Address," *National Committee on North Korea,* https://www.ncnk.org/node/1427

to his sole authority to launch nuclear weapons and signaling that he had a command-and-control system that rivaled the U.S. president's.

In touting the North's nuclear-related accomplishments and the apparent fulfillment of a longstanding element of the North's dual-track policy, Kim's speech also suggested that the North's nuclear development would necessarily slow as it opened the door for dialogue with the South. Foreshadowing a formal change in the government's policy line in the spring, Kim noted that the U.S.-led maximum pressure campaign was having a negative impact on the economy.[2] The "life-threatening sanctions and blockade" were leading to "difficult living conditions" in the North, a message intended for a domestic audience that would need to continue to bear the burden of the sanctions pressure as Kim turned his focus to improving the economy.[3]

In South Korea, Kim's New Year's address was generally met with a positive response, as Moon directed his administration to begin a dialogue with North Korean negotiators at Panmunjom and engage as if the PyeongChang Olympics proposal could serve "as a turning point in improving South–North relations and promoting peace."[4] The North soon reopened a border hotline with Seoul, a valuable channel for direct dialogue. In Washington, the Trump administration reacted with a nod toward simply continuing "maximum pressure," as officials promised that the United States would not deviate from its policy of no dialogue unless maximalist preconditions were met by the North. As in 2017, Trump overlaid his inflammatory rhetoric on the U.S. position, lobbing a tweet at Kim and telling him to take note of Trump's own nuclear button that was a "much bigger & more powerful one than his, and my Button works!" The public U.S. response betrayed no nuanced understanding of the potentially momentous policy changes in the North that Kim's speech foretold.

2. Robert Carlin, "A New Enchilada," *38 North* (January 2, 2018), https://www.38north.org/2018/01/rcarlin010218/; Ruediger Frank, "Kim Jong Un's 2018 New Year's Speech: Self-Confidence After a Tough Year," *38 North*, (January 3, 2018), https://www.38north.org/2018/01/rfrank010318/

3. "Kim Jong Un's 2018 New Year's Address."

4. Choe Sang-Hun, "South Korea Proposes Border Talks with North Korea After Kim's Overture," *New York Times* (January 2, 2018), https://www.nytimes.com/2018/01/02/world/asia/south-north-korea-olympics-talks.html

THE NORTH–SOUTH DIALOGUE BUILDS MOMENTUM

Inter-Korean talks on January 9 at Panmunjom set in motion a significant series of events, beginning with the Winter Olympics in February, to which the North agreed to send a delegation. The sight of athletes from the two Koreas marching together under the Korean unification flag drew enthusiastic cheers from the spectators and from Chairman Kim's sister, Kim Yo Jong, and the North's nominal head of state, Kim Yong Nam, representing their country. In stark contrast to two clapping North Koreans and a similarly jubilant President Moon, an expressionless Vice President Pence sat in silence.

North–South high-level dialogue continued after the Olympics with National Security Advisor Chung Eui Yong and Director of the National Intelligence Service Suh Hoon meeting Kim Jong Un in Pyongyang. The South Korean envoys traveled to the White House the same week to brief the Trump administration and meet with the president and other high-level officials in the Oval Office. Chung explained that Kim had made four explicit promises in his meeting with them in Pyongyang—namely, a commitment to denuclearization; a commitment to halt nuclear and missile tests; acceptance of ongoing routine U.S.–ROK military exercises; and most importantly, an express desire to meet with Trump. The remarkable statement from Chung that Kim was willing to meet may well have been a direct response to Trump's December message via Jeffrey Feltman, spurred on by the diplomatic efforts of the Moon administration and the technical achievements of the North's nuclear scientists and engineers. Despite McMaster's skepticism of Kim's promises, Trump immediately stated that he would be willing to meet with Kim and directed Chung to make a public announcement. Chung appeared for a statement on the front lawn of the White House on the evening of March 9. He announced on national television the four ideas that Kim had conveyed to the South Koreans and that Trump agreed to Kim's offer to meet.

Trump's acceptance of Kim's invitation for a direct meeting stunned the international community; his overture to Kim via Feltman was not public knowledge, and thus there had been no indication that the United States was prepared to align more closely with the policy of engagement that Seoul was pursuing. Trump did a 180-degree turn from threatening Kim with "fire and fury" to falling back on his belief in his extraordinarily persuasive skills, suggesting that he could develop a strong personal relationship with

Kim and reach a deal that would garner significant media attention and international acclaim. I had to modify my Stanford lectures on North Korea to reflect this new reality. Where I had once described Mattis and Tillerson as the "control rods" that would keep an eruptive President Trump in check, now I had to give Trump some credit for inserting the control rods to prevent a political meltdown.

THE ROAD TO SINGAPORE

During the next three months, South Korea made a major push to help prepare for a successful Kim–Trump summit. North Korea was also ready to engage. At the Olympics, Kim's sister had delivered a handwritten invitation to President Moon to visit the North. Moon and Kim took the first step toward engagement by meeting at Panmunjom in late April. That summit jumpstarted a whirlwind of North Korea's summit diplomacy and prompted a new wave of hope that diplomacy could be effective after years of confrontation and tensions.

Pyongyang and Washington eventually agreed on Singapore as the venue for the first meeting of a sitting U.S. president with the leader of North Korea. But the road to Singapore was chaotic on the American side. Washington was entering uncharted territory with little planning or discipline. Trump had asked CIA Director Mike Pompeo to make a secret trip to Pyongyang over Easter weekend to lay the groundwork for the summit. Pompeo was waiting for U.S. Senate confirmation to replace fired Secretary of State Rex Tillerson. Pompeo traveled with the head of the agency's newly established Korea Mission Center, Sung Hyun (Andy) Kim. Kim was a career CIA analyst whose most recent assignment was CIA section chief in Seoul. A fluent Korean language speaker who had grown up in South Korea, he had an exceptionally good grasp of the issues and problems on the Korean Peninsula. Pompeo was able to get confirmation from Kim Jong Un that he intended to denuclearize. Kim didn't miss a beat by explaining to the Americans that nuclear weapons were a heavy burden that he and his children would have to bear, suggesting that he desired to lift this weight off the backs of future generations of North Koreans. At Pompeo's suggestion, they also agreed to set up a working-level meeting to come up with an agenda.[5]

5. Andy Kim, "Prices for Denuclearization of North Korea," speaking at Stanford Uni-

Later in April, Pompeo officially took over as secretary of state. Whatever his private misgivings might have been about the chances of diplomacy with North Korea, he was the president's man and displayed a positive front. National Security Advisor General H. R. McMaster was replaced by John Bolton, the former Bush administration official who had held senior positions in the State Department and continued to burnish his brand as a hawkish advocate for U.S. supremacy since leaving public service. Trump had clearly soured on McMaster, and Bolton couldn't wait to get back into government but insisted it would be only as secretary of state or national security advisor. He had to settle for the latter as Pompeo had been chosen to head the State Department.

The timing of the change from McMaster to Bolton made little sense, as the United States was entertaining a serious diplomatic push, and Trump remained fixated on a summit meeting with Kim. The conservative McMaster, who had helped to fashion the "maximum pressure" North Korea policy and had great misgivings about Trump meeting with Kim, was replaced by Bolton, who was dead set against such a meeting. McMaster believed that Kim wanted nuclear weapons not just as a deterrent, but as a tool to drive the United States out of South Korea and take over the peninsula. Like many before him, he viewed negotiations as a mechanism that the North abused to buy time to craft more favorable conditions on the Korean Peninsula for its revisionist goals. Bolton, for his part, was deeply skeptical of diplomacy and was one of the most forceful proponents of using military force against North Korea. In one of his opinion pieces authored just before he joined the Trump administration, Bolton made what in his mind was a legal case for a preventive strike on North Korea's nuclear program. Because the North would soon have a robust capability to strike the United States with nuclear weapons, he wrote that it would be "perfectly legitimate for the United States to respond . . . by striking first."[6] Bringing Bolton on board at this moment did not look like a positive step toward arranging a meeting with Kim Jong Un.

versity's Shorenstein Asia-Pacific Research Center (February 22, 2019); Bob Woodward, *Rage* (New York: Simon & Schuster, 2020), 99.

6. John Bolton, "The Legal Case for Striking North Korea First," *Wall Street Journal* (February 28, 2018), https://www.wsj.com/articles/the-legal-case-for-striking-north-korea-first-1519862374

As Trump's advisors played musical chairs, Chairman Kim took notable steps in April to reposition the North on a new policy trajectory. Kim told the Central Committee of the Workers' Party of Korea that the North had "verified the completion of nuclear weapons. . . . We no longer need any nuclear test or test launches of intermediate and intercontinental range ballistic missiles, and because of this the northern nuclear test site has finished its mission."[7] Kim Jong Un also announced a shift in the party line that some Korea watchers had been anticipating. His parallel policy approach, *byungjin*, was formally replaced in favor of a "new strategic line" that focused on the North's economy. Some Korea watchers, including Bob Carlin, had been arguing that Kim had laid the foundation for this eventual pivot to a new economic policy ever since 2012, and they could sense this shift coming as the North's rhetoric about its nuclear program changed in late 2017.[8]

In early May, Mike Pompeo made another trip to Pyongyang, this time as the newly appointed secretary of state, to lay additional groundwork for the Trump–Kim summit. This trip did not conclude successfully. Pompeo was trying to get firm commitments such as a list of the sites developing and testing nuclear weapons, a discussion that his North Korea counterparts said was strictly the purview of Chairman Kim. Conveniently, Kim was at that time traveling to Beijing to meet for the second time in as many months with President Xi Jinping. After a frosty relationship with Xi during the first several years of his term, Kim was now reaching out to shore up Chinese support or at least give Beijing a heads-up of the upcoming summit with Trump.

After Pompeo left Pyongyang empty-handed in May, momentum for the Singapore summit slowed considerably. The North responded negatively to comments by John Bolton that compared the North's path to denuclearization to the Libyan case. On May 24, Vice Minister Choe Son Hui issued a sharp-edged statement attacking Vice President Pence, who had extolled

7. Anna Fifield, "North Korea Says It Will Suspend Nuclear and Missile Tests, Shut Down Test Site," *Washington Post* (April 20, 2018), https://www.washingtonpost.com/world/north-korean-leader-suspends-nuclear-and-missile-tests-shuts-down-test-site/2018/04/20/71ff2eea-44e7-11e8-baaf-8b3c5a3da888_story.html

8. Robert Carlin, "Kim Jong Un's New Strategic Line," *38 North* (April 23, 2018), https://www.38north.org/2018/04/rcarlin042318/

the Libya model and stated the military option for North Korea has never come off the table. She wrote, "We could surmise more than enough what a political dummy he is as he is trying to compare the DPRK, a nuclear weapon state, to Libya that had simply installed a few items of equipment and fiddled around with them."[9] When that arrived at the White House, Trump and a small group of advisors quickly agreed that this attack was unacceptable. The president sent a message to Kim saying their meeting was off. At the same time, Kim and Moon hurriedly met and Kim Gye Gwan, on authorization from above, issued a statement in effect apologizing for Choe's comments.

Trump's interest in establishing a relationship with Kim and the spectacle of that effort compelled him to reverse course. As he explained to his advisors, he did not want to "risk the momentum. . . . This is a big win here. If we make a deal, it will be one of the greatest deals in history." Bolton observed after Trump's change of heart, "It was depressing. We had come so close to escaping the trap" of holding a meeting with Kim in Singapore.[10] In *The Room*, Bolton states that he realized that since Singapore would be going ahead, he would make a determined effort "to stop anything legally binding, and also to minimize the damage of whatever objectionable document Trump might agree to."

Notwithstanding the whiplash of Trump's apparent cancellation and immediate reversal, the North went ahead with the destruction of the test tunnels at Punggye-ri in the presence of international journalists. The disablement of Punggye-ri followed from Kim's claim in May that the test site would no longer be needed to advance North Korea's nuclear program. The North claimed to have collapsed the three remaining usable tunnels at the site and destroyed numerous support facilities, but there were no foreign experts present to verify these claims. A few weeks later, the North appeared to make good on its other key promise in the runup to the Singapore meeting: destroying a missile engine test stand and dismantling elements of its

9. "Press Statement by Vice-Minister of Foreign Affairs of DPRK," *KCNA* (May 24, 2018), http://www.uriminzokkiri.com/index.php?lang=eng&ptype=cfodoc&m-type=view&no=11445

10. John Bolton, *The Room Where It Happened: A White House Memoir* (New York: Simon & Schuster, 2020), 92.

launch facility at Sohae.[11] Bolton was very skeptical of the value of the North blowing up the test tunnels. He called it another "sham" concession, "pure fluff." I thought it was a big deal. The nuclear testing and long-range missile testing moratoria were critical steps toward reducing the nuclear risk posed by Pyongyang. Blowing up some of the tunnels at the nuclear test site made a return to nuclear testing less likely, although not impossible.

In the spring of 2018, I, along with my Stanford University colleagues Bob Carlin and Elliot Serbin, completed a study we termed "A Comprehensive History of North Korea's Nuclear Program."[12] We combined what Carlin and I had learned over the years from our visits to North Korea (seven for me and more than thirty for Carlin) with an extensive literature review to map out the evolution of North Korea's program. Beginning with 1992, we showed the development of the North's nuclear and missile programs side by side with key diplomatic changes. We posted a narrative of nearly one hundred pages along with a color-coded set of charts that provided a readily comprehensible graphic summary. The color charts provided a visual interpretation of the year-by-year diplomatic, technical, and political developments. We chose the color coding—three shades of green for good developments and three shades of red for bad developments, all from a U.S. perspective—in the hope of being able to reach those policymakers in Washington who don't read.

The key takeaways from the study informed my policy advice to the Trump administration and U.S. elected officials in the lead-up to the Singapore summit. First, we concluded that North Korea's pursuit of nuclear weapons had been deliberate, determined, and patient. The nuclear program was not the most secretive in the world. Second, despite North Korea's nuclear progress not being a surprise, U.S. diplomacy since 2000 had been sporadic, reactive, and often motivated by a desire for avoiding risk instead of managing it. North Korea's nuclear program had been slowed, sometimes reversed, during periods of diplomacy, but it had never been

11. Choe Sang-Hun, "North Korea Razes Missile Test Facility Ahead of Meeting with Trump," *New York Times* (June 7, 2018), https://www.nytimes.com/2018/06/07/world/asia/north-korea-missile-test-site.html

12. Siegfried S. Hecker, Robert Carlin, and Elliot Serbin, "A Comprehensive History of North Korea's Nuclear Program," Center for International Security and Cooperation, Stanford University, https://cisac.fsi.stanford.edu/content/cisac-north-korea

abandoned. One of the most important factors in slowing North Korea's nuclear program had been U.S. and IAEA presence in Yongbyon—and that should again be one of the immediate goals of U.S.–DPRK talks. The charts also showed that nuclearization in North Korea was a massive enterprise. It took roughly twenty-five years, and thus we should expect denuclearization to take time as well.

The charts helped clarify how Washington might further its goal of denuclearization. No one quite knew what "denuclearization" even meant. Did it mean no weapons, no deployed weapons, no fissile materials, no missiles, no people, and no civilian nuclear program? It would be helpful for the United States to clarify its definition of this term, even if it did not align with the North's immediately. In addition, it would be easier to advance denuclearization if Washington understood that the narrative that North Korea "has cheated on every agreement" was neither accurate nor useful. The color charts elucidated a better understanding of the history of North Korea's nuclear program so as not to repeat the mistakes. Finally, we observed that as bad as it was in 2018, the situation could get worse. The United States had missed several opportunities in the past by not managing the incremental risks, and it must approach any denuclearization talks with an awareness of this history and a desire to manage those risks to prevent the situation from worsening.

We demonstrated that sanctions had little measurable effect on the evolution of the North's weapon program. We also found that contrary to common belief, Washington had spent only modest sums during times it had diplomatic agreements with the North. We identified the most important initial steps to be no nuclear tests; no intermediate- or long-range missile tests; no more production of plutonium and highly enriched uranium; and no export of nuclear weapons, materials, or technologies. We recommended a phased "halt, roll back, and eliminate" approach that would stretch over a decade to eliminate North Korea's nuclear weapons program because of the enormity of its nuclear weapon enterprise and the huge trust deficit between Washington and Pyongyang.

We briefed our findings in several offices in Washington in the spring of 2018, including to Matt Pottinger and Allison Hooker at the National Security Council, the State Department, the Pentagon, and the National Nuclear Security Administration. We received ample interest in Washington and a polite reception at the NSC. We did not meet with John Bolton during an April visit. He had just become the national security advisor. However, our recommended phased approach was the direct opposite of Bolton's views. He believed any "action for action" steps must be avoided because he claimed they benefited North Korea by frontloading economic benefits while dragging out the dismantlement of the nuclear program into the indefinite future.[13] Bolton told Trump that any benefits the North might receive should come only *after* accomplishing complete, verifiable, and irreversible denuclearization. He continued to tout the "Libya model" for complete denuclearization. He also argued that dismantlement of the North's nuclear program should take only six to nine months based on the experience in Libya. Such an unrealistic time schedule is yet another example of either Bolton's lack of nuclear technical literacy or his willingness to let ideology drive political decisions regardless of technical realities.

Our study got worldwide publicity when William Broad and David Sanger featured it in a front-page *New York Times* story with the headline "North Korea Nuclear Disarmament Could Take 15 Years, Expert Warns."[14] The headline writers used the "15" years because in response to one of Broad's questions as to whether or not denuclearization can actually be achieved in the ten-year time frame we used in our study, I responded that "we don't really know, it may take longer, perhaps fifteen years." As often happens with newswire stories, it is the headline that is remembered.

In late May, U.S. technical and diplomatic experts led by special envoy Sung Kim traveled to North Korea and Singapore to begin laying the groundwork for the summit. President Moon Jae In's "shuttle diplomacy" had helped to get the meeting back on track after both Trump and the North had threatened cancelation.[15] In the runup to Singapore, Sung Kim was "seeking detailed commitments" about Kim Jong Un's willingness to abandon his nuclear weapons. The North also sent officials to the United States around this time, as Kim Yong Chol met with Secretary of State

13. Bolton, *The Room*, 78.

14. William J. Broad and David E. Sanger, "North Korea Nuclear Disarmament Could Take 15 Years, Expert Warns," *New York Times* (May 28, 2018), https://www.nytimes.com/2018/05/28/us/politics/north-korea-nuclear-disarmament-could-take-15-years-expert-warns.html

15. Woodward, *Rage*, 107.

Pompeo in New York. They billed the summit as an opportunity to work on strengthening their personal relationship.[16]

THE SINGAPORE SUMMIT

Trump arrived tired in Singapore having come directly from a contentious G7 summit in Charlevoix, Canada. The Singapore meeting began with a dramatic, slow walk of Trump and Kim across a red-carpeted stage against a backdrop of American and North Korean flags for a handshake. After an initial one-on-one session with interpreters that lasted less than an hour, the two sides engaged in a larger meeting and working lunch with lower-level officials on both sides. Trump, ever focused on the personal aspect, promised ahead of the meeting, "I think we will have a terrific relationship." Kim displayed a more tempered, yet notably optimistic, outlook about the impact of the meeting, as the United States and North Korea overcame the "old prejudices and practices" that had historically inhibited the relationship.[17]

During the meeting, Kim affirmed his commitment to denuclearization and explained that those who distrusted him because of the actions of his predecessors should know that he is different. He promised Trump that "they could work to dispel mistrust and accelerate the pace of denuclearization" as they met "frequently."[18] Kim also explained to Trump that hard-liners in Pyongyang posed "domestic political hurdles he could not easily overcome," and he would have to build public support in North Korea for his denuclearization plans. Trump agreed with Kim's suggestion to curtail the military exercises, promising not to hold the exercises during good faith negotiations, and Kim replied that the hard-liners in Pyongyang would be impressed by Trump's decision about the exercises. Toward the end of the meeting, as the two leaders were waiting to sign their statement, Kim asked if UN sanctions would be the next step, and Trump said he was open to it and wanted to think about it, according to Bolton.

16. Jane Perlez and Choe Sang-Hun, "Top Aide to North Korean Leader Is Expected in U.S. to Meet Pompeo," *New York Times* (May 29, 2018): A5.

17. "Trump to Suspend Military Exercises on Korean Peninsula," Live Briefing, *New York Times* (June 11, 2018), https://www.nytimes.com/2018/06/11/world/asia/trump-kim-live-updates.html

18. Bolton, *The Room*, 109.

The summit produced a joint statement that was signed by both leaders committing to normalization of relations and denuclearization. The core agreement was as follows:

1. Commit to establish new U.S.–DPRK relations in accordance with the desire of the peoples of the two countries for peace and prosperity.
2. Join their efforts to build a lasting and stable peace regime on the Korean Peninsula.
3. Reaffirming the April 27, 2018, Panmunjom Declaration, the DPRK commits to work toward complete denuclearization of the Korean Peninsula.
4. Commit to recovery and repatriation of the remains of American prisoners of war and soldiers missing in action in North Korea, including the immediate repatriation of those already identified.

Kim in his first visit to a foreign country, other than his two earlier trips to China, had to walk a diplomatic tightrope in front of a hungry group of some 3,000 international journalists. He handled himself like a seasoned statesman and shattered the portrait of a reclusive madman with nukes.

In *The Room*, Bolton describes how even at the more business-like events, Trump and Kim hit it off splendidly, creating a strong personal relationship. Bolton shows Kim to be an engaging, clever head of state, who appeared to have taken the correct measure of Mr. Trump and his giant ego.[19] Bolton writes that Trump told Kim that he knew almost immediately that the two of them would get along. And then Trump asked Kim how he assessed him. (I heard a slightly different rendition of this exchange: Kim turned to Trump and said, "Mr. President, I understand you can judge people quickly, in a minute or so." Kim continued speaking and then asked Trump how he judged him. Trump said that he loved the question, "But no, it does not take me that long.") Bolton has Trump telling Kim that he viewed him as "really smart, quite secretive, a very good person, totally sincere, with a great personality." In Bolton's view, Kim showed he had Trump hooked.

Trump was maligned by much of Washington's foreign policy establishment for having ceded Kim the publicity bonanza with few demonstrable reductions in the nuclear threat. The goal of denuclearization of

19. Ibid.

the Korean Peninsula was affirmed but without details, timetables, or a road map. Contrary to these critiques, I saw the summit as a bold step by Trump that dramatically reduced tensions and created time and space for diplomacy. No doubt, the hard work was yet ahead, but things were moving in the right direction. In Singapore, the United States (and for that matter, the world) learned more about Kim Jong Un than it had learned throughout the previous five years, during which the only Americans who had met Kim, in addition to Pompeo and Andy Kim, were the eccentric basketball player Dennis Rodman and his entourage.

Trump concluded the summit with a solo, rambling one-hour plus news conference. He declared victory with exaggerated claims and his usual disregard for the truth. For example, he said that he helped to prevent a catastrophe in which 30, 40, 50 million people could have died. What I found interesting was Trump's apparent reference to our Stanford study. When he was asked about how long it will take for the North to denuclearize, he answered that we can do it fast, as quickly as science and mechanics will allow. He added, "Whoever wrote it would take 15 years," in apparent reference to the *New York Times* headline on our work, "is wrong." By July, Trump had changed his mind. Referring to negotiations for denuclearization of North Korea, he told CBS News, "This has been going on for many, many decades, but I'm in no real rush."[20]

In *The Room*, Bolton concluded his coverage of the summit by noting that the news coverage of the declaration signing was extraordinary. Then "we were off to Washington, my fondest wish, before anything else went wrong."[21] Just as Bolton had planned, the Singapore statement did not contain anything legally binding so as to minimize the damage of whatever objectionable document Trump might agree to. And he had avoided the "step-by-step, simultaneous actions" the North had extolled.

North Korea saw the Singapore summit as a great step forward. North Korean state media lauded the meeting as a resounding success in a detailed report that read like a formal communiqué for the record. It stated:

20. Sarah Kim, "After Helsinki, Trump Says He's in No Hurry for Denuclearization of North Korea," *Korea JoongAng Daily* (July 17, 2018), https://koreajoongangdaily.joins.com/news/article/article.aspx?aid=3050692

21. Bolton, *The Room*, 113.

The two top leaders had a candid exchange of views on the practical issues of weighty significance in putting an end to the decades-long hostile relations between the DPRK and the U.S. and making peace and stability settle on the Korean Peninsula. Trump expressed his intention to halt the U.S.–South Korea joint military exercises, which the DPRK side regards as provocation, over a period of good-will dialogue between the DPRK and the U.S., offer security guarantees to the DPRK and lift sanctions against it, along with advance in improving the mutual relationship through dialogue and negotiation. . . . There was a comprehensive and in-depth discussion over the issues of establishing new DPRK–U.S. relations and building a permanent and durable peace mechanism at the talks.[22]

It added, "Kim Jong Un and Trump had the shared recognition to the effect that it is important to abide by the principle of step-by-step and simultaneous action in achieving peace, stability and denuclearization of the Korean Peninsula."[23]

Upon his return from Singapore, Trump's outlandish claims diminished the real accomplishments of the summit. "Everybody can now feel much safer than the day I took office," Trump said on Twitter. "There is no longer a nuclear threat from North Korea. Meeting with Kim Jong Un was an interesting and very positive experience. North Korea has great potential for the future!" Trump was criticized for these comments, and rightfully so, but they unfortunately dominated media coverage of what had otherwise been a serious, if incremental, step forward in U.S.–DPRK negotiations.

Now the hard diplomatic work of realizing the promise of the summit would begin. But progress would be plagued by the divergence in how the two sides viewed the meeting of the two leaders. Trump's remarks focused primarily on what he considered his achievements at the summit—his claim to have made the world safer and on having established a personal relationship with Kim. For North Korea, as the full statement clearly showed, this was an opportunity to strike a new relationship with Washington and to resolve the decades' old enmities on the peninsula.

22. "Historic First DPRK–U.S. Summit Meeting and Talks Held," *KCNA* (June 13, 2018), https://kcnawatch.org/newstream/1528840973-311086573/historic-first-dprk-u-s-summit-meeting-and-talks-held/
23. Ibid.

20 The Train Wreck in Hanoi

THE LOVE LETTERS

The next step in the diplomatic dance, as agreed in Singapore, was to hold a follow-up meeting between a Pompeo-led American team and the North. It was at this meeting that the veneer of goodwill from the Singapore summit began to crack. But before this meeting, and even as the two sides began to follow a downward trajectory at the negotiating table, Donald Trump and Kim Jong Un continued a dialogue—friendly and optimistic in tone—through personal letters that played a significant role in the lead-up to, and subsequent failure, of the Hanoi summit.

Little was known about the details in the letters. The White House would occasionally refer to one of them, but they were for the most part dismissed as not serious. I was deeply skeptical that the letters had serious diplomatic content, particularly when Trump praised them as "beautiful letters" from Kim, adding that he and Kim had "fallen in love." I expected the letters to demonstrate Bob Woodward's description of Trump in *Rage:* "The oversized personality. The failure to organize. The lack of discipline. The lack of trust in others he picked, in experts."[1] As for Kim, I thought he would focus on playing to Trump's vanities and ego. I was wrong on both accounts.

1. Bob Woodward, *Rage* (New York: Simon & Schuster, 2020), 386.

Although Kim knew how to play Trump, he demonstrated a seriousness about diplomacy and a good understanding of the key nuclear issues. Trump demonstrated good instincts about the importance of engaging Kim personally and building bonds that might lead to diplomatic progress. The letters did feed his ego, and they also showed he had little understanding of the real issues and failed to follow the openings that Kim gave him in the letters.

In wide-ranging interviews with Bob Woodward, Trump gave him full access to the twenty-seven letters exchanged between April 2018 to August 2019. Woodward provided some of the details in *Rage*, but the full impact of those letters was not assessed until Woodward gave my colleague, Bob Carlin, access to the letters (although neither Woodward nor Carlin were allowed to make copies of the letters).[2] Carlin points out that whereas they contained flattery and psychological ploys typical in such letters, they also contained the core perceptions and misperceptions by each side as they tried to bring decades of U.S.–North Korean hostility to something approaching more normal relations. Carlin called the letters "a highly illuminating reflection of the fundamental misperceptions between the two sides."

Trump used one of his early letters to urge Kim to work with Pompeo to follow up on the Singapore joint statement during Pompeo's upcoming visit. He asked that they advance three key objectives: the return of American POW remains from the Korean War, a visit by technical experts to the missile test site at Sohae that Kim had promised to shutter, and the development of a more detailed plan describing first steps toward a robust agreement on denuclearization.[3] A few days later, Kim replied to Trump that Singapore was the "start of a meaningful journey" and that his trust in Trump would increase as he took practical actions to help bring the next summit to fruition. He added, there could be "epochal progress" in relations. As Carlin points out, Trump's focus in most of his letters was to remind

2. Robert Carlin, "The Real Lessons of the Trump–Kim Love Letters," *Foreign Policy* (August 13, 2021), https://foreignpolicy.com/2021/08/13/north-korea-trump-kim-jong-un-love-letters-diplomacy-nuclear-talks/ There appears to be one more letter from Trump to Kim that was not part of the collection to which Woodward had access. In a *KCNA* article dated March 22, 2020, Kim Yo Jong, Kim's sister and first vice department director of the Central Committee, states that Kim received a personal letter from Trump.

3. Woodward, *Rage*, 171.

Kim of his denuclearization obligations. Trump rarely brought up his own obligations to work toward normalization of the two countries.

In parallel and in almost direct opposition to the letters, John Bolton wanted to prevent a deal. Bolton told Pompeo as he was preparing to return to Pyongyang in early July that no serious negotiations should begin until the United States had secured a commitment from Pyongyang "to provide a full, baseline declaration on their nuclear and ballistic missile programs" while maintaining that the disarming work "could then be done in one year or less."[4] Bolton said this would be a test of good faith in the negotiations, a way to ascertain Kim's real commitment to the Singapore agreement. The effect of this advice—which, according to Bolton, Pompeo agreed with in principle and adopted into his negotiating approach—was to put a chill on the entire process. The fundamental disconnect in how the two sides viewed the outlines of what had been agreed to in Singapore surfaced quickly when Kim Yong Chol, North Korea's lead negotiator, hosted Pompeo in Pyongyang. Pompeo, who privately expressed great doubt that Kim would ever give up nuclear weapons, pushed an aggressive agenda on a baseline declaration and denuclearization timelines.

A DPRK Foreign Ministry spokesman characterized Pompeo's position as a "unilateral and brigandish demand for denuclearization," and Kim Yong Chol pushed back during the meeting, instead proposing "balanced implementation" of the Singapore agreement.[5] In the North's view, this meant a process that focused less at the beginning on concrete denuclearization steps and more on establishing a "peace regime" through an end-of-war declaration. Although Pyongyang criticized Washington's policy, it was careful to continue praising Kim's personal relations with Trump and emphasizing its "good faith" in the U.S. president. It was the Trump–Kim letters that kept the dialogue afloat.

The North continued to tout steps Pyongyang had already taken as a sign of goodwill and serious commitment to denuclearization. In the North's view, they had made the first move before Singapore, and their expectation

4. John Bolton, *The Room Where It Happened: A White House Memoir* (New York: Simon & Schuster, 2020), 117.

5. "FM Spokesman on DPRK–U.S. High-Level Talks," *KCNA* (July 7, 2018), http://www.uriminzokkiri.com/index.php?lang=eng&ptype=cfodoc&mtype=view&no=12300; the "brigandish" quote is found in Carlin, "The Real Lessons of the Trump–Kim Love Letters."

was for a reciprocal, if not immediate, U.S. response. But within Trump's national security team, Bolton and Pompeo did not view the North's steps as significant. Contrary to Kim's optimistic letter, they believed the process held "zero probability of success."[6]

The truth was somewhere in between. The steps Pyongyang had taken, such as the self-declared moratorium on nuclear and long-range missile testing, were positive. In fact, North Korea had refrained from launching missiles of any range in 2018. They also began dismantling the missile-engine test stand and rail-mounted processing building for preparing launch vehicles at the Sohae site.[7] All of these were legitimate confidence-building measures, but they were all reversible. The return of remains of fifty-five American servicemen who were killed during the Korean War also was a concrete step following Singapore, though it was a resumption of a previous program for remains recoveries, ended during the Bush administration, rather than something new.

Cognizant of these moves and interested in prompting reciprocal U.S. actions, Kim wrote to Trump on July 30 to remind him of his Singapore commitments, noting his "sense of regret for the lack of anticipated declaration on the termination of war."[8] In an early August speech to the ASEAN Regional Forum, DPRK Foreign Minister Ri Yong Ho called the end-of-war declaration a "very basic and primary step for providing peace on the Korean Peninsula." Much in the same way that the United States sought to test the North's commitment to denuclearization in the proposal put forward by Pompeo, Pyongyang's focus on the end-of-war declaration was characterized by Ri as a test of Washington's "strong will" to build trust with the North.[9]

On September 6, Kim sent Trump his longest letter to date, one with specific reference to denuclearization. He told Trump it would be more

6. Bolton, *The Room*, 119.

7. Joseph Bermudez, "North Korea Begins Dismantling Key Facilities at the Sohae Satellite Launching Station," *38 North* (July 23, 2018), https://www.38north.org/2018/03/sohae032018/

8. Woodward, *Rage*, 172.

9. "DPRK Foreign Minister Makes Speech at ASEAN Regional Forum," *KCNA* (August 5, 2018), https://kcnawatch.org/newstream/1533450055-893152373/dprk-foreign-minister-makes-speech-at-asean-regional-forum

constructive to meet again in person because he didn't think Pompeo could "fully represent Your Excellency's mind." It may also have been an early signal that other North Korean officials were not going to be empowered to talk in detail about the nuclear issue: That would be reserved for discussion between Kim and Trump. In the letter, Kim described the steps he was prepared to take, and what he needed from the United States to proceed. He stated,

> "In addition to the steps we have taken up front, we are willing to take further meaningful steps one at a time in a phased manner, such as the complete shutdown of the Nuclear Weapons Institute or the Satellite Launch District and the irreversible closure of the nuclear materials production facility."[10]

The dismantlement of the Sohae launch facility had already been put on the table over the summer. The statement on irreversible closure of the nuclear materials production facility appeared more definitive than before.

The complete shutdown of the Nuclear Weapons Institute (NWI) had never come up before. It was a remarkable offer because I believed (and still believe) it to be the brain center of the North's nuclear program—that is, their Los Alamos (in the United States, these duties are split between the Los Alamos and the Lawrence Livermore national labs). What is so significant about Kim's offer is that shutting down the NWI (like shutting down Los Alamos and Lawrence Livermore labs) means the eventual end of the nuclear weapons program. It is not possible to deploy nuclear weapons without the scientists and engineers from the labs: those who designed them, those who helped to assemble them, and those who oversee their maintenance and disassembly. While suggesting a willingness to move forward with denuclearization, Kim also warned in the letter that in order "to sustain the momentum . . . we need to feel some changes in our surroundings, even a little to prove that the efforts we made are by no means in vain."

It seems that Trump's senior national security team was unimpressed with the letter from Kim. Bolton recounts in *The Room* that he, Pompeo, and John Kelly (chief of staff at the time) handed Trump the letter and that Trump praised the "wonderful" and "nice" letter as he read out loud "one oleaginous passage after another." After reading the letter, Trump wanted

10. Woodward, *Rage*, 172.

another meeting with Kim and chastised Bolton for opposing the idea. Trump told Bolton, "John, you have a lot of hostility," to which Bolton replied, "The letter is written by a dictator of a rat-shit little country. He doesn't deserve another meeting with you until he has met with Pompeo."

As Trump pushed for a second meeting with Kim after the mid-term elections in November, it was Pompeo who next met with Kim in mid-October. The main outcome of the meeting was to restart working-level discussions, which Bolton "considered inevitable but bad news, nonetheless," because he expected the United States to begin making concessions to the North's diplomats, displaying his well-known disdain for the work done at the State Department.[11] Bolton mentions none of the denuclearization specifics Kim had offered in the letter. In fact, Bolton never mentioned the Nuclear Weapons Institute in his book.

Kim Jong Un provided a glimpse of plans for next steps when he met with President Moon at the Pyongyang summit September 18 to 20. As surreal as it must have been, Kim arranged for President Moon to address a wildly cheering crowd of some 150,000 North Koreans in Pyongyang. Kim also took Moon to visit Mount Paektu—the famous and revered volcano on the border with China—for a symbolic step toward peace. The two leaders released a joint declaration to pursue peace, agree to military cooperation, establish new communication channels, and develop new economic ties. Not reported in any detail in the media were the denuclearization discussions at the summit. I had the benefit of learning about the details from people intimately familiar with the summit discussions when I visited Seoul a week later.

Much as in his letter to Trump, Kim was bold on the nuclear front with the South Korean delegation. He said he was changing DPRK's strategic direction. He planned to denuclearize and concentrate fully on the economy. Kim told Moon he wanted to demonstrate his commitment to this goal by undertaking significant steps that would allay skepticism in the United States. He was frustrated that he had already signed the Panmunjom declaration with Moon and the Singapore declaration with Trump, and yet there was still much skepticism. Kim repeated the offer to dismantle the Yongbyon facilities. He had previously offered to dismantle an engine

11. Bolton, *The Room*, 125.

test stand at the Sohae Satellite Launching Station. Now, he would offer to dismantle the entire launch site because he realized that if they only dismantled the test stand, it would be heavily criticized by the United States. Kim was concerned about how he would explain this to his people because the DPRK had made such a big deal of having put satellites into space. He suggested to Moon that since they both had capabilities for space and satellites, perhaps they could do things together later. Kim told Moon that the DPRK would not give up the weapons until the end, as it would be too vulnerable otherwise. The weapons would go last, after a peace treaty, Kim said. The general contours of Kim's position on denuclearization in his talks with the South Korean delegation were consistent with the content of his September 6 letter to Trump, revealed much later in Woodward's *Rage*. My South Korean colleagues, who at the time of the Pyongyang summit almost surely had no knowledge of the letter contents, made no mention of the Nuclear Weapons Institute having come up in the Kim–Moon discussions.

They did tell me that Moon and his delegation believed that Kim was serious about the strategic shift he described. One day after the summit ended, however, Kim in another letter to Trump complained of the "excessive interest" and "unnecessary" role that President Moon was taking in the denuclearization matter. Hence, despite being quite specific on denuclearization with Moon, Kim made it clear that these issues were reserved for him and Trump to decide. Kim went on to state that although many were skeptical of the prospects for improving U.S.–DPRK bilateral relations and progressing on denuclearization, he was confident that together with "Your Excellency" he would "definitely prove them wrong."

In early September, the administration had appointed a new special representative for North Korea, Stephen Biegun, who transitioned from several government posts to head international governmental affairs at the Ford Motor Company. Bob Carlin and I met Steve at the State Department during his first official day in the office. As it turned out, it was September 6, the date Kim penned the long letter to Trump. Biegun was an experienced foreign policy expert, having spent time in Moscow in the early 1990s and serving as executive secretary of the NSC during Condoleezza Rice's term as national security advisor. As we met in the State Department lobby and I extended my hand to introduce myself, Biegun replied, "I know who you are, and I need your help." He reminded me that we had met when I testified as Los Alamos director at Senate hearings on the Comprehensive Nuclear Test Ban Treaty in the mid-1990s. He was on Senator Jesse Helms's staff at the time.

The meeting with Biegun offered an early sign of how he would conduct business as special representative—very thoughtful, always listening, and mindful of advice on a path forward. With the aid of his able staff, Biegun took a deep dive into Korean Peninsula matters, soliciting advice within and outside the United States. He took a pragmatic approach to the North Korea issue, driven by a desire to attain results rather than remain beholden to a distinct ideological bent. Biegun had a big job to get to know his counterparts in South Korea, Japan, China, and Russia, and he had to start from scratch with the North's diplomats, who had been dealing with Pompeo. Kim Jong Un, of course, had been dealing with Trump directly.

By this time in September, several competing agendas were at play. The Pyongyang summit demonstrated that, at the time, Kim and Moon were aligned on a path forward. Kim was pivoting toward the economy, and Moon had grand plans for economic integration of the South and North. The photos from the summit showed an almost brotherly friendship. But Kim did not want Moon involved in the nuclear issue. Thus, Washington's policy would play a more decisive role on that question. As he got up to speed on the diplomatic and nuclear files with North Korea, Biegun set out to help Trump make the deal. Despite facing enormous complexities on the diplomatic front, Biegun's greatest challenge was inside Washington. Bolton was determined to stop any deal short of the North's total capitulation. Bolton's view was nominally shared by many officials in the NSC as well as, to a large degree, Biegun's boss, Secretary Pompeo. But at the top, Trump maintained his own agenda, one focused on making a grand deal that would captivate the media and satisfy his domestic political interests.

THE ROAD TO HANOI

As the United States and North Korea moved toward a second leader-level summit in early 2019, the correspondence between Trump and Kim transcended the deep disagreements and doubts that prevailed at lower levels in their governments. Kim and Trump stayed engaged through the exchange of letters throughout the fall and into 2019. Kim continued to pledge to denuclearize. Trump told him he looked forward to the next summit and to making real progress on denuclearization and "a really bright future for your people under your leadership in the year ahead." In early 2019, Trump gave Kim every indication that "great results will be accomplished between our two countries, and that the only two leaders who can do it are you and me." One of Trump's letters was handwritten and signed: "Your friend, Donald J. Trump."

John Bolton did not share Trump's "your friend" sentiment for Kim. In *The Room*, Bolton wrote that he made a determined effort to prepare Trump for Hanoi to avoid a debacle. He described that Trump was much more engaged during three 45-minute briefings than was customary, the first of which was held two weeks before the summit. Bolton worked hard on Trump's psyche to make certain that he understood that standing firm was critical. He told Trump that Kim was the one more desperate for a deal. To make the point, Bolton showed Trump clips of President Reagan describing the 1986 Reykjavik summit with Mikhail Gorbachev extolling the virtues of hanging tough. Trump summarized his take-aways from the briefing: "I don't need to be rushed," and "I could walk away." Bolton wrote, "I couldn't have scripted it better."[12]

In the second briefing, Bolton focused on the meaning of "complete denuclearization." Bolton stressed the importance of getting a full baseline declaration and the dismantling of everything, including chemical and biological weapons. Trump was attentive and asked Bolton to write it all on a single piece of paper, which Trump later gave to Kim in Hanoi. Bolton patted himself on the back for how well the second briefing went. He stated that they accomplished getting "Trump into the right frame of mind so as not to give away the store in Hanoi." Bolton was equally pleased with the third briefing but concluded, "Whether they [the briefings] would suffice to prevent catastrophic concessions to Kim remained to be seen."

Although Bolton felt confident that Trump had gotten the main message about taking a hard line from the briefings in the runup to Hanoi, he continued to be alarmed about what Biegun and the working-level team were offering the North Koreans before the summit. He was incensed by what Biegun presented at the end of January at Stanford University in his first public policy statement. Biegun said that Washington needed "to advance

12. Ibid., 320–323.

our diplomacy alongside our plans for denuclearization in a manner that sends that message clearly to North Korea as well." He was aware of Pyongyang's insistence that actions must be taken step by step toward complete denuclearization "simultaneously and in parallel" toward peace in Korea, starting with a peace declaration.[13] This was very much in line with the Singapore joint statement and what Carlin, Serbin, and I had concluded in our comprehensive history of the North's nuclear program.

Biegun and his team met with the North's working-level team in Washington and Pyongyang in the lead-up to the Hanoi summit. The week before the summit, Biegun took a sixteen-member interagency team to meet with their North Korean counterparts. He reported subsequently that the North brought some creative ideas on how they "could improve people-to-people cooperation and transform relations on the Korean peninsula."[14] On the issue of sanctions, Biegun stated, "what the North Koreans asked, and what they have been asking for several weeks in our working-level negotiations, is the lifting of the United Nations Security Council sanctions imposed since March of 2016."[15] As we will see, that was interpreted differently by the two sides at the summit.

Biegun said that the key driver of the Singapore summit had been denuclearization, and the North Korean team was "not authorized to discuss denuclearization issues, which is just absurd." Yet, in the post-summit news brief, he stated, on the definition of denuclearization, "it's a matter that we discussed at length in the working-level negotiations, but it wasn't in the North Korean proposal yesterday." Biegun and his team had developed a road map, largely based on the ideas he presented at Stanford, that included all facets of what they believed had to be discussed in detail before the

13. Stephen E. Biegun, "Remarks on the DPRK," Stanford University, Freeman Spogli Institute (January 31, 2019), https://fsi-live.s3.us-west-1.amazonaws.com/s3fs-public/transcript_stephen_bieugn_discussion_on_the_dprk_20190131.pdf

14. "Negotiating with North Korea: An Interview with Former U.S. Deputy Secretary of State Stephen Biegun," *Arms Control Association* (June 2021), https://www.armscontrol.org/act/2021-06/interviews/negotiating-north-korea-interview-former-us-deputy-secretary-state-stephen

15. "Senior State Department Official Remarks to Traveling Press," *U.S. State Department* (February 28, 2019), https://2017-2021.state.gov/senior-state-department-official-remarks-to-traveling-press-3/index.html Although he was not identified as such in the official remarks, it was clearly Steve Biegun who was the senior State Department official.

leaders met at the summit. They gave an unofficial copy (called table-dropping in the diplomatic trade) to the North Korean team.

Biegun's ideas couldn't have been more at odds with how Bolton had prepped Trump for the summit. Bolton was determined to intervene prior to Hanoi to avoid Trump's endorsement of this approach with what he called its "dangerous consequences." In *The Room*, Bolton lashed out at Biegun for having operated without authority and in deliberate violation of the established interagency process to "table-drop" the draft statement with the North Koreans. Bolton was furious, calling it a "massive process foul."[16] He said it read as if it was drafted by the North Koreans.

At this point, Bolton moved into a sabotage mode of anything the State Department and its team had planned. Bolton reports that he conferred with Trump's new chief of staff, Mick Mulvaney, and got word to Vice President Pence. Mulvaney gave a copy of Biegun's draft to Trump on Air Force One on the way to Hanoi. Bolton states that Trump told Pompeo he didn't like Biegun's comments (the table-dropped draft)—it was "too much." Bolton takes particular delight in sharing in his book, "For the record, when he [Trump] saw Biegun the next morning, he didn't recognize him."[17] That's a sad testament of how well Trump was prepared for the summit if he apparently did not recognize his chief negotiator, who also happened to be the only one aligned with him to get a deal.

It wasn't until more than two years later that Biegun responded to Bolton's "table-drop" accusation in an interview with *NK News*.[18] Biegun said the document was cleared through the appropriate deputies' committee channel and shared with the North Koreans at the Hanoi meeting of the working teams the week before the summit. Biegun said that the contents were agreed to by Bolton's NSC staff present at the meeting. Even after the passing of two years, Biegun was hesitant to discuss how Bolton sabotaged his every move on North Korea. He simply stated that Bolton "was prone

16. Bolton, *The Room*, 323.

17. Ibid., 324.

18. Bryan Betts, "An Interview with Stephen Biegun, Former US Special Envoy to North Korea," *NK News* (July 14, 2021), https://www.nknews.org/2021/07/an-interview-with-stephen-biegun-former-us-envoy-to-north-korea/

336 The Train Wreck in Hanoi

to follow his own approach and operate on his own assumptions."[19] As we shall see, that is exactly what Bolton did in Hanoi.

Let's review the state of play for both sides on the eve of the summit. The American side was bitterly divided. Trump wanted a deal. He had raised expectations in his January letter to Kim with "great results will be accomplished between our two countries." Biegun supported Trump's desire for a deal by working with his North Korean counterparts. He shared the road map for a deal with them, but he was not able to get the North Korean team to negotiate key denuclearization details ahead of the summit. Bolton sabotaged Biegun's every move, and it was Bolton who prepped Trump for Hanoi and took pride that he had convinced Trump that he needn't be rushed and could walk away. Trump also faced major challenges at home with hearings scheduled during the summit dates by the House of Representatives Oversight Committee on Russian interference in the 2016 U.S. elections. A star witness was to be Michael Cohen, Trump's personal attorney, generally known as his "fixer."

Kim must have come to the summit supremely confident. He had conducted himself like a seasoned statesman at the Singapore summit. He had successfully engaged the leaders of China, Russia, and South Korea in multiple summits. He conducted personal diplomacy with Trump through the exchange of letters. North Korea's expectations for the summit were captured well in the pro-DPRK Tokyo *Choson Sinbo* newspaper in an article by the well-connected journalist Kim Chi Yong, published as the summit began.[20] It reminded the reader that Trump said the talks will be "very successful, while claiming 'there is no hurry' when it comes to denuclearization." It stated that President Trump is heading to Hanoi with the belief that a deal will follow "the principle of step-by-step, simultaneous action." It listed the preemptive denuclearization measures that Pyongyang had already taken during the past year. These included the suspension of nuclear tests and ballistic rocket test launches, and the dismantlement of a nuclear test site. The article stated that North Korea had already clarified its willingness to dismantle an engine test site and rocket launcher and to dismantle the Yongbyon nuclear facilities following corresponding measures by the United

---

19. Ibid.

20. Kim Chi-yong, "Second North Korea–US Summit Talks in Hanoi, Vietnam from Today," *Choson Sinbo* (online in Korean) (February 27, 2019).

States. It also reminded the reader that in his 2019 New Year's address, Kim reaffirmed the position "to no longer make, test, use, or propagate nuclear weapons." If the United States wants to realize these, "surely it should take corresponding actions and measures," Kim Chi Yong added.

Kim Jong Un also must have been encouraged by what his team had heard of Biegun's Stanford University policy speech and the working-level talks. He may well have been overconfident that he could wait to negotiate details of denuclearization and the corresponding measures directly with Trump. He had previously informed Trump in his September 6 letter that the denuclearization details must be discussed in person because Secretary Pompeo would not be able to represent the president's mind. And, although Kim knew that Bolton opposed the president's desire for a deal, he would not have known that Bolton had seized the upper hand in preparing Trump.

TRUMP WALKS AWAY IN HANOI

On February 26, Kim arrived in Hanoi after a sixty-hour train ride from Pyongyang. President Trump arrived on Air Force One that evening. Both held separate meetings in Hanoi with Vietnamese officials on Wednesday. They began with a short one-on-one meeting between the two leaders followed by dinner, at which Trump was accompanied by Pompeo and Chief of Staff Mick Mulvaney. According to Bolton, the North Koreans excluded him from the dinner.

Mulvaney told Bolton after dinner that Trump had wanted to avoid substantive discussions with Kim until the next morning, but that Kim expanded on his previous proposal to irreversibly close the Yongbyon nuclear center in return for the removal of all post–2016 UN Security Council sanctions. Bolton states that this type of deal was precisely what he was determined to prevent—what he called the typical "action for action" ploy, giving the North economic relief they needed while the United States received, in his view, very little in return. What exactly transpired that first evening is important so as to understand the dynamics of the rest of the summit, but the details remain unknown. Trump appeared prepared to go for a big deal or walk, while Kim must have been anxious to present the "big present" his team had told Biegun that he was bringing to Hanoi.[21]

21. Betts, "Negotiating with North Korea: Interview with Biegun."

Bolton reports in *The Room* that Trump had stayed up well into the night watching Michael Cohen's incriminating testimony. Bolton states that Trump canceled the morning briefings, and on the way to the Metropole hotel, the venue for the summit, he asked whether it was a bigger story if he got a small deal or if he walked away. Bolton assured him that "walking away was a far bigger story."[22] Trump and Kim began with another one-on-one meeting before they were joined by Pompeo and Kim Yong Chol. Bolton reports that after about an hour, the two sides took a break. Trump headed for the holding room and "immediately switched on Fox News to see how the late-night shows were covering Cohen's testimony, as well as events in Hanoi." According to Bolton, Trump was visibly tired and irritated and apparently felt there was no satisfactory deal at hand.

After the break, the two sides convened for the larger session, which along with Trump included Pompeo, Mulvaney, and, for the only time, Bolton. Kim Yong Chol and Minister Ri Yong Ho joined Kim. Unfortunately, as of this writing, Bolton's account, which is hardly an unbiased history, is the only one available with details of the meeting. Bolton reports that Trump asked Kim what they had come up with during the break. Kim indicated he was unhappy since he had traveled all the way to Hanoi and was offering a proposal incomparable to all those his predecessors had put on the table, but Trump was still not satisfied. Bolton states that at that point, Trump asked for the one-pager Bolton had prepared on the definition of denuclearization and another on the bright economic future for North Korea, which he then passed on to Kim. Unmoved, according to Bolton, Kim stressed again the significance of the Yongbyon concession. Bolton states that Trump asked Kim if he could add something to his offer, such as a percentage reduction in the sanctions rather than completely removing them.

The details of how this discussion proceeded are crucial. Did Kim indicate in some manner that he was mainly concerned at that point with sanctions that inhibited the civilian economy and the livelihood of his people? Foreign Minister Ri Yong Ho explained that's what the North had been requesting at his hastily called midnight news conference following the summit. Whether there was nuance in Kim's response that was missed by the U.S. side, whether Kim was holding back to unveil this as a compromise

22. Bolton, *The Room*, 326.

position once he judged the moment was ripe, or whether he simply misplayed his hand, we don't know. Although Bolton doesn't provide a description of the discussion in any detail, he does strongly state his own views: "This was beyond doubt the worst moment of the meeting. If Kim Jong Un had said yes there, they might have had a deal, disastrously for America." Bolton adds, "fortunately Kim wasn't biting, saying he was getting nothing."

Trump tried again to have Kim improve his denuclearization package. According to Bolton, he suggested Kim should offer to eliminate long-range missiles. Again, we are left to wonder if Kim replied that he was offering up the Sohae launch site and reminded Trump that he had already taken unilateral actions to halt long-range missile testing and nuclear testing. Bolton doesn't say.

Bolton writes that after failing to get Kim to budge on his position, Trump asked Bolton what he thought. Bolton states, he "was not going to miss his chance." He laid out what he had put in the one-pager that Trump handed Kim, which focused on the need for a "full baseline declaration of North Korea's nuclear, chemical, biological, and ballistic-missile programs." In Bolton's view, prior negotiations had failed without receiving such a declaration up front. From the North's perspective, of course, this was a non-starter. Bolton reports that Kim responded that a step-by-step process "would ultimately give the U.S. a comprehensive picture." Kim's response was what Pyongyang had stressed for the past year, and what Kim had repeatedly told Trump in his letters. It was also the approach developed by Biegun for the road map. Bolton states in *The Room* that Kim replied to Trump that they couldn't do what Bolton asked since "they had no legal guarantees to safeguard their country's security. They had no diplomatic relations; seventy years of hostility and only eight months of personal relations."

Bob Woodward reports in *Rage* that Trump had his own version of events in Hanoi. He told Woodward that almost from the start of the summit, he instinctively knew "Kim wasn't ready to get where we needed him to go." Whereas Kim was ready to give up one nuclear site, Trump said he had five we needed him to give up. "Listen, one doesn't help and two doesn't help and three doesn't help and four doesn't help." Trump told Kim, "Five does help." Kim replied that Yongbyon was their biggest site, to which Trump retorted, "Yeah, it's also your oldest." Trump went on to tell Kim, "I know every one of your sites. I know all of them, better than any of my people I know them. You understand that."[23] That, of course, was pure nonsense.

It is also a testament to how unprepared Trump was for the summit and how unwilling Bolton was to negotiate a denuclearization deal. I imagine that at this point, Kim would have countered by telling Trump that he had already taken four or five denuclearization actions without reciprocity from the United States. And maybe Kim repeated the offer to permanently close the Nuclear Weapons Institute as he had proposed in his September 6 letter. If he didn't propose that, why not? And why did the American side not bring it up? It was, in my opinion, the most consequential offer Kim had made in the past year, particularly when combined with the dismantlement of Yongbyon. Yet, Bolton either did not comprehend the seriousness of that offer, or he didn't want to know.

I did not find out until I had the opportunity to ask Bolton about that offer during a seminar he presented on North Korea in February 2022.[24] I asked Bolton about the September 6 letter and specifically if he could tell me what the Nuclear Weapons Institute was. Somewhat uncharacteristically, Bolton fumbled a bit and said, "that term had come up in a couple of places, but it was never defined by North Korea." He went to say, "I can't speak for others, but I understood it as a general reference to their entire [nuclear] program." That's nonsense. It demonstrates that Bolton neither knew what the Nuclear Weapons Institute was, nor did he care to ask and find out.

In his later discussion with Bob Woodward, Trump said that Kim wouldn't budge on his position. Finally, Trump told Kim, "You are not ready to make a deal, you are not there." Kim's face was in utter shock as he asked, "What do you mean?" Trump replied, "I've got to leave. You are my friend. I think you are a wonderful guy. But we've got to leave because you're not ready to make a deal."[25] That, I believe, was a monumental misreading. Kim came prepared to make a deal, although he may have been overconfident in how far he could persuade Trump to move in his direction.

23. Woodward, *Rage*, 175.

24. Institute for Corean-American Studies (ICAS) seminar featuring John Bolton (February 4, 2022), https://www.icasinc.org/2022/2022v/v220204a.html

25. Woodward, *Rage*, 176.

At this point, Trump and Kim tried to put the best spin on why they did not reach a deal. They went back and forth as to whether to issue a joint statement or separate ones. Pompeo and Kim Yong Chol were sent out to compose a joint statement, a virtually impossible job given the circumstances and the time pressure. Not surprisingly, they failed. While they were out, off in the holding rooms, Biegun tried to get a definitive answer from Vice Foreign Minister Choe Son Hui of what shutting down Yongbyon entailed. She replied that only Chairman Kim could answer that. Biegun reported that, after some back and forth, including trips to check with Kim in his holding room, she returned to tell Biegun that Kim said it meant, "everything at Yongbyon." Biegun recounted that he told Choe, "That's great, let's talk." But at that moment, Trump, who was not involved in these discussions, decided it was time to go—he walked past Biegun and Choe on the way out the door. The summit was over. Later, Biegun told me that if Kim would have said earlier that everything at Yongbyon was included, "it would have changed history."[26] Maybe, maybe not. Bolton had the cards stacked against Biegun and a deal. He had convinced Trump that walking away was in his best interest.

Trump and Pompeo tried to put a positive spin on the summit in their news conference.[27] We learned little about critical details of the negotiations from Trump's rambling, mostly incoherent account. Secretary Pompeo tried to paint a confident picture of the summit at the news conference and to set the stage for future meetings with, "I'm very optimistic that the progress that we made . . . I'm hopeful that the teams will get back together in the days and weeks ahead, and continue to work out what's a very complex problem."

In contrast, at their midnight news conference, Foreign Minister Ri and First Vice Minister Choe expressed their, and almost certainly Kim Jong Un's, frustrations. They asserted that the North had asked only for "an initial, partial lifting of the United Nations' sanctions." Ri stated that

"[I]f the United States lifts some UN sanctions—that is to say, sanctions on

26. Biegun, personal communications with author, U.S. State Department (May 18, 2019).

27. "Remarks by President Trump in Press Conference," Hanoi, Vietnam (February 28, 2019), https://trumpwhitehouse.archives.gov/briefings-statements/remarks-president-trump-press-conference-hanoi-vietnam/

items that disrupt the civilian economy and public welfare—we will permanently dismantle, in their entirety, all facilities that produce nuclear materials, including plutonium and uranium, in Yongbyon in the presence of US experts through the joint operation by the technicians of the two countries."[28]

They viewed their proposal as a realistic way to proceed in confidence building and resolving issues in a phased manner, which had been jointly agreed upon in Singapore. Ms. Choe reiterated that their proposal was to close the entire Yongbyon facility. She concluded:

> "What I want to stress is that a nuclear expert, Dr. Hecker, once visited our enriched uranium plant in Yongbyon. We even suggested that we could permanently close this plant that is capable of producing highly enriched uranium. But the response from the U.S is not good enough. I cannot promise that such a golden opportunity will come again, to be laid right in front of the U.S. again."

HANOI—ANOTHER HINGE POINT

Trump walking away in Hanoi was another in a series of hinge points— bad decisions with bad consequences—rather than what Trump viewed as a temporary setback. Kim returned to Pyongyang bruised and angry. It must have been particularly agonizing for him to have to wait around Hanoi after the summit collapsed on Thursday—to have his train serviced, meet with Vietnamese leaders, and then make the two-and-a-half-day journey home, not arriving until 3 AM on Tuesday March 5. The train ride must have been hell for his staff since the summit did not go as planned. However, for some, like General Kim Yong Chol, it may have been preferable to incur the leader's wrath rather than have him give away the store in Hanoi. Kim Yong Chol may well have been North Korea's answer to John Bolton, playing a similar role as spoiler. The general was an old spymaster who had opposed compromising with Washington going back some thirty

---

28. This is the wording used in the post-summit article written by Kim Chi-yong for *Choson Sinbo* (online in Korean) (March 1, 2019): "The Points of Arguments for the Second Summit Between the Democratic People's Republic of Korea and the United States and the Way of Resolving the Issues—The First Step Toward DPRK-US Cooperation Is Confidence Building Through Phase-by-Phase Simultaneous Actions."

years when he opposed Kim Il Sung's overture to South Korea. He likely never deviated much from that stance or from preferring not to deal with the Americans.

In Washington, Trump won praise for walking away from what was almost uniformly considered a bad deal. The common belief in Washington was that the Yongbyon facilities that Kim offered were old and "used up." I disagreed then and still do now. During my last visit to Yongbyon in 2010, I was shown a new, ultramodern centrifuge facility. The North was building a new reactor. Many more construction projects could be observed during the next ten years via satellite in this sprawling nuclear site of 3 square miles with 300-some buildings. There was no question in my mind that Yongbyon was neither used up nor obsolete.

Much of the North's nuclear program—such as the weaponization facilities (R&D, weapons manufacture, and assembly) and missile production and testing facilities—were known to be outside of Yongbyon. But I believed the Yongbyon facilities were still the heart of the North's nuclear materials production complex. Yongbyon housed all of the North's nuclear reactors capable of producing plutonium and tritium. The modern centrifuge facility I visited that had doubled in size a few years later was there. I concluded in 2010 that the North had additional centrifuge facilities outside of Yongbyon; how many, their capacities, and their location remained uncertain. These sites likely depend on the Yongbyon chemical processing facilities to help produce most of the uranium hexafluoride feed material for all centrifuge operations. Hence, Yongbyon continued to be critical to the North's capacity to produce highly enriched uranium and influence the size of its stockpile. More importantly, however, was that without Yongbyon, the North could not produce additional plutonium and tritium, thereby limiting its ability to enhance the sophistication of its nuclear weapons.

Had Trump taken the North's offer in Hanoi, operations would have been halted in Yongbyon, and an American technical team would have been able to return to the site for the first time in ten years. That would have allowed Washington to resolve many of the uncertainties about the North's nuclear capabilities. For example, how sophisticated and capable were their centrifuge facilities? Inspecting those in Yongbyon would have provided a much better idea of what the North had elsewhere. Being back in Yongbyon would have shed light on why the 5 MWe reactor was not operating at that time and if it could be restarted. In addition, it would have provided much needed insight about the status and role the experimental light water reactor was expected to play.

Beyond the Yongbyon facilities, Minister Ri pointed out, they had offered to put in writing that North Korea would end all nuclear and long-range missile tests. I believed that was important because North Korea still needed more of both kinds of testing in order to achieve a militarily useful nuclear-tipped ICBM. A written guarantee would not be ironclad, but it would still be an important milestone along the way. The North had also dismantled its Punggye-ri nuclear test site, at least to the point of blowing up the entrances to several test tunnels. A deal in Hanoi would have made it highly unlikely that they would reconstitute some of the tunnels for further nuclear testing. But what topped all these concessions was Kim's offer in his September 6 letter to completely shut down the Nuclear Weapons Institute. Kim had put enough in play before going to Hanoi that it should have been sufficient to pave the way for constructive negotiations.

From Singapore through to Hanoi, Kim showed that, like his father and grandfather, he saw the potential of strategic accommodation with Washington—one that would allow his regime to normalize relations with the United States, to improve the country's economy, and to get out of the undue influence of China. Trump's unconventional approach to develop personal relations with Kim Jong Un opened the door to progress on halting and eventually eliminating the North's nuclear weapons program. At Hanoi, Trump walked away instead of walking through that open door.

Trump chose not to ease up on the maximum pressure sanctions campaign, instead doubling down to continue a policy that had failed for the past two decades. Had Trump chosen to offer Kim specific enticements through sanctions relief for concrete steps toward denuclearization, it would have cost Washington little. However, as much as the Trump administration's actions in Hanoi resulted in negative consequences that we are liable to feel for many years, Kim Jong Un also missed the mark. He had several opportunities to appeal to Trump's instinct and desire for a deal, and to counteract Bolton's outsized influence by working with Biegun's team, but he missed them.

The issue of sanctions relief was pivotal in the failure of the Hanoi summit. According to Bolton, Trump told Kim it was his proposal to lift the sanctions that was the deal breaker. We don't know how Kim pitched the lifting of sanctions to Trump in his sessions. On the American side, there seemed to be unanimity, even from Biegun, that the price was too high for what Kim was asking. Whereas Pyongyang wanted sanctions relief for the civilian side, Washington believed it was precisely these sanctions that applied the maximum pressure necessary to bring the North to denuclearize. Yet, it had consistently failed. The hard-line sanctions proponents always had the same answer for the failure—not stringent enough and not applied long enough.

In a subsequent interview, Biegun said the North Korean working-level team discussed the lifting of sanctions at their pre-summit meeting in Hanoi. Biegun claimed the North Korean team requested lifting all sanctions, although it isn't clear from Biegun's remarks if that was the North's initial request or its bottom line. His economic analysts calculated that the sanctions Pyongyang wanted lifted would give them a financial windfall in the billions. According to Biegun, "In effect, the only remaining strictures on trade would be actively doing business with the weapons of mass destruction facilities and enterprises themselves." He added, what the North was implicitly proposing "would in effect accept North Korea as a nuclear weapons state."[29] Quite frankly, that sounds more like something out of John Bolton's playbook.

The North Korean side viewed the lifting of sanctions very differently. They saw it as an initial step for confidence building, which is the "touchstone for determining the United States' will for improving relations."[30] What is perplexing is that Minister Ri stated at the news conference that sanctions relief was not the North's highest priority. Instead, security guarantees were more important to allow the DPRK to take denuclearization measures. Ri said that they requested sanctions relief because they thought this would be easier for the Americans. In that case, why did Kim and Trump not more fully explore sanctions relief or security guarantees in Hanoi? In the final analysis, the Americans saw the "gap" between what Pyongyang was willing to offer on denuclearization and what it demanded on sanctions relief as too big to solve in Hanoi. And they didn't appear inclined to decrease that gap through negotiations.

29. Betts, "Negotiating with North Korea: Interview with Biegun."
30. Kim Chi-yong, "The Points of Arguments for the Second Summit."

President Trump, Secretary Pompeo, and Special Representative Biegun were optimistic that the differences could be resolved soon after the summit. Not so, John Bolton. He not only viewed the failure to make a deal as a success but took credit for it. In *The Room,* he states "that perhaps most important, through the pre-Hanoi briefing process we [in describing the briefings, Bolton made it clear in *The Room* that it was "he," not the generic "we"] had helped Trump conclude that walking away was no failure, thereby derailing the unhealthy negotiation path Biegun was on."[31]

"SUCH A GOLDEN OPPORTUNITY
MAY NOT COME AGAIN"

President Trump did what he could before leaving Hanoi to assure Kim that the breakdown was not irrevocable. Woodward reports that after Hanoi, letters between Trump and Kim were cordial but infrequent. When Kim returned home, although bitterly disappointed, he kept up a good front and did not criticize the summit. That came to an end in the speech he gave in early April, in which he took a hard line on what happened in Hanoi and what the future held. North Korea had by then also severed almost all contacts with Seoul—whose "meddling" mediation Kim mocked in the April speech.[32] In June, Kim wrote his first letter to Trump in many months, looking back at Singapore at its first anniversary. Kim wrote, "Today's reality is that without a new approach and the courage it takes, the prospect for resolution of the issues will only be bleak." He dangled the hope that another meeting may "build a lasting and stable peace regime on the Korean Peninsula."

Two weeks later, Trump invited Kim via Twitter to meet him at the DMZ "with no special agenda" following the G20 summit meeting he attended in Japan. Kim accepted to meet Trump for what may well have been the highlight of photo ops during Trump's presidency—accepting Kim's invitation to step across the dividing line at the joint security area in Panmunjom into North Korean territory. Yet, progress appeared to be elusive. On August 5, Kim wrote Trump his longest letter yet. As Carlin points out, in Kim's

31. Bolton, *The Room,* 331.

32. "On Socialist Construction and the Internal and External Policies of the Government of the Republic at the Present Stage," First Session of the 14th Supreme People's Assembly of the DPRK, posted by National Committee on North Korea (April 12, 2019), https://www.ncnk.org/resources/publications/kju_april2019_policy_speech.pdf/file_view

letter of unrelenting woe, Kim laid out his concerns and the obstacles that he accused the United States and South Korea of creating.[33] Kim wrote, "he remembers clearly" promising President Trump at the DMZ meeting "to have the experts meet in a few weeks, but times are different now." He accused Washington of proceeding with "provocative combined military exercises" that targeted his country. Kim expressed his disappointment to Trump that he would allow these to proceed when, as Kim said, "I have no intention of either attacking South Korea or of starting a war." He added that what he objected to even more was that "the US military is engaged in these paranoid and hypersensitive actions with the South Korean people."

Kim became even more emotional in the rest of the letter. He stated, "I am clearly offended and do not want to hide this feeling from you. I am really, very offended." He added,

> I do not wish to do anything to disappoint you any time soon nor do I plan to do so. If you do not think of our relationship as a steppingstone that only benefits you, then you would not make me look like an idiot that will only give without getting anything in return.

Kim concluded by telling Trump that "regrettably now is not the time to have working level talks." Kim stressed that because of "what has transpired, we are in a different situation, and we are not in a hurry." The high-level correspondence and the relationship it had fostered between Trump and Kim, which in turn had sustained a diplomatic process that was otherwise hollow, had now fractured as well.

At this point, relations between North Korea and the United States were running on fumes. Secretary Pompeo tried to continue the dialogue, but he did not seem to win the North Koreans' hearts. Foreign Minister Ri Yong Ho, usually the consummate diplomat, denounced Pompeo as the "poisonous plant of American diplomacy" and "disrupter" of North Korea–U.S. negotiations.[34] It was never clear to me what side Pompeo was on—was he in lockstep with the president to

33. Robert Carlin, "The Real Lessons of the Trump–Kim Love Letters," *Foreign Policy* (August 13, 2021), https://foreignpolicy.com/2021/08/13/north-korea-trump-kim-jong-un-love-letters-diplomacy-nuclear-talks/

34. Kim Hyung-Jin, "North Korea Foreign Minister Calls Pompeo 'Poisonous Plant,'" *Asociated Press* (August 23, 2019), https://abcnews.go.com/International/wireStory/north-korea-foreign-minister-calls-pompeo-poisonous-plant-65138219

get a deal or with Bolton to prevent one? Unsurprisingly, in public, he was always supportive of President Trump and his agenda. Bolton, however, indicated that in private conversations with Pompeo, the secretary of state did not differ much from Bolton's views. Minister Ri must have experienced the same.

I had occasion to meet with Secretary Pompeo in his office suite in May after the summit. Pompeo was forever the politician, extending his hand with a "Hi, I'm Mike" firm handshake and a ready smile. But when pushed on North Korea, his mood turned sour, and he showed a total disdain for Kim and his regime. Pompeo said there was basically "no hope with this guy. You couldn't believe anything they say or promise." In Pompeo's view, "the North had a twenty-five-year history of lying, and Kim was simply playing us along." I tried to make the point that targeted sanctions relief could yield rollbacks of the nuclear program. Pompeo said the only way to get Kim to change paths was to increase the pressure. We had to make "Kim feel the pain. Otherwise, we would just be writing Kim a check for sanctions relief, but he would not follow through on serious actions." Whereas Pompeo may not have undermined the president's attempt to get a deal as did Bolton, his remarks made it clear that he must have been relieved to have Trump walk in Hanoi. I told Pompeo that I was concerned about Hanoi becoming another hinge point. I explained the consequences of missed opportunities during the Bush and Obama administrations. He nodded and said, "Yeah, Hanoi will likely be another hinge point."

Nevertheless, Steve Biegun made another valiant attempt to hold working-level meetings with his North Korean counterparts. He reiterated the administration's commitment to the search for a lasting peace on the Korean Peninsula in a policy speech at the University of Michigan on September 6. Almost everything that Biegun proposed for next steps was diametrically opposed to what Bolton had been promoting, but Bolton managed to get on Trump's bad side and was on his way out a few days later—undoubtedly to begin work on his tell-all book.

Following his speech, Biegun managed to get the North Koreans to meet one more time, in Stockholm in early October, but as Bob Carlin explains, "It was an ambush at which the North Koreans announced that the possibility for further dialogue had vanished."[35] North Korea had already resumed a

---

35. Robert Carlin, "Distant Thunder: The Crisis Coming in Korea," *38 North* (October 17, 2019), https://www.38north.org/2019/10/rcarlin101719/

robust missile test schedule in May 2019 after a nearly eighteen-month hiatus during which diplomacy had the upper hand. The flurry of missile launches beginning in May looked like operational exercises to qualify solid-fueled short-range missiles. The North still had not launched any long-range rockets nor conducted additional nuclear tests, but in January 2020, Pyongyang announced that it felt no longer bound to these moratoriums. The nuclear prong of the North's dual-track strategy had regained dominance.

Pyongyang was silent as it learned about Biden's election victory in November. As Biden prepared to take office in early January, Kim stressed at the Eighth Congress of the Workers' Party of Korea (WPK) that the first order of business for the North Korean leadership was the economy.[36] However, all eyes in the United States were on his nuclear pronouncements, and Kim gave Washington much to think about. He called for a massive military buildup, arguing that it would be "foolish and dangerous" not to keep North Korea's defense capabilities at the highest possible level, while "the number of the enemy's advanced weapons targeting the nation is increasing."

Kim specifically mentioned the Hwasong-class ICBMs and the Pukguksong submarine-launched ballistic missiles. Kim lauded progress in miniaturizing nuclear weapons and making them "standardized, tactical, and weaponized." He announced the development of "super-large hydrogen bombs" and mid- and long-range cruise missiles, anti-aircraft rocket systems, heavy tanks, howitzers, multiple-warhead missiles, new types of ballistic missiles, "hypersonic gliding flight warheads," electronic weapons, drones with a 500-kilometer range, and military reconnaissance satellites.[37] He further stressed the military need to destroy targets within a range of 15,000 kilometers (covering all of the United States). Kim also claimed that

36. R. L. Carlin, "North Korea's Eighth Workers' Party Congress: Putting Things into Context," 38 North (January 19, 2021), https://www.38north.org/2021/01/north-koreas-eighth-workers-party-congress-putting-things-into-context/; Ruediger Frank, "Key Results of the Eighth Party Congress in North Korea" (part 2 of 2), 38 North (January 19, 2021), https://www.38north.org/2021/01/key-results-of-the-eighth-party-congress-in-north-korea-part-2-of-2/

37. "Great Programme for Struggle Leading Korean-style Socialist Construction to Fresh Victory on Report Made by Supreme Leader Kim Jong Un at Eighth Congress of WPK," KCNA Watch (January 10, 2021), https://kcnawatch.org/newstream/1610261416-871234007/great-programme-for-struggle-leading-korean-style-socialist-construction-to-fresh-victory-on-report-made-by-supreme-leader-kim-jong-un-at-eighth-congress-of-wpk/

they were in the final stages of developing a new submarine and that they would operate a military reconnaissance satellite in the near future.

This, of course, was a wish list, most likely targeting Kim's domestic audience. It would demonstrate that he was more determined than ever to guard North Korea's security and sovereignty, no matter who was the U.S. president. Although pollyannaish, Pyongyang has demonstrated a dogged determination over the years to work toward what appear to be unrealistic goals—and eventually achieve success.

Kim entered his tenth year as Supreme Leader in 2021, once again with the nuclear track having priority over the diplomatic track. The high hopes for normalization with Washington that were clearly demonstrated in his letter correspondence with Trump had been dashed in Hanoi by John Bolton. Kim's plan to turn to the economy was upended by the pandemic that resulted in the nearly complete lockdown of the country in 2020 and extended through 2021. Despite the announcement of his military plans, Kim kept the possibility of the diplomatic track alive by toning down his rhetoric from previous years. At the Eighth Party Congress, the United States was portrayed as the "principal" enemy, whereas at the previous one, in 2016, it was referred to as the "sworn enemy." He also backed off from brushing aside previous U.S.–DPRK summits as worthless because, he claimed, Washington had never been serious. Instead, Kim implied that the June 2018 Singapore joint statement was still a valid basis for improving U.S.–DPRK relations.

21 Closing Observations: Hinge Points and Missteps

I landed feet first in North Korea's Yongbyon nuclear complex in January 2004 with little knowledge of the country. My years of experience dealing with Russian nuclear scientists and engineers after the collapse of the Soviet Union turned out to be good preparation, but only up to a point. There was much I needed to learn. Seven visits on the ground in the DPRK over seven years provided an education that could not be duplicated by looking at satellite photographs. During those visits, I was given remarkable access to the North's nuclear facilities and its nuclear technical staff. Traveling with Americans who had experience with North Korea, I came face to face with the DPRK's top diplomats. Those years were both an exhilarating and depressing phase of my career. I entered the picture when the North's nuclear weapons program was going downhill, but over the next two decades, I watched as their nuclear capabilities grew. Meanwhile, American diplomacy remained largely mired in indecision, repeatedly short-circuiting itself by dismissing the North Koreans as duplicitous and regarding engagement with Pyongyang as a waste of time.

In this book, I have taken the reader along on the complex journey of tracking the North's nuclear developments side by side with political

developments, revealing how the two fed into each other and how, ultimately, that produced a North Korean policy that should have been viewed
never as only one or the other but *both*. Because I was in the rare position to
observe these two streams as they flowed—sometimes in parallel, sometimes
as one—I concluded that North Korea has followed a dual-track strategy of
diplomacy *and* nuclear development, variously emphasizing one or the other
but never completely abandoning either. The Bush, Obama, and Trump
administrations failed to see that strategy, much less to cope effectively
with it. Their misguided assumptions and deep suspicions about North
Korea repeatedly caused all three administrations to miss opportunities
to mitigate risk and to alter the trajectory of the North's nuclear program
during times when Pyongyang favored the diplomatic track. Washington
had a fixed belief that Pyongyang pursued diplomacy primarily to buy time
and resources from the United States so that it could advance its nuclear
arsenal. That meant even when Washington did engage Pyongyang, the
attempts were at best halfhearted and usually riddled with doubt. These
efforts were never long enough or effective enough to bear fruit.

Smart, senior officials in three U.S. administrations were highly skeptical
about making progress with North Korea. So why was I convinced that at
key times each of the three Kim regimes pursued diplomacy that offered
the United States real possibilities? The answer is simple: because Pyongyang saw the diplomatic track as vital to improving the country's external
security situation. That meant achieving regime security not through its
nuclear arsenal but rather through rapprochement with its main adversary,
something that could provide North Korea with breathing room to develop
its economy and to slip out from under China's shadow. In other words,
Pyongyang believed that whereas nuclear weapons would help it survive, it
would take diplomacy to make it thrive. This calculus provided opportunities for Washington; in every case, they were squandered.

Pyongyang's dual-track strategy produced a steady stream of nuclear
advances, both while it prioritized the nuclear track and while it hedged to
preserve options with diplomacy. To a surprising degree, the North Koreans
openly discussed and displayed these advances during my visits. After my
visits stopped, the country continued to demonstrate advances in the nuclear weapons sphere through its media. These persistent nuclear activities
should have been countered by technically informed risk/benefit analysis in

Washington that sought to manage the risk. Instead, the policy responses for the past twenty years have been reactive and primarily politically driven. Three administrations had a singular focus on denuclearization—to drive the nuclear risk to zero—rather than realistically managing risk. Influenced by this line of thinking, time and again Washington made unfortunate calls at key decision points. It failed to constrain the program when it could have. The result has been exactly the opposite of what Washington wanted. The North has been handed opportunities to expand its program relatively unfettered.

Every policy is complex, made up of different streams of decisions that come together over time. In the case of U.S. policy on North Korea, obviously there were other factors in play than the phenomenon I focused on throughout this book—the hinge points. At least three other factors are worth mentioning, each of which played a part in the overall decision-making process and fed into the hinge point problem. First, from the second Bush administration up to the present, Washington turned to China and to increasing sanctions to rein in North Korea's nuclear program. That failed. It pushed Pyongyang toward China instead of pulling it toward South Korea. Second, Washington did not pursue a holistic approach to peace on the Korean Peninsula—one that included economic, educational, and cultural dialogue, as well as promoting inter-Korean relations. Instead, the U.S. policy was driven by a singular focus on denuclearization. Pyongyang has made it clear that elimination of nuclear weapons must be accompanied by normalization of relations. Third, despite their steady nuclear and missile advances, the United States has not made North Korea a top-tier security priority.

Important as each of those are, I have focused on "hinge points"—the term I use to describe forks in the road of the nuclear–diplomatic history—for good reason. These periods of potential opportunity were wasted by shortsighted decisions in Washington and often exacerbated by poor judgment in Pyongyang. Much of the U.S.-based analysis of the North Korean nuclear issue locates blame solely with the North, placing the responsibility for failed diplomatic initiatives on Pyongyang and not the United States. While this framing is sometimes true—and I have identified throughout the book those times when North Korea blundered—I also turn the lens inward to critically appraise Washington's role so as to construct an improved

U.S. policy for the future. An honest account of the history is not kind to Washington. The hinge points were moments when Washington might have been able to effectively channel Pyongyang further down the diplomatic road toward the elimination of nuclear weapons at a manageable level of risk. Instead, through its decisions, the U.S. policies exacerbated the nuclear threat on the Korean Peninsula.

OCTOBER 2002: SHATTERING THE AGREED FRAMEWORK

The most fateful hinge point occurred in October 2002, when the Bush administration dealt a fatal blow to the 1994 Agreed Framework without either fully evaluating or properly appreciating the risks of walking away. At the end of the Clinton administration, North Korea had no nuclear weapons, less than a few kilograms of plutonium, and no active plutonium production. It likely possessed no enriched uranium stockpile and only a fledgling centrifuge program. It was in its fourth year of a unilaterally declared missile launch moratorium, which limited its ability to expand the range and sophistication of its missiles. This was the best opportunity to convince North Korea give up its nuclear weapons program because it didn't have much.

The Bush administration's stated reason for walking away was that Pyongyang was violating the framework by clandestinely pursuing uranium enrichment. The real reason was largely political, as stated later by John Bolton: It was to "drive a stake through the Agreed Framework," one of the major foreign policy accomplishments of the Clinton administration.

The technical ramifications of killing of the Agreed Framework were disastrous. These were made clear to me during my first visit in 2004. The Bush administration had traded the long-term threat of Pyongyang developing a centrifuge program to produce highly enriched uranium, which would have taken another decade to come to fruition, for a free pass to resume operations at Yongbyon and build a plutonium bomb in less than a year. The international inspectors and American technical teams were expelled, the known facilities were rapidly brought back into operation, and the clandestine operations continued. The tragedy is that these risks should have been fully understood by senior national security officials in Washington because the Americans had good access to Yongbyon during the Agreed Framework.

Not surprisingly, as part of its dual-track strategy, Pyongyang had kept a hedge during the Agreed Framework to be able to reconstitute its nuclear weapons program, which Kim Jong Il did essentially unconstrained once Washington walked away. He also kept diplomacy alive through the China-brokered Six-Party Talks so that he could stay engaged, measure Washington's temperature, and manage the risk generated by his increasingly aggressive steps on the nuclear front. In the second term of the Bush administration, those talks resulted in the September 2005 joint statement.

SEPTEMBER 2005: WALKING BACK THE JOINT STATEMENT

The world would never know whether the joint statement held promise for resolving the nuclear crisis because the Bush administration almost immediately undermined its implementation. The U.S. government issued a unilateral statement that walked back major six-party commitments almost before the ink on Ambassador Hill's signature had dried. In addition, almost concurrently, the Treasury Department imposed sanctions on Banco Delta Asia designed to discourage other banks from dealing with North Korea. These decisions convinced Pyongyang to reject the deal and its stated denuclearization commitments.

This was another hinge point—the technical benefits of the deal greatly outweighed the potential risks to Washington. Pyongyang had committed to abandoning all nuclear weapons and existing nuclear programs and to returning at an early date to the Nuclear Nonproliferation Treaty and to IAEA safeguards. Whether or not one believed that the North would live up to that deal, the ill-advised decisions in Washington freed Pyongyang to move full speed ahead on its nuclear track. North Korea continued to produce plutonium for more bombs instead of getting international inspectors back into Yongbyon and halting operations. It continued nuclear test preparations and proceeded with the centrifuge program, the very program that the Bush administration originally insisted it wanted to halt. A year later, in October 2006, the North conducted its first nuclear test.

Although only partially successful, the test seemed to garner a modicum of diplomatic leverage rather than a military response from Washington. Domestically the test was billed as the North's arrival as a nuclear power. Vice Minister Kim Gye Gwan agreed to work with Christopher Hill to revive the Six-Party Talks a few months later, resulting in two six-party agreements in 2007 aimed at facilitating the implementation of the 2005 joint statement. The 2007 agreements resulted in the temporary disablement of the Yongbyon nuclear facilities, as I was able to verify during my visits in 2007 and 2008. IAEA inspectors and American technical teams returned to Yongbyon.

Diplomatic progress during the first half of 2008 was slowed by bitter division and dysfunction within the Bush administration, which resulted in moving the disablement agreement's verification goalposts that Ambassador Hill had negotiated with the North. Hill had made a pragmatic, and in my view correct, risk/benefit decision to focus on plutonium, but he did so pretty much in a freelance mode because of opposition from much of the administration. Ultimately, Hill was not able to overcome Washington's deep suspicions of Pyongyang, and the deal began to fall apart.

Already on shaky ground because Pyongyang believed the Americans failed again to deliver on a deal, the death knell for diplomacy in 2008 came when Kim Jong Il suffered a serious stroke in August. With Kim's life in danger, succession planning motivated North Korea's decision-making. Apparently, the moment for reconciliation had passed. Pyongyang was no longer willing to deal because it was determined to put succession planning on a solid track, which probably entailed a second nuclear test to establish the credibility of the North's nuclear deterrent, leaving a nuclear crisis for the incoming Obama administration.

APRIL 2009: CONDEMNING
THE NORTH'S ROCKET LAUNCH

North Korea greeted President Obama with an attempted satellite launch on April 5, 2009, the same day the president gave his seminal speech in Prague on the elimination of nuclear weapons. The launch was unsuccessful, yet it poisoned the relationship as Obama saw it as a manifestation of Pyongyang's "cycle of provocation, extortion, and reward," which he was determined to end. Washington response to the launch was to orchestrate a UN Security Council condemnation of the launch, which was just what Pyongyang had expected and which paved the way to move its nuclear program forward. The North restored the disabled Yongbyon facilities to their original state. It expelled the IAEA and Americans from the country. Six weeks later, Pyongyang detonated its second nuclear device, this one successfully.

Pyongyang may well have already been on an unstoppable path to the second nuclear test as the Bush administration left office, but Obama's response to the rocket launch closed more options for the United States than it did for North Korea. During the rest of 2009 and 2010, the disablement actions the North had taken in Yongbyon were reversed, the missile program was ramped up, and the uranium enrichment program was taken to the next stage—as my Stanford colleagues and I discovered when the North revealed a remarkably modern, small industrial-scale uranium centrifuge plant and the construction of an indigenous light water reactor during our November 2010 visit to Yongbyon.

Obama's response to the North's satellite launch resulted in a hinge point. North Korea took a huge leap forward with its successful nuclear test and the uranium enrichment facilities that demonstrated it had the second path to the bomb. But it was a hinge point forced by Pyongyang's timing the launch to just when Obama was settling into the White House. We will never know if postponing the launch would have put the two countries on a different track. As it was, the Obama administration settled on a policy of "strategic patience," which amounted to containment, watchful waiting, and a stated aversion to rewarding the "bad behavior" of North Korea.

APRIL 2012: WALKING AWAY FROM THE LEAP DAY DEAL

Having shored up the nuclearization prong of its dual-track strategy, Pyongyang mounted another diplomatic effort in 2011. It appeared that Kim Jong Il was attempting to reach a less confrontational relationship with Washington to pave the way for a better leadership transition for his son. The diplomatic effort, interrupted by Kim Jong Il's sudden death in December 2011, resulted in a deal under the leadership of Kim Jong Un. On February 29, 2012, the two capitals issued separate press statements about the Leap Day Deal that would have shut down Yongbyon and have placed observers back on the ground at the Yongbyon nuclear complex. It also called for a moratorium on nuclear and long-range missile tests, all for the promise of a couple of hundred thousand tons of U.S. nutritional aid.

Unfortunately, the two sides had different understandings of what constituted a missile test. Six weeks after the Leap Day signing, Pyongyang attempted to launch an Earth observation satellite. Although the launch failed, it confirmed the administration's conviction that Pyongyang was an unreliable negotiating partner, a view that lasted throughout the rest of Obama's time in office.

The administration's decision to scupper the deal led yet to another hinge point with serious consequences. Moving forward with the Leap Day Deal would have meant shutting down operations and regaining access to Yongbyon so that the United States and the IAEA could learn critical technical details about the centrifuge program and why the 5 MWe plutonium production reactor still stood dormant. Instead, the North doubled the size of the centrifuge facility and managed to get the reactor back in operation. Washington was left watching the construction of the experimental light water reactor through satellite images, never learning how the reactor was designed, whether it had adequate safety features, and whether it had provisions for both electricity and plutonium production. Instead of shutting down Yongbyon, the North mounted a torrid pace of renovation and new construction at the nuclear complex. It accelerated highly enriched uranium production and resumed plutonium and tritium production. Without a nuclear test moratorium, it prepared for another nuclear test, which it conducted in a little less than a year. North Korea test-launched over sixty missiles during President Obama's second term after not having conducted any missile tests in 2010 and 2011.

The heavy price paid was not a matter of a lack of intelligence that Pyongyang could proceed rapidly with its nuclear program. Although the intelligence community had missed the construction of the centrifuge facility and light water reactor in 2010, by this time it had sufficient information about how fast the North's program was progressing. The failure, instead, resulted from American policymakers relying on their longstanding belief in Pyongyang's insincere motives rather than assessing the technical risk that would ensue from walking away after the attempted satellite launch. Barely four months after taking power, Kim Jong Un may have felt compelled to conduct the launch planned by his father to commemorate his grandfather's centenary. He was either misled or greatly misjudged the Obama administration's reaction to the launch.

JANUARY 2015: PASSING ON A NUCLEAR TESTING MORATORIUM

During the rest of 2013 and 2014, North Korea continued to produce fissile materials for bombs and to enhance its missile capabilities. In January 2015, Kim Jong Un appeared to circle back to explore diplomacy with Washington, perhaps to give his new economic policies a boost. He proposed a moratorium on nuclear testing in return for a moratorium on U.S.–South Korea joint military exercises. Unfortunately, by this time the Obama administration was so determined not to get trapped by what it considered the North's insincere proposals that it rejected Kim's offer out of hand. It was another hinge point. Washington was left watching from the sidelines as the North responded with two more nuclear tests and a flurry of missile launches before the end of Obama's presidency. Despite not having mounted a serious diplomatic initiative with the North, President Obama and his team understood that North Korea had become a significantly greater threat on their watch. Obama told President-elect Trump at their transition meeting in November 2016 that North Korea would be his biggest national security problem.

FEBRUARY 2019: WALKING AWAY AT THE HANOI SUMMIT

With President Trump's ascent to the White House, the year 2017 turned into the most dangerous year yet on the Korean Peninsula. Trump's "fire and fury" countered by Kim's equally menacing replies threatened to escalate into real conflict. North Korea for the first time successfully test-launched ICBM-capable missiles. In September, it detonated its sixth nuclear device, likely a hydrogen bomb, with more than ten times the explosive yield of the Hiroshima and Nagasaki bombs. Then in December, Trump turned the tables and sent a secret message to Kim Jong Un via UN envoy Jeffrey Feltman that he was willing to meet with Kim.

At the Singapore summit in June 2018, Trump and Kim signed a joint statement, though leaving specific details of timing and sequence for the future, linked normalization *and* denuclearization. The difficult work of realizing the promise of the Singapore statement was left for another summit, this one in Hanoi at the end of February 2019. Trump wanted a deal with Kim. Steve Biegun, the special representative for North Korea matters, was working with the North Koreans to develop a deal along the lines of the Singapore summit. But reenter John Bolton as Trump's national security advisor. He had helped to kill the Agreed Framework during the Bush administration, and he was determined that no deal would be reached in Hanoi.

Kim came to Hanoi supremely confident. He had conducted serious diplomacy directly with Trump and stayed on friendly terms through their letter correspondence. It all crashed in Hanoi. The president's advisors were at each other's throats. Bolton's knives proved sharper, and the president, distracted by the growing impeachment threat, became convinced that it was to his advantage to walk away, making the disastrous assumption that when he met Kim again, the North's leader would be more pliable.

Hanoi turned out to be another hinge point, a lost opportunity to turn back the threat of the North's nuclear program. The Yongbyon nuclear complex, which in my opinion was still the key to the North's fissile materials production, continued to operate and expand. In Hanoi, the Americans did not explore shuttering the Nuclear Weapon Institute, the brain center of the North's nuclear program, which Kim offered to close in his September 6, 2018, letter to Trump. Pyongyang's self-declared moratorium on nuclear testing and long-range missile testing was not formalized. The Sohae rocket launch site was not permanently dismantled.

What makes Hanoi the most serious hinge point yet is that by the time of the summit, North Korea's nuclear arsenal had grown immensely in size and sophistication. The nuclear complex had shown itself to be remarkably successful by testing a series of increasingly powerful nuclear devices. The Strategic Rocket Forces and supporting military/industrial complex continued to deliver impressive missile advances. They had grown to a size and likely to an influence within the regime that would be difficult to shut down. Yet, in Hanoi, Kim had appeared willing to take big steps to scale back the nuclear weapons program. As he told Trump, that couldn't be done all at once, but he was ready to move in that direction in parallel with U.S. steps toward normalization. This is what was at stake in Hanoi, but Washington was not willing to take the risk to find out. It should have learned the lessons from previous hinge points to manage the risk rather than walk—but it didn't. Hanoi was a big opportunity, but it was squandered. Senior North Korean diplomats publicly warned, "Such an opportunity may not come again"—and it didn't during the rest of Trump's term.

In the end, the policies of three U.S. administrations since 2001 led to North Korea becoming one of only three nations that could threaten the United States and its allies with nuclear weapons. Those policies also did nothing to help lift ordinary North Koreans out of poverty and did not improve their human condition. The Korean Peninsula remained divided, a dangerous place in an increasingly dangerous Northeast Asia, with the goals of peace and stability no closer and the two Koreas as far from reconciliation as they have ever been. That was the situation inherited by the Biden administration in January 2021.

Epilogue

As I write in May 2022, the North Korean nuclear problem has become alarmingly worse. When President Trump walked away at the Hanoi summit, diplomacy stopped. The historical record strongly suggests that when there is no dialogue, Pyongyang ramps up both its nuclear and its missile programs. Since 2019, neither sanctions nor the pandemic have slowed the North's military advances. In the past, nuclear buildups were followed by diplomatic openings. But immediately after the Hanoi summit, the North warned that the steps it had offered toward denuclearization may not be on the table again. If that turns out to be the case, the situation will indeed be bleak in Northeast Asia.

Just weeks before President Biden's inauguration, Kim Jong Un announced ambitious plans for his nuclear program at the Eighth Congress of the Workers' Party of Korea. He called for an increased number of nuclear weapons and greater sophistication. Since then, North Korea produced enough additional highly enriched uranium for about six more nuclear weapons. At the Yongbyon nuclear complex, which Hanoi summit critics called a "used up" facility, the restarted 5 MWe nuclear reactor produced additional plutonium and tritium, materials required for much more destructive hydrogen bombs. At the October 2021 Defense Development Exhibition, the North rolled out an impressive array of missile systems accompanied by a robust testing program in the fall and winter. At this current pace, by 2024 the North could have sixty-five bombs. This puts the Biden administration in line with the failures of the Bush administration (which resulted in the North's first five bombs), the Obama administration (an increase to roughly twenty-five bombs), and the Trump administration (up to forty-five bombs). Each time, the North not only had more weapons, but they had longer reach, greater destructive power, and improved sophistication.

There were signs at the beginning of the Biden administration that Kim was keeping the door cracked open for reengagement with Washington, even while he ordered a five-year defense plan that would result in a significant upgrade of the North's nuclear and missile programs across the board. Whether Kim was waiting to achieve a new level of defense capability before going back to diplomacy remains an open question. It is worth recalling that in 2017, as things appeared to be reaching a boiling point between North Korea and the United States, Kim was already planning his switch to the diplomatic track and to a greater focus on the economy.

But neither side moved quickly early in the Biden administration to seriously explore whether the diplomatic track that led to the Singapore summit could be resumed. It became increasingly unlikely that Kim was serious about working out—and sustaining—a diplomatic way forward. Kim's position strengthens, not weakens, with time, while for Washington, the path to even approaching the first steps of denuclearization becomes longer and more difficult. In other words, the risks grow as the North's nuclear arsenal grows, while the prospects of denuclearization diminish.

The one ray of light is that over the years the North Koreans have showed that they tend to be pragmatic and to quickly adapt to changing circumstances. Kim Jong Un knew that whatever plans he had for reviving the North Korean economy could not succeed without improvement in the external security environment. For that, he has to push for a less hostile relationship with the United States. Domestic developments will also play a role along with Kim's external security priorities. He has continued to press for economic reforms but has been challenged by the recent COVID-19 outbreak, requiring a lockdown and threatening to ravage North Korea's unvaccinated public.

At the start of 2022, Kim began a major, very visible drive to enhance his nuclear and missile programs, with more than fifteen missile launches and what appear to be preparations for a nuclear test—the seventh since 2006 and the first in five years. Kim also more clearly stated his nuclear doctrine, reminding Washington that the North's nuclear arsenal is not only for deterrence but is also for use if its fundamental interests are threatened. Moreover, Kim has signaled that he is aligning his nation with Russia (supporting its invasion of Ukraine) and China, an indication that he sees a change in the global political power balance. If Kim has indeed given up attempting to reach strategic accommodation with Washington to improve the external security environment and is positioning himself more solidly with Beijing and Moscow, we will have a North Korean nuclear problem that will threaten us well into the twenty-first century.

Acknowledgments

My thanks go to Stanford University, particularly the Center for International Security and Cooperation and its parent organization, the Freeman Spogli Institute for International Studies. They gave me the opportunity for new horizons after nearly four decades at the Los Alamos National Laboratory. Special thanks go to Professor Scott Sagan with whom I had the privilege of serving as co-director of CISAC for six years, and who convinced me that there was science in political science. The department of Management Science and Engineering allowed me to teach students in the School of Engineering and across the university. I taught classes on technology and nuclear security to over three thousand students during my fifteen years at Stanford, and this has been the most rewarding part of my time at the university. Thanks go to former Secretary of Defense and retired Stanford University professor, William Perry, who recruited me to take over his class. Watching my students spellbound in their seats as I reported upon returning from my seven visits to North Korea convinced me I had a story to tell that the American public should hear.

Special thanks go to student interns, research assistants, and postdoctoral fellows who contributed to the book with their own research and by collaborating with me – namely Niko Milonopoulos, Peter Davis, Isabella Uria, Chris Lawrence, Frank Willey, Julien de Troullioud de Lanversin, and Sulgiye Park. I want to thank my professional colleagues and affiliates at CISAC. Chaim Braun was instrumental in helping me assess North Korea's nuclear programs and facilities, Nick Hansen in understanding the North's missile program, and Frank Pabian and Allison Puccioni in interpreting the increasing volume of satellite imagery that became available after my last trip to North Korea in 2010.

I benefitted enormously in understanding North Korea from my tireless mentors, John Lewis and Robert Carlin. I learned much from my travel companions to North Korea in addition to Lewis and Carlin, namely Charles (Jack) Pritchard, W. Keith Luse, Frank Jannuzi, David Straub, John Merrill, Joel Wit, and Paul Carroll. From my first trip to North Korea in 2004 through my last in 2010, I was encouraged by numerous officials in the U.S. Government to travel to the North and had informative discussions with them upon my return. I have received encouragement from South Korean scholars, educators, and government officials for my work in North Korea. I have learned immensely from my interactions with them over the years. Likewise, continuing discussions with Chinese and Russian scholars and officials provided a broader perspective of North Korean issues. Three Stanford University scholars and affiliates were especially helpful on understanding China's views of North Korea – namely Thomas Fingar, Larry Brandt, and Jason Reinhardt.

My research, analysis, and travel on the North Korea projects was supported by the Carnegie Corporation of New York and the John D. and Catherine T. MacArthur Foundation. The encouragement and support of the project monitors at the foundations is gratefully acknowledged.

I am deeply indebted to Elliot Serbin, my co-author, for his meticulous research into the history of North Korea's nuclear program and his writing skills to help me tell many of the stories in the book. His analytical skills in satellite imagery analysis were instrumental in deciphering much of what North Korea accomplished in the nuclear arena. I thank Robert Carlin, my frequent traveling companion to North Korea, who freely shared his knowledge of North Korea and critically reviewed all chapters. My close scientific collaborator from our days at the Los Alamos National Laboratory, James Toevs, reviewed the scientific content of the book, as did my Stanford University colleague, Chaim Braun. Any errors in the book, however, are of my own doing. My Stanford University colleagues, Alla Kassianova, and student intern Frank Willey provided essential help in collecting references and citations along with overseeing the development of a website that will accompany the book. I thank Jennifer Gordon for doing a masterful job of copyediting the book.

Last but not least, I would like to thank my wife, Nina. She has been the foundation of our family as we raised four daughters while I was finishing graduate school, began careers in Los Alamos and Michigan, then tackled increasingly demanding jobs at Los Alamos and traveled the world to promote nuclear cooperation. She was there to provide the love and comfort of home and family after each of those trips, whether to North Korea, Russia, Kazakhstan, Uzbekistan, China, Mongolia, Pakistan, India, or less exotic places.

Index

ABOUT THE AUTHORS

Siegfried S. Hecker is senior fellow and professor emeritus at Stanford University and director emeritus of the Los Alamos National Laboratory. His expertise ranges from plutonium science to nuclear weapons and international security. Hecker has documented the history of post-Soviet Russian–American nuclear cooperation in his highly acclaimed *Doomed to Cooperate*. His scientific and diplomatic achievements have been recognized internationally, including with the presidential Enrico Fermi Award, the American Nuclear Society's Eisenhower Medal, and election to the National Academy of Engineering.

Elliot A. Serbin worked with Siegfried S. Hecker at Stanford University from 2016 to 2020. At Stanford, Serbin supported the Nuclear Risk Reduction Project and assisted Hecker's research and analysis of North Korea's nuclear program. Serbin has most recently worked at the U.S. Nuclear Regulatory Commission and Lawrence Livermore National Laboratory. He is currently a student at Harvard University where he is pursuing a J.D. and a Master in Public Policy.